D0998502

BRITISH POLITICAL FACTS
1900–1960

BRITISH POLITICAL FACTS 1900-1960

BY

DAVID BUTLER

AND

JENNIE FREEMAN

LONDON

MACMILLAN & CO LTD

NEW YORK · ST MARTIN'S PRESS

1964

—

First Edition 1963
Reprinted with corrections 1964

MACMILLAN AND COMPANY LIMITED
St Martin's Street London WC 2
also Bombay Calcutta Madras Melbourne

THE MACMILLAN COMPANY OF CANADA LIMITED
70 Bond Street Toronto 2

ST MARTIN'S PRESS INC
175 Fifth Avenue New York 10 NY

PRINTED IN GREAT BRITAIN

CONTENTS

INTRODUCTION

THE table of contents offers the simplest justification for this book — but inevitably it is a book that will justify itself in different ways to different readers. The scholar, the journalist, the politician and the club bore were all in the authors' minds at one point or another during its compilation. Some of those who look at this book will, we hope, be delighted to find in compact and reliable form data that might still have eluded them after searching through a dozen standard works of reference; others will at least discover from our pages where the information they seek may be found; a few, we fear, will be infuriated by our omissions and, despite all our efforts at checking, by our errors.

The idea of writing this book grew gradually in the mind of one of its authors as, in the course of twelve years as a student and a teacher at Nuffield College (which is devoted to research in contemporary subjects), he noticed the amount of time that he and others wasted in searching for seemingly obvious facts about twentieth-century Britain. If, therefore, any one reader has been especially in our minds, he is the graduate student writing a thesis on any domestic theme in the last sixty years. We hope he will find here not only an expeditious way of checking basic facts but also, if he finds time to browse through our lists and tables, a stimulating reminder of people and considerations that must have played a part, perhaps only as background, in the situations he is analysing.

But we are not concerned solely with academic needs. Experience of checking facts in newspaper offices and broadcasting studios, and the anecdotes of friends in Whitehall and Westminster have made plain to us how much elementary political data is annoyingly elusive. Many admirable works of reference exist but the right one is not always to hand; most of them, moreover, are compiled on an annual basis — which can be very frustrating for those who are trying to trace an office or a statistic over a number of years.

The compiler of any work of reference is limited by space and time. How much data shall be included? How far shall other works be duplicated? How many hours is it worth devoting to any particular compilation? In this book we have had to exclude interesting information either because it would fill a disproportionate number of pages or because it could not be obtained without more labour than we thought justified. We have consoled ourselves for setting out data in abbreviated form by giving exact references to more exhaustive sources.

Indeed, since the compilation of reference books is, even more than other research, systematised plagiarism, perhaps the most valuable part of these pages lies in these citations. We have not attempted an exhaustive bibliography — except for a compilation of bibliographies and general reference books — but we have throughout tried to list all major authorities.

The title, *British Political Facts 1900–1960*, provides a reasonably close delimitation of the scope of this book. *British* indicates that we have been concerned with the domestic history of the United Kingdom. But it is not possible to set precise boundaries to the term 'domestic' and we have perhaps strayed beyond them by listing Colonies, Governors-General, and some Ambassadors.

Political is potentially ambiguous, but we have used it to stress that our interest is in the power of the state. We have tried to list the principal people who were involved in the government of Britain at any moment in this century; we have recorded election results — as providing the basis for political authority — and major legislation — as representing its use; we have assembled, in summary form, statistical data which show some of the social and economic background to all political action.

Facts indicates that we have tried to eschew political judgements as far as possible. Some value judgements may be implicit in our selection of material, but we believe that virtually everything here would be acceptable as non-controversial evidence in debates over the nature of twentieth-century British history. It is a waste of time to argue about verifiable questions of fact. But it is also a waste of time to assemble facts except as a basis for argument. Because in this book we have stuck rigidly to facts, it does not mean that we overrate them. Analysis of our past and present situation is far more important than mere fact-gathering. Unlike Martha we are fully aware which is the better part.

1900–1960 is a somewhat arbitrary period — but any historical period must be arbitrary. Our terminal date, December 31, 1960, was determined by the availability of material in 1961–2; perhaps a second edition will carry the record forward. Our opening date was a numerological accident — but it would be hard to find a better watershed without going back at least to 1885, which because of space, and still more because of the availability of data, was impracticable. We have endeavoured to treat every one of our sixty years equally, providing as full and exact data about 1901 as about 1959. With some statistics this has proved impossible and some of our time-series are regrettably discontinuous. But in general it will be found that we have resisted the temptation to make a special favourite of the more recent past — it is not our fault that there were no Gallup polls before 1938 and that local election results cannot usefully be pursued very far back.

In compiling this book we have become very conscious of the strengths and weaknesses of other reference books — and particularly of the importance of pedantic accuracy and clear presentation. We have certainly not avoided all the pitfalls into which we have observed others falling; therefore, by way both of excuse and of warning, it may be worth describing a few of the diffculties we have faced.

The general problems of finding exact data on British politics were best exemplified in the gathering of complete lists of ministries over the last sixty years — the most time-consuming of all our operations. There are a number of publications which purport to list all ministerial appointments — the most useful of these are the two Parliamentary handbooks, *Dod* and *Vacher*. There is also the Stationery Office publication *H.M. Ministers and Heads of Public Departments* which has appeared four or five times a year since 1946. Lists of ministers are also printed in *Hansard* once a fortnight during sessions. But all these sources have the same disadvantage — no indication is given of the date when a minister was appointed or left office. A man may indeed be appointed and leave office between the publication of these lists, so that there is no record whatever of his elevation. *Keesing's Contemporary Archives* have since 1931 recorded most government appointments — but they depend solely on newspaper sources and are not altogether infallible. The *Indexes* to *The Times* are the best means of checking on ministerial changes, though here too there are problems. *Palmer's Index to the Times* which was not superseded by the *Official Index* until 1906 is far from satisfactory; under the heading 'Official Appointments' is the depressing injunction 'See every issue'. From 1906 the *Official Index* is much more thorough, although misprints and references to different editions of the paper do occur. Even *The Times*, moreover, has occasionally missed a minor government change. An additional complication lies in the range of possible days which might be considered the date of appointment: there is the announcement from Downing Street, the press report the following day, the official gazetting a week or more later, the exchange of seals and the kissing of hands. None of these may represent the precise date on which the new minister took over his duties, but wherever possible, we have decided to use the date of *The Times* report, as being the earliest and most public announcement. Peerages sometimes cause further confusion, since weeks usually elapse before a newly elevated minister's title is announced. Care has also to be taken when a familiar minister disappears behind a new name — the fact that Mr Ivor Guest, Lord Ashby St Ledgers, and Viscount Wimborne were one and the same person is not immediately apparent. Another snag arises, particularly in wartime, when the titles and functions of ministries change kaleidoscopically.

In many other fields the sources of confusion were almost equally numerous. The search for reliable and consistent evidence about newspaper circulations, religious affiliations and trade disputes caused us particular trouble and we were surprised at the difficulties involved in compiling lists of all permanent secretaries of departments and assessing the size of the various grades of the civil service. But it would be tedious to quote all the gaps in existing works of reference which we have — with very varying success — tried to fill. We must, however, mention the complications which arise from the structure of the United Kingdom. The changes in Ireland in 1922 inevitably cause a break in all national statistical time-series and since then many tables have, perforce, to exclude Northern Ireland as well as

Eire; but the administrative separation of Scotland causes almost as many difficulties. Statistics are compiled independently north and south of the Border, quite often on different bases. Sometimes this arises from the different legal or administrative systems — as with education; but in the case of population and vital statistics the Registrars-General seem unnecessarily perverse in presenting their census findings in differing forms.

In preparing this book we have had assistance from many quarters — most notably from the Fellows and Students of Nuffield College, but also from officials in Parliament, in the Party Headquarters, in Government Departments and in newspaper offices, from many friends in the academic world, and from our publishers. We are also deeply indebted to anonymous compilers of the many works of reference from which we have so freely drawn. The statistical section of the book was largely prepared by Mrs Barbara Williamson with some invaluable advice from Mr Brian Mitchell and Mr Graham Pyatt of the Department of Applied Economics at Cambridge. The data for elections before 1918 was prepared by Mr Neal Blewett. The section on the courts was mainly the work of Mr Yash Ghai. Indispensable secretarial aid came from Miss Audrey Carruthers. And here is an incomplete list of others to whom we are indebted.

R. F. Allen
F. M. Barlow
Professor M. Beloff
H. B. Berrington
N. Birnbaum
G. D. M. Block
P. A. Bromhead
Professor P. Campbell
D. N. Chester
H. A. Clegg
P. C. Collison
Miss S. J. Conwill
T. Evans
H. R. M. Farmer
Sir Edward Fellowes
A. Fox
Sir Michael Fraser
S. Gordon
M. Harrison
S. C. Hawtrey
B. Keith-Lucas
A. S. King
K. E. Kitchen
U. W. Kitzinger
Professor F. Lawson
Sir Donald McDougall
A. MacIntyre
A. F. Madden
G. Marshall
D. L. Munby
H. G. Nicholas
H. Pelling
Miss M. F. Perham
P. G. Richards
C. Seymour-Ure
D. M. Shapiro
R. J. A. Skidelsky
N. D. Walker
P. M. Williams

While we could not have completed this book without these far-flung helpers, we should stress our sole responsibility for its inevitable errors. Our readers are earnestly invited to let us know of any that they may detect.[1]

DAVID BUTLER
JENNIE FREEMAN

NUFFIELD COLLEGE, OXFORD
June 1962

[1] *June 1964.* We must express our gratitude to the many people, friends and strangers, who answered this request. Several of those listed above have suggested *corrigenda* and we would like to add these names to their number: A. N. Cass, A. Deyermond, C. Driver, R. Jenkins, A. L. Lamaison, J. S. Milner, J. Morland Craig, J. Palmer, C. Pannell, M. B. Parker, J. C. Sainty, and A. H. Warren. We hope for still more suggestions of corrections and editions before the next edition.

I

MINISTRIES[1]

CONSERVATIVE GOVERNMENT, 1900–1905

	MINISTERS IN CABINET			JUNIOR MINISTERS ATTACHED	
P.M.	**M of Salisbury (3rd)**	1900–11 Jul 02			
	A. Balfour	12 Jul 02–4 Dec 05			
1st Ld of Treasury[2]	**A. Balfour**	1900			
	(*office combined with P.M. when Balfour succeeded Salisbury*)				
Ld Pres.	**D of Devonshire**	1900			
	M of Londonderry	13 Oct 03			
Ld Chanc.	**E of Halsbury**	1900			
Privy S.	**Vt Cross**	1900			
	M of Salisbury (3rd) (P.M.)	1 Nov 00			
	A. Balfour (P.M.)	12 Jul 02			
	M of Salisbury (4th)	11 Oct 03			
Exch.	**Sir M. Hicks-Beach**	1900	*Treasury:*		
	C. Ritchie	8 Aug 02	*F.S.*	R. Hanbury	1900
	A. Chamberlain	6 Oct 03		A. Chamberlain	7 Nov 00
				W. Hayes Fisher	8 Aug 02
				A. Elliott	10 Apr 03
				V. Cavendish	9 Oct 03
For. O.	**M of Salisbury (3rd) (P.M.)**	1900	*U-S.*	St J. Brodrick	1900
	M of Lansdowne	1 Nov 00		Vt Cranborne[3] (4th M of Salisbury)	7 Nov 00
				Earl Percy[3]	9 Oct 03
Home O.	**Sir M. White Ridley**	1900	*U-S.*	J. Collings	1900
	C. Ritchie	1 Nov 00		T. Cochrane	8 Aug 02
	A. Akers-Douglas	8 Aug 02			
Admir.	**G. Goschen**	1900	*P.&F.S.:*	Sir W. Macartney	1900
	E of Selborne	1 Nov 00		H. Arnold-Forster	7 Nov 00
	Earl Cawdor	5 Mar 05		E. Pretyman	11 Oct 03
			Civil Ld:	A. Chamberlain	1900
				E. Pretyman	7 Nov 00
				A. Lee	11 Oct 03
Bd Ag. & Fish.	**W. Long**	1900			
	R. Hanbury	14 Nov 00			
	E of Onslow	19 May 03			
	A. Fellowes	12 Mar 05			

[1] Ministers in the cabinet are printed throughout this section in heavy type. Ministers outside the cabinet and Ministers of State are printed in capitals. Junior ministers are in ordinary print. The seven leading offices are placed first in each ministry; the remainder are arranged alphabetically, except that the Law offices and the political appointments to the Royal Household are placed at the end, together with the Treasury appointments which are held by Whips. (Unpaid assistant Whips are not listed, being technically party, not government, appointees.) In these tables (and throughout the book) titles are placed in brackets if acquired during the tenure of a particular office or on transfer to the next office. U-S. Under Secretary: F.S. Financial Secretary: P.S. Parliamentary Secretary.

This section has been subdivided chronologically at changes of Prime Minister, except when few other offices changed hands, as in 1902, 1923, 1937 and 1957; further subdivisions are made for the drastic reconstructions of 1915, 1931 and May 1945.

[2] The only occasion from 1900 to 1960 when 1st Ld of Treasury was not combined with P.M.

[3] Not a member of the House of Lords.

CONSERVATIVE GOVERNMENT, 1900–1905 (*contd.*)

	MINISTERS IN CABINET			JUNIOR MINISTERS ATTACHED	
Col. O.	**J. Chamberlain**	1900	*U-S.*	E of Selborne	1900
	A. Lyttelton	6 Oct 03		E of Onslow	12 Nov 00
				D of Marlborough	23 Jul 03
Bd Educ.	**D of Devonshire**	1900	*Sec.*	(*office not established*)	
	M of Londonderry	8 Aug 02		Sir W. Anson	8 Aug 02
				(*previously Vice-President of Committee of Council—Sir J. Gorst* 1900-8 *Aug* 02)	
India O.	**Ld G. Hamilton**[1]	1900	*U-S.*	E of Onslow	1900
	St J. Brodrick	6 Oct 03		E of Hardwicke	12 Nov 00
				Earl Percy[1]	8 Aug 02
				E of Hardwicke	15 Oct 03
				M of Bath	19 Jan 05
Chief Sec. Ireland	(*office not in cabinet*)		*V. Pres. Dept. Agric. for Ireland:*	(Sir) H. Plunkett	1900
	G. Wyndham	8 Aug 02			
	W. Long	12 Mar 05			
Ld Chanc. Ireland	**Ld Ashbourne**	1900			
Ld Lieut. Ireland	**Earl Cadogan** (*E of Dudley* 8 *Aug* 02 *& office not in cabinet*)	1900			
D. Lanc.	**Ld James of Hereford** (*Sir W. Walrond* 8 *Aug* 02 *& office not in cabinet*)	1900			
Loc. Govt. Bd	**H. Chaplin**	1900	*P.S.*	T. Russell	1900
	W. Long	7 Nov 00		(Sir) J. Lawson	11 Nov 00
	G. Balfour	12 Mar 05		A. Jeffreys	27 Jun 05
Postm.-Gen.	(*office not in cabinet*)				
	M of Londonderry	7 Nov 00			
	A. Chamberlain	8 Aug 02			
	Ld Stanley[1]	6 Oct 03			
Scotland	**Ld Balfour of Burleigh**	1900			
	A. Murray	6 Oct 03			
	M of Linlithgow	2 Feb 05			
B.o.T.	**C. Ritchie**	1900	*P.S.*	E of Dudley	1900
	G. Balfour	7 Nov 00		A. Bonar Law	8 Aug 02
	M of Salisbury (4th)	12 Mar 05			
War O.	**M of Lansdowne**	1900	*F.S.*	J. Powell Williams	1900
	St J. Brodrick	1 Nov 00		Ld Stanley[1]	7 Nov 00
	H. Arnold-Forster	6 Oct 03		W. Bromley-Davenport	11 Oct 03
			P.S.	G. Wyndham	1900
				Ld Raglan	12 Nov 00
				E of Hardwicke	8 Aug 02
				E of Donoughmore	15 Oct 03
1st *C. Works*	**A. Akers-Douglas** (*Ld Windsor* 8 *Aug* 02 *& office out of cabinet*)	1900			

	MINISTERS NOT IN CABINET		
Chief Sec. Ireland	G. Balfour	1900	(*for Junior Ministers see above*)
	G. Wyndham	7 Nov 00	
	(8 *Aug* 02 *office in cabinet*)		
D. Lanc.	(*office in cabinet*)		
	Sir W. Walrond	8 Aug 02	
Paym.-Gen.	D of Marlborough	1900	
	Sir S. Crossley	11 Mar 02	
Postm.-Gen.	D of Norfolk	1900	
	M of Londonderry	2 Apr 00	
	(7 *Nov* 00 *office in cabinet*)		

[1] Not a member of the House of Lords.

CONSERVATIVE GOVERNMENT, 1900–1905 (*contd.*)

MINISTERS NOT IN CABINET

1st C. Works	(*office in cabinet*)	
	LD WINDSOR	8 Aug 02
Law Officers:		
Att. Gen.	SIR R. WEBSTER	1900
	SIR R. FINLAY	7 May 00
Sol. Gen.	SIR R. FINLAY	1900
	SIR E. CARSON	7 May 00
Ld Advoc.	A. MURRAY	1900
	S. DICKSON	18 Oct 03
Sol. Gen. Scotland	S. DICKSON	1900
	D. DUNDAS	18 Oct 03
	E. SALVESEN	30 Jan 05
	J. CLYDE	16 Oct 05
Att. Gen. Ireland	J. ATKINSON	1900
Sol. Gen. Ireland	D. BARTON	1900
	G. WRIGHT	30 Jan 00
	J. CAMPBELL	8 Jul 03
H.M. Household:		
Treas.	VT CURZON[1] (Earl Howe)	1900
	V. CAVENDISH	3 Dec 00
	M OF HAMILTON[1]	11 Oct 03
Comptr.	VT VALENTIA[1]	1900
V. Chamb.	A. FELLOWES	1900
	SIR A. ACLAND HOOD	3 Dec 00
	LD WOLVERTON	17 Nov 02
Ld Chamb.	E OF HOPETOUN	1900
	E OF CLARENDON	12 Nov 00
Ld Steward	E OF PEMBROKE & MONTGOMERY	1900
Capt. Gents at Arms	LD BELPER	1900
Capt. Yeomen of Guard	EARL WALDEGRAVE	1900
Master of Horse	D OF PORTLAND	1900
Master of Buckhounds	E OF COVENTRY	1900
	LD CHESHAM	2 Nov 00
	(*office abolished* 1901)	

P.S. to Treasury:		
	Sir W. Walrond	1900
	Sir A. Acland Hood	8 Aug 02
Junior Lds of Treasury:		
	W. Hayes Fisher	1900–8 Aug 02
	H. Anstruther	1900–11 Oct 03
	Ld Stanley[1]	1900–7 Nov 00
	A. Fellowes	7 Nov 00–15 Mar 05
	H. Forster	8 Aug 02–4 Dec 05
	Ld Balcarres[1]	11 Oct 03–4 Dec 05
	Ld E. Talbot[1]	16 Jun 05–4 Dec 05
Lds in Waiting:		
	E of Clarendon	1900–30 Oct 00
	Ld Harris	1900–4 Dec 00
	Vt Bridport	1900–18 Feb 01
	Ld Bagot	1900–14 Feb 05
	E of Denbigh	1900–4 Dec 05
	Earl Howe	30 Oct 00–1 Oct 03
	Ld Churchill (Vt)	1900–4 Dec 05
	Ld Kenyon	4 Dec 00–4 Dec 05
	E of Kintore	1900–4 Dec 05
	Ld Lawrence	1900–4 Dec 05
	Ld Suffield	18 Feb 01–4 Dec 05
	E of Erroll	19 Oct 03–4 Dec 05

LIBERAL GOVERNMENT, 1905–1908

MINISTERS IN CABINET

P.M.	**Sir H. Campbell-Bannerman**	5 Dec 05–5 Apr 08
Ld Pres.	**E of Crewe**	10 Dec 05
Ld Chanc.	**Sir R. Reid** (*Ld Loreburn*)	10 Dec 05
Privy S.	**M of Ripon**	10 Dec 05
Exch.	**H. Asquith**	10 Dec 05

JUNIOR MINISTERS ATTACHED

Treasury:		
F.S.	R. McKenna	12 Dec 05
	W. Runciman	29 Jan 07

[1] Not a member of the House of Lords.

LIBERAL GOVERNMENT, 1905–1908 (*contd.*)

MINISTERS IN CABINET			JUNIOR MINISTERS ATTACHED		
For. O.	**Sir E. Grey**	10 Dec 05	*U-S.*	Ld E. Fitzmaurice[1] (Ld)	18 Dec 05
Home O.	**H. Gladstone**	10 Dec 05	*U-S.*	H. Samuel	12 Dec 05
Admir.	**Ld Tweedmouth**	10 Dec 05	*P. & F.S.:*	E. Robertson	12 Dec 05
			Civil Ld:	G. Lambert	18 Dec 05
Bd Ag. & Fish.	**Earl Carrington**	10 Dec 05			
Col. O.	**E of Elgin**	10 Dec 05	*U-S.*	W. Churchill	12 Dec 05
Bd Educ.	**A. Birrell** **R. McKenna**	10 Dec 05 23 Jan 07	*P.S.*	T. Lough	18 Dec 05
India O.	**J. Morley**	10 Dec 05	*U-S.*	J. Ellis C. Hobhouse	12 Dec 05 29 Jan 07
Chief Sec. Ireland	**J. Bryce** **A. Birrell**	10 Dec 05 23 Jan 07	*Vice-Pres. Dept. Agric. for Ireland:*	Sir H. Plunkett T. Russell	12 Dec 05 21 May 07
D. Lanc.	**Sir H. Fowler**	10 Dec 05			
Loc. Govt. Bd.	**J. Burns**	10 Dec 05	*P.S.*	W. Runciman T. Macnamara	18 Dec 05 29 Jan 07
Postm.-Gen.	**S. Buxton**	10 Dec 05			
Scotland	**J. Sinclair**	10 Dec 05			
B.o.T.	**D. Lloyd George**	10 Dec 05	*P.S.*	H. Kearley	18 Dec 05
War O.	**R. Haldane**	10 Dec 05	*P.S.*	E of Portsmouth	12 Dec 05
			F.S.	T. Buchanan	14 Dec 05
1st C. Works	(*office not in cabinet*) **L. Harcourt**	27 Mar 07			

MINISTERS NOT IN CABINET					
Paym.-Gen.	R. Causton	12 Dec 05			
1st C. Works	L. Harcourt (27 *Mar* 07 *office in cabinet*)	10 Dec 05			
Law Officers:			*P.S. to Treasury:*	G. Whiteley	12 Dec 05
Att. Gen.	Sir J. Walton Sir W. Robson	12 Dec 05 28 Jan 08			
Sol. Gen.	Sir W. Robson Sir S. Evans	12 Dec 05 28 Jan 08			
Ld Advoc.	T. Shaw	12 Dec 05	*Junior Lds of Treasury:*	H. Lewis	18 Dec 05–5 Apr 08
Sol. Gen. Scotland	A. Ure	18 Dec 05		J. Pease	18 Dec 05–5 Apr 08
				F. Freeman-Thomas	21 Dec 05–2 Feb 06
Att. Gen. Ireland	R. Cherry	20 Dec 05		C. Norton	21 Dec 05–5 Apr 08
				J. Fuller	2 Feb 06–27 Feb 07
Sol. Gen. Ireland	R. Barry	20 Dec 05		J. Whitley	27 Feb 07–5 Apr 08
H.M. Household:			*Lds in Waiting:*		
Treas.	Sir E. Strachey	18 Dec 05		Ld Denman	18 Dec 05–31 Jul 07
Comptr.	Master of Elibank	18 Dec 05		E of Granard	18 Dec 05–21 Aug 07
V. Chamb.	W. Beaumont (*Ld Allendale*) J. Fuller	18 Dec 05 27 Feb 07		Ld Acton Earl Granville Ld Hamilton of Dalzell	18 Dec 05–5 Apr 08 18 Dec 05–5 Apr 08 18 Dec 05–5 Apr 08
Ld Chamb.	Vt Althorp	18 Dec 05		Ld Colebrooke	20 Dec 05–5 Apr 08
Ld Steward	Ld Hawkesbury (*1st E of Liverpool*) Earl Beauchamp	18 Dec 05 31 Jul 07		Ld Suffield Ld Farquhar	Feb 06–5 Apr 08 31 Jul 07–5 Apr 08

[1] Not a member of the House of Lords.

LIBERAL GOVERNMENT, 1905–1908 (*contd.*)

MINISTERS NOT IN CABINET

H.M. Household:

Master of Horse	E of Sefton	18 Dec 05	Ld Herschell	31 Jul 07–5 Apr 08
	E of Granard	6 Sep 07	Ld O'Hagan	1 Nov 07–5 Apr 08
Capt. Gents at Arms	Earl Beauchamp	18 Dec 05		
	Ld Denman	31 Jul 07		
Capt. Yeomen of Guard	D of Manchester	18 Dec 05		
	Ld Allendale	29 Apr 07		

LIBERAL GOVERNMENT, 1908–1915

MINISTERS IN CABINET			JUNIOR MINISTERS ATTACHED		
P.M.	**H. Asquith**	5 Apr 08–25 May 15			
Ld Pres.	**Ld Tweedmouth**	12 Apr 08			
	Vt Wolverhampton	13 Oct 08			
	Earl Beauchamp	16 Jun 10			
	Vt Morley	3 Nov 10			
	Earl Beauchamp	5 Aug 14			
Ld Chanc.	**Ld Loreburn** (*Earl*)	12 Apr 08			
	Vt Haldane	10 Jun 12			
Privy S.	**M of Ripon**	12 Apr 08			
	E of Crewe	9 Oct 08			
	Earl Carrington	23 Oct 11			
	M of Crewe	13 Feb 12			
Exch.	**D. Lloyd George**	12 Apr 08	*Treasury:*		
			F.S.	C. Hobhouse	12 Apr 08
				T. M'Kinnon Wood	23 Oct 11
				C. Masterman	13 Feb 12
				E. Montagu	11 Feb 14
				F. Acland	3 Feb 15
For. O.	**Sir E. Grey**	12 Apr 08	*U-S.*	Ld Fitzmaurice	12 Apr 08
				T. M'Kinnon Wood	19 Oct 08
				F. Acland	23 Oct 11
				N. Primrose	4 Feb 15
Home O.	**H. Gladstone**	12 Apr 08	*U-S.*	H. Samuel	12 Apr 08
	W. Churchill	14 Feb 10		C. Masterman	7 Jul 09
	R. McKenna	23 Oct 11		E. Griffith	19 Feb 12
				C. Harmsworth	4 Feb 15
Admir.	**R. McKenna**	12 Apr 08	*P. & F.S.:*		
	W. Churchill	23 Oct 11		T. Macnamara	13 Apr 08
			Civil Ld:		
				G. Lambert	12 Apr 08
Bd Ag. & Fish.	**Earl Carrington**	12 Apr 08	*P.S.*	(*post not established*)	
				Sir E. Strachey (*Ld Strachie*)	20 Dec 09
	W. Runciman	23 Oct 11		Ld Lucas	23 Oct 11
	Ld Lucas	6 Aug 14		Sir H. Verney	10 Aug 14
Att. Gen.	(*office not in cabinet*)				
	Sir R. Isaacs	4 Jun 12			
	Sir J. Simon	19 Oct 13			
Col. O.	**E of Crewe**	12 Apr 08	*U-S.*	J. Seely	12 Apr 08
	L. Harcourt	3 Nov 10		Ld Lucas	23 Mar 11
				Ld Emmott	23 Oct 11
				Ld Islington	10 Aug 14
Bd Educ.	**W. Runciman**	12 Apr 08	*P.S.*	T. M'Kinnon Wood	13 Apr 08
	J. Pease	23 Oct 11		C. Trevelyan	19 Oct 08
				C. Addison	10 Aug 14
India O.	**J. Morley (Vt)**	12 Apr 08	*U-S.*	T. Buchanan	12 Apr 08
	E of Crewe	3 Nov 10		Master of Elibank	25 Jun 09
	Vt Morley	7 Mar 11		E. Montagu	20 Feb 10
	E of Crewe (M)	25 May 11		C. Roberts	17 Feb 14

LIBERAL GOVERNMENT, 1908–1915 (*contd.*)

MINISTERS IN CABINET			JUNIOR MINISTERS ATTACHED		
Chief Sec. Ireland	**A. Birrell**	12 Apr 08	*V. Pres. Dept. Agric. Ireland:*	T. Russell	12 Apr 08
D. Lanc.	**Sir H. Fowler** (*Vt Wolverhampton*)	12 Apr 08			
	Ld Fitzmaurice	13 Oct 08			
	H. Samuel	25 Jun 09			
	J. Pease	14 Feb 10			
	C. Hobhouse	23 Oct 11			
	C. Masterman	11 Feb 14			
	E. Montagu	3 Feb 15			
Loc. Govt. Bd	**J. Burns**	12 Apr 08	*P.S.*	C. Masterman	12 Apr 08
	H. Samuel	11 Feb 14		H. Lewis	7 Jul 09
Postm.-Gen.	**S. Buxton**	12 Apr 08	*Ass.*	(*post not established*)	
	H. Samuel	14 Feb 10		Sir H. Norman	3 Jan 10
	C. Hobhouse	11 Feb 14		C. Norton	20 Feb 10
Scotland	**J. Sinclair** (*Ld Pentland*)	12 Apr 08			
	T. M'Kinnon Wood	13 Feb 12			
B.o.T.	**W. Churchill**	12 Apr 08	*P.S.*	(Sir) H. Kearley	12 Apr 08
	S. Buxton	14 Feb 10		H. Tennant	10 Jan 09
	J. Burns	11 Feb 14		J. Robertson	25 Oct 11
	W. Runciman	5 Aug 14			
War O.	**R. Haldane (Vt)**	12 Apr 08	*F.S.*	F. Acland	12 Apr 08
	J. Seely	12 Jun 12		C. Mallet	4 Mar 10
	H. Asquith (P.M.)	30 Mar 14		F. Acland	31 Jan 11
	Earl Kitchener	5 Aug 14		H. Tennant	25 Oct 11
				H. Baker	14 Jun 12
			U-S.	Ld Lucas	12 Apr 08
				J. Seely	23 Mar 11
				H. Tennant	14 Jun 12
1st C. Works	**L. Harcourt**	12 Apr 08			
	Earl Beauchamp	3 Nov 10			
	Ld Emmott	6 Aug 14			

MINISTERS NOT IN CABINET		
Paym.-Gen.	R. Causton (*Ld Southwark*)	12 Apr 08
	I. Guest (*Ld Ashby St Ledgers*)	23 Feb 10
	Ld Strachie	23 May 12
Law Officers:		
Att. Gen.	Sir W. Robson	12 Apr 08
	Sir R. Isaacs	7 Oct 10
	(*4 Jun 12 office in cabinet*)	
Sol. Gen.	Sir S. Evans	12 Apr 08
	Sir R. Isaacs	6 Mar 10
	Sir J. Simon	7 Oct 10
	Sir S. Buckmaster	19 Oct 13
Ld Advoc.	T. Shaw	12 Apr 08
	A. Ure	14 Feb 09
	R. Munro	30 Oct 13
Sol. Gen. Scotland	A. Ure	12 Apr 08
	A. Dewar	18 Feb 09
	W. Hunter	18 Apr 10
	A. Anderson	3 Dec 11
	T. Morison	30 Oct 13
Att. Gen Ireland	R. Cherry	12 Apr 08
	R. Barry	2 Dec 09
	C. O'Connor	26 Sep 11
	I. O'Brien	24 Jun 12

JUNIOR MINISTERS ATTACHED		
P.S. to Treasury:		
	G. Whiteley	12 Apr 08
	J. Pease	3 Jun 08
	Master of Elibank	14 Feb 10
	P. Illingworth	7 Aug 12
	J. Gulland	24 Jan 15
Junior Lds of Treasury:		
	J. Pease	12 Apr 08–3 Jun 08
	H. Lewis	12 Apr 08–7 Jul 09
	C. Norton	12 Apr 08–20 Feb 10
	J. Whitley	12 Apr 08–20 Feb 10
	O. Partington	6 Jul 09–19 Jan 11
	J. Gulland	7 Jul 09–24 Jan 15
	W. Benn	20 Feb 10–25 May 15
	E. Soares	20 Feb 10–16 Apr 11
	P. Illingworth	28 Feb 10–7 Aug 12
	W. Jones	19 Jan 11–25 May 15
	F. Guest	16 Apr 11–21 Feb 12
	Sir A. Haworth	21 Feb 12–16 Apr 12
	H. Webb	16 Apr 12–25 May 15

LIBERAL GOVERNMENT, 1908–1915 (*contd.*)

MINISTERS NOT IN CABINET

	T. Molony	10 Apr 13
	J. Moriarty	20 Jun 13
	J. Pim	1 Jul 14
Sol. Gen. Ireland	R. Barry	12 Apr 08
	C. O'Connor	2 Dec 09
	I. O'Brien	19 Oct 11
	T. Molony	24 Jun 12
	J. Moriarty	25 Apr 13
	J. Pim	20 Jun 13
	J. O'Connor	1 Jul 14
H.M. Household:		
Treas.	Sir E. Strachey	12 Apr 08
	W. Dudley Ward	20 Dec 09
	F. Guest	21 Feb 12
Comptr.	Master of Elibank	12 Apr 08
	E of Liverpool (2nd)	12 Jul 09
	Ld Saye & Sele	1 Nov 12
V. Chamb.	(Sir) J. Fuller	12 Apr 08
	G. Howard	6 Feb 11
Ld Chamb.	Vt Althorp (*Earl Spencer*)	12 Apr 08
	Ld Sandhurst	14 Feb 12
Ld Steward	Earl Beauchamp	12 Apr 08
	E of Chesterfield	22 Jun 10
Master of Horse	E of Granard	12 Apr 08
Capt. Gents at Arms	Ld Denman	12 Apr 08
	Ld Colebrooke	26 Jun 11
Capt. Yeomen of Guard	Ld Allendale (Vt)	12 Apr 08
	E of Craven	2 Oct 11

JUNIOR MINISTERS ATTACHED

C. Beck	3 Feb 15–25 May 15
W. Rea	3 Feb 15–25 May 15

Lds in Waiting:

Ld O'Hagan	12 Apr 08–15 Apr 10
Ld Suffield	12 Apr 08–7 May 10
Ld Hamilton of Dalzell	12 Apr 08–2 Oct 11
Ld Colebrooke	12 Apr 08–19 Jun 11
Ld Farquhar	12 Apr 08–25 May 15
Ld Herschell	12 Apr 08–25 May 15
Ld Acton	12 Apr 08–25 May 15
Earl Granville	12 Apr 08–25 May 15
Ld Tweedmouth	15 Apr 10–4 Dec 11
Ld Willingdon	19 Jun 11–31 Jan 13
Vt Allendale	2 Oct 11–25 May 15
Ld Loch	4 Dec 11–1 May 14
Ld Ashby St Ledgers	31 Jan 13–8 Feb 15
Ld Stanmore	1 May 14–25 May 15
Ld Ranksborough	8 Feb 15–25 May 15

COALITION GOVERNMENT, 1915–1916

MINISTERS IN CABINET

P.M.	**H. Asquith** (Lib)	25 May 15–5 Dec 16
Ld Pres.	**M of Crewe** (Lib)	25 May 15
Ld Chanc.	**Ld Buckmaster** (Lib)	25 May 15
Privy S.	**Earl Curzon** (C)	25 May 15
Exch.	**R. McKenna** (Lib)	25 May 15
For. O.	**Sir E. Grey** (Lib) (*Vt*)	25 May 15
Home O.	**Sir J. Simon** (Lib)	25 May 15
	Sir H. Samuel (Lib)	10 Jan 16
Admir.	**A. Balfour** (C)	25 May 15

JUNIOR MINISTERS ATTACHED

Treasury:		
F.S.	E. Montagu (Lib) (*also D. Lanc., in cabinet from 11 Jan 16*)	26 May 15
	T. M'Kinnon Wood (Lib) (*also D. Lanc. in cabinet*)	9 Jul 16
U-S.	Ld R. Cecil[1] (C) (*also Blockade, in cabinet from 23 Feb 16*)	30 May 15
Ass.	Ld Newton (C)	18 Aug 16
U-S.	W. Brace (Lab)	30 May 15
P. & F.S.:		
	T. Macnamara (Lib)	30 May 15
Civil Ld:		
	D of Devonshire (C)	9 Jun 15
	E of Lytton (C)	26 Jul 16

[1] Not a member of the House of Lords.

COALITION GOVERNMENT, 1915–1916 (*contd.*)

MINISTERS IN CABINET			JUNIOR MINISTERS ATTACHED		
Bd Ag. & Fish.	**E of Selborne** (C)	25 May 15	*P.S.*	F. Acland (Lib)	30 May 15
	E of Crawford (C)	11 Jul 16			
Att. Gen.	**Sir E. Carson** (C)	25 May 15			
	Sir F. Smith (C)	3 Nov 15			
Blockade	**Ld R. Cecil**[1] (C) (*also U-S. at F.O.*)	23 Feb 16			
Col. O.	**A. Bonar Law** (C)	25 May 15	*U-S.*	A. Steel-Maitland (C)	30 May 15
Bd Educ.	**A. Henderson** (Lab)	25 May 15	*P.S.*	H. Lewis (Lib)	30 May 15
	M of Crewe (Lib)	18 Aug 16			
Health & Loc. Govt Bd	**W. Long** (C)	25 May 15	*P.S.*	W. Hayes Fisher (C)	30 May 15
India O.	**A. Chamberlain** (C)	25 May 15	*U-S.*	Ld Islington (Lib)	30 May 15
Chief Sec. Ireland	**A. Birrell** (Lib)	25 May 15	*V. Pres. Dept. Agric. & Technical Instruction, Ireland:*		
	H. Duke (C)	31 Jul 16		T. Russell (Lib)	30 May 15
D. Lanc.	**W. Churchill** (Lib)	25 May 15			
	H. Samuel (Lib)	25 Nov 15			
	E. Montagu (Lib) (*also F.S. at Treasury*)	11 Jan 16			
	T. M'Kinnon Wood (Lib) (*also F.S. at Treasury*)	9 Jul 16			
Munitions	**D. Lloyd George** (Lib)	25 May 15	*P.S.*	C. Addison (Lib)	30 May 15–8 Dec 16
	E. Montagu (Lib)	9 Jul 16		A. Lee (C)	11 Nov 15[1]–9 Jul 16
Paym.-Gen.	(*office not in cabinet*)				
	A. Henderson (Lab)	18 Aug 16			
Min. without Portfolio	**M of Lansdowne** (C)	25 May 15			
Scotland	**T. M'Kinnon Wood** (Lib)	25 May 15			
	H. Tennant (Lib)	9 Jul 16			
B.o.T.	**W. Runciman** (Lib)	25 May 15	*P.S.*	E. Pretyman (C)	30 May 15
War O.	**Earl Kitchener**	25 May 15	*U-S.*	H. Tennant (Lib)	30 May 15
	D. Lloyd George (Lib)	6 Jul 16		E of Derby (C)	6 Jul 16
			F.S.	H. Forster (C)	30 May 15
1st C. Works	**L. Harcourt (Vt)** (Lib)	25 May 15			

MINISTERS NOT IN CABINET			JUNIOR MINISTERS ATTACHED		
Paym.-Gen.	Ld Newton (C) (*A. Henderson 18 Aug 16 & office in cabinet*)	9 Jun 15			
Postm.-Gen.	H. Samuel (Lib)	26 May 15	*Ass.*	H. Pike Pease (C)	30 May 15
	J. Pease (Lib)	18 Jan 16			
Law Officers:			*P.S. to Treasury:*		
Att. Gen.	(*office in cabinet*)			J. Gulland (Lib)	30 May 15–5 Dec 16
Sol. Gen.	Sir F. Smith (C)	2 Jun 15		Ld E. Talbot[2] (C)	30 May 15–5 Dec 16
	(Sir) G. Cave (C)	8 Nov 15	*Junior Lds of Treasury:*		
Ld Advoc.	R. Munro (Lib)	8 Jun 15		G. Howard (Lib)	27 May 15–5 Dec 16
Sol. Gen. Scotland	T. Morison (Lib)	8 Jun 15		G. Roberts (Lab)	27 May 15–5 Dec 16
Att. Gen. Ireland	J. Gordon (C)	8 Jun 15		W. Bridgeman (C)	27 May 15–5 Dec 16
	J. Campbell (C)	9 Apr 16			
Sol. Gen. Ireland	J. O'Connor (Nat)	8 Jun 15		W. Rea (Lib)	27 May 15–5 Dec 16

[1] Date of first reply in Commons as *Parliamentary (Military) Secretary to the Munitions Department.*

[2] Not a member of the House of Lords.

COALITION GOVERNMENT, 1915–1916 (*contd.*)

MINISTERS NOT IN CABINET

H.M. Household:

Treas.	J. HOPE (C)	30 May 15
Comptr.	C. ROBERTS (Lib)	30 May 15
V. Chamb.	C. BECK (Lib)	30 May 15
Ld Chamb.	LD SANDHURST (Lib)	9 Jun 15
Ld Steward	LD FARQUHAR (C)	9 Jun 15
Master of Horse	E OF CHESTERFIELD (Lib)	9 Jun 15
Capt. Gents at Arms	LD COLEBROOKE (Lib)	9 Jun 15
Capt. Yeomen of Guard	LD SUFFIELD (C)	9 Jun 15

JUNIOR MINISTERS ATTACHED

Lds in Waiting:

Ld Herschell (Lib) 9 Jun 15–5 Dec 16
Vt Allendale (Lib) 9 Jun 15–5 Dec 16
Ld Stanmore (Lib) 9 Jun 15–5 Dec 16
Ld Ranksborough (Lib) 9 Jun 15–5 Dec 16
Vt Valentia[1] (C) 9 Jun 15–5 Dec 16
Ld Hylton (C) 9 Jun 15–5 Dec 16

COALITION GOVERNMENT, 1916–1922

Note.—From 6 Dec 1916 to 10 Jan 1919 there was a war cabinet of 5–7 ministers.

MINISTERS IN WAR CABINET

P.M.	**D. Lloyd George** (Lib)	6 Dec 16–19 Oct 22
Ld Pres.	**Earl Curzon** (C)	10 Dec 16
	A. Balfour (C)	23 Oct 19
Ld Chanc.	(*office not in war cabinet: see below*)	
Privy S.	(*office not in war cabinet: see below*)	
Exch.	**A. Bonar Law** (C)	10 Dec 16
	A. Chamberlain (C)	10 Jan 19
	Sir R. Horne (C)	1 Apr 21
For. O.	(*office not in war cabinet: see below*)	
Home O.	(*office not in war cabinet: see below*)	
Nat. S.	**N. Chamberlain** (C)[1]	19 Dec 16
	(*Sir A. Geddes 17 Aug 17 & office not in war cabinet*)	
Min. without Portfolio	**A. Henderson** (Lab)	10 Dec 16–12 Aug 17
	Vt Milner (C)	10 Dec 16–18 Apr 18
	Sir E. Carson (C)	17 Jul 17–21 Jan 18
	J. Smuts[1]	22 Jun 17–10 Jan 19
	G. Barnes (Lab)	13 Aug 17–27 Jan 20
	A. Chamberlain (C)	18 Apr 18–10 Jan 19
	Sir L. Worthington-Evans (C)	2 Apr 20–13 Feb 21
	C. Addison (Lib)	1 Apr 21–14 Jul 21

JUNIOR MINISTERS ATTACHED

Treasury:

F.S.	Sir H. Lever	15 Dec 16–19 May 19
	S. Baldwin (C)	18 Jun 17–1 Apr 21
	E. Young (Lib)	1 Apr 21–19 Oct 22
P.S.	Vt Peel (C)	15 Apr 18–Dec 18
	S. Walsh (Lab)	17 Mar 17–28 Jun 17
	C. Beck (Lib)	28 Jun 17–Dec 19
	(*post abolished* 1919)	

MINISTERS OF CABINET RANK 1916–1919 & MINISTERS IN CABINET 1919–1922

Ld Chanc.	**Ld Finlay** (C)	10 Dec 16
	Ld Birkenhead (Vt) (C)	10 Jan 19

JUNIOR MINISTERS ATTACHED

[1] Not a member of the House of Commons.

COALITION GOVERNMENT, 1916–1922 (*contd.*)

MINISTERS OF CABINET RANK 1916–1919 & MINISTERS IN CABINET 1919–1922			JUNIOR MINISTERS ATTACHED		
Privy S.	**E of Crawford** (C)	15 Dec 16			
	A. Bonar Law (C)	10 Jan 19			
	A. Chamberlain (C)	23 Mar 21			
For. O.	**A. Balfour** (C)	10 Dec 16	*U-S.*	Ld R. Cecil[1] (C)	10 Dec 16
	Earl Curzon (C)	23 Oct 19		C. Harmsworth (Lib)	10 Jan 19
	(*Marquess*)		*Ass. U-S.:*		
				Ld Newton (C)	10 Dec 16
				(*post abolished* 10 *Jan* 1919)	
Home O.	**Sir G. Cave (Vt)** (C)	10 Dec 16	*U-S.*	W. Brace (Lab)	10 Dec 16
	E. Shortt (Lib)	10 Jan 19		Sir H. Greenwood (Lib)	10 Jan 19
				(Sir) J. Baird (C)	29 Apr 19
Admir.	**Sir E. Carson** (C)	10 Dec 16	*P. & F.S.:*		
	Sir E. Geddes (C)	17 Jul 17		T. Macnamara (Lib)	10 Dec 16
	W. Long (C)	10 Jan 19		Sir J. Craig (C)	2 Apr 20
	Ld Lee (C)	13 Feb 21		L. Amery (C)	1 Apr 21
			P.S. Addit.:		
				E of Lytton (C)	7 Feb 17
				(*post abolished* 27 *Jan* 1919)	
			Civil Ld:		
				E. Pretyman (C)	14 Dec 16
				E of Lytton (C)	27 Jan 19
				E of Onslow (C)	26 Oct 20
				B. Eyres-Monsell (C)	1 Apr 21
			2nd Civil Ld:		
				A. Pease (C)	10 Dec 16
				(*post abolished* 10 *Jan* 1919)	
Bd Ag. & Fish.	**R. Prothero** (C)	10 Dec 16	*P.S.*	Sir R. Winfrey (Lib)	14 Dec 16
	(*Ld Ernle*)			D of Marlborough (C)	18 Feb 17
	Ld Lee (C)	15 Aug 19		Vt Goschen (C)	26 Mar 18
	(*Min.* 15 *Aug* 19)			Ld Clinton (C)	18 Jun 18
	Sir A. Griffith-Boscawen (C)	13 Feb 21		Sir A. Griffith-Boscawen (C)	10 Jan 19
				(*& Dep. Min. Fisheries* 18 *Nov* 19)	
				E of Onslow (C)	5 Apr 21
				E of Ancaster (C)	7 Apr 21
				(*& Dep. Min. Fisheries* 28 *Oct* 21)	
Att. Gen.	(*office not in cabinet*)				
	Sir G. Hewart (Lib)	7 Nov 21			
	(*Sir E. Pollock* (*C*) 6 *Mar* 22 *& office not in cabinet*)				
Col. O.	**W. Long** (C)	10 Dec 16	*U-S.*	(Sir) A. Steel-Maitland (C)	10 Dec 16
	Vt Milner (C)	10 Jan 19		W. Hewins (C)	26 Sep 17
	W. Churchill (Lib)	13 Feb 21		L. Amery (C)	10 Jan 19
				E. Wood (C)	1 Apr 21
Bd Educ.	**H. Fisher** (Lib)	10 Dec 16	*P.S.*	(Sir) H. Lewis (Lib)	10 Dec 16
Health	(*Dept. under Loc. Govt Bd: see below*)		*P.S.* (*Loc. Govt Bd*)*:*		
				W. Hayes Fisher (C)	10 Dec 16
				S. Walsh (Lab)	28 Jun 17
	C. Addison (Lib)	24 Jun 19		W. Astor (Vt) (C)	27 Jan 19
	Sir A. Mond (Lib)	1 Apr 21		E of Onslow (C)	7 Apr 21
India O.	**A. Chamberlain** (C)	10 Dec 16	*U-S.*	Ld Islington (Lib)	10 Dec 16
	E. Montagu (Lib)	17 Jul 17		Ld Sinha (Lib)	10 Jan 19
	Vt Peel (C)	19 Mar 22		E of Lytton (C)	22 Sep 20
				Earl Winterton[1] (C)	20 Mar 22
Chief Sec. Ireland	**(Sir) H. Duke** (C)	10 Dec 16	*V. Pres. Dept. Agric. & Technical Instruction for Ireland:*		
	E. Shortt (Lib)	5 May 18			
	I. Macpherson (Lib)	10 Jan 19		(Sir) T. Russell (Lib)	10 Dec 16
	Sir H. Greenwood (Lib)	2 Apr 20		H. Barrie (C)	15 Jan 19

[1] Not a member of the House of Lords.

COALITION GOVERNMENT, 1916–1922 (*contd.*)

MINISTERS OF CABINET RANK 1916–1919 & MINISTERS IN CABINET 1919–1922			JUNIOR MINISTERS ATTACHED		
Ld Lieut. Ireland	**Ld Wimborne** (Lib)	10 Dec 16			
	Vt French (*E of Ypres*)	5 May 18			
	Vt Fitzalan (C)	1 Apr 21			
Lab.	**J. Hodge** (Lab)	10 Dec 16	*P.S.*	W. Bridgeman (C)	22 Dec 16
	G. Roberts (Lab)	17 Aug 17		G. Wardle (Lab)	10 Jan 19
	Sir R. Horne (C)	10 Jan 19		Sir A. Montague-Barlow (C)	2 April 20
	T. Macnamara (Lib)	19 Mar 20			
D. Lanc.	**Sir F. Cawley** (Lib)	10 Dec 16			
	Ld Beaverbrook (C)	10 Feb 18			
	(*& Min. of Propaganda/Information*)				
	Ld Downham (C)	4 Nov 18			
	(*E of Crawford (C) 10 Jan 19 & office not in cabinet*)				
Loc. Govt. Bd	**Ld Rhondda** (Lib)	10 Dec 16		(*for Junior Ministers see above, under Health*)	
	W. Hayes Fisher (C)	28 Jun 17			
	(*Ld Downham*)				
	Sir A. Geddes (C)	4 Nov 18			
	C. Addison (Lib)	10 Jan 19			
	(*24 Jun 19 became Min. of Health: see above*)				
Munitions (Supply)	**C. Addison** (Lib)	10 Dec 16	*P.S.*	Sir L. Worthington-Evans (C)	14 Dec 16–30 Jan 18
	W. Churchill (Lib)	17 Jul 17		F. Kellaway (Lib)	14 Dec 16–1 Apr 21
	(*10 Jan 19 became Min. of Supply*)			J. Seely (Lib)	18 Jul 18–10 Jan 19
	Ld Inverforth (Con)	10 Jan 19		J. Baird (C)	10 Jan 19–27 Jan 19
	(*office abolished 21 Mar 21*)		*P. & F.S.:*	Sir L. Worthington-Evans (C)	30 Jan 18–13 May 18
				J. Hope (C)	27 Jan 19–4 Apr 21
Scotland	**R. Munro** (Lib)	10 Dec 16	*P.S. Min. of Health for Scotland:*	(Sir) J. Pratt (Lib)	8 Aug 19
B.o.T.	**Sir A. Stanley** (Lib)	10 Dec 16	*P.S.*	G. Roberts (Lab)	14 Dec 16
	Sir A. Geddes (C)	26 May 19		G. Wardle (Lab)	17 Aug 17
	Sir R. Horne (C)	19 Mar 20		W. Bridgeman (C)	10 Jan 19
	S. Baldwin (C)	1 Apr 21		Sir P. Lloyd-Greame (C)	22 Aug 20
				Sir W. Mitchell-Thomson (C)	1 Apr 21
			Sec. Dept. Overseas Trade:	Sir A. Steel-Maitland (C)	14 Sep 17
				Sir H. Greenwood (Lib)	29 Apr 19
				F. Kellaway (Lib)	2 Apr 20
				Sir P. Lloyd-Greame (C)	1 Apr 21
				(*Director Overseas Trade Dept.*)	
			P.S. Mines Dept.:	W. Bridgeman (C)	22 Aug 20
Transp.	(*office not established*)		*P.S.*	Sir R. Williams (Lib)	23 Sep 19
	Sir E. Geddes (C)	17 Aug 19		A. Neal (Lib)	28 Nov 19
	(*Vt Peel 7 Nov 21 & office not in cabinet*)				
War O	**E of Derby** (C)	10 Dec 16	*U-S.*	I. Macpherson (Lib)	14 Dec 16
	Vt Milner (C)	18 Apr 18		Vt Peel (C)	10 Jan 19
	(*10 Jan 19 War O. & Air Min. combined*)			Sir R. Sanders (C)	1 Apr 21
			F.S.	H. Forster (Ld) (C)	10 Dec 16
	W. Churchill (Lib)	10 Jan 19		Sir A. Williamson (Lib)	18 Dec 19
	(*13 Feb 21 War O. only*)			G. Stanley (C)	1 Apr 21
	Sir L. Worthington-Evans (C)	13 Feb 21	*P.S.*	Earl Stanhope (C)	14 Dec 16
				(*post abolished 10 Jan 1919*)	
1st C. Works	(*office not in cabinet*)				
	E of Crawford (C)	7 Apr 22			

COALITION GOVERNMENT, 1916–1922 (*contd.*)

	MINISTERS NOT IN CABINET			JUNIOR MINISTERS ATTACHED	
Air	Ld Rothermere (Lib)	26 Nov 17	*P.S. Air Council:*		
	Ld Weir (Lib)	26 Apr 18		J. Baird (C)	14 Dec 16
	(*War O. & Air Min. combined 10 Jan 19, see above*)			(*post abolished 10 Jan 19*)	
	W. Churchill (Lib)	10 Jan 19	*U-S.*	J. Seely (Lib)	10 Jan 19
	F. Guest (Lib)	1 Apr 21		G. Tryon (C)	22 Dec 19
				M of Londonderry (C)	2 Apr 20
				Ld Gorell (Lib)	18 Jul 21
Blockade	Ld R. Cecil[1] (C)	10 Dec 16	*P.S.*	F. Leverton Harris	22 Dec 16
	(*also U-S. at F.O.*)			(*post abolished 10 Jan 19*)	
	Sir L. Worthington-Evans (C)	18 Jul 18			
	(*office abolished 10 Jan 1919*)				
Food Control	Vt Devonport (Lib)	10 Dec 16	*P.S.*	(Sir) C. Bathurst (C)	12 Dec 16
	Ld Rhondda (Vt) (Lib)	19 Jun 17		J. Clynes (Lab)	2 Jul 17
	J. Clynes (Lab)	9 Jul 18		W. Astor (C)	18 Jul 18
	G. Roberts (Lab)	10 Jan 19		C. McCurdy (Lib)	27 Jan 19
	C. McCurdy (Lib)	19 Mar 20		Sir W. Mitchell-Thomson (C)	19 Apr 20
	(*office abolished 31 Mar 21*)				
Ld Chanc. Ireland	Sir I. O'Brien (Lib)	10 Dec 16			
	Sir J. Campbell (C)	4 Jun 18			
	Sir J. Ross (C)	27 Jun 21			
D. Lanc.	(*office of cabinet rank see above*)				
	E of Crawford (C)	10 Jan 19			
	Vt Peel (C)	1 Apr 21			
	Sir W. Sutherland (Lib)	7 Apr 22			
Nat. S.	(*office in cabinet*)			(*for Junior Ministers see above*)	
	Sir A. Geddes (C)	17 Aug 17			
	(*Jan 1919 & Min. of Reconstruction*)				
Paym.-Gen.	Sir J. Compton-Rickett (Lib)	15 Dec 16			
	Sir T. Walters (Lib)	26 Oct 19			
Pensions	G. Barnes (Lab)	10 Dec 16	*P.S.*	Sir A. Griffith-Boscawen (C)	22 Dec 16
	J. Hodge (Lab)	17 Aug 17		Sir J. Craig (C)	10 Jan 19
	Sir L. Worthington-Evans (C)	10 Jan 19		G. Tryon (C)	2 Apr 20
	I. Macpherson (Lib)	2 Apr 20			
Min. without Portfolio	Sir E. Geddes (C)	10 Jan 19–19 May 19			
Postm.-Gen.	A. Illingworth (Lib)	10 Dec 16	*Ass.*	H. Pike Pease (C)	10 Dec 16
	F. Kellaway (Lib)	1 Apr 21			
Reconstruction	C. Addison (Lib)	17 Jul 17		(*for Junior Ministers see above, under National Service & Reconstruction*)	
	(*office abolished 10 Jan 1919*)				
Shipping	Sir J. Maclay (Ld) (Lib)	10 Dec 16	*P.S.*	Sir L. Chiozza Money (Lib)	22 Dec 16
	(*office abolished 31 Mar 21*)			L. Wilson (C)	10 Jan 19
Transp.	(*office in cabinet from 17 Aug 19*)			(*for Junior Ministers see above*)	
	Vt Peel (C)	7 Nov 21			
	E of Crawford (C)	12 Apr 22			
1st C. Works	Sir A. Mond (Lib)	10 Dec 16			
	E of Crawford (C)	1 Apr 21			
	(*office in cabinet 7 Apr 22*)				
Law Officers:			*P.S. to Treasury:*		
Att. Gen.	Sir F. Smith (C)	10 Dec 16		Ld E. Talbot[1] (C)	14 Dec 16–1 Apr 21
	(*Ld Birkenhead*)			N. Primrose (Lib)	14 Dec 16–2 Mar 17
	Sir G. Hewart (Lib)	10 Jan 19		F. Guest (Lib)	2 Mar 17–1 Apr 21
	(*office in cabinet 7 Nov 21*)			C. McCurdy (Lib)	1 Apr 21–19 Oct 22
	Sir E. Pollock (C)	6 Mar 22		L. Wilson (C)	1 Apr 21–19 Oct 22

[1] Not a member of the House of Lords.

COALITION GOVERNMENT, 1916–1922 (*contd.*)

MINISTERS NOT IN CABINET

Law Officers:

Sol. Gen.	Sir G. Hewart (Lib)	10 Dec 16
	Sir E. Pollock (C)	10 Jan 19
	(Sir) L. Scott (C)	6 Mar 22
Ld Advoc.	J. Clyde (C)	10 Dec 16
	T. Morison (Lib)	25 Mar 20
	C. Murray (C)	5 Mar 22
Sol. Gen. Scotland	T. Morison (Lib)	10 Dec 16
	C. Murray (C)	25 Mar 20
	A. Briggs Constable (C)	16 Mar 22
	W. Watson (C)	Jun 22
Att. Gen. Ireland	J. Campbell (C)	20 Dec 16
	J. O'Connor (Nat)	8 Jan 17
	A. Samuels (C)	7 Apr 18
	D. Henry (C)	6 Jul 19
	T. Brown (C)	5 Aug 21
	(*post vacant from* 16 *Nov* 21)	
Sol. Gen. Ireland	J. Chambers (C)	19 Mar 17
	A. Samuels (C)	12 Sep 17
	J. Powell (C)	7 Apr 18
	D. Henry (C)	27 Nov 18
	D. Wilson (C)	6 Jul 19
	T. Brown (C)	12 Jun 21

H.M. Household:

Treas.	(Sir) J. Craig (C)	14 Dec 16
	R. Sanders (C)	10 Jun 18
	B. Eyres-Monsell (C)	5 Feb 19
	G. Gibbs (C)	1 Apr 21
Comptr.	Sir E. Cornwall (Lib)	14 Dec 16
	G. Stanley (C)	28 Feb 19
	H. Barnston (C)	7 Apr 21
V. Chamb.	C. Beck (Lib)	14 Dec 16
	W. Dudley Ward (Lib)	9 Dec 17
Ld Chamb.	Ld Sandhurst (Vt) (Lib)	14 Dec 16
	D of Atholl (C)	20 Nov 21
Ld Steward	Ld Farquhar (Vt) (C)	14 Dec 16
Master of Horse	E of Chesterfield (Lib)	14 Dec 16
Capt. Gents at Arms	Ld Colebrooke (Lib)	14 Dec 16
Capt. Yeomen of Guard	Ld Suffield (C)	14 Dec 16
	Ld Hylton (C)	21 May 18

JUNIOR MINISTERS ATTACHED

Junior Lds of Treasury:

G. Howard (Lib)	10 Dec 16–27 Dec 16
G. Roberts (Lab)	10 Dec 16–27 Dec 16
W. Bridgeman (C)	10 Dec 16–27 Dec 16
W. Rea (Lib)	10 Dec 16–27 Dec 16
S. Walsh (Lab)	14 Dec 16–27 Dec 16
J. Hope (C)	14 Dec 16–27 Jan 19
J. Pratt (Lib)	14 Dec 16–8 Aug 19
S. Baldwin (C)	29 Jan 17–21 Jun 17
J. Parker (Lab)	29 Jan 17–19 Oct 22
J. Towyn Jones (Lib)	29 Jan 17–4 Jul 22
(Sir) R. Sanders (C)	5 Feb 19–1 Apr 21
Sir G. Collins (Lib)	8 Aug 19–10 Feb 20
Sir W. Sutherland (Lib)	15 Feb 20–7 Apr 22
Sir J. Gilmour (C)	1 Apr 22–19 Oct 22
T. Lewis (Lib)	4 Jul 22–19 Oct 22

Lds in Waiting:

Ld Herschell (Lib)	14 Dec 16–11 Feb 19
Ld Stanmore (Lib)	14 Dec 16–19 Oct 22
Ld Ranksborough (Lib)	14 Dec 16–4 Apr 21
Vt Valentia[1] (C)	14 Dec 16–19 Oct 22
Ld Hylton (C)	14 Dec 16–18 May 18
Ld Kenyon (C)	14 Dec 16–11 Sep 18
Ld Somerleyton (C)	18 May 18–19 Oct 22
Ld Elphinstone (C)	10 Sep 18–21 Nov 18
E of Jersey (C)	11 Jan 19–17 Aug 19
E of Bradford (C)	11 Feb 19–19 Oct 22
E of Onslow (C)	17 Aug 19–12 Nov 20
E of Lucan (C)	12 Nov 20–19 Oct 22
E of Clarendon (C)	7 Apr 21–19 Oct 22

CONSERVATIVE GOVERNMENT, 1922–1924

MINISTERS IN CABINET

P.M.	**A. Bonar Law**	23 Oct 22–20 May 23
	S. Baldwin	22 May 23–22 Jan 24
Ld Pres.	**M of Salisbury**	24 Oct 22
Ld Chanc.	**Vt Cave**	24 Oct 22
Privy S.	(*office vacant*)	
	Ld R. Cecil[1]	25 May 23

JUNIOR MINISTERS ATTACHED

[1] Not a member of the House of Lords. Viscount Valentia became a U.K. Peer (Ld Annesley) in 1917.

CONSERVATIVE GOVERNMENT, 1922–1924 (*contd.*)

	MINISTERS IN CABINET			JUNIOR MINISTERS ATTACHED	
Exch.	**S. Baldwin**	24 Oct 22	*Treasury:*		
	(*& P.M. from 22 May 23*)		*F.S.*	J. Hills	6 Nov 22
	N. Chamberlain	27 Aug 23		A. Boyd-Carpenter	12 Mar 23
F.S. to Treasury	(*office not in cabinet*)			(*Sir W. Joynson-Hicks 25 May 23 & seat in cabinet*)	
	Sir W. Joynson-Hicks	25 May 23		W. Guinness	5 Oct 23
	(*W. Guinness 5 Oct 23 & office not in cabinet*)				
For. O.	**Marquess Curzon**	24 Oct 22	*U-S.*	R. McNeill	31 Oct 22
Home O.	**W. Bridgeman**	24 Oct 22	*U-S.*	G. Stanley	31 Oct 22
				G. Locker-Lampson	12 Mar 23
Admir.	**L. Amery**	24 Oct 22	*P. & F.S.:*		
				B. Eyres-Monsell	31 Oct 22
				A. Boyd-Carpenter	25 May 23
			Civil Ld:		
				M of Linlithgow	31 Oct 22
Ag. & Fish.	**Sir R. Sanders**	24 Oct 22	*P.S. Ag. & Deputy Min. Fisheries:*		
				E of Ancaster	31 Oct 22
Air	(*office not in cabinet*)		*U-S.*	D of Sutherland	31 Oct 22
	Sir S. Hoare	25 May 23			
Col. O.	**D of Devonshire**	24 Oct 22	*U-S.*	W. Ormsby-Gore	31 Oct 22
Bd Educ.	**E. Wood**	24 Oct 22	*P.S.*	Ld E. Percy [1]	21 Mar 23
				E of Onslow	25 May 23
Health	**Sir A. Griffith-Boscawen**	24 Oct 22	*P.S.*	E of Onslow	31 Oct 22
	N. Chamberlain	7 Mar 23		Ld E. Percy [1]	25 May 23
	Sir W. Joynson-Hicks	27 Aug 23			
India O.	**Vt Peel**	24 Oct 22	*U-S.*	Earl Winterton [1]	31 Oct 22
Lab.	**Sir A. Montague-Barlow**	31 Oct 22	*P.S.*	A. Boyd-Carpenter	6 Nov 22
				H. Betterton	12 Mar 23
D. Lanc.	**M of Salisbury**	24 Oct 22			
	(*J. Davidson & office not in cabinet 25 May 23*)				
Postm.-Gen.	(*office not in cabinet*)				
	Sir L. Worthington-Evans	28 May 23			
Scotland	**Vt Novar**	24 Oct 22	*P.S. Min. of Health for Scotland:*		
				J. Kidd	31 Oct 22
				W. Elliot	15 Jan 23
B.o.T.	**Sir P. Lloyd-Greame**	24 Oct 22	*P.S.*	Vt Wolmer [1]	31 Oct 22
			Sec. Overseas Trade Dept.:		
				Sir W. Joynson-Hicks	31 Oct 22–12 Mar 23
				A. Buckley	12 Mar 23–18 Nov 23
			P.S. Mines Dept.:		
				G. Lane-Fox	6 Nov 22
War O	**E of Derby**	24 Oct 22	*U-S.*	W. Guinness	31 Oct 22
				W. Ashley	8 Oct 23
			F.S.	S. Jackson	31 Oct 22
				R. Gwynne	15 Mar 23

	MINISTERS NOT IN CABINET		JUNIOR MINISTERS ATTACHED
Air	SIR S. HOARE	31 Oct 22	(*for Junior Ministers see above*)
	(*office in cabinet 25 May 23*)		
D. Lanc.	(*office in cabinet*)		
	J. DAVIDSON	25 May 23	

[1] Not a member of the House of Lords.

CONSERVATIVE GOVERNMENT, 1922–1924 (*contd.*)

MINISTERS NOT IN CABINET			JUNIOR MINISTERS ATTACHED		
Paym. Gen.	(*office vacant*)				
	N. CHAMBERLAIN	5 Feb 23			
	SIR W. JOYNSON-HICKS	15 Mar 23			
	A. BOYD-CARPENTER	25 May 23			
Pensions	G. TRYON	31 Oct 22	*P.S.*	C. Craig	13 Feb 23
Postm.-Gen.	N. CHAMBERLAIN	31 Oct 22			
	SIR W. JOYNSON-HICKS	7 Mar 23			
	(*Sir L. Worthington-Evans & office in cabinet* 28 *May* 23)				
Transp.	SIR J. BAIRD	31 Oct 22	*P.S. Office of Works & Min. of Transp.:*		
				W. Ashley	31 Oct 22
1st *C. Works*	SIR J. BAIRD	31 Oct 22		J. Moore-Brabazon	8 Oct 23
				(*to Min. Transp. only*)	
Law Officers:			*P.S. to Treasury:*		
Att. Gen.	SIR D. HOGG	24 Oct 22		L. Wilson	31 Oct 22
Sol. Gen.	SIR T. INSKIP	31 Oct 22		B. Eyres-Monsell	25 Jul 23
Ld Advoc.	W. WATSON	24 Oct 22	*Junior Lds of Treasury:*		
Sol. Gen. Scotland	D. FLEMING	6 Nov 22		D. King	31 Oct 22–22 Jan 24
	F. THOMSON	5 Apr 23		A. Buckley	31 Oct 22–12 Mar 23
				F. Thomson	7 Feb 23–25 May 23
				G. Hennessy	11 Dec 22–22 Jan 24
				W. Cope	20 Mar 23–22 Jan 24
				P. Ford	25 May 23–20 Dec 23
				Sir J. Gilmour	20 Dec 23–22 Jan 24
H.M. Household:			*Lds in Waiting:*		
Treas.	G. GIBBS	6 Nov 22		Vt Valentia	20 Nov 22–22 Jan 24
Comptr.	H. BARNSTON	31 Oct 22		Ld Somerleyton	20 Nov 22–22 Jan 24
V. Chamb.	D. HACKING	20 Nov 22		E of Bradford	20 Nov 22–22 Jan 24
Ld Chamb.	E OF CROMER	20 Nov 22		E of Lucan	20 Nov 22–22 Jan 24
Ld Steward	E OF SHAFTESBURY	20 Nov 22		E of Malmesbury	20 Nov 22–22 Jan 24
Master of Horse	M OF BATH	20 Nov 22		E of Albemarle	20 Nov 22–22 Jan 24
Capt. Gents at Arms	E OF CLARENDON	20 Nov 22			
Capt. Yeomen of Guard	LD HYLTON	20 Nov 22			

LABOUR GOVERNMENT, 1924

MINISTERS IN CABINET			JUNIOR MINISTERS ATTACHED		
P.M.	**J. R. MacDonald**	22 Jan 24–3 Nov 24			
Ld Pres.	**Ld Parmoor**	22 Jan 24			
Ld Chanc.	**Vt Haldane**	22 Jan 24			
Privy S.	**J. Clynes**	22 Jan 24			
Exch.	**P. Snowden**	22 Jan 24	*Treasury:*		
			F.S.	W. Graham	23 Jan 24
For. O.	**J. R. MacDonald (P.M.)**	22 Jan 24	*U-S.*	A. Ponsonby	23 Jan 24
Home O.	**A. Henderson**	22 Jan 24	*U-S.*	R. Davies	23 Jan 24
Admir.	**Vt Chelmsford**	22 Jan 24	*P. & F.S.:*		
				C. Ammon	23 Jan 24
			Civil Ld:		
				F. Hodges	24 Jan 24
Ag. & Fish	**N. Buxton**	22 Jan 24	*P.S.*	W. Smith	23 Jan 24

LABOUR GOVERNMENT, 1924 (*contd.*)

MINISTERS IN CABINET			JUNIOR MINISTERS ATTACHED		
Air	**Ld Thomson**	22 Jan 24	*U-S.*	W. Leach	23 Jan 24
Col. O.	**J. Thomas**	22 Jan 24	*U-S.*	Ld Arnold	23 Jan 24
Bd Educ.	**C. Trevelyan**	22 Jan 24	*P.S.*	M. Jones	23 Jan 24
Health	**J. Wheatley**	22 Jan 24	*P.S.*	A. Greenwood	23 Jan 24
India O.	**Ld Olivier**	22 Jan 24	*U-S.*	R. Richards	23 Jan 24
Lab.	**T. Shaw**	22 Jan 24	*P.S.*	Miss M. Bondfield	23 Jan 24
D. Lanc.	**J. Wedgwood**	22 Jan 24			
Postm.-Gen.	**V. Hartshorn**	22 Jan 24			
Scotland	**W. Adamson**	22 Jan 24	*U-S. Health for Scotland:*	J. Stewart	23 Jan 24
B.o.T.	**S. Webb**	22 Jan 24	*P.S.*	A. Alexander	23 Jan 24
			P.S. Overseas Trade Dept.:	W. Lunn	23 Jan 24
			P.S. Mines Dept.:	E. Shinwell	23 Jan 24
War O.	**S. Walsh**	22 Jan 24	*U-S.*	C. Attlee	23 Jan 24
			F.S.	J. Lawson	23 Jan 24
1st C. Works	**F. Jowett**	22 Jan 24			

MINISTERS NOT IN CABINET			JUNIOR MINISTERS ATTACHED		
Paym.-Gen.	H. Gosling	6 May 24			
Pensions	F. Roberts	23 Jan 24	*P.S.*	J. Muir	28 Jan 24
Transp.	H. Gosling	24 Jan 24	*P.S.*	(*vacant*)	
Law Officers:			*P.S. to Treasury:*	B. Spoor	23 Jan 24
Att. Gen.	Sir P. Hastings	23 Jan 24	*Junior Lds of Treasury:*	F. Hall	2 Feb 24
Sol. Gen.	Sir H. Slesser	23 Jan 24		T. Kennedy	2 Feb 24
Ld Advoc.	H. Macmillan[1]	8 Feb 24		J. Robertson	2 Feb 24
Sol. Gen. Scotland	J. Fenton[1]	18 Feb 24		G. Warne	24 Feb 24
				W. Graham	2 Feb 24
H.M. Household:			*Lds in Waiting:*	Earl De La Warr	8 Feb 24
Treas.	T. Griffiths	2 Feb 24		Ld Muir-Mackenzie	8 Feb 24
Comptr.	J. Parkinson	2 Feb 24			
V. Chamb.	J. Davison	2 Feb 24			
Capt. Gents at Arms	E of Dunmore[1]	2 Feb 24			
Capt. Yeomen of Guard	Ld Loch[1]	2 Feb 24			

CONSERVATIVE GOVERNMENT, 1924–1929

MINISTERS IN CABINET		
P.M.	**S. Baldwin**	4 Nov 24–4 Jun 29
Ld Pres.	**Marquess Curzon**	6 Nov 24
	E of Balfour	27 Apr 25
Ld Chanc.	**Vt Cave**	6 Nov 24
	Ld Hailsham (Vt)	28 Mar 28
Privy S.	**M of Salisbury**	6 Nov 24

[1] Non-political appointments.

CONSERVATIVE GOVERNMENT, 1924–1929 (*contd.*)

	MINISTERS IN CABINET			JUNIOR MINISTERS ATTACHED	
Exch.	**W. Churchill**	6 Nov 24	*Treasury:*		
			F.S.	W. Guinness	11 Nov 24
				R. McNeill (*Ld Cushendun*)	5 Nov 25
				A. Samuel	1 Nov 27
For. O.	**(Sir) A. Chamberlain**	6 Nov 24	*U-S.*	R. McNeill	11 Nov 24
				G. Locker Lampson	7 Dec 25
Home O.	**Sir W. Joynson-Hicks**	6 Nov 24	*U-S.*	G. Locker Lampson	11 Nov 24
				D. Hacking	8 Dec 25
				Sir V. Henderson	9 Nov 27
Admir.	**W. Bridgeman**	6 Nov 24	*P. & F.S.:*		
				J. Davidson	11 Nov 24
				C. Headlam	16 Dec 26
			Civil Ld:		
				Earl Stanhope	11 Nov 24
Ag. & Fish.	**E. Wood**	6 Nov 24	*P.S. Ag. & Deputy Min. of Fisheries:*		
	W. Guinness	4 Nov 25		Ld Bledisloe	11 Nov 24
				E of Stradbroke	5 Feb 28
Air	**Sir S. Hoare**	6 Nov 24	*U-S.*	Sir P. Sassoon	11 Nov 24
Att. Gen.	**Sir D. Hogg** (*Ld Hailsham*) (28 *Mar* 28 *Sir T. Inskip & office not in cabinet*)	6 Nov 24			
Col. O.	**L. Amery**	6 Nov 24	*U-S.*	W. Ormsby-Gore	12 Nov 24
Dom. O.	**L. Amery**	11 Jun 25	*U-S.*	E of Clarendon	5 Aug 25
				Ld Lovat	5 May 27
				E of Plymouth	1 Jan 29
Bd Educ.	**Ld E. Percy**[1]	6 Nov 24	*P.S.*	Duchess of Atholl	11 Nov 24
Health	**N. Chamberlain**	6 Nov 24	*P.S.*	Sir K. Wood	11 Nov 24
India O.	**E of Birkenhead**	6 Nov 24	*U-S.*	Earl Winterton[1]	11 Nov 24
	Vt Peel	18 Oct 28			
Lab.	**Sir A. Steel-Maitland**	6 Nov 24	*P.S.*	H. Betterton	11 Nov 24
D. Lanc.	**Vt Cecil**	10 Nov 24			
	Ld Cushendun	19 Oct 27			
Scot. O.	**Sir J. Gilmour** (*became Sec. of State for Scotland* 15 *Jul* 26)	6 Nov 24	*U-S.*	W. Elliot	26 Jul 26
			P.S. Health for Scotland:		
				W. Elliot (*post abolished* 26 *Jul* 26)	11 Nov 24
B.o.T.	**Sir P. Lloyd-Greame** (*changed name to Sir P. Cunliffe-Lister* 27 *Nov* 24)	6 Nov 24	*P.S.*	Sir B. Chadwick	11 Nov 24
				H. Williams	13 Jan 28
			P.S. Overseas Trade Dept.:		
				A. Samuel	11 Nov 24
				D. Hacking	9 Nov 27
			P.S. Mines Dept.:		
				G. Lane-Fox	11 Nov 24
				D. King	13 Jan 28
War O.	**Sir L. Worthington-Evans**	6 Nov 24	*U-S.*	E of Onslow	11 Nov 24
				D of Sutherland	2 Dec 28
			F.S.	D. King	11 Nov 24
				A. Duff Cooper	13 Jan 28
1*st C. Works*	**Vt Peel**	10 Nov 24			
	M of Londonderry	18 Oct 28			

	MINISTERS NOT IN CABINET			JUNIOR MINISTERS ATTACHED	
Paym.-Gen.	(*office vacant*)				
	D OF SUTHERLAND	28 Jun 25			
	E OF ONSLOW	2 Dec 28			
Pensions	G. TRYON	11 Nov 24	*P.S.*	G. Stanley	11 Nov 24

[1] Not a member of the House of Lords.

CONSERVATIVE GOVERNMENT, 1924–1929 (*contd.*)

MINISTERS NOT IN CABINET

Postm.-Gen.	Sir W. Mitchell-Thomson	11 Nov 24
Transp.	W. Ashley	11 Nov 24
Law Officers:		
Att. Gen.	(*office in cabinet*)	
	Sir T. Inskip	28 Mar 28
Sol. Gen.	Sir T. Inskip	11 Nov 24
	Sir F. Merriman	28 Mar 28
Ld Advoc.	W. Watson	11 Nov 24
	A. MacRobert	23 Apr 29
Sol. Gen. Scotland	D. Fleming	11 Nov 24
	A. MacRobert	30 Dec 25
	W. Normand	23 Apr 29
H.M. Household:		
Treas.:	G. Gibbs	13 Nov 24
	Sir G. Hennessy	13 Jan 28
Comptr.	Sir H. Barnston	13 Nov 24
	Sir W. Cope	13 Jan 28
V. Chamb.	D. Hacking	13 Nov 24
	(Sir) G. Hennessy	10 Dec 25
	(Sir) F. Thomson	13 Jan 28
Capt. Gents at Arms	E of Clarendon	1 Dec 24
	E of Plymouth	26 Jun 25
	E of Lucan	1 Jan 29
Capt. Yeomen of Guard	Ld Desborough	1 Dec 24

JUNIOR MINISTERS ATTACHED

Ass.	Vt Wolmer[1]	11 Nov 24
P.S.	J. Moore-Brabazon	11 Nov 24
	(*post vacant from 14 Jan 27*)	
P.S. to Treasury:	B. Eyres-Monsell	7 Nov 24
Junior Lds of Treasury:	G. Hennessy	13 Nov 24–10 Dec 25
	Ld Stanley[1]	13 Nov 24–9 Nov 27
	F. Thomson	13 Nov 24–14 Jan 28
	(Sir) W. Cope	13 Nov 24–14 Jan 28
	Vt Curzon[1]	13 Nov 24–15 Jan 29
	D. Margesson	28 Aug 26–4 Jun 29
	M of Titchfield[1]	9 Nov 27–4 Jun 29
	G. Bowyer	28 Dec 27–4 Jun 29
	F. Penny	13 Jan 28–4 Jun 29
	E. Wallace	13 Jan 28–4 Jun 29
Lds in Waiting:	Vt Gage	1 Dec 24–4 Jun 29
	Ld Somers	1 Dec 24–23 Mar 26
	E of Lucan	1 Dec 24–1 Jan 29
	E of Airlie	1 Apr 26–4 Jun 29
	Ld Templemore	1 Jan 29–4 Jun 29

LABOUR GOVERNMENT, 1929–1931

	MINISTERS IN CABINET			JUNIOR MINISTERS ATTACHED	
P.M.	**J. R. MacDonald**	5 Jun 29–24 Aug 31			
Ld Pres.	**Ld Parmoor**	7 Jun 29			
Ld Chanc.	**Ld Sankey**	7 Jun 29			
Privy S.	**J. Thomas**	7 Jun 29			
	V. Hartshorn	5 Jun 30			
	T. Johnston	24 Mar 31			
Exch.	**P. Snowden**	7 Jun 29	*Treasury:*		
			F.S.	F. Pethick-Lawrence	11 Jun 29
For. O.	**A. Henderson**	7 Jun 29	*U-S.*	H. Dalton	11 Jun 29
Home O.	**J. Clynes**	7 Jun 29	*U-S.*	A. Short	11 Jun 29
Admir.	**A. Alexander**	7 Jun 29	*P. & F.S.:*	C. Ammon	11 Jun 29
			Civil Ld:	G. Hall	11 Jun 29
Ag. & Fish.	**N. Buxton**	7 Jun 29	*P.S.*	C. Addison	11 Jun 29
	C. Addison	5 Jun 30		Earl De La Warr	5 Jun 30

[1] Not a member of the House of Lords.

LABOUR GOVERNMENT, 1929–1931 (*contd.*)

	MINISTERS IN CABINET			JUNIOR MINISTERS ATTACHED	
Air	**Ld Thomson**	7 Jun 29	*U-S.*	F. Montague	11 Jun 29
	Ld Amulree	14 Oct 30			
Col. O.	**Ld Passfield**	7 Jun 29	*U-S.*	W. Lunn	11 Jun 29
				D. Shiels	1 Dec 29
Dom. O.	**Ld Passfield**	7 Jun 29	*U-S.*	A. Ponsonby	11 Jun 29
	J. Thomas	5 Jun 30		W. Lunn	1 Dec 29
Bd Educ.	**Sir C. Trevelyan**	7 Jun 29	*P.S.*	M. Jones	11 Jun 29
	H. Lees-Smith	2 Mar 31			
Health	**A. Greenwood**	7 Jun 29	*P.S.*	Miss S. Lawrence	11 Jun 29
India O.	**W. Benn**	7 Jun 29	*U-S.*	D. Shiels	11 Jun 29
				Earl Russell	1 Dec 29
				Ld Snell	13 Mar 31
Lab.	**Miss M. Bondfield**	7 Jun 29	*P.S.*	J. Lawson	11 Jun 29
Scot. O.	**W. Adamson**	7 Jun 29	*U-S.*	T. Johnston	7 Jun 29
				J. Westwood	25 Mar 31
B.o.T.	**W. Graham**	7 Jun 29	*P.S.*	W. Smith	11 Jun 29
			P.S. Overseas Trade Dept.:		
				G. Gillett	7 Jul 29
			P.S. Mines Dept.:		
				B. Turner	11 Jun 29
				E. Shinwell	5 Jun 30
Transp.	(*office not in cabinet*)		*P.S.*	Earl Russell	11 Jun 29
	H. Morrison	19 Mar 31		A. Ponsonby (Ld)	1 Dec 29
				J. Parkinson	1 Mar 31
War O.	**T. Shaw**	7 Jun 29	*U-S.*	Earl De La Warr	11 Jun 29
				Ld Marley	5 Jun 30
			F.S.	E. Shinwell	11 Jun 29
				W. Sanders	5 Jun 30
1st C. Works	**G. Lansbury**	7 Jun 29			

	MINISTERS NOT IN CABINET			JUNIOR MINISTERS ATTACHED	
D. Lanc.	Sir O. Mosley	7 Jun 29			
	C. Attlee	23 May 30			
	Ld Ponsonby	13 Mar 31			
Paym.-Gen.	Ld Arnold	7 Jun 29			
Pensions	F. Roberts	7 Jun 29	*P.S.*	(*post vacant*)	
Postm.-Gen.	H. Lees-Smith	7 Jun 29	*Ass.*	S. Viant	7 Jul 29
	C. Attlee	2 Mar 31			
Transp.	H. Morrison	7 Jun 29		(*for Junior Ministers see above*)	
	(*office in cabinet* 19 *Mar* 31)				
Law Officers:			*P.S. to Treasury:*		
Att. Gen.	Sir W. Jowitt	7 Jun 29		T. Kennedy	14 Jun 29
			Junior Lds of Treasury:		
Sol. Gen.	Sir J. Melville	7 Jun 29		J. Parkinson	11 Jun 29–13 Mar 31
	Sir S. Cripps	22 Oct 30		C. Edwards	11 Jun 29–24 Aug 31
				A. Barnes	11 Jun 29–23 Oct 30
Ld Advoc.	C. Aitchison	17 Jun 29		W. Whiteley	27 Jun 29–24 Aug 31
Sol. Gen. Scotland	J. Watson	17 Jun 29		W. Paling	27 Jun 29–24 Aug 31
				E. Thurtle	23 Oct 30–24 Aug 31
				H. Charleton	13 Mar 31–24 Aug 31
H.M. Household:			*Lds in Waiting:*		
Treas.	B. Smith	24 Jun 29		Earl De La Warr	18 Jul 29–24 Aug 31

LABOUR GOVERNMENT, 1929–1931 (*contd.*)

MINISTERS NOT IN CABINET			JUNIOR MINISTERS ATTACHED	
H.M. Household:			Ld Muir-Mackenzie	18 Jul 29–17 Jan 30
Comptr.	T. HENDERSON	24 Jun 29	Ld Marley	17 Jan 30–24 Aug 31
V. Chamb.	J. HAYES	24 Jun 29		
Capt Gents at Arms	E OF CAVAN[1]	24 Jun 29		
Capt. Yeomen of Guard	LD LOCH[1]	24 Jun 29		

NATIONAL GOVERNMENT, 1931–1935

MINISTERS IN CABINET			JUNIOR MINISTERS ATTACHED		
P.M.	**J. R. MacDonald** (N. Lab)	24 Aug 31–7 Jun 35			
Ld Pres.	**S. Baldwin** (C)	25 Aug 31			
Ld Chanc.	**Ld Sankey (Vt)** (N. Lab)	25 Aug 31			
Privy S	(*office not in cabinet*)				
	Vt Snowden (N. Lab)	5 Nov 31			
	S. Baldwin (C)	29 Sep 32			
	(31 *Dec* 33 *A. Eden & office not in cabinet*)				
Exch.	**P. Snowden (Vt)** (N. Lab)	25 Aug 31	*Treasury:* *F.S.*	W. Elliot (C)	3 Sep 31
	N. Chamberlain (C)	5 Nov 31		L. Hore-Belisha (L. Nat)	29 Sep 32
				A. Duff Cooper (C)	29 Jun 34
For. O.	**M of Reading** (Lib)	25 Aug 31	*U-S.*	A. Eden (C)	3 Sep 31
	Sir J. Simon (L. Nat)	5 Nov 31		Earl Stanhope (C)	18 Jan 34
Home O.	**Sir H. Samuel** (Lib)	25 Aug 31	*U-S.*	O. Stanley (C)	3 Sep 31
	Sir J. Gilmour (C)	28 Sep 32		D. Hacking (C)	22 Feb 33
				H. Crookshank (C)	29 Jun 34
Admir.	(*office not in cabinet*)		*P. & F.S.:*		
	Sir B. Eyres-Monsell (C)	5 Nov 31		Earl Stanhope (C)	3 Sep 31
				Ld Stanley[2] (C)	10 Nov 31
			Civil Ld:	(*vacant*)	
				E. Wallace (C)	10 Nov 31
Ag. & Fish.	(*office not in cabinet*)		*P.S.*	(*vacant*)	
	Sir J. Gilmour (C)	5 Nov 31		Earl De La Warr (N. Lab)	10 Nov 31
	W. Elliot (C)	28 Sep 32			
Air	(*office not in cabinet*)		*U-S.*	Sir P. Sassoon (C)	3 Sep 31
	M of Londonderry (C)	5 Nov 31			
Col. O.	**J. Thomas** (N. Lab)	25 Aug 31	*U-S.*	Sir R. Hamilton (Lib)	3 Sep 31
	Sir P. Cunliffe-Lister (C)	5 Nov 31		E of Plymouth (C)	29 Sep 32
Dom. O.	**J. Thomas** (N. Lab)	25 Aug 31	*U-S.*	M. MacDonald (N. Lab)	3 Sep 31
Bd Educ.	(*office not in cabinet*)		*P.S.*	Sir K. Wood (C)	3 Sep 31
	Sir D. Maclean (Lib)	5 Nov 31		H. Ramsbotham (C)	10 Nov 31
	Ld Irwin (*Vt Halifax*) (C)	15 Jun 32			
Health	**N. Chamberlain** (C)	25 Aug 31	*P.S.*	E. Simon (Lib)	22 Sep 31
	Sir E. Young (C)	5 Nov 31		E. Brown (L. Nat.)	10 Nov 31
				G. Shakespeare (L. Nat)	30 Sep 32
India O.	**Sir S. Hoare** (C)	25 Aug 31	*U-S.*	(*vacant*)	
				M of Lothian (Lib)	10 Nov 31
				R. Butler (C)	29 Sep 32
Lab.	(*office not in cabinet*)		*P.S.*	M. Gray (Lib)	3 Sep 31
	Sir H. Betterton (C)	5 Nov 31		R. Hudson (C)	10 Nov 31
	O. Stanley (C)	29 Jun 34			
Postm.-Gen.	(*office not in cabinet*)		*Ass.*	G. White (Lib)	3 Sep 31
	Sir K. Wood (C)	20 Dec 33		Sir E. Bennett (N. Lab)	21 Oct 32

[1] Non-political appointments.

[2] Not a member of the House of Lords.

NATIONAL GOVERNMENT, 1931–1935 (*contd.*)

	MINISTERS IN CABINET		JUNIOR MINISTERS ATTACHED
Scot. O.	(*office not in cabinet*) **Sir A. Sinclair** (Lib) 5 Nov 31 **Sir G. Collins** (L. Nat) 28 Sep 32	*U-S.*	N. Skelton (C) 3 Sep 31
B.o.T.	**Sir P. Cunliffe-Lister** (C) 25 Aug 31 **W. Runciman (Ld)** (L. Nat.) 5 Nov 31	*P.S.*	G. Lloyd-George (Lib) 3 Sep 31 L. Hore-Belisha (L. Nat) 10 Nov 31 L. Burgin (L. Nat) 29 Sep 32
		P.S. Overseas Trade Dept.:	Sir E. Young (C) 3 Sep 31 J. Colville (C) 10 Nov 31
		P.S. Mines Dept.:	I. Foot (Lib) 3 Sep 31 E. Brown (L. Nat) 30 Sep 32
War O.	(*office not in cabinet*) **Vt Hailsham** (C) 5 Nov 31	*U-S.*	(*vacant*) Earl Stanhope (C) 10 Nov 31 Ld Strathcona & Mount Royal (C) 24 Jan 34
		F.S.	A. Duff Cooper (C) 3 Sep 31 D. Hacking (C) 29 Jun 34
1st C. Works	(*office not in cabinet*) **W. Ormsby-Gore** (C) 5 Nov 31		

	MINISTERS NOT IN CABINET		JUNIOR MINISTERS ATTACHED
Admir.	SIR A. CHAMBERLAIN (C) 25 Aug 31 (*5 Nov 31 Sir B. Eyres-Monsell & office in cabinet*)		(*for Junior Ministers see above*)
Ag. & Fish	SIR J. GILMOUR (C) 25 Aug 31 (*5 Nov 31 office in cabinet*)		(*for Junior Ministers see above*)
Air	LD AMULREE (N. Lab) 25 Aug 31 (*5 Nov 31 M of Londonderry & office in cabinet*)		(*for Junior Ministers see above*)
Bd Educ.	SIR D. MACLEAN (Lib) 25 Aug 31 (*5 Nov 31 office in cabinet*)		(*for Junior Ministers see above*)
Lab.	SIR H. BETTERTON (C) 25 Aug 31 (*5 Nov 31 office in cabinet*)		(*for Junior Ministers see above*)
D. Lanc.	M OF LOTHIAN (Lib) 25 Aug 31 (SIR) J. DAVIDSON (C) 10 Nov 31		
Paym.-Gen.	SIR T. WALTERS (Lib) 4 Sep 31 LD ROCHESTER (N. Lab) 23 Nov 31		
Pensions	G. TRYON (C) 3 Sep 31	*P.S.*	(*vacant*) C. Headlam (C) 10 Nov 31 (*vacant from 29 Sep 32*)
Postm.-Gen.	W. ORMSBY-GORE (C) 3 Sep 31 SIR K. WOOD (C) 10 Nov 31 (*20 Dec 33 office in cabinet*)		(*for Junior Ministers see above*)
Privy S.	EARL PEEL (C) 3 Sep 31 (*5 Nov 31 Vt Snowden & office in cabinet* A. EDEN (C) 31 Dec 33		
Scot. O.	SIR A. SINCLAIR (Lib) 25 Aug 31 (*5 Nov 31 office in cabinet*)		(*for Junior Ministers see above*)
Transp.	J. PYBUS (L. Nat) 3 Sep 31 O. STANLEY (C) 22 Feb 33 L. HORE-BELISHA (L. Nat) 29 Jun 34	*P.S.*	(Sir) G. Gillett (N. Lab) 4 Sep 31 E of Plymouth (C) 25 Nov 31 C. Headlam (C) 29 Sep 32 (*5 Jul 34 vacant*) A. Hudson (C) 12 Apr 35
War O.	M OF CREWE (Lib) 26 Aug 31 (*5 Nov 31 Vt Hailsham & office in cabinet*)		(*for Junior Ministers see above*)
1st C. Works	M OF LONDONDERRY (C) 25 Aug 31 (*5 Nov 31 W. Ormsby-Gore & office in cabinet*)		

NATIONAL GOVERNMENT, 1931–1935 (*contd.*)

MINISTERS NOT IN CABINET

Law Officers:

Att. Gen.	Sir W. Jowitt (N. Lab)	3 Sep 31
	Sir T. Inskip (C)	26 Jan 32
Sol. Gen.	Sir T. Inskip (C)	3 Sep 31
	Sir F. Merriman (C)	26 Jan 32
	Sir D. Somervell (C)	29 Sep 33
Ld Advoc.	C. Aitchison (N. Lab)	3 Sep 31
	W. Normand (C)	2 Oct 33
	D. Jamieson (C)	28 Mar 35
Sol. Gen. Scotland	J. Watson (N. Lab)	4 Sep 31
	W. Normand (C)	10 Nov 31
	D. Jamieson (C)	2 Oct 33
	T. Cooper (C)	15 May 35

H.M. Household:

Treas.:	Sir G. Hennessy (C)	3 Sep 31
	Sir F. Thomson (C)	12 Nov 31
	Sir F. Penny (C)	1 May 35
Comptr.	G. Owen (Lib)	14 Sep 31
	W. Rea (Lib)	12 Nov 31
	Sir F. Penny (C)	30 Sep 32
	Sir V. Warrender (C)	1 May 35
V. Chamb.	Sir F. Thomson (C)	3 Sep 31
	Sir F. Penny (C)	12 Nov 31
	Sir V. Warrender (C)	30 Sep 32
	Sir L. Ward (C)	1 May 35
Capt. Gents at Arms	E of Cavan (C)	3 Sep 31
	E of Lucan (C)	12 Nov 31
Capt. Yeomen of Guard	Ld Loch (Lib)	3 Sep 31
	Ld Strathcona & Mount Royal (C)	12 Nov 31
	Ld Templemore (C)	24 Jan 34

JUNIOR MINISTERS ATTACHED

P.S. to Treasury:

Sir B. Eyres-Monsell (C)	3 Sep 31
D. Margesson (C)	10 Nov 31

Junior Lds of Treasury:

D. Margesson (C)	26 Aug 31–10 Nov 31
Sir F. Penny (C)	3 Sep 31–12 Nov 31
A. Glassey (Lib)	14 Sep 31–12 Nov 31
M of Titchfield [1] (C)	3 Sep 31–12 Nov 31
E. Wallace (C)	3 Sep 31–12 Nov 31
(Sir) W. Womersley (C)	12 Nov 31–7 Jun 35
Sir V. Warrender (C)	12 Nov 31–30 Sep 32
G. Shakespeare (L. Nat)	12 Nov 31–30 Sep 32
A. Hudson (C)	12 Nov 31–12 Apr 35
Sir L. Ward (C)	12 Nov 31–1 May 35
G. Davies (C)	11 Oct 32–7 Jun 35
J. Blindell (L. Nat)	30 Sep 32–7 Jun 35
J. Stuart (C)	1 May 35–7 Jun 35
A. Southby (C)	23 Apr 35–7 Jun 35

Lds in Waiting:

Vt Hampden (C)	12 Nov 31–7 Jun 35
Ld Colebrooke (Lib)	12 Nov 31–7 Jun 35
E of Dunmore (C)	12 Nov 31–7 Jun 35
Vt Gage (C)	12 Nov 31–7 Jun 35
E of Munster (C)	25 Oct 32–7 Jun 35
E of Feversham (C)	24 Jan 34–7 Jun 35
Vt Allendale (Lib)	12 Nov 31–28 Sep 32
Ld Templemore (C)	12 Nov 31–24 Jan 34

NATIONAL GOVERNMENT, 1935–1940

MINISTERS IN CABINET

P.M.	**S. Baldwin**	7 Jun 35–28 May 37
	[2] **N. Chamberlain**	28 May 37–10 May 40
Ld Pres.	**J. R. MacDonald**	7 Jun 35
	Vt Halifax	28 May 37
	Vt Hailsham	9 Mar 38
	Vt Runciman	31 Oct 38
	Earl Stanhope	3 Sep 39
Ld Chanc.	**Vt Hailsham**	7 Jun 35
	Ld Maugham	9 Mar 38
	Vt Caldecote	3 Sep 39

[1] Not a member of the House of Lords.

[2] Denotes member of the War Cabinet. Following the British declaration of war against Germany on 3 Sep 39, all members of the cabinet formally surrendered their portfolios to the P.M.; in the evening of the same day the formation of a war cabinet was announced.

NATIONAL GOVERNMENT, 1935–1940 (*contd.*)

	MINISTERS IN CABINET			JUNIOR MINISTERS ATTACHED	
Privy S.	**M of Londonderry**	7 Jun 35			
	Vt Halifax	22 Nov 35			
	Earl De La Warr	28 May 37			
	Sir J. Anderson	31 Oct 38			
	[2] **Sir S. Hoare**	3 Sep 39			
	Sir K. Wood	3 Apr 40			
Exch.	**N. Chamberlain**	7 Jun 35	*Treasury:*		
	[2] **Sir J. Simon**	28 May 37	*F.S.*	A. Duff Cooper	18 Jun 35
				W. Morrison	22 Nov 35
				J. Colville	29 Oct 36
				E. Wallace	16 May 38
				H. Crookshank	21 Apr 39
For. O.	**Sir S. Hoare**	7 Jun 35	*U-S.*	Earl Stanhope	18 Jun 35–16 Jun 36
	A. Eden	22 Dec 35		Vt Cranborne [1]	6 Aug 35–20 Feb 38
	[2] **Vt Halifax**	21 Feb 38		(*for League of Nations Affairs*)	
				E of Plymouth	30 Jul 36–May 39
				R. Butler	25 Feb 38–10 May 40
Home O.	**Sir J. Simon**	7 Jun 35	*U-S.*	E. Wallace	18 Jun 35
	Sir S. Hoare	28 May 37		G. Lloyd	28 Nov 35
	Sir J. Anderson	3 Sep 39		O. Peake	21 Apr 39
			P.S. Min. Home Security:		
				A. Lennox-Boyd	6 Sep 39
				W. Mabane	24 Oct 39
Admir.	**Sir B. Eyres-Monsell**	7 Jun 35	*P. & F.S.:*		
	(*Vt Monsell*)			Sir V. Warrender	18 Jun 35
	Sir S. Hoare	5 Jun 36		Ld Stanley [1]	28 Nov 35
	A. Duff Cooper	28 May 37		G. Shakespeare	28 May 37
	Earl Stanhope	27 Oct 38		Sir V. Warrender	3 Apr 40
	[2] **W. Churchill**	3 Sep 39	*Civil Ld:*		
				K. Lindsay	18 Jun 35
				J. Llewellin	28 May 37
				A. Hudson	14 Jul 39
Ag. & Fish.	**W. Elliot**	7 Jun 35	*P.S.*	Earl De La Warr	18 Jun 35
	W. Morrison	29 Oct 36		H. Ramsbotham	28 Nov 35
	Sir R. Dorman-Smith	29 Jan 39		E of Feversham	30 Jul 36
				Ld Denham	19 Sep 39
Air	**Sir P. Cunliffe-Lister**		*U-S.*	Sir P. Sassoon	18 Jun 35
	(*Vt Swinton*)	7 Jun 35		A. Muirhead	28 May 37
	[2] **Sir K. Wood**	16 May 38		H. Balfour	16 May 38
	Sir S. Hoare	3 Apr 40			
Col. O.	**M. MacDonald**	7 Jun 35	*U-S.*	E of Plymouth	18 Jun 35
	J. Thomas	22 Nov 35		Earl De La Warr	30 Jul 36
	W. Ormsby-Gore	28 May 36		M of Dufferin & Ava	28 May 37
	M. MacDonald	16 May 38			
Min. for Co-ordination of Defence	(*office not established*)				
	Sir T. Inskip	13 Mar 36			
	[2] **Ld Chatfield**	29 Jan 39			
Dom. O.	**J. Thomas**	7 Jun 35	*U-S.*	Ld Stanley [1]	18 Jun 35
	M. MacDonald	22 Nov 35		D. Hacking	28 Nov 35
	Ld Stanley [1]	16 May 38		M of Hartington [1]	4 Mar 36
	M. MacDonald	31 Oct 38		(*D of Devonshire*)	
	Sir T. Inskip	29 Jan 39			
	(*Vt Caldecote*)				
	A. Eden	3 Sep 39			
Bd Educ.	**O. Stanley**	7 Jun 35	*P.S.*	H. Ramsbotham	18 Jun 35
	Earl Stanhope	28 May 37		Earl De La Warr	28 Nov 35
	Earl De La Warr	27 Oct 38		G. Shakespeare	30 Jul 36
	H. Ramsbotham	3 Apr 40		K. Lindsay	28 May 37

[1] Not a member of the House of Lords.

[2] Denotes member of the War Cabinet. Following the British declaration of war against Germany on 3 Sep 39, all members of the cabinet formally surrendered their portfolios to the P.M.; in the evening of the same day the formation of a war cabinet was announced.

NATIONAL GOVERNMENT, 1935–1940 (*contd.*)

	MINISTERS IN CABINET			JUNIOR MINISTERS ATTACHED	
Food	(*combined with D. Lanc.* 4 *Sep* 39)		*P.S.*	A. Lennox-Boyd	11 Oct 39
	Ld Woolton	3 Apr 40			
Health	**Sir K. Wood**	7 Jun 35	*P.S.*	G. Shakespeare	18 Jun 35
	W. Elliot	16 May 38		R. Hudson	30 Jul 36
				R. Bernays	28 May 37
				Miss F. Horsbrugh	14 Jul 39
India O. (& Burma O. 1937–)	**M of Zetland**	7 Jun 35	*U-S.*	R. Butler	18 Jun 35
				Ld Stanley[1]	28 May 37
				A. Muirhead	16 May 38
				Sir H. O'Neill	11 Sep 39
Information	(*office not established*)		*P.S.*	Sir E. Grigg	19 Sep 39
	Ld Macmillan	4 Sep 39		(*office vacant* 3 *Apr* 40)	
	Sir J. Reith	5 Jan 40			
Lab.	**E. Brown**	7 Jun 35	*P.S.*	A. Muirhead	18 Jun 35
	(3 *Sep* 39 *Lab. & Nat S.*)			R. Butler	28 May 37
				A. Lennox-Boyd	25 Feb 38
				R. Assheton	6 Sep 39
D. Lanc.	(*office not in cabinet*)				
	Earl Winterton[1]	11 Mar 38			
	W. Morrison	29 Jan 39			
	(4 *Sep* 39–3 *Apr* 40 *combined with Min. of Food*)				
	G. Tryon	3 Apr 40			
Min. without Portfolio for League of Nations Affairs	**A. Eden**	7 Jun 35–22 Dec 35			
Min. without Portfolio	**Ld E. Percy**[1]	7 Jun 35–31 Mar 36			
	L. Burgin	21 Apr 39–14 Jul 39			
	[2]**Ld Hankey**	3 Sep 39–10 May 40			
Scot. O.	**Sir G. Collins**	7 Jun 35	*U-S.*	N. Skelton	18 Jun 35
	W. Elliot	29 Oct 36		J. Colville	28 Nov 35
	J. Colville	16 May 38		H. Wedderburn	29 Oct 36
				J. McEwen	6 Sep 39
Shipping	(*office not established*)		*P.S.*	Sir A. Salter	13 Nov 39
	Sir J. Gilmour	13 Oct 39			
	R. Hudson	3 Apr 40			
Supply	(*office not established*)		*P.S.*	J. Llewellin	14 Jul 39
	L. Burgin	14 Jul 39			
B.o.T.	**Ld Runciman (Vt)**	7 Jun 35	*P.S.*	L. Burgin	18 Jun 35
	O. Stanley	28 May 37		E. Wallace	28 May 37
	Sir A. Duncan	5 Jan 40		R. Cross	16 May 38
				G. Lloyd-George	6 Sep 39
			P.S. Overseas Trade Dept.:		
				J. Colville	18 Jun 35
				E. Wallace	28 Nov 35
				R. Hudson	28 May 37
				G. Shakespeare	3 Apr 40
			P.S. Mines Dept.:		
				H. Crookshank	18 Jun 35
				G. Lloyd	21 Apr 39
Transp.	(*office not in cabinet*)		*P.S.*	A. Hudson	18 Jun 35
	L. Hore-Belisha	29 Oct 36		R. Bernays	14 Jul 39

[1] Not a member of the House of Lords.
[2] Denotes member of the War Cabinet. Following the British declaration of war against Germany on 3 Sep 39, all members of the cabinet formally surrendered their portfolios to the P.M.; in the evening of the same day the formation of a war cabinet was announced.

NATIONAL GOVERNMENT, 1935–1940 (*contd.*)

	MINISTERS IN CABINET			JUNIOR MINISTERS ATTACHED	
	L. Burgin	28 May 37			
	E. Wallace	21 Apr 39			
War O.	**Vt Halifax**	7 Jun 35	*U-S.*	Ld Strathcona & Mount Royal	18 Jun 35
	A. Duff Cooper	22 Nov 35		E of Munster	29 Jan 39
	[2] **L. Hore-Belisha**	28 May 37		Vt Cobham	19 Sep 39
	O. Stanley	5 Jan 40	*F.S.*	D. Hacking	18 Jun 35
				Sir V. Warrender	28 Nov 35
				Sir E. Grigg	3 Apr 40
1st C. Works	**W. Ormsby-Gore**	7 Jun 35			
	Earl Stanhope	16 Jun 36			
	(28 *May* 37 *Sir P. Sassoon & office out of cabinet*)				

	MINISTERS NOT IN CABINET			JUNIOR MINISTERS ATTACHED	
Econ. Warfare	R. Cross	3 Sep 39			
D. Lanc.	Sir J. Davidson	18 Jun 35			
	Earl Winterton [1]	28 May 37			
	(*office in cabinet* 11 *Mar* 38)				
Paym.-Gen.	Ld Rochester	18 Jun 35			
	Ld Hutchison	6 Dec 35			
	E of Munster	2 Jun 38			
	Earl Winterton [1]	29 Jan 39			
	(*office vacant from Nov* 39)				
Pensions	R. Hudson	18 Jun 35			
	H. Ramsbotham	30 Jul 36			
	Sir W. Womersley	7 Jun 39			
Postm.-Gen.	G. Tryon	7 Jun 35	*Ass.*	Sir E. Bennett	18 Jun 35
	W. Morrison	3 Apr 40		Sir W. Womersley	6 Dec 35
				W. Mabane	7 Jun 39
				C. Waterhouse	24 Oct 39
Transp.	L. Hore-Belisha	18 Jun 35			
	(*office in cabinet* 29 *Oct* 36)				
1st C. Works	(*office in cabinet*)				
	Sir P. Sassoon	28 May 37			
	H. Ramsbotham	7 Jun 39			
	Earl De La Warr	3 Apr 40			
Law Officers:			*P.S. to Treasury:*		
				D. Margesson	18 Jun 35
Att. Gen.	Sir T. Inskip	18 Jun 35	*Junior Lds of Treasury:*		
	Sir D. Somervell	18 Mar 36		J. Stuart	18 Jun 35–10 May 40
Sol. Gen.	Sir D. Somervell	18 Jun 35		(Sir) A. Southby	18 Jun 35–28 May 37
	Sir T. O'Connor	19 Mar 36		Sir W. Womersley	18 Jun 35–6 Dec 35
Ld Advoc.	D. Jamieson	18 Jun 35		G. Davies	18 Jun 35–6 Dec 35
	T. Cooper	25 Oct 35		(Sir) J. Blindell	18 Jun 35–28 May 37
Sol. Gen. Scotland	T. Cooper	18 Jun 35		A. Hope	6 Dec 35–28 May 37
	A. Russell	29 Nov 35		(Sir) H. Morris-Jones	6 Dec 35–28 May 37
	J. Reid	25 Jun 36		C. Kerr	28 May 37–4 Apr 39
				T. Dugdale	28 May 37–12 Feb 40
				C. Waterhouse	28 May 37–18 Oct 37
				R. Cross	28 May 37–18 Oct 37
				P. Munro	18 Oct 37–10 May 40

[1] Not a member of the House of Lords.

[2] Denotes member of the War Cabinet. Following the British declaration of war against Germany on 3 Sep 39, all members of the cabinet formally surrendered their portfolios to the P.M.; in the evening of the same day the formation of a war cabinet was announced.

NATIONAL GOVERNMENT, 1935–1940 (*contd.*)

MINISTERS NOT IN CABINET

H.M. Household:

Treas.	Sir F. Penny	18 Jun 35
	Sir L. Ward	28 May 37
	A. Hope	18 Oct 37
	C. Waterhouse	4 Apr 39
	R. Grimston	12 Nov 39
Comptr.	Sir G. Bowyer	21 Jun 35
	Sir L. Ward	6 Dec 35
	Sir G. Davies	28 May 37
	C. Waterhouse	18 Oct 37
	C. Kerr	4 Apr 39
V. Chamb.	Sir L. Ward	18 Jun 35
	(Sir) G. Davies	6 Dec 35
	A. Hope	28 May 37
	R. Cross	18 Oct 37
	R. Grimston	18 May 38
	Sir J. Edmondson	12 Nov 39
Capt. Gents at Arms	E of Lucan	18 Jun 35
Capt. Yeomen of Guard	Ld Templemore	18 Jun 35

JUNIOR MINISTERS ATTACHED

Junior Lds of Treasury:

R. Grimston	18 Oct 37–18 May 38
S. Furness	20 May 38–10 May 40
Sir J. Edmondson	4 Apr 39–13 Nov 39
P. Buchan-Hepburn	13 Nov 39–10 May 40
W. Boulton	12 Feb 40–10 May 40

Lds in Waiting:

Vt Gage	18 Jun 35–11 Apr 39
E of Munster	18 Jun 35–2 Jun 38
Ld Colebrooke	18 Jun 35–21 Jul 36
E of Dunmore	18 Jun 35–21 Jul 36
Vt Hampden	18 Jun 35–21 Jul 36
E of Feversham	18 Jun 35–30 Jul 36
Ld Brownlow	21 Jul 36–1 Mar 37
E of Sefton	21 Jul 36–1 Mar 37
M of Dufferin & Ava	29 Oct 36–28 May 37
E of Erne	29 Oct 36–25 Jul 39
E of Eldon	1 Mar 37–10 May 40
Vt Allendale	1 Mar 37–10 May 40
Earl Fortescue	26 Aug 37–10 May 40
E of Birkenhead	12 Jul 38–10 May 40
Vt Bridport	11 Apr 39–10 May 40
Ld Ebury	25 Jul 39–10 May 40

COALITION GOVERNMENT, 1940–1945

MINISTERS IN WAR CABINET

P.M.	**W. Churchill** (C)	10 May 40–23 May 45
Ld Pres.	**N. Chamberlain** (C)	11 May 40
	Sir J. Anderson (Nat)	3 Oct 40
	C. Attlee (Lab)	24 Sep 43
Ld Chanc.	(*office not in war cabinet*)	
Privy S.	**C. Attlee** (Lab)	11 May 40
	Sir S. Cripps (Lab)	19 Feb 42
	(*Vt Cranborne 22 Nov 42 & office not in war cabinet*)	
Exch.	(*office not in war cabinet*)	
	Sir K. Wood (C)	3 Oct 40
	(19 *Feb 42 office not in war cabinet*)	
	Sir J. Anderson (Nat)	24 Sep 43
For. O.	**Vt Halifax** (C)	11 May 40
	A. Eden (C)	22 Dec 40
Min. of State	**Ld Beaverbrook** (C)	1 May 41
	O. Lyttelton (C)	29 Jun 41
	(*became Min. of Production*) 12 *Mar* 42 *& remained in war cabinet*)	
Home O. & Home Security	(*office not in war cabinet*)	
	H. Morrison (Lab)	22 Nov 42

JUNIOR MINISTERS ATTACHED

Treasury:

F.S.	H. Crookshank (C)	15 May 40
	R. Assheton (C)	7 Feb 43
	O. Peake (C)	29 Oct 44
Min. of State:	R. Law (C)	24 Sep 43
U-S.	R. Butler (C)	15 May 40
	R. Law (C)	20 Jul 41
	G. Hall (Lab)	25 Sep 43
U-S.	O. Peake (C)	15 May 40
	E of Munster (C)	31 Oct 44
P.S. Home Security:	W. Mabane (L. Nat)	15 May 40–3 Jun 42

COALITION GOVERNMENT, 1940–1945 *(contd.)*

	MINISTERS IN WAR CABINET		JUNIOR MINISTERS ATTACHED
			Miss E. Wilkinson (Lab) 8 Oct 40–23 May 45
Aircraft Production	*(office not in war cabinet)* **Ld Beaverbrook** (C) 2 Aug 40 *(J. Moore-Brabazon 1 May 41 & office not in war cabinet)*		*(for Junior Ministers see below)*
Def.	**W. Churchill (P.M.)** (C) 10 May 40		
Dom. O.	*(office not in war cabinet)* **C. Attlee** (Lab) 19 Feb 42 *(Vt Cranborne 24 Sep 43 & office not in war cabinet)*		*(for Junior Ministers see below)*
Lab. & Nat. S.	*(office not in war cabinet)* **E. Bevin** (Lab) 3 Oct 40	*P.S.*	R. Assheton (C) 15 May 40–4 Feb 42 G. Tomlinson (Lab) 8 Feb 41–23 May 45 M. McCorquodale (C) 4 Feb 42–23 May 45
Min. resident in Mid. East	*(office not in war cabinet)* **O. Lyttelton** (C) 19 Feb 42 **R. Casey**[1] 19 Mar 42 *(office not in war cabinet 23 Dec 43)*	*Deputy Min. of State:*	Ld Moyne (C) 27 Aug 42–28 Jan 44
Min. without Portfolio	**A. Greenwood** (Lab) 11 May 40–22 Feb 42 *(Sir W. Jowitt appointed 30 Dec 42 not in war cabinet)*		
Reconstruction	*(office not established)* **Ld Woolton** (C) 11 Nov 43		
Supply	*(office not in war cabinet)* **Ld Beaverbrook** (C) 29 Jun 41 *(Sir A. Duncan & office not in war cabinet 4 Feb 42)*		*(for Junior Ministers see below)*
(War) Production	*(office not established)* **Ld Beaverbrook** (C) 4 Feb 42 *(office vacant 19 Feb 42)* **O. Lyttelton** (C) 12 Mar 42 *(Minister of Production)*	*P.S.*	G. Garro-Jones (Lab) 10 Sep 42

	MINISTERS NOT IN WAR CABINET		JUNIOR MINISTERS ATTACHED
Admir.	A. ALEXANDER (Lab) 11 May 40	*P. & F.S.:*	Sir V. Warrender (C) 17 May 40 *(Ld Bruntisfield)*
		Civil Ld:	A. Hudson (C) 15 May 40 R. Pilkington (C) 4 Mar 42
		F.S.	G. Hall (Lab) 4 Feb 42 J. Thomas (C) 25 Sep 43
Ag. & Fish.	R. HUDSON (C) 14 May 40	*P.S.*	Ld Moyne (C) 15 May 40–8 Feb 41 T. Williams (Lab) 15 May 40–23 May 45 D of Norfolk (C) 8 Feb 41–23 May 45
Air	SIR A. SINCLAIR (Lib) 11 May 40	*P.S.*	H. Balfour (C) 15 May 40–21 Nov 44 Ld Sherwood (Lib) 20 Jul 41–23 May 45 R. Brabner (C) 21 Nov 44–27 Mar 45 Q. Hogg (C) 12 Apr 45–23 May 45

[1] Not a member of the House of Commons.

COALITION GOVERNMENT, 1940–1945 (*contd.*)

MINISTERS NOT IN WAR CABINET			JUNIOR MINISTERS ATTACHED		
Aircraft Production	Ld Beaverbrook (C)	14 May 40	*P.S.*	J. Llewellin (C)	15 May 40
	(*office in war cabinet* 2 *Aug* 40)			F. Montague (Lab)	1 May 41
	J. Moore-Brabazon (C)	1 May 41		B. Smith (Lab)	4 Mar 42
	J. Llewellin (C)	22 Feb 42		A. Lennox-Boyd (C)	11 Nov 43
	Sir S. Cripps (Lab)	22 Nov 42			
Civil Av.	(*office not established*)		*P.S.*	R. Perkins (C)	22 Mar 45
	Vt Swinton (C)	8 Oct 44			
Col. O.	Ld Lloyd (C)	12 May 40	*U-S.*	G. Hall (Lab)	15 May 40
	Ld Moyne (C)	8 Feb 41		H. Macmillan (C)	4 Feb 42
	Vt Cranborne (C)	22 Feb 42		D of Devonshire (C)	1 Jan 43
	O. Stanley (C)	22 Nov 42			
Dom. O.	Vt Caldecote (C)	14 May 40	*U-S.*	G. Shakespeare (L. Nat)	15 May 40
	Vt Cranborne[1] (C)	3 Oct 40		P. Emrys-Evans (C)	4 Mar 42
	(*C. Attlee* 19 *Feb* 42 *& office in war cabinet*)				
	Vt Cranborne (C)	24 Sep 43			
Economic Warfare	H. Dalton (Lab)	15 May 40	*P.S.*	D. Foot (Lib)	17 May 40
	Vt Wolmer (*E of Selborne*)	22 Feb 42			
Bd Educ.	H. Ramsbotham (C)	14 May 40	*P.S.*	C. Ede (Lab)	15 May 40
	R. Butler (C)	20 Jul 41			
	(3 *Aug* 44 *becomes Min. of Educ.*)				
Exch.	Sir K. Wood (C)	12 May 40		(*for Financial Secretary to Treasury see above*)	
	(3 *Oct* 40 *office in war cabinet,* 19 *Feb* 42 *out of war cabinet again*)				
	(24 *Sep* 43 *Sir J. Anderson & office in war cabinet*)				
Food	Ld Woolton (C)	13 May 40	*P.S.*	R. Boothby (C)	15 May 40
	J. Llewellin (C)	11 Nov 43		G. Lloyd-George (Ind. L)	22 Oct 40
				W. Mabane (L. Nat)	3 Jun 42
Fuel, Light & Power	(*office not established*)		*P.S.*	G. Lloyd (C)	3 Jun 42–23 May 45
	G. Lloyd-George (Ind L.)	3 Jun 42		T. Smith (Lab)	3 Jun 42–23 May 45
Health	M. MacDonald (N. Lab)	13 May 40	*P.S.*	Miss F. Horsbrugh (C)	15 May 40
	E. Brown (L. Nat)	8 Feb 41			
	H. Willink (C)	11 Nov 43			
Home O. & Home Security	Sir J. Anderson (C)	12 May 40		(*for Junior Ministers see above*)	
	H. Morrison (Lab)	3 Oct 40			
	(22 *Nov* 42 *office in war cabinet*)				
India & Burma O.	L. Amery (C)	13 May 40	*P.S.*	D of Devonshire (C)	17 May 40
				E of Munster (C)	1 Jan 43
				E of Listowel (Lab)	31 Oct 44
Information	A. Duff Cooper (C)	12 May 40	*P.S.*	H. Nicolson (N. Lab)	17 May 40
	(*attended war cabinet from* 28 *May* 40)			E. Thurtle (Lab)	20 Jul 41
	B. Bracken (C)	20 Jul 41			
Lab. & Nat. S.	E. Bevin (Lab)	13 May 40		(*for Junior Ministers see above*)	
	(*office in war cabinet* 3 *Oct* 40)				
D. Lanc.	Ld Hankey (Ind)	14 May 40			
	A. Duff Cooper (C)	20 Jul 41			
	E. Brown (L. Nat)	11 Nov 43			
Ld Chanc.	Vt Simon (L. Nat)	12 May 40			
Min. resident at Allied H.Q. in N.W. Africa	H. Macmillan (C)	30 Dec 42			

[1] Not a member of the House of Lords. Viscount Wolmer was moved to the House of Lords by writ of acceleration in October 1940. The same was done for Viscount Cranborne in January 1941.

COALITION GOVERNMENT, 1940–1945 (*contd.*)

MINISTERS NOT IN WAR CABINET			JUNIOR MINISTERS ATTACHED		
Min. resident in Washington for Supply	J. Llewellin (C)	22 Nov 42			
	B. Smith (Lab)	11 Nov 43			
Min. resident in W. Africa	Vt Swinton (C)	8 Jun 42			
	H. Balfour (C)	21 Nov 44			
Min. of State in Mid. East	(*office in war cabinet*)			(*for Junior Ministers see above*)	
	Ld Moyne (C)	28 Jan 44			
	Sir E. Grigg (C)	21 Nov 44			
Paym.-Gen.	Vt Cranborne [1] (C)	15 May 40			
	(*office vacant* 3 Oct 40)				
	Ld Hankey	20 Jul 41			
	Sir W. Jowitt (Lab)	4 Mar 42			
	Ld Cherwell (C)	30 Dec 42			
Pensions	Sir W. Womersley (C)	15 May 40		Miss E. Wilkinson (Lab)	17 May 40
				Ld Tryon (C)	8 Oct 40
				W. Paling (Lab)	8 Feb 41
Min. without Portfolio	(*in war cabinet* 11 *May* 40–22 *Feb* 42)				
	Sir W. Jowitt (Lab)	30 Dec 42–8 Oct 44			
Postm.-Gen.	W. Morrison (C)	15 May 40	*Ass.*	C. Waterhouse (C)	17 May 40
	H. Crookshank (C)	30 Dec 42		A. Chapman (C)	1 Mar 41
				R. Grimston (C)	4 Mar 42
Privy S.	(*office in war cabinet*)				
	Vt Cranborne (C)	22 Nov 42			
	Ld Beaverbrook (C)	24 Sep 43			
Scot. O.	E. Brown (L. Nat)	14 May 40	*P.S.*	.Westwood (Lab)	17 May 40–23 May 45
	T. Johnston (Lab)	8 Feb 41		H. Wedderburn (C)	8 Feb 41–4 Mar 42
				A. Chapman (C)	4 Mar 42–23 May 45
Shipping	R. Cross (C)	14 May 40	*P.S.*	Sir A. Salter (Ind)	15 May 40
	(1 *May* 41 *combined with Min. of Transport, as Min. of War Transport see below*)				
Soc. Insur.	(*office not established*)		*P.S.*	C. Peat (C)	22 Mar 45
	Sir W. Jowitt (Lab)	8 Oct 44			
	(*renamed National Insurance Nov* 44)				
Supply	H. Morrison (Lab)	12 May 40	*P.S.*	H. Macmillan (C)	15 May 40–4 Feb 42
	Sir A. Duncan (C)	3 Oct 40		Ld Portal (C)	4 Sep 40–4 Mar 42
	(*Ld Beaverbrook* 29 *Jun* 41 *& office in war cabinet*)			R. Assheton (C)	4 Feb 42–30 Dec 42
	Sir A. Duncan (C)	4 Feb 42		C. Peat (C)	4 Mar 42–22 Mar 45
				D. Sandys (C)	30 Dec 42–21 Nov 44
				J. Wilmot (Lab)	21 Nov 44–23 May 45
				J. de Rothschild (Lib)	22 Mar 45–23 May 45
T. & C. Planning	(*office not established*)		*P.S.*	H. Strauss (C)	30 Dec 42
	W. Morrison (C)	30 Dec 42		A. Jenkins (Lab)	22 Mar 45
	(*Minister designate*)				
B.o.T.	Sir A. Duncan (C)	12 May 40	*P.S.*	G. Lloyd-George (Ind L.)	15 May 40
	O. Lyttelton (C)	3 Oct 40		(*& P.S. Food* 22 Oct 40)	
	Sir A. Duncan (C)	29 Jun 41		C. Waterhouse (C)	8 Feb 41
	J. Llewellin (C)	4 Feb 42	*Sec. Bd Overseas Trade:*		
	H. Dalton (Lab)	22 Feb 42		H. Johnstone (Lib)	15 May 40
				S. Summers (C)	22 Mar 45

[1] Not a member of the House of Lords.

COALITION GOVERNMENT, 1940–1945 (*contd.*)

MINISTERS NOT IN WAR CABINET			JUNIOR MINISTERS ATTACHED	
			Mines Dept.:	D. Grenfell (Lab) 15 May 40
			Sec. Petrol Dept.:	G. Lloyd (C) 15 May 40–3 Jun 42 (*3 Jun 42 combined in Min. of Fuel, Light & Power*)
Transp.	SIR J. REITH (Nat) J. MOORE-BRABAZON (C) (*1 May 41 became Min. of War Transport, see below*)	14 May 40 3 Oct 40		(*for Junior Ministers see below, under War Transport*)
War O.	A. EDEN (C) D. MARGESSON (C) SIR J. GRIGG (C)	11 May 40 22 Dec 40 22 Feb 42	*U-S.*	Sir H. Page-Croft (C) (*Ld Croft*) 17 May 40–23 May 45 Sir E. Grigg (C) 17 May 40–4 Mar 42 A. Henderson (Lab) 4 Mar 42–30 Dec 42
			F.S.	R. Law (C) 17 May 40 D. Sandys (C) 20 Jul 41 A. Henderson (Lab) 7 Feb 43
War Transp.	LD LEATHERS (C)	1 May 41	*P.S.*	F. Montague (Lab) 18 May 40–1 May 41 (*renamed War Transport 1 May 41*) J. Llewellin (C) 1 May 41–4 Feb 42 Sir A. Salter (Ind) 29 Jun 41–4 Feb 42 P. Noel-Baker (Lab) 4 Feb 42–23 May 45
1st.C.Works	LD TRYON (C) SIR J. REITH (LD) (Nat) (*Min. of Works & Buildings & 1st C. Works 3 Oct 40*) LD PORTAL (*Min. of Works and Planning 11 Feb 42. Min. of Works Feb 43*) D. SANDYS (C)	18 May 40 3 Oct 40 22 Feb 42 21 Nov 44	*P.S.*	G. Hicks (Lab) 19 Nov 40–23 May 45 H. Strauss (C) 4 Mar 42–30 Dec 42
Law Officers:			*P.S. to Treasury:*	D. Margesson (C) 17 May 40–22 Dec 40 Sir C. Edwards (Lab) 17 May 40–12 Mar 42 J. Stuart (C) 14 Jan 41–23 May 45 W. Whiteley (Lab) 12 Mar 42–23 May 45
Att. Gen.	SIR D. SOMERVELL (C)	15 May 40		
Sol. Gen.	SIR W. JOWITT (Lab) D. MAXWELL FYFE (C)	15 May 40 4 Mar 42		
Ld Advoc.	T. COOPER (C) J. REID (C)	15 May 40 5 Jun 41		
Sol. Gen. Scotland	J. REID (C) (SIR) D. MURRAY (C)	15 May 40 5 Jun 41	*Junior Lds of Treasury:*	S. Furness (L. Nat) 12 May 40–18 May 40 J. Stuart (C) 12 May 40–14 Jan 41 P. Munro (C) 12 May 40–13 Mar 42 P. Buchan-Hepburn (C) 12 May 40–26 Jun 40 W. Boulton (C) 12 May 40–13 Mar 42 W. Paling (Lab) 18 May 40–8 Feb 41 J. Thomas (C) 26 Jun 40–25 Sep 43 T. Dugdale (C) 8 Feb 41–23 Feb 42 W. Adamson (Lab) 1 Mar 41–2 Oct 44 A. Young (C) 23 Feb 42–3 Jul 44 J. McEwen (C) 13 Mar 42–6 Dec 44 L. Pym (C) 13 Mar 42–23 May 45 A. Beechman (L. Nat) 25 Sep 43–23 May 45 C. Drewe (C) 3 Jul 44–23 May 45

COALITION GOVERNMENT, 1940–1945 (*contd.*)

MINISTERS NOT IN WAR CABINET

H.M. Household:

Treas.	R. Grimston (C)	17 May 40
	Sir J. Edmondson (C)	12 Mar 42
Comptr.	W. Whiteley (Lab)	17 May 40
	W. John (Lab)	12 Mar 42
	G. Mathers (Lab)	2 Oct 44
V. Chamb.	Sir J. Edmondson (C)	17 May 40
	W. Boulton (C)	12 Mar 42
	A. Young (C)	13 Jul 44
Capt. Gents at Arms	Ld Snell (Lab)	31 May 40
Capt. Yeomen of Guard	Ld Templemore (C)	31 May 40

JUNIOR MINISTERS ATTACHED

	W. John (Lab)	2 Oct 44–23 May 45
	P. Buchan-Hepburn (C)	6 Dec 44–23 May 45
Lds in Waiting:		
	E of Eldon	31 May 40–23 May 45
	Vt Allendale	31 May 40–23 May 45
	Earl Fortescue	31 May 40–22 Mar 45
	Vt Clifden	31 May 40–23 May 45
	Ld Alness	31 May 40–23 May 45
	M of Normanby	22 Mar 45–23 May 45

CARETAKER GOVERNMENT, 1945

MINISTERS IN CABINET			JUNIOR MINISTERS ATTACHED		
P.M.	**W. Churchill**	23 May 45–26 Jul 45			
Ld Pres.	**Ld Woolton**	25 May 45			
Ld Chanc.	(*office not in cabinet*)				
Privy S.	**Ld Beaverbrook**	25 May 45			
Exch.	**Sir J. Anderson**	25 May 45	*Treasury:*		
			F.S.	O. Peake	26 May 45
For. O.	**A. Eden**	25 May 45	*Min. of State:*		
				W. Mabane	25 May 45
			U-S.	Ld Dunglass[1]	26 May 45
				Ld Lovat	26 May 45
Home O.	**Sir D. Somervell**	25 May 45	*U-S.*	E of Munster	26 May 45
Admir.	**B. Bracken**	25 May 45	*P. & F.S.:*		
				Ld Bruntisfield	26 May 45
			Civil Ld:		
				R. Pilkington	26 May 45
			F.S.	J. Thomas	26 May 45
Ag. & Fish.	**R. Hudson**	25 May 45	*P.S.*	D of Norfolk	26 May 45
				D. Scott	26 May 45
Air	**H. Macmillan**	25 May 45	*U-S.*	Q. Hogg	26 May 45
				Earl Beatty	26 May 45
Col. O.	**O. Stanley**	25 May 45	*U-S*	D of Devonshire	26 May 45
Def.	**W. Churchill (P.M.)**	25 May 45			
Dom. O.	**Vt Cranborne**	25 May 45	*U-S.*	P. Emrys-Evans	26 May 45
India & Burma O.	**L. Amery**	25 May 45	*P.S.*	E of Scarbrough	26 May 45
Lab. & Nat. S.	**R. Butler**	25 May 45	*P.S.*	M. McCorquodale	26 May 45
Production	**O. Lyttelton** (*& Pres. B.o.T.*)	25 May 45	*P.S.*	J. Maclay	28 May 45
Scot. O.	**E of Rosebery**	25 May 45	*P.S.*	A. Chapman	26 May 45
				T. Galbraith	26 May 45
B.o.T.	**O. Lyttelton** (*& Min. of Production*)	25 May 45	*P.S.*	C. Waterhouse	26 May 45
			Sec. Bd Overseas Trade:		
				S. Summers	26 May 45

[1] Not a member of the House of Lords.

CARETAKER GOVERNMENT, 1945 (*contd.*)

	MINISTERS IN CABINET			JUNIOR MINISTERS ATTACHED	
War O.	**Sir J. Grigg**	25 May 45	*U-S.*	Ld Croft	26 May 45

	MINISTERS NOT IN CABINET			JUNIOR MINISTERS ATTACHED	
Aircraft Production	E. Brown	25 May 45	*P.S.*	A. Lennox-Boyd	26 May 45
Civil Av.	Vt Swinton	25 May 45	*P.S.*	R. Perkins	26 May 45
Educ.	R. Law	25 May 45	*P.S.*	Mrs T. Cazalet-Keir	26 May 45
Food	J. Llewellin	25 May 45	*P.S.*	Miss F. Horsbrugh	26 May 45
Fuel & P.	G. Lloyd-George	25 May 45	*P.S.*	Sir A. Hudson	26 May 45
Health	H. Willink	25 May 45	*P.S.*	H. Kerr	26 May 45
Information	G. Lloyd	25 May 45			
D. Lanc.	Sir A. Salter	25 May 45			
Ld Chanc.	Vt Simon	25 May 45			
Min. resident in Mid. East	Sir E. Grigg	25 May 45			
Min. resident in W. Africa	H. Balfour	25 May 45			
Nat. Ins.	L. Hore-Belisha	25 May 45	*P.S.*	C. Peat	26 May 45
Paym.-Gen.	Ld Cherwell	25 May 45			
Pensions	Sir W. Womersley	25 May 45	*P.S.*	W. Sidney (Ld de Lisle)	26 May 45
Postm.-Gen.	H. Crookshank	25 May 45	*Ass.*	W. Anstruther-Gray	26 May 45
Supply	Sir A. Duncan	25 May 45	*P.S.*	R. Grimston	26 May 45
T. & C. Planning	W. Morrison	25 May 45	*P.S.*	R. Tree	26 May 45
War Transp.	Ld Leathers	25 May 45	*P.S.*	P. Thorneycroft	26 May 45
Works	D. Sandys	25 May 45	*P.S.*	R. Manningham-Buller	26 May 45
Law Officers:			*P.S. to Treasury:*		
Att. Gen.	Sir D. Maxwell Fyfe	25 May 45		J. Stuart	26 May 45
Sol. Gen.	Sir W. Monckton [1]	25 May 45	*Junior Lds of Treasury:*		
Advoc. Gen.	J. Reid	25 May 45		A. Beechman	28 May 45
Sol. Gen. Scotland	Sir D. Murray	25 May 45		C. Drewe	25 May 45
				P. Buchan-Hepburn	25 May 45
				R. Cary	28 May 45
				C. Mott-Radclyffe	28 May 45
H.M. Household:			*Lds in Waiting:*		
Treas.	Sir J. Edmondson	28 May 45		Ld Alness	28 May 45
Comptr.	L. Pym	28 May 45		M of Normanby	28 May 45
V. Chamb.	A. Young	28 May 45		D of Northumberland	28 May 45
Capt. Gents at Arms	Earl Fortescue	28 May 45			
Capt. Yeomen of Guard	Ld Templemore	28 May 45			

LABOUR GOVERNMENT, 1945–1951

	MINISTERS IN CABINET		JUNIOR MINISTERS ATTACHED
P.M.	**C. Attlee**	26 Jul 45–26 Oct 51	
Ld Pres.	**H. Morrison**	27 Jul 45	
	Vt Addison	9 Mar 51	

[1] Not a member of the House of Commons.

LABOUR GOVERNMENT, 1945–1951 (*contd.*)

	MINISTERS IN CABINET			JUNIOR MINISTERS ATTACHED	
Ld Chanc.	**Ld Jowitt**	27 Jul 45			
Privy S.	**A. Greenwood**	27 Jul 45			
	Ld Inman	17 Apr 47			
	Vt Addison	7 Oct 47			
	E. Bevin	9 Mar 51			
	R. Stokes	26 Apr 51			
	(*also Min. of Materials from 6 Jul* 51)				
Exch.	**H. Dalton**	27 Jul 45	*Min. Econ. Affairs:*		
	Sir S. Cripps	13 Nov 47		H. Gaitskell	28 Feb 50–19 Oct 50
	H. Gaitskell	19 Oct 50			
Min. Econ. Affairs	(*office not established*)		*Treasury:*		
	Sir S. Cripps	29 Sep 47	*F.S.*	W. Hall	4 Aug 45
	(*office combined with Exch* 13 *Nov* 47)			D. Jay	2 Mar 50
			Econ. S.:		
				D. Jay	5 Dec 47
				(*post vacant* 28 *Feb* 50)	
				J. Edwards	19 Oct 50
For. O.	**E. Bevin**	27 Jul 45	*Min. of State:*		
	H. Morrison	9 Mar 51		P. Noel-Baker	3 Aug 45
				H. McNeil	4 Oct 46
				K. Younger	28 Feb 50
			U-S.	H. McNeil	4 Aug 45–4 Oct 46
				C. Mayhew	4 Oct 46–2 Mar 50
				Ld Henderson	7 Jun 48–26 Oct 51
				E. Davies	2 Mar 50–26 Oct 51
Home O.	**C. Ede**	3 Aug 45	*U-S.*	G. Oliver	4 Aug 45
				K. Younger	7 Oct 47
				G. de Freitas	2 Mar 50
Admir.	**A. Alexander**	3 Aug 45		(*for Junior Ministers see below*)	
	(*office not in cabinet* 4 *Oct* 46)				
Ag. & Fish.	**T. Williams**	3 Aug 45	*P.S.*	E of Huntingdon	4 Aug 45–22 Nov 50
				P. Collick	5 Sep 45–7 Oct 47
				G. Brown	7 Oct 47–26 Apr 51
				E of Listowel	22 Nov 50–26 Oct 51
				A. Champion	26 Apr 51–26 Oct 51
Air	**Vt Stansgate**	3 Aug 45		(*for Junior Ministers see below*)	
	(*office not in cabinet* 4 *Oct* 46)				
Civil Av.	(*office not in cabinet*)		*P.S.*	I. Thomas	10 Aug 45
	Ld Pakenham	31 May 48		G. Lindgren	4 Oct 46
	(*office not in cabinet* 28 *Feb* 50)			F. Beswick	2 Mar 50
Col. O.	**G. Hall**	3 Aug 45	*Min.*	E of Listowel	4 Jan 48
	A. Creech Jones	4 Oct 46		J. Dugdale	28 Feb 50
	J. Griffiths	28 Feb 50	*U-S.*	A. Creech Jones	4 Aug 45
				I. Thomas	4 Oct 46
				D. Rees-Williams	7 Oct 47
				T. Cook	2 Mar 50
C.R.O.	(*office not established*)		*Min.*	A. Henderson	14 Aug 47
	Vt Addison	7 Jul 47		(*office in cabinet* 7 *Oct* 47)	
	P. Noel-Baker	7 Oct 47	*U-S.*	P. Gordon Walker	7 Oct 47
	P. Gordon Walker	28 Feb 50		Ld Holden	2 Mar 50
				D. Rees-Williams (*Ld Ogmore*)	4 Jul 50
				E of Lucan	1 Jun 51
Def.	**C. Attlee (P.M.)**	27 Jul 45			
	A. Alexander (Vt)	20 Dec 46			
	E. Shinwell	28 Feb 50			
Dom. O.	**Vt Addison**	3 Aug 45	*U-S.*	J. Parker	4 Aug 45
	(*became C.R.O.* 7 *Jul* 47 *see above*)			A. Bottomley	10 May 46
Educ.	**Miss E. Wilkinson**	3 Aug 45	*P.S.*	A. Jenkins	4 Aug 45
	G. Tomlinson	10 Feb 47		D. Hardman	30 Oct 45

LABOUR GOVERNMENT, 1945–1951 *(contd.)*

	MINISTERS IN CABINET			JUNIOR MINISTERS ATTACHED	
Fuel & P.	**E. Shinwell**	3 Aug 45		*(for Junior Ministers see below)*	
	(H. Gaitskell 7 Oct 47 & office not in cabinet)				
Health	**A. Bevan**	3 Aug 45	*P.S.*	C. Key	4 Aug 45
	(H. Marquand 17 Jan 51 & office not in cabinet)			J. Edwards	12 Feb 47
				A. Blenkinsop	1 Feb 49
India O. & Burma O.	**Ld Pethick-Lawrence**	3 Aug 45	*U-S.*	A. Henderson	4 Aug 45
	E of Listowel	17 Apr 47			
	(4 Jan 48 offices wound up)				
Lab. & Nat. S.	**G. Isaacs**	3 Aug 45	*P.S.*	N. Edwards	4 Aug 45
	A. Bevan	17 Jan 51		F. Lee	2 Mar 50
	A. Robens	24 Apr 51			
D. Lanc.	*(office not in cabinet)*				
	H. Dalton	31 May 48			
	Vt Alexander	28 Feb 50			
Paym.-Gen.	*(office vacant)*				
	A. Greenwood	9 Jul 46			
	(H. Marquand 5 Mar 47 & office not in cabinet)				
	Vt Addison	2 Jul 48			
	(Ld Macdonald 1 Apr 49 & office not in cabinet)				
Min. without Portfolio	**A. Alexander**	4 Oct 46–20 Dec 46			
	A. Greenwood	17 Apr 47–29 Sep 47			
Scot. O.	**J. Westwood**	3 Aug 45	*U-S.*	G. Buchanan	4 Aug 45–7 Oct 47
	A. Woodburn	7 Oct 47		T. Fraser	4 Aug 45–26 Oct 51
	H. McNeil	28 Feb 50		J. Robertson	7 Oct 47–2 Mar 50
				Miss M. Herbison	2 Mar 50–26 Oct 51
T. & C. Planning	*(office not in cabinet)*		*P.S.*	F. Marshall	10 Aug 45
	H. Dalton	28 Feb 50		E. King	7 Oct 47
	(recast as Local Government & Planning 31 Jan 51)			G. Lindgren	2 Mar 50
B.o.T.	**Sir S. Cripps**	27 Jul 45	*P.S.*	E. Smith	4 Aug 45
	H. Wilson	29 Sep 47		J. Belcher	12 Jan 46
	Sir H. Shawcross	24 Apr 51		J. Edwards	1 Feb 49
				H. Rhodes	2 Mar 50
			Sec. Overseas Trade Dept.:		
				H. Marquand	4 Aug 45
				H. Wilson	5 Mar 47
				A. Bottomley	7 Oct 47
War O.	**J. Lawson**	3 Aug 45		*(for Junior Ministers see below)*	
	(office not in cabinet 4 Oct 46)				

	MINISTERS NOT IN CABINET			JUNIOR MINISTERS ATTACHED	
Admir.	*(office in cabinet)*		*P. & F.S.:*		
	Vt Hall	4 Oct 46		J. Dugdale	4 Aug 45
	Ld Pakenham	24 May 51		J. Callaghan	2 Mar 50
			Civil Ld:		
				W. Edwards	4 Aug 45
Air	*(office in cabinet)*		*U-S.*	J. Strachey	4 Aug 45
	P. Noel-Baker	4 Oct 46		G. de Freitas	27 May 46
	A. Henderson	7 Oct 47		A. Crawley	2 Mar 50
Civil Av.	Ld Winster	4 Aug 45		*(for Junior Ministers see above)*	
	Ld Nathan	4 Oct 46			
	(Ld Pakenham 31 May 48 & office in cabinet)				
	Ld Pakenham	28 Feb 50			
	Ld Ogmore	1 Jun 51			

LABOUR GOVERNMENT, 1945–1951 (*contd.*)

MINISTERS NOT IN CABINET			JUNIOR MINISTERS ATTACHED		
Food	Sir B. Smith	3 Aug 45	*P.S.*	Edith Summerskill	4 Aug 45
	J. Strachey	27 May 46		S. Evans	2 Mar 50
	M. Webb	28 Feb 50		F. Willey	18 Apr 50
Fuel & P.	(*office in cabinet*)		*P.S.*	W. Foster	4 Aug 45
	H. Gaitskell	7 Oct 47		H. Gaitskell	10 May 46
	P. Noel-Baker	28 Feb 50		A. Robens	7 Oct 47
				H. Neal	26 Apr 51
Health	(*office in cabinet*)			(*for Junior Ministers see above*)	
	H. Marquand	17 Jan 51			
Information	E. Williams	4 Aug 45			
	(*office wound up* 31 *Mar* 46)				
D. Lanc.	J. Hynd	4 Aug 45			
	Ld Pakenham	17 Apr 47			
	(*H. Dalton* 31 *May* 48 *& office in cabinet*)				
Nat. Ins.	J. Griffiths	4 Aug 45	*P.S.*	G. Lindgren	4 Aug 45
	Edith Summerskill	28 Feb 50		T. Steele	4 Oct 46
				H. Taylor	2 Mar 50
Paym.-Gen.	(*office in cabinet*)				
	H. Marquand	5 Mar 47			
	(*Vt Addison* 2 *Jul* 48 *& office in cabinet*)				
	Ld Macdonald of Gwaenysgor	1 Apr 49			
Pensions	W. Paling	3 Aug 45	*P.S.*	Mrs J. Adamson	4 Aug 45
	J. Hynd	17 Apr 47		A. Blenkinsop	10 May 46
	G. Buchanan	7 Oct 47		C. Simmons	1 Feb 49
	H. Marquand	2 Jul 48			
	G. Isaacs	17 Jan 51			
Postm.-Gen.	E of Listowel	4 Aug 45	*Ass.*	W. Burke	10 Aug 45
	W. Paling	17 Apr 47		C. Hobson	7 Oct 47
	N. Edwards	28 Feb 50			
Supply	J. Wilmot	3 Aug 45	*P.S.*	W. Leonard A. Woodburn	4 Aug 45
	G. Strauss	7 Oct 47		J. Freeman J. Jones	7 Oct 47
				J. Freeman	2 Mar 50
				M. Stewart	2 May 51
T. & C. Planning	L. Silkin	4 Aug 45		(*for Junior Ministers see above*)	
	(*H. Dalton* 28 *Feb* 50 *& office in cabinet*)				
Transp.	A. Barnes	3 Aug 45	*P.S.*	G. Strauss	4 Aug 45
				J. Callaghan	7 Oct 47
				Ld Lucas of Chilworth	2 Mar 50
War O.	(*office in cabinet*)		*U-S.*	Ld Nathan	4 Aug 45
	F. Bellenger	4 Oct 46		Ld Pakenham	4 Oct 46–17 Apr 47
	E. Shinwell	7 Oct 47	*F.S.*	F. Bellenger	4 Aug 45
	J. Strachey	28 Feb 50		J. Freeman	4 Oct 46–17 Apr 47
			U. & F.S.	J. Freeman	17 Apr 47
				M. Stewart	7 Oct 47
				W. Wyatt	2 May 51
Works	G. Tomlinson	4 Aug 45	*P.S.*	H. Wilson	4 Aug 45
	C. Key	10 Feb 47		E. Durbin	5 Mar 47
	R. Stokes	28 Feb 50		Ld Morrison	26 Sep 48
	G. Brown	26 Apr 51			
Law Officers:			*P.S. to Treasury:*		
Att. Gen.	Sir H. Shawcross	4 Aug 45		W. Whiteley	3 Aug 45
	Sir F. Soskice	24 Apr 51	*Junior Lds of Treasury:*		
Sol. Gen.	Sir F. Soskice	4 Aug 45		R. Taylor	4 Aug 45–26 Oct 51
	Sir L. Ungoed-Thomas	24 Apr 51		J. Henderson	4 Aug 45–1 Jan 50
				M. Stewart	10 Aug 45–30 Mar 46

LABOUR GOVERNMENT, 1945–1951 (*contd.*)

MINISTERS NOT IN CABINET

Law Officers:

Ld Advoc.	G. Thomson	10 Aug 45[1]
	J. Wheatley	7 Oct 47
Sol. Gen. Scotland	D. Blades	10 Sep 45[1]
	J. Wheatley	19 Mar 47
	D. Johnston	24 Oct 47

H.M. Household:

Treas.	G. Mathers	4 Aug 45
	A. Pearson	30 Mar 46
Comptr.	A. Pearson	4 Aug 45
	M. Stewart	30 Mar 46
	F. Collindridge	9 Dec 46
V. Chamb.	J. Snow	10 Aug 45
	M. Stewart	9 Dec 46
	E. Popplewell	16 Oct 47
Capt. Gents at Arms	Ld Ammon	4 Aug 45
	Ld Shepherd	18 Oct 49
Capt. Yeomen of Guard	Ld Walkden	4 Aug 45
	Ld Shepherd	6 Jul 49
	Ld Lucas of Chilworth	18 Oct 49
	E of Lucan	5 Mar 50
	Ld Archibald	8 Jun 51

JUNIOR MINISTERS ATTACHED

A. Blenkinsop	10 Aug 45–10 May 46
F. Collindridge	10 Aug 45–9 Dec 46
C. Simmons	30 Mar 46–1 Feb 49
W. Hannan	10 May 46–26 Oct 51
J. Snow	9 Dec 46–3 Mar 50
R. Adams	1 Feb 49–23 Apr 50
W. Wilkins	1 Jan 50–26 Oct 51
H. Bowden	3 Mar 50–26 Oct 51
C. Royle	23 Apr 50–26 Oct 51

Lds in Waiting:

Ld Westwood	10 Sep 45–17 Jan 47
Ld Pakenham	14 Oct 45–4 Oct 46
Ld Henderson	21 Oct 45–7 Jun 48
Ld Chorley	11 Oct 46–31 Mar 50
Ld Morrison	17 Jan 47–26 Sep 48
Ld Lucas of Chilworth	9 Jul 48–18 Oct 49
Ld Shepherd	14 Oct 48–6 Jul 49
Ld Kershaw	6 Jul 49–26 Oct 51
Ld Darwen	18 Oct 49–26 Dec 50
Ld Burden	31 Mar 50–26 Oct 51
Ld Haden-Guest	13 Feb 51–26 Oct 51

CONSERVATIVE GOVERNMENT, 1951–1955

MINISTERS IN CABINET			JUNIOR MINISTERS ATTACHED		
P.M.	**(Sir) W. Churchill**	26 Oct 51–5 Apr 55			
Ld Pres.	**Ld Woolton**	28 Oct 51			
	M of Salisbury	24 Nov 52			
Ld Chanc.	**Ld Simonds**	30 Oct 51			
	Vt Kilmuir	18 Oct 54			
Privy S.	**M of Salisbury**	28 Oct 51			
	H. Crookshank	7 May 52			
Exch.	**R. Butler**	28 Oct 51	*Min. Econ. Affs.:*	Sir A. Salter	31 Oct 51 (24 *Nov* 52 *post extinct*)
			Treasury: F.S.	J. Boyd-Carpenter	31 Oct 51
				H. Brooke	28 Jul 54
			Econ.S.:	R. Maudling	24 Nov 52
For. O.	**(Sir) A. Eden**	28 Oct 51	*Min. of State:*	S. Lloyd	30 Oct 51–18 Oct 54
				M of Reading	11 Nov 53–5 Apr 55
				A. Nutting	18 Oct 54–5 Apr 55
			U-S.	M of Reading	31 Oct 51–11 Nov 53
				A. Nutting	31 Oct 51–18 Oct 54
				A. Dodds-Parker	11 Nov 53–18 Oct 54
				R. Turton	18 Oct 54–5 Apr 55
				Ld J. Hope[2]	18 Oct 54–5 Apr 55

[1] Non-political appointments.

[2] Not a member of the House of Lords.

CONSERVATIVE GOVERNMENT, 1951–1955 (*contd.*)

	MINISTERS IN CABINET			JUNIOR MINISTERS ATTACHED	
Home O. & Welsh Affs.	**Sir D. Maxwell Fyfe** (*Vt Kilmuir*)	28 Oct 51	*U-S.*	D. Llewellyn	5 Nov 51–14 Oct 52
				Sir H. Lucas-Tooth	3 Feb 52–5 Apr 55
	G. Lloyd-George	18 Oct 54		Ld Lloyd	24 Nov 52–18 Oct 54
				Ld Mancroft	18 Oct 54–5 Apr 55
Ag. & Fish.	(*office not in cabinet*)		*P.S.*	Ld Carrington	5 Nov 51–18 Oct 54
	Sir T. Dugdale	3 Sep 53		R. Nugent	5 Nov 51–5 Apr 55
	D. Heathcoat Amory	28 Jul 54		Earl St Aldwyn	18 Oct 54–5 Apr 55
	(18 *Oct* 54 *Min. of Ag. & Fish.* (*combined with Min. of Food*)				
Col. O.	**O. Lyttelton**	28 Oct 51	*Min.*	A. Lennox-Boyd	2 Nov 51
	A. Lennox-Boyd	28 Jul 54		H. Hopkinson	7 May 52
			U-S.	E of Munster	5 Nov 51
				Ld Lloyd	18 Oct 54
C.R.O.	**Ld Ismay**	28 Oct 51	*U-S*	J. Foster	3 Nov 51
	M of Salisbury	12 Mar 52		A. Dodds-Parker	18 Oct 54
	Vt Swinton	24 Nov 52			
Co-ordination of Transport, Fuel & Power	**Ld Leathers**	30 Oct 51			
	(3 *Sep* 53 *office extinct*)				
Def.	**W. Churchill (P.M.)**	28 Oct 51	*P.S.*	N. Birch	28 Feb 52
	Earl Alexander	1 Mar 52		Ld Carrington	18 Oct 54
	H. Macmillan	18 Oct 54			
Educ.	(*office not in cabinet*)		*P.S.*	K. Pickthorn	5 Nov 51
	Miss F. Horsbrugh	3 Sep 53		D. Vosper	18 Oct 54
	Sir D. Eccles	18 Oct 54			
Food	(*office not in cabinet*)		*P.S.*	C. Hill	31 Oct 51
	G. Lloyd-George	3 Sep 53			
	D. Heathcoat Amory	18 Oct 54			
	(*& combined with Min. of Ag. & Fish.*)				
Health	**H. Crookshank**	30 Oct 51	*P.S.*	Miss P. Hornsby-Smith	3 Nov 51
	(7 *May* 52 *office not in cabinet*)				
Housing & Loc. Govt.	**H. Macmillan**	30 Oct 51	*P.S.*	E. Marples	3 Nov 51
	D. Sandys	18 Oct 54		W. Deedes	18 Oct 54
Lab. & Nat. S.	**Sir W. Monckton**	28 Oct 51	*P.S.*	Sir P. Bennett	31 Oct 51
				H. Watkinson	28 May 52
D. Lanc.	(*office not in cabinet*)				
	Ld Woolton (Vt)	24 Nov 52			
	(3 *Sep* 53–15 *Jul* 54 *also Min. of Materials*)				
Paym.-Gen.	**Ld Cherwell**	30 Oct 51			
	(11 *Nov* 53 *E of Selkirk & office not in cabinet*)				
Pensions & Nat. Ins.	(*office not in cabinet*)			(*for Junior Ministers see below*)	
	O. Peake	18 Oct 54			
Scot. O.	**J. Stuart**	30 Oct 51	*Min.*	E of Home	2 Nov 51
			U-S.	T. Galbraith	2 Nov 51–5 Apr 55
				W. Snadden	2 Nov 51–5 Apr 55
				J. Henderson Stewart	4 Feb 52–5 Apr 55
B.o.T.	**P. Thorneycroft**	30 Oct 51	*Min.*	D. Heathcoat Amory	3 Sep 53
				T. Low	28 Jul 54
			P.S.	H. Strauss	3 Nov 51
			Sec. Overseas Trade:	H. Hopkinson	3 Nov 51
				H. Mackeson	28 May 52
				(3 *Sep* 53 *office extinct, Min. of State established*)	

CONSERVATIVE GOVERNMENT, 1951–1955 (*contd.*)

MINISTERS NOT IN CABINET			JUNIOR MINISTERS ATTACHED		
Admir.	J. Thomas	31 Oct 51	*P. & F.S.:*	A. Noble	5 Nov 51
			Civil Ld:	S. Wingfield Digby	5 Nov 51
Ag. & Fish	Sir T. Dugdale (3 *Sep* 53 *office in cabinet*)	31 Oct 51		(*for Junior Ministers see above*)	
Air	Ld De L'Isle and Dudley	31 Oct 51	*U-S.*	N. Birch G. Ward	3 Nov 51 29 Feb 52
Educ.	Miss F. Horsbrugh (3 *Sep* 53 *office in cabinet*)	2 Nov 51		(*for Junior Ministers see above*)	
Food	G. Lloyd-George (3 *Sep* 53 *office in cabinet*)	31 Oct 51		(*for Junior Ministers see above*)	
Fuel & P.	G. Lloyd	31 Oct 51	*P.S.*	L. Joynson-Hicks	5 Nov 51
Health	(*office in cabinet*) I. Macleod	 7 May 52		(*for Junior Ministers see above*)	
D. Lanc.	Vt Swinton (*also Min. of Materials.* 24 *Nov* 52, *Ld Woolton became D. Lanc. & office in cabinet*)	31 Oct 51–24 Nov 52			
Materials	Vt Swinton (*also D. Lanc.*)	31 Oct 51–24 Nov 52			
	Sir A. Salter (1 *Sep* 53–15 *Jul* 54 *Ld Woolton combined Materials with D. Lanc. in cabinet.* 15 *Jul* 54 *Min.* of *Materials wound up*)	24 Nov 52–1 Sep 53			
Min. without Portfolio	E of Munster	18 Oct 54–5 Apr 55			
Nat. Ins.	O. Peake (3 *Sep* 53 *combined with Min. of Pensions, see below*)	31 Oct 51	*P.S.*	R. Turton	5 Nov 51–3 Sep 53
Paym.-Gen.	(*office in cabinet*) E of Selkirk	 11 Nov 53			
Pensions (& Nat. Ins.)	D. Heathcoat Amory (1 *Sep* 53 *combined Min. of Pensions & National Insurance*)	5 Nov 51	*P.S.*	J. Smyth R. Turton E. Marples	5 Nov 51–5 Apr 55 3 Sep 53–18 Oct 54 18 Oct 54–5 Apr 55
	O. Peake (18 *Oct* 54 *office in cabinet*)	3 Sep 53			
Postm.-Gen.	Earl De La Warr	5 Nov 51	*Ass.*	D. Gammans	5 Nov 51
Supply	D. Sandys S. Lloyd	31 Oct 51 18 Oct 54	*P.S.*	T. Low Sir E. Boyle	3 Nov 51 28 Jul 54
Transp. & Civil Av.	J. Maclay A. Lennox-Boyd (*Ministries of Transport & Civil Aviation merged* 1 *Oct* 53) J. Boyd-Carpenter	31 Oct 51 7 May 52 28 Jul 54	*P.S.*	J. Gurney Braithwaite R. Maudling J. Profumo H. Molson	5 Nov 51–1 Nov 53 18 Apr 52–24 Nov 52 24 Nov 52–5 Apr 55 11 Nov 53–5 Apr 55
War O.	A. Head	31 Oct 51	*U-S. & F.S.:*	J. Hutchison F. Maclean	5 Nov 51 18 Oct 54
Works	D. Eccles N. Birch	1 Nov 51 18 Oct 54	*P.S.*	H. Molson J. Bevins	3 Nov 51 11 Nov 53
Law Officers:			*P.S. to Treasury:*		
Att. Gen.	Sir L. Heald Sir R. Manningham-Buller	3 Nov 51 18 Oct 54		P. Buchan-Hepburn	30 Oct 51
Sol. Gen.	Sir R. Manningham-Buller Sir H. Hylton-Foster	3 Nov 51 18 Oct 54	*Junior Lds of Treasury:*	H. Mackeson (Sir) H. Butcher E. Heath T. Galbraith	7 Nov 51–28 May 52 7 Nov 51–3 Jul 53 7 Nov 51–5 Apr 55 7 Nov 51–4 Jun 54

CONSERVATIVE GOVERNMENT, 1951–1955 (*contd.*)

MINISTERS NOT IN CABINET

Law Officers:

Ld Advoc.	J. Clyde	2 Nov 51
	W. Milligan	30 Dec 54
Sol. Gen. Scotland	W. Milligan	3 Nov 51
	W. Grant	10 Jan 55

H.M. Household:

Treas.	(Sir) C. Drewe	7 Nov 51
Comptr.	R. Conant	7 Nov 51
	T. Galbraith	7 Jun 54
V. Chamb.	H. Studholme	7 Nov 51
Capt. Gents at Arms	Earl Fortescue	5 Nov 51
Capt. Yeomen of Guard	E of Onslow	5 Nov 51

JUNIOR MINISTERS ATTACHED

D. Vosper	7 Nov 51–18 Oct 54
H. Oakshott	28 May 52–5 Apr 55
M. Redmayne	3 Jul 53–5 Apr 55
R. Thompson	28 Jul 54–5 Apr 55
G. Wills	26 Oct 54–5 Apr 55

Lds in Waiting:

E of Birkenhead	5 Nov 51–28 Jan 55
E of Selkirk	5 Nov 51–11 Nov 53
Ld Lloyd	7 Nov 51–24 Nov 52
Ld Mancroft	15 Dec 52–18 Oct 54
Ld Hawke	11 Nov 53–5 Apr 55
Ld Fairfax	18 Oct 54–5 Apr 55
Ld Chesham	28 Jan 55–5 Apr 55

CONSERVATIVE GOVERNMENT, 1955–1960

MINISTERS IN CABINET

P.M.	**Sir A. Eden**	6 Apr 55–9 Jan 57
	H. Macmillan	10 Jan 57–
Ld Pres.	**M of Salisbury**	7 Apr 55
	E of Home	29 Mar 57
	Vt Hailsham	17 Sep 57
	E of Home	14 Oct 59
	Vt Hailsham	27 Jul 60
	(*also Min. for Science*)	
Ld Chanc.	**Vt Kilmuir**	7 Apr 55
Privy S.	**H. Crookshank**	7 Apr 55
	R. Butler	20 Dec 55
	(*also Home Sec. from 13 Jan 57*)	
	Vt Hailsham	14 Oct 59
	(*also Min. for Science*)	
	E. Heath	27 Jul 60
Exch.	**R. Butler**	7 Apr 55
	H. Macmillan	20 Dec 55
	P. Thorneycroft	13 Jan 57
	D. Heathcoat Amory	6 Jan 58
	S. Lloyd	27 Jul 60
For. O.	**H. Macmillan**	7 Apr 55
	S. Lloyd	20 Dec 55
	E of Home	27 Jul 60

JUNIOR MINISTERS ATTACHED

Treasury:

F.S.	H. Brooke	7 Apr 55
	E. Powell	16 Jan 57
	J. Simon	6 Jan 58
	Sir E. Boyle	22 Oct 59
Econ.S.:	Sir E. Boyle	7 Apr 55
	D. Walker-Smith	11 Nov 56
	N. Birch	16 Jan 57
	(*vacant 6 Jan 58*)	
	F. Erroll	23 Oct 58
	A. Barber	22 Oct 59

Min. of State:

	M of Reading	7 Apr 55–16 Jan 57
	A. Nutting	7 Apr 55–3 Nov 56
	A. Noble	9 Nov 56–16 Jan 59
	D. Ormsby-Gore	16 Jan 57–
	J. Profumo	16 Jan 59–27 Jul 60
U-S.	R. Turton	7 Apr 55–20 Dec 55
	Ld J. Hope[1]	7 Apr 55–9 Nov 56
	A. Dodds-Parker	20 Dec 55–18 Jan 57
	D. Ormsby-Gore	9 Nov 56–16 Jan 57
	E of Gosford	18 Jan 57–23 Oct 58

[1] Not a member of the House of Lords.

CONSERVATIVE GOVERNMENT, 1955–1960 (*contd.*)

	MINISTERS IN CABINET			JUNIOR MINISTERS ATTACHED	
				I. Harvey	18 Jan 57–24 Nov 58
				J. Profumo	28 Nov 58–16 Jan 59
				M of Lansdowne	23 Oct 58–
				R. Allan	16 Jan 59–7 Oct 60
				J. Godber	28 Oct 60–
Home O. & Welsh Affs.	**G. Lloyd-George**	7 Apr 55	*Min. Home Affs.:*	D. Vosper	28 Oct 60
	R. Butler	13 Jan 57	*U-S.*	Sir H. Lucas-Tooth	7 Apr 55–20 Dec 55
	(*13 Jan 57 Home O. only. Welsh Affs. combined with Housing & Local Government — see below*)			Ld Mancroft	7 Apr 55–18 Jan 57
				W. Deedes	20 Dec 55–18 Jan 57
				Miss P. Hornsby-Smith	18 Jan 57–22 Oct 59
				J. Simon	18 Jan 57–6 Jan 58
				D. Renton	17 Jan 58–
				D. Vosper	22 Oct 59–28 Oct 60
Ag. Fish. & Food	**D. Heathcoat Amory**	7 Apr 55	*P.S.*	Earl St Aldwyn	7 Apr 55–27 Jun 58
	J. Hare	6 Jan 58		H. Nicholls	7 Apr 55–18 Jan 57
	C. Soames	27 Jul 60		R. Nugent	7 Apr 55–18 Jan 57
				J. Godber	18 Jan 57–28 Oct 60
				Earl Waldegrave	27 Jun 58–
				W. Vane	28 Oct 60–
Aviation	(*see Transp. & Civil Av.*)			(*for Junior Ministers see below—Transp. & Civil Aviation*)	
	D. Sandys	14 Oct 59	*P.S.*	G. Rippon	22 Oct 59
	P. Thorneycroft	27 Jul 60			
Col. O.	**A. Lennox-Boyd**	7 Apr 55	*Min.*	H. Hopkinson	7 Apr 55
	I. Macleod	14 Oct 59		J. Hare	20 Dec 55
				J. Maclay	18 Oct 56
				E of Perth	16 Jan 57
			U-S.	Ld Lloyd	7 Apr 55
				J. Profumo	18 Jan 57
				J. Amery	28 Nov 58
				H. Fraser	28 Oct 60
C.R.O.	**E of Home**	7 Apr 55	*Min.*	C. Alport	22 Oct 59
	D. Sandys	27 Jul 60	*U-S.*	A. Dodds-Parker	7 Apr 55
				A. Noble	20 Dec 55
				Ld J. Hope[1]	9 Nov 56
				C. Alport	18 Jan 57
				R. Thompson	22 Oct 59
				D of Devonshire	28 Oct 60
Def.	**S. Lloyd**	7 Apr 55	*P.S.*	Ld Carrington	7 Apr 55
	Sir W. Monckton	20 Dec 55		E of Gosford	22 May 56
	A. Head	18 Oct 56		Ld Mancroft	18 Jan 57
	D. Sandys	13 Jan 57		(*11 Jun 57 office vacant*)	
	H. Watkinson	14 Oct 59			
Educ.	**Sir D. Eccles**	7 Apr 55	*P.S.*	D. Vosper	7 Apr 55
	Vt Hailsham	13 Jan 57		Sir E. Boyle	18 Jan 57
	G. Lloyd	17 Sep 57		K. Thompson	22 Oct 59
	Sir D. Eccles	14 Oct 59			
Housing & Loc. Govt.	**D. Sandys**	7 Apr 55	*Min.*	Ld Brecon	12 Dec 57
	H. Brooke	13 Jan 57	*P.S.*	W. Deedes	7 Apr 55
	(*& Min. for Welsh Affairs*)			E. Powell	20 Dec 55
				J. Bevins	18 Jan 57
				Sir K. Joseph	22 Oct 59
Lab. & Nat. S.	**Sir W. Monckton**	7 Apr 55	*P.S.*	H. Watkinson	7 Apr 55
	I. Macleod	20 Dec 55		R. Carr	20 Dec 55
	E. Heath	14 Oct 59		R. Wood	14 Apr 58
	(12 *Nov 59—Min. of Labour*)			P. Thomas	22 Oct 59
	J. Hare	27 Jul 60			

[1] Not a member of the House of Lords.

CONSERVATIVE GOVERNMENT, 1955–1960 (*contd.*)

	MINISTERS IN CABINET		JUNIOR MINISTERS ATTACHED	
D. Lanc.	**Vt Woolton**	7 Apr 55		
	E of Selkirk	20 Dec 55		
	C. Hill	13 Jan 57		
Paym.-Gen.	(*office not in cabinet*)			
	Sir W. Monckton	18 Oct 56		
	(16 *Jan* 57 *R. Maudling & office not in cabinet*)			
	R. Maudling	17 Sep 57		
	Ld Mills	14 Oct 59		
Pensions & Nat. Ins.	**O. Peake**	7 Apr 55	(*for Junior Ministers see below*)	
	(20 *Dec* 55 *J. Boyd-Carpenter & office not in cabinet*)			
Power	(*see Fuel & Power below*)		(*for Junior Ministers see Fuel & Power below*)	
	Ld Mills	13 Jan 57		
	(14 *Oct* 59 *R. Wood & office not in cabinet*)			
Scot. O.	**J. Stuart**	7 Apr 55	*Min.* T. Galbraith (*Ld Strathclyde*)	7 Apr 55
	J. Maclay	13 Jan 57	Ld Forbes	23 Oct 58
			J. Browne (*Ld Craigton*)	22 Oct 59
			U-S. W. Snadden	7 Apr 55–13 Jun 55
			J. Browne	7 Apr 55–22 Oct 59
			N. Macpherson	13 Jun 55–28 Oct 60
			J. Henderson Stewart	7 Apr 55–18 Jan 57
			Ld J. Hope[1]	18 Jan 57–22 Oct 59
			T. Galbraith	22 Oct 59–
			G. Leburn	22 Oct 59–
			R. Brooman-White	28 Oct 60–
B.o.T	**P. Thorneycroft**	7 Apr 55	*Min.* T. Low	7 Apr 55
	Sir D. Eccles	13 Jan 57	D. Walker-Smith	16 Jan 57
	R. Maudling	14 Oct 59	J. Vaughan-Morgan	17 Sep 57
			F. Erroll	22 Oct 59
			P.S. D. Kaberry	7 Apr 55
			D. Walker-Smith	19 Oct 55
			F. Erroll	11 Nov 56
			J. Rodgers	23 Oct 58
			N. Macpherson	28 Oct 60
Transp. & Civil Av.	(*office not in cabinet*)		*P.S.* H. Molson	7 Apr 55–16 Jan 57
	H. Watkinson	13 Jan 57	J. Profumo	7 Apr 55–18 Jan 57
	(14 *Oct* 59 *Min. of Transp. only*)		R. Nugent	18 Jan 57–22 Oct 59
	E. Marples	14 Oct 59	A. Neave	18 Jan 57–16 Jan 59
	(*see above Min. of Aviation*)		J. Hay	16 Jan 59–
			Ld Chesham	22 Oct 59–
Works	(*office not in cabinet*)		(*for Junior Ministers see below*)	
	P. Buchan-Hepburn	20 Dec 55		
	(16 *Jan* 57 *H. Molson & office not in cabinet*)			

	MINISTERS NOT IN CABINET		JUNIOR MINISTERS ATTACHED	
Admir.	J. Thomas (*Vt Cilcennin*)	7 Apr 55	*P. & F.S.:*	
	Vt Hailsham	2 Sep 56	A. Noble	7 Apr 55
	E of Selkirk	16 Jan 57	G. Ward	20 Dec 55
	Ld Carrington	16 Oct 59	C. Soames	18 Jan 57
			R. Allan	17 Jan 58
			C. Orr Ewing	16 Jan 59
			(16 *Oct* 59 *office vacant*)	
			Civil Ld:	
			S. Wingfield Digby	7 Apr 55
			T. Galbraith	18 Jan 57
			C. Orr Ewing	16 Oct 59

[1] Not a member of the House of Lords.

CONSERVATIVE GOVERNMENT, 1955–1960 (*contd.*)

MINISTERS NOT IN CABINET			JUNIOR MINISTERS ATTACHED		
Air	Ld De L'Isle and Dudley	7 Apr 55	*U-S.*	G. Ward	7 Apr 55
	N. Birch	20 Dec 55		C. Soames	20 Dec 55
	G. Ward	16 Jan 57		C. Orr Ewing	18 Jan 57
	J. Amery	28 Oct 60		A. Neave	16 Jan 59
				W. Taylor	16 Oct 59
Fuel & P.	G. Lloyd	7 Apr 55	*P.S.*	L. Joynson-Hicks	7 Apr 55
	A. Jones	20 Dec 55		D. Renton	20 Dec 55
	(13 *Jan* 57 *renamed, Min. of Power & Ld Mills in cabinet*)			Sir I. Horobin	17 Jan 58
	R. Wood	14 Oct 59		J. George	22 Oct 59
Health	I. Macleod	7 Apr 55	*P.S.*	Miss P. Hornsby-Smith	7 Apr 55
	R. Turton	20 Dec 55		J. Vaughan-Morgan	18 Jan 57
	D. Vosper	16 Jan 57		R. Thompson	17 Sep 57
	D. Walker-Smith	17 Sep 57		Miss E. Pitt	22 Oct 59
	E. Powell	27 Jul 60			
Paym.-Gen.	E of Selkirk	7 Apr 55			
	(20 *Dec* 55 *office vacant. Sir W. Monckton* 18 *Oct* 56 *& office in cabinet*)				
	R. Maudling	16 Jan 57			
	(17 *Sep* 57 *office in cabinet*)				
Pensions & Nat. Ins.	(*office in cabinet*)		*P.S.*	J. Smyth	7 Apr 55–20 Dec 55
	J. Boyd-Carpenter	20 Dec 55		E. Marples	7 Apr 55–20 Dec 55
				Miss E. Pitt	20 Dec 55–22 Oct 59
				R. Wood	20 Dec 55–14 Apr 58
				W. Vane	14 Apr 58–28 Oct 60
				Miss P. Hornsby-Smith	22 Oct 59–
				B. Braine	28 Oct 60–
Min. without Portfolio	E of Munster	7 Apr 55			
	Ld Mancroft	11 Jun 57			
	E of Dundee	23 Oct 58			
Postm.-Gen.	C. Hill	7 Apr 55	*Ass.*	D. Gammans	7 Apr 55
	E. Marples	16 Jan 57		C. Alport	20 Dec 55
	J. Bevins	22 Oct 59		K. Thompson	18 Jan 57
				Miss M. Pike	22 Oct 59
Power	(*see Fuel & Power above*)				
Supply	R. Maudling	7 Apr 55	*P.S.*	F. Erroll	7 Apr 55
	A. Jones	16 Jan 57		I. Harvey	11 Nov 56
	(*office wound up* 22 *Oct* 59)			W. Taylor	18 Jan 57
				(*office wound up* 22 *Oct* 59)	
Transp. & Civil Av.	J. Boyd-Carpenter	7 Apr 55		(*for Junior Ministers see above*)	
	H. Watkinson	20 Dec 55			
	(13 *Jan* 57 *office in cabinet*)				
War O.	A. Head	7 Apr 55	*U-S. & F.S.:*		
	J. Hare	18 Oct 56		F. Maclean	7 Apr 55
	C. Soames	6 Jan 58		J. Amery	18 Jan 57
	J. Profumo	27 Jul 60		H. Fraser	28 Nov 58
				J. Ramsden	28 Oct 60
Works	N. Birch	7 Apr 55	*P.S.*	J. Bevins	7 Apr 55
	(20 *Dec* 55 *P. Buchan-Hepburn & office in cabinet*)			H. Nicholls	18 Jan 57
	H. Molson	16 Jan 57		R. Thompson	28 Oct 60
	Ld J. Hope[1]	22 Oct 59			
Law Officers:			*P.S. to Treasury:*		
Att. Gen.	Sir R. Manningham-Buller	7 Apr 55		P. Buchan-Hepburn	7 Apr 55
				E. Heath	20 Dec 55
				M. Redmayne	14 Oct 59

[1] Not a member of the House of Lords.

MINISTERS NOT IN CABINET

Law Officers:

Sol. Gen.	SIR H. HYLTON-FOSTER	7 Apr 55
	SIR J. SIMON	22 Oct 59
Ld Advoc.	W. MILLIGAN	7 Apr 55
	W. GRANT	5 Apr 60
Sol. Gen. Scotland	W. GRANT	7 Apr 55
	D. ANDERSON	11 May 60

JUNIOR MINISTERS ATTACHED

Junior Lds of Treasury:

H. Oakshott	7 Apr 55–13 Jun 55
E. Heath	7 Apr 55–20 Dec 55
M. Redmayne	7 Apr 55–14 Oct 59
R. Thompson	7 Apr 55–8 Apr 56
G. Wills	7 Apr 55–19 Jan 57
P. Legh	13 Jun 55–17 Sep 57
E. Wakefield	24 Jan 56–23 Oct 58
H. Harrison	8 Apr 56–16 Jan 59
A. Barber	9 Apr 57–19 Feb 58
R. Brooman-White	28 Oct 57–21 Jun 60
P. Bryan	19 Feb 58–
M. Hughes-Young	23 Oct 58–
G. Finlay	16 Jan 59–28 Oct 60
D. Gibson-Watt	22 Oct 59–
R. Chichester-Clark	21 Jun 60–
J. Hill	28 Oct 60–

H.M. Household:

Treas.	SIR C. DREWE	7 Apr 55
	T. GALBRAITH	13 Jun 55
	H. OAKSHOTT	19 Jan 57
	P. LEGH (*Ld Newton*)	16 Jan 59
	E. WAKEFIELD	21 Jun 60
Comptr.	T. GALBRAITH	7 Apr 55
	H. OAKSHOTT	13 Jun 55
	(SIR) G. WILLS	19 Jan 57
	E. WAKEFIELD	23 Oct 58
	H. HARRISON	16 Jan 59
V. Chamb.	H. STUDHOLME	7 Apr 55
	R. THOMPSON	8 Apr 56
	P. LEGH	17 Sep 57
	E. WAKEFIELD	16 Jan 59
	R. BROOMAN-WHITE	21 Jun 60
	G. FINLAY	28 Oct 60
Capt. Gents at Arms	EARL FORTESCUE	7 Apr 55
	EARL ST ALDWYN	27 Jun 58
Capt. Yeomen of Guard	E OF ONSLOW	7 Apr 55
	LD NEWTON	28 Oct 60

Lds in Waiting:

Ld Hawke	7 Apr 55–11 Jun 57
Ld Fairfax	7 Apr 55–31 Jun 57
Ld Chesham	7 Apr 55–22 Oct 59
M of Lansdowne	11 Jun 57–23 Oct 58
E of Gosford	23 Oct 58–22 Oct 59
Earl Bathurst	17 Sep 57–
Ld St Oswald	22 Oct 59–

Parliamentary Private Secretaries to Prime Ministers, 1900–1960

1900–02	E. Cecil
1906–08	H. Carr-Gomm
1908–10	G. Howard
1910–15	C. Lyell
1915–16	Sir J. Barran
1916–17	D. Davies
1918	W. Astor
1918–20	(Sir) W. Sutherland
1920–22	Sir P. Sassoon
1922–23	J. Davidson
1923–24	S. Herbert
1924	L. MacNeil Weir
1924–27	S. Herbert
1927–29	C. Rhys
1929–31	L. MacNeil Weir and R. Morrison
1931–32	R. Glyn and F. Markham
1932–35	(Sir) R. Glyn and J. Worthington
1935	G. Lloyd
1935–37	T. Dugdale
1937–40	Ld Dunglass
1940–41	B. Bracken
1941–45	G. Harvie-Watt
1945–46	G. de Freitas
1946–51	A. Moyle
1952–55	C. Soames
1955	R. Carr
1955–58	R. Allan
1958–59	A. Barber
1959–	S. Cunningham

SOURCES.—*Whitaker's Almanack, 1900–61; His/Her Majesty's Ministers & Heads of Public Departments* (*H.M.S.O.*)*, 1946–61; British Imperial Calendar & Civil Service List* (*H.M.S.O.*)*, 1900–61; Who's Who, 1961; Who Was Who, 1900–60.*

Size of Cabinets and Governments

	1900	1910	1917	1920	1930	1940	1950	1960
Cabinet Ministers	19	19	5	19	19	9	18	19
Non-Cabinet Ministers	10 [a]	7	33	15	9	25	20	20
Junior Ministers	15	22	33	33	27	32	35	35
Royal Household	16	14	14	14	7 [b]	8	8	8
Total	60	62	85	81	62	74	81	82
No. of M.P.s in the Government	33	43	60	58	50	58	68	65
No. of Peers included in the Government	27	19	25	22	12	19	13	18
Parliamentary Private Secretaries	9	16	12	13	26	25	27	36
Total No. of M.P.s involved in Government	42	59	72	71	76	83	95	101

[a] Including the Paymaster-General, though the post was considered a Royal Household appointment until 1905.

[b] Since 1924 the offices of Lord Chamberlain, Lord Steward, and Master of the Horse have been non-political. There have always been some non-political Lords-in-Waiting.

SOURCES.—Members of the Government from *Hansard*, the first volume of each year. P.P.S.s from *Whitaker's Almanack* (the figures for 1900–40 are only approximate), and from *H.M. Ministers and Heads of Public Departments, 1946–61* (H.M.S.O.).

Ministerial Offices, 1900–1960

Admiralty. First Lord of the Admiralty, 1900–

Agriculture. President of the Board of Agriculture, 1900–3; President of the Board of Agriculture and Fisheries, 1903–19; Minister of Agriculture and Fisheries, 1919–1955; Minister of Agriculture, Fisheries and Food, 1955– (see *Food*)

Air. Secretary of State, 1918–

Aircraft Production. Minister, 1940–46

Attorney-General, 1900–

Attorney-General for Ireland, 1900–22

Aviation. Minister, 1959– (see *Civil Aviation*)

Blockade. Minister, 1916–19

Burma. Secretary of State for India and Burma, 1937–47

Civil Aviation. Minister, 1944–53; Minister of Transport and Civil Aviation, 1953–59; Minister of Aviation, 1959–

Colonies. Secretary of State, 1900–

Commonwealth Relations. Secretary of State, 1947–

Co-ordination of Defence. Minister, 1936–40

Co-ordination of Transport, Fuel and Power. Secretary of State, 1951–53

Defence. Minister, 1940– [1]

Dominions. Secretary of State, 1925–47

Duchy of Lancaster. Chancellor, 1900–

Economic Affairs. Minister, 1947

Economic Warfare. Minister, 1939–45

Education. President of the Board of Education, 1900–44; Minister of Education, 1944–

Food. Minister, 1916–21, and 1939–55 (see *Agriculture*)

Foreign Affairs. Secretary of State, 1900–

Fuel and Power. Minister, 1944–57; Minister of Power, 1957–

Fuel, Light and Power. Minister, 1942–4 (see *Fuel and Power*)

Health. Minister, 1919–

Home Affairs. Secretary of State, 1900–

Home Security. Minister, 1939–45

Housing and Local Government. Minister of Town and Country Planning, 1943–51; Minister of Local

[1] From 1940 to 1946 the office was held by the Prime Minister. A permanent department for Defence was not established until 1946.

Government and Planning, 1951; Minister of Housing and Local Government, 1951–

India. Secretary of State for India, 1900–37; Secretary of State for India and Burma, 1937–47

Information. Minister, Mar–Nov 1918 and 1939–46

Ireland. Chief Secretary to the Lord Lieutenant of Ireland, 1900–22 (*Irish Office wound up 1924*).

Labour. Minister of Labour, 1916–39; Minister of Labour and National Service, 1939–59; Minister of Labour, 1959–

Local Government. President of the Local Government Board, 1900–19 (see *Housing and Local Government*)

Local Government and Planning. Minister, 1951 (see *Housing and Local Government*)

Lord Advocate, 1900–

Lord Chancellor, 1900–

Lord Chancellor of Ireland, 1900-22

Lord President of the Council, 1900–

Lord Privy Seal, 1900–

Materials. Minister, 1951–54

Mines. Secretary for Mines Department, 1920–42

Munitions. Minister, 1915–19 (see *Supply*)

National Insurance. Minister, 1944–53; Minister of Pensions and National Insurance, 1953–

National Service. Minister, 1917–19; Minister of Labour and National Service, 1939–59

Overseas Trade. Secretary for Overseas Trade, 1917–53

Paymaster-General, 1900–

Pensions. Minister of Pensions, 1916–1953; Minister of Pensions and National Insurance, 1953–

Petroleum. Secretary for Petroleum Department, 1940–42

Portfolio. Minister without portfolio, 1915–21, 1935–36, 1939–42, 1942–1944, 1946, 1947, 1954–

Post Office. Postmaster-General, 1900–

Power. Minister, 1957– (see *Fuel and Power*)

Prime Minister, 1900–

Production. Minister, 1942–45

Reconstruction. Minister, 1917–19 and 1944–45

Science. Minister, 1959–

Scotland. Secretary, 1900–26; Secretary of State, 1926–

Shipping. Minister, 1916–21 and 1939–1941 (see *War Transport*)

Social Insurance. Minister, Oct–Nov 1944 (see *National Insurance*)

Solicitor-General, 1900–

Solicitor-General for Ireland, 1900–22

Solicitor-General for Scotland, 1900–

Supply. Minister, 1919–21 and 1939–59

Town and Country Planning. Minister of Town and Country Planning, 1943–51 (see *Local Government and Planning*)

Trade. President of the Board of Trade, 1900–

Transport. Minister of Transport, 1919–41; Minister of War Transport, 1941–46; Minister of Transport, 1946–53; Minister of Transport and Civil Aviation, 1953–59; Minister of Transport, 1959–

Treasury. Chancellor of the Exchequer, 1900–

War. Secretary of State, 1900–

War Transport. Minister, 1941–46 (see *Shipping* and *Transport*)

Welsh Affairs. Minister, 1951–

Works. First Commissioner of Works, 1900–40; Minister of Works and Buildings, 1940–42; Minister of Works and Planning, 1942–43; Minister of Works, 1943–

SOURCE.—For a full table of changes within the central administration between 1914–56 see *The Organisation of British Central Government, 1914–1956*, by D. N. Chester and F. M. G. Willson (1957), especially Appendix C, pp. 385-420.

Holders of Ministerial Offices

Prime Minister

1900	M of Salisbury (3rd)
12 Jul 02	A. Balfour
5 Dec 05	Sir H. Campbell-Bannerman
5 Apr 08	H. Asquith
6 Dec 16	D. Lloyd George
23 Oct 22	A. Bonar Law
22 May 23	S. Baldwin
22 Jan 24	J. R. MacDonald
4 Nov 24	S. Baldwin
5 Jun 29	J. R. MacDonald
7 Jun 35	S. Baldwin
28 May 37	N. Chamberlain
10 May 40	W. Churchill
26 Jul 45	C. Attlee
26 Oct 51	(Sir) W. Churchill

6 Apr	55	Sir A. Eden
10 Jan	57	H. Macmillan

Lord President of the Council

	1900	D of Devonshire
13 Oct	03	M of Londonderry
10 Dec	05	E of Crewe
12 Apr	08	Ld Tweedmouth
13 Oct	08	Vt Wolverhampton
16 Jun	10	Earl Beauchamp
3 Nov	10	Vt Morley
5 Aug	14	Earl Beauchamp
25 May	15	M of Crewe
10 Dec	16	Earl Curzon
23 Oct	19	A. Balfour
24 Oct	22	M of Salisbury (4th)
22 Jan	24	Ld Parmoor
6 Nov	24	Marquess Curzon
27 Apr	25	E of Balfour
7 Jun	29	Ld Parmoor
25 Aug	31	S. Baldwin
7 Jun	35	J. R. MacDonald
28 May	37	Vt Halifax
9 Mar	38	Vt Hailsham (1st)
31 Oct	38	Vt Runciman
3 Sep	39	Earl Stanhope
11 May	40	N. Chamberlain
3 Oct	40	Sir J. Anderson
24 Sep	43	C. Attlee
25 May	45	Ld Woolton
27 Jul	45	H. Morrison
9 Mar	51	Vt Addison
28 Oct	51	Ld Woolton
24 Nov	52	M of Salisbury (5th)
29 Mar	57	E of Home
17 Sep	57	Vt Hailsham (2nd)
14 Oct	59	E of Home
27 Jul	60	Vt Hailsham (2nd)

Lord Chancellor

	1900	E of Halsbury
10 Dec	05	Ld Loreburn (Earl)
10 Jun	12	Vt Haldane
25 May	15	Ld Buckmaster
10 Dec	16	Ld Finlay
10 Jan	19	Ld Birkenhead (Vt)
24 Oct	22	Vt Cave
22 Jan	24	Vt Haldane
6 Nov	24	Vt Cave
28 Mar	28	Ld Hailsham (Vt)
7 Jun	29	Ld Sankey (Vt)
7 Jun	35	Vt Hailsham
9 Mar	38	Ld Maugham (Vt)
3 Sep	39	Vt Caldecote
12 May	40	Vt Simon
27 Jul	45	Ld Jowitt
30 Oct	51	Ld Simonds
18 Oct	54	Vt Kilmuir

Lord Privy Seal

	1900	Vt Cross
1 Nov	00	M of Salisbury (3rd)
12 Jul	02	A. Balfour
11 Oct	03	M of Salisbury (4th)
10 Dec	05	M of Ripon
9 Oct	08	E of Crewe
23 Oct	11	Earl Carrington
13 Feb	12	M of Crewe
25 May	15	Earl Curzon
15 Dec	16	E of Crawford
10 Jan	19	A. Bonar Law
23 Mar	21	A. Chamberlain
24 Oct	22	(*office vacant*)
25 May	23	Ld R. Cecil
22 Jan	24	J. Clynes
6 Nov	24	M of Salisbury (4th)
7 Jun	29	J. Thomas
5 Jun	30	V. Hartshorn
24 Mar	31	T. Johnston
3 Sep	31	Earl Peel
5 Nov	31	Vt Snowden
29 Sep	32	S. Baldwin
31 Dec	33	A. Eden
7 Jun	35	M of Londonderry
22 Nov	35	Vt Halifax
28 May	37	Earl De La Warr
31 Oct	38	Sir J. Anderson
3 Sep	39	Sir S. Hoare
3 Apr	40	Sir K. Wood
11 May	40	C. Attlee
19 Feb	42	Sir S. Cripps
22 Nov	42	Vt Cranborne (5th M of Salisbury)
24 Sep	43	Ld Beaverbrook
27 Jul	45	A. Greenwood
17 Apr	47	Ld Inman
7 Oct	47	Vt Addison
9 Mar	51	E. Bevin
26 Apr	51	R. Stokes
28 Oct	51	M of Salisbury (5th)
7 May	52	H. Crookshank
20 Dec	55	R. Butler
14 Oct	59	Vt Hailsham
27 Jul	60	E. Heath

Chancellor of the Exchequer

	1900	Sir M. Hicks-Beach
8 Aug	02	C. Ritchie
6 Oct	03	A. Chamberlain
10 Dec	05	H. Asquith
12 Apr	08	D. Lloyd George
25 May	15	R. McKenna
10 Dec	16	A. Bonar Law
10 Jan	19	A. Chamberlain
1 Apr	21	Sir R. Horne
24 Oct	22	S. Baldwin
27 Aug	23	N. Chamberlain
22 Jan	24	P. Snowden
6 Nov	24	W. Churchill
7 Jun	29	P. Snowden
5 Nov	31	N. Chamberlain
28 May	37	Sir J. Simon
12 May	40	Sir K. Wood
24 Sep	43	Sir J. Anderson
27 Jul	45	H. Dalton
13 Nov	47	Sir S. Cripps
19 Oct	50	H. Gaitskell
28 Oct	51	R. Butler
20 Dec	55	H. Macmillan
13 Jan	57	P. Thorneycroft
6 Jan	58	D. Heathcoat Amory
27 Jul	60	S. Lloyd

Secretary of State for Foreign Affairs

	1900	M of Salisbury
1 Nov	00	M of Lansdowne
10 Dec	05	Sir E. Grey (Vt)
10 Dec	16	A. Balfour
23 Oct	19	Earl Curzon (Marquess)
22 Jan	24	J. R. MacDonald
6 Nov	24	(Sir) A. Chamberlain
7 Jun	29	A. Henderson
25 Aug	31	M of Reading
5 Nov	31	Sir J. Simon
7 Jun	35	Sir S. Hoare
22 Dec	35	A. Eden
21 Feb	38	Vt Halifax
22 Dec	40	A. Eden
27 Jul	45	E. Bevin
9 Mar	51	H. Morrison
28 Oct	51	(Sir) A. Eden
7 Apr	55	H. Macmillan
20 Dec	55	S. Lloyd
27 Jul	60	E of Home

Secretary of State for the Home Department

	1900	Sir M. White-Ridley
1 Nov	00	C. Ritchie
8 Aug	02	A. Akers-Douglas
10 Dec	05	H. Gladstone
14 Feb	10	W. Churchill
23 Oct	11	R. McKenna
25 May	15	Sir J. Simon
10 Jan	16	Sir H. Samuel
10 Dec	16	Sir G. Cave (Vt)
10 Jan	19	E. Shortt
24 Oct	22	W. Bridgeman
22 Jan	24	A. Henderson
6 Nov	24	Sir W. Joynson-Hicks
7 Jun	29	J. Clynes
25 Aug	31	Sir H. Samuel
28 Sep	32	Sir J. Gilmour
7 Jun	35	Sir J. Simon
28 May	37	Sir S. Hoare
3 Sep	39	Sir J. Anderson
3 Oct	40	H. Morrison
25 May	45	Sir D. Somervell
3 Aug	45	C. Ede

28 Oct 51	Sir D. Maxwell Fyfe
18 Oct 54	G. Lloyd-George
13 Jan 57	R. Butler

First Lord of the Admiralty

1900	G. Goschen
1 Nov 00	E of Selborne
5 Mar 05	Earl Cawdor
10 Dec 05	Ld Tweedmouth
12 Apr 08	R. McKenna
23 Oct 11	W. Churchill
25 May 15	A. Balfour
10 Dec 16	Sir E. Carson
17 Jul 17	Sir E. Geddes
10 Jan 19	W. Long
13 Feb 21	Ld Lee
24 Oct 22	L. Amery
22 Jan 24	Vt Chelmsford
6 Nov 24	W. Bridgeman
7 Jun 29	A. Alexander
25 Aug 31	Sir A. Chamberlain
5 Nov 31	Sir B. Eyres-Monsell (Vt Monsell)
5 Jun 36	Sir S. Hoare
28 May 37	A. Duff Cooper
27 Oct 38	Earl Stanhope
3 Sep 39	W. Churchill
11 May 40	A. Alexander
25 May 45	B. Bracken
3 Aug 45	A. Alexander
4 Oct 46	Vt Hall
24 May 51	Ld Pakenham
31 Oct 51	J. Thomas (Vt Cilcennin)
2 Sep 56	Vt Hailsham
16 Jan 57	E of Selkirk
16 Oct 59	Ld Carrington

President of the Board of Agriculture and Fisheries

1900	W. Long
14 Nov 00	R. Hanbury
19 May 03	E of Onslow
12 Mar 05	A. Fellowes
10 Dec 05	Earl Carrington
23 Oct 11	W. Runciman
6 Aug 14	Ld Lucas
25 May 15	E of Selborne
11 Jul 16	E of Crawford
10 Dec 16	R. Prothero (Ld Ernle)

(Minister of Agriculture and Fisheries)

(*and Food, since* 18 *Oct* 54)

15 Aug 19	Ld Lee of Fareham
13 Feb 21	Sir A. Griffith-Boscawen
24 Oct 22	Sir R. Sanders
22 Jan 24	N. Buxton
6 Nov 24	E. Wood
4 Nov 25	W. Guinness
7 Jun 29	N. Buxton
5 Jun 30	C. Addison
25 Aug 31	Sir J. Gilmour
28 Sep 32	W. Elliot
29 Oct 36	W. Morrison
29 Jan 39	Sir R. Dorman-Smith
14 May 40	R. Hudson
3 Aug 45	T. Williams
31 Oct 51	Sir T. Dugdale
28 Jul 54	D. Heathcoat Amory
6 Jan 58	J. Hare
27 Jul 60	C. Soames

Secretary of State for Air

26 Nov 17	Ld Rothermere
26 Apr 18	Ld Weir
10 Jan 19	W. Churchill
1 Apr 21	F. Guest
31 Oct 22	Sir S. Hoare
22 Jan 24	Ld Thomson
6 Nov 24	Sir S. Hoare
7 Jun 29	Ld Thomson
14 Oct 30	Ld Amulree
5 Nov 31	M of Londonderry
7 Jun 35	Sir P. Cunliffe-Lister (Vt Swinton)
16 May 38	Sir K. Wood
3 Apr 40	Sir S. Hoare
11 May 40	Sir A. Sinclair
25 May 45	H. Macmillan
3 Aug 45	Vt Stansgate
4 Oct 46	P. Noel-Baker
7 Oct 47	A. Henderson
31 Oct 51	Ld De L'Isle
20 Dec 55	N. Birch
16 Jan 57	G. Ward
28 Oct 60	J. Amery

Minister of Aircraft Production

14 May 40	Ld Beaverbrook
1 May 41	J. Moore-Brabazon
22 Feb 42	J. Llewellin
22 Nov 42	Sir S. Cripps
25 May 45	E. Brown

(*office abolished* 26 *Jul* 45)

Attorney-General

1900	Sir R. Webster
7 May 00	Sir R. Finlay
12 Dec 05	Sir J. Walton
28 Jan 08	Sir W. Robson
7 Oct 10	Sir R. Isaacs
19 Oct 13	Sir J. Simon
25 May 15	Sir E. Carson
3 Nov 15	Sir F. Smith
10 Jan 19	Sir G. Hewart
6 Mar 22	Sir E. Pollock
24 Oct 22	Sir D. Hogg
23 Jan 24	Sir P. Hastings
6 Nov 24	Sir D. Hogg
28 Mar 28	Sir T. Inskip
7 Jun 29	Sir W. Jowitt
26 Jan 32	Sir T. Inskip
18 Mar 36	Sir D. Somervell
25 May 45	Sir D. Maxwell Fyfe
4 Aug 45	Sir H. Shawcross
24 Apr 51	Sir F. Soskice
3 Nov 51	Sir L. Heald
18 Oct 54	Sir R. Manningham-Buller

Minister of Blockade

10 Dec 16	Ld R. Cecil
18 Jul 18	Sir L. Worthington-Evans

(*office abolished* 10 *Jan* 19)

Minister of Civil Aviation

8 Oct 44	Vt Swinton
4 Aug 45	Ld Winster
4 Oct 46	Ld Nathan
31 May 48	Ld Pakenham
1 Jun 51	Ld Ogmore
31 Oct 51	J. Maclay
7 May 52	A. Lennox-Boyd

(Minister of Transport and Civil Aviation)

1 Oct 53	A. Lennox-Boyd
28 Jul 54	J. Boyd-Carpenter
20 Dec 55	H. Watkinson

(Minister of Aviation)

14 Oct 59	D. Sandys
27 July 60	P. Thorneycroft

Secretary of State for the Colonies

1900	J. Chamberlain
6 Oct 03	A. Lyttelton
10 Dec 05	E of Elgin
12 Apr 08	E of Crewe
3 Nov 10	L. Harcourt
25 May 15	A. Bonar Law
10 Dec 16	W. Long
10 Jan 19	Vt Milner
13 Feb 21	W. Churchill
24 Oct 22	D of Devonshire
22 Jan 24	J. Thomas
6 Nov 24	L. Amery
7 Jun 29	Ld Passfield
25 Aug 31	J. Thomas
5 Nov 31	Sir P. Cunliffe-Lister
7 June 35	M. MacDonald
22 Nov 35	J. Thomas
28 May 36	W. Ormsby-Gore
16 May 38	M. MacDonald
12 May 40	Ld Lloyd
8 Feb 41	Ld Moyne
22 Feb 42	Vt Cranborne
22 Nov 42	O. Stanley
3 Aug 45	G. Hall
4 Oct 46	A. Creech Jones
28 Feb 50	J. Griffiths
28 Oct 51	O. Lyttelton
28 Jul 54	A. Lennox-Boyd
14 Oct 59	I. Macleod

Minister for Co-ordination of Defence

13 Mar 36 Sir T. Inskip
29 Jan 39 Ld Chatfield

(Minister of Defence)

10 May 40 W. Churchill
27 Jul 45 C. Attlee
20 Dec 46 A. Alexander
28 Feb 50 E. Shinwell
28 Oct 51 W. Churchill
1 Mar 52 Earl Alexander
18 Oct 54 H. Macmillan
7 Apr 55 S. Lloyd
20 Dec 55 Sir W. Monckton
18 Oct 56 A. Head
13 Jan 57 D. Sandys
14 Oct 59 H. Watkinson

Secretary of State for Dominion Affairs

11 Jun 25 L. Amery
7 Jun 29 Ld Passfield
5 Jun 30 J. Thomas
22 Nov 35 M. MacDonald
16 May 38 Ld Stanley
31 Oct 38 M. MacDonald
29 Jan 39 Sir T. Inskip (Vt Caldecote)
3 Sep 39 A. Eden
14 May 40 Vt Caldecote
3 Oct 40 Vt Cranborne
19 Feb 42 C. Attlee
24 Sep 43 Vt Cranborne
3 Aug 45 Vt Addison
(*7 Jul* 1947 *the Dominions Office became the Commonwealth Relations Office*)

(Secretary of State for Commonwealth Relations)

7 Jul 47 Vt Addison
7 Oct 47 P. Noel-Baker
28 Feb 50 P. Gordon Walker
28 Oct 51 Ld Ismay
12 Mar 52 M of Salisbury
24 Nov 52 Vt Swinton
7 Apr 55 E of Home
27 Jul 60 D. Sandys

Minister of Economic Warfare

3 Sep 39 R. Cross
15 May 40 H. Dalton
22 Feb 42 Vt Wolmer (E of Selborne)
(*office wound up* 23 *May* 45)

President of the Board of Education

1900 D of Devonshire
8 Aug 02 M of Londonderry
10 Dec 05 A. Birrell
23 Jan 07 R. McKenna
12 Apr 08 W. Runciman
23 Oct 11 J. Pease
25 May 15 A. Henderson
18 Aug 16 M of Crewe
10 Dec 16 H. Fisher
24 Oct 22 E. Wood
22 Jan 24 C. Trevelyan
6 Nov 24 Ld E. Percy
7 Jun 29 Sir C. Trevelyan
2 Mar 31 H. Lees-Smith
25 Aug 31 Sir D. Maclean
15 Jun 32 Ld Irwin (Vt Halifax)
7 Jun 35 O. Stanley
28 May 37 Earl Stanhope
27 Oct 38 Earl De La Warr
3 Apr 40 H. Ramsbotham
20 Jul 41 R. Butler

(Minister of Education)

3 Aug 44 R. Butler
25 May 45 R. Law
3 Aug 45 Miss E. Wilkinson
10 Feb 47 G. Tomlinson
2 Nov 51 Miss F. Horsbrugh
18 Oct 54 Sir D. Eccles
13 Jan 57 Vt Hailsham
17 Sep 57 G. Lloyd
14 Oct 59 Sir D. Eccles

Minister of Food Control

10 Dec 16 Vt Devonport
19 Jun 17 Ld Rhondda (Vt)
9 Jul 18 J. Clynes
10 Jan 19 G. Roberts
19 Mar 20 C. McCurdy
(*office abolished* 31 *Mar* 21)

Minister of Food

4 Sep 39 W. Morrison
3 Apr 40 Ld Woolton
11 Nov 43 J. Llewellin
3 Aug 45 Sir B. Smith
27 May 46 J. Strachey
28 Feb 50 M. Webb
31 Oct 51 G. Lloyd-George
18 Oct 54 D. Heathcoat Amory
(*and combined with Minister of Agriculture and Fisheries*)

Minister of Fuel, Light and Power

3 Jun 42 G. Lloyd-George

(Minister of Fuel and Power)

25 May 45 G. Lloyd-George
3 Aug 45 E. Shinwell
7 Oct 47 H. Gaitskell
28 Feb 50 P. Noel-Baker
31 Oct 51 G. Lloyd
20 Dec 55 A. Jones

(Minister of Power)

13 Jan 57 Ld Mills
14 Oct 59 R. Wood

Minister of Health

(*see below*, under *Local Government*)

Secretary of State for India (and Burma 1937-48)

1900 Ld G. Hamilton
6 Oct 03 St J. Brodrick
10 Dec 05 J. Morley (Vt)
3 Nov 10 E of Crewe
7 Mar 11 Vt Morley
25 May 11 E of Crewe (M)
25 May 15 A. Chamberlain
17 Jul 17 E. Montagu
19 Mar 22 Vt Peel
22 Jan 24 Ld Olivier
6 Nov 24 E of Birkenhead
18 Oct 28 Vt Peel
7 Jun 29 W. Benn
25 Aug 31 Sir S. Hoare
7 Jun 35 M of Zetland
13 May 40 L. Amery
3 Aug 45 Ld Pethick-Lawrence
17 Apr 47 E of Listowel
(4 *Jan* 1948 *India & Burma Offices wound up*)

Minister of Information

10 Feb 18 Ld Beaverbrook
4 Nov 18 Ld Downham
(*office abolished* 10 *Jan* 19)
4 Sep 39 Ld Macmillan
5 Jan 40 Sir J. Reith
12 May 40 A. Duff Cooper
20 Jul 41 B. Bracken
25 May 45 G. Lloyd
4 Aug 45 E. Williams
(*office abolished* 31 *Mar* 46)

Chief Secretary for Ireland

1900 G. Balfour
7 Nov 00 G. Wyndham
12 Mar 05 W. Long
10 Dec 05 J. Bryce
23 Jan 07 A. Birrell
31 Jul 16 (Sir) H. Duke
5 May 18 E. Shortt
10 Jan 19 I. Macpherson
2 Apr 20 Sir H. Greenwood
(*Irish Office wound up* 1922)

Minister of Labour

10 Dec 16 J. Hodge
17 Aug 17 G. Roberts
10 Jan 19 Sir R. Horne
19 Mar 20 T. Macnamara
31 Oct 22 Sir A. Montague-Barlow
22 Jan 24 T. Shaw
6 Nov 24 Sir A. Steel-Maitland
7 Jun 29 Miss M. Bondfield
25 Aug 31 Sir H. Betterton

29 Jun 34 O. Stanley
7 Jun 35 E. Brown

(Minister of Labour and National Service)

3 Sep 39 E. Brown
13 May 40 E. Bevin
25 May 45 R. Butler
3 Aug 45 G. Isaacs
17 Jan 51 A. Bevan
24 Apr 51 A. Robens
28 Oct 51 Sir W. Monckton
20 Dec 55 I. Macleod
14 Oct 59 E. Heath

(Minister of Labour)

12 Nov 59 E. Heath
27 Jul 60 J. Hare

Chancellor of the Duchy of Lancaster

1900 Ld James of Hereford
8 Aug 02 Sir W. Walrond
10 Dec 05 Sir H. Fowler (Vt Wolverhampton)
13 Oct 08 Ld Fitzmaurice
25 Jun 09 H. Samuel
14 Feb 10 J. Pease
23 Oct 11 C. Hobhouse
11 Feb 14 C. Masterman
3 Feb 15 E. Montagu
25 May 15 W. Churchill
25 Nov 15 H. Samuel
11 Jan 16 E. Montagu
9 Jul 16 T. McKinnon Wood
10 Dec 16 Sir F. Cawley
10 Feb 18 Ld Beaverbrook
4 Nov 18 Ld Downham
10 Jan 19 E of Crawford
1 Apr 21 Vt Peel
7 Apr 22 Sir W. Sutherland
24 Oct 22 M of Salisbury
25 May 23 J. Davidson
22 Jan 24 J. Wedgwood
10 Nov 24 Vt Cecil
19 Oct 27 Ld Cushendun
7 Jun 29 Sir O. Mosley
23 May 30 C. Attlee
13 May 31 Ld Ponsonby
25 Aug 31 M of Lothian
10 Nov 31 (Sir) J. Davidson
28 May 37 Earl Winterton
29 Jan 39 W. Morrison
3 Apr 40 G. Tryon
14 May 40 Ld Hankey
20 Jul 41 A. Duff Cooper
11 Nov 43 E. Brown
25 May 45 Sir A. Salter
4 Aug 45 J. Hynd
17 Apr 47 Ld Pakenham
31 May 48 H. Dalton
28 Feb 50 Vt Alexander
31 Oct 51 Vt Swinton
24 Nov 52 Ld Woolton (Vt)

20 Dec 55 E of Selkirk
13 Jan 57 C. Hill

President of the Local Government Board

1900 H. Chaplin
7 Nov 00 W. Long
12 Mar 05 G. Balfour
10 Dec 05 J. Burns
11 Feb 14 H. Samuel
25 May 15 W. Long
10 Dec 16 Ld Rhondda
28 Jun 17 W. Hayes Fisher
4 Nov 18 Sir A. Geddes
10 Jan 19 C. Addison
(24 *Jun* 19 *the Local Government Board became the Ministry of Health*)

Minister of Health

24 Jun 19 C. Addison
1 Apr 21 Sir A. Mond
24 Oct 22 Sir A. Griffith Boscawen
7 Mar 23 N. Chamberlain
27 Aug 23 Sir W. Joynson-Hicks
22 Jan 24 J. Wheatley
6 Nov 24 N. Chamberlain
7 Jun 29 A. Greenwood
25 Aug 31 N. Chamberlain
5 Nov 31 Sir E. Young
7 Jun 35 Sir K. Wood
16 May 38 W. Elliot
13 May 40 M. MacDonald
8 Feb 41 E. Brown
11 Nov 43 H. Willink
3 Aug 45 A. Bevan
17 Jan 51 H. Marquand
30 Oct 51 H. Crookshank
7 May 52 I. Macleod
20 Dec 55 R. Turton
16 Jan 57 D. Vosper
17 Sep 57 D. Walker-Smith
27 Jul 60 E. Powell

Minister of Local Government and Planning

31 Jan 51 H. Dalton

(Minister of Housing and Local Government)

30 Oct 51 H. Macmillan
18 Oct 54 D. Sandys
13 Jan 57 H. Brooke

Minister of Materials

6 Jul 51 R. Stokes
31 Oct 51 Vt Swinton
24 Nov 52 Sir A. Salter
1 Sep 53 Ld Woolton
(15 *Jul* 54 *office wound up*)

Minister of Munitions

25 May 15 D. Lloyd George
9 Jul 16 E. Montagu
10 Dec 16 C. Addison
17 Jul 17 W. Churchill
10 Jan 19 Ld Inverforth
(*and Minister designate for Ministry of Supply. Office abolished* 21 *Mar* 21)

Paymaster-General

1900 D of Marlborough
11 Mar 02 Sir S. Crossley
12 Dec 05 R. Causton (Ld Southwark)
23 Feb 10 I. Guest (Ld Ashby St Ledgers)
23 May 12 Ld Strachie
9 Jun 15 Ld Newton
18 Aug 16 A. Henderson
15 Dec 16 Sir J. Compton-Rickett
26 Oct 19 Sir T. Walters
24 Oct 22 (*office vacant*)
5 Feb 23 N. Chamberlain
15 Mar 23 Sir W. Joynson-Hicks
25 May 23 A. Boyd-Carpenter
6 May 24 H. Gosling
6 Nov 24 (*office vacant*)
28 Jul 25 D of Sutherland
2 Dec 28 E of Onslow
7 Jun 29 Ld Arnold
4 Sep 31 Sir T. Walters
23 Nov 31 Ld Rochester
6 Dec 35 Ld Hutchison
2 Jun 38 E of Munster
29 Jan 39 Earl Winterton
Nov 39 (*office vacant*)
15 May 40 Vt Cranborne
3 Oct 40 (*office vacant*)
20 Jul 41 Ld Hankey
4 Mar 42 Sir W. Jowitt
30 Dec 42 Ld Cherwell
3 Aug 45 (*office vacant*)
9 Jul 46 A. Greenwood
5 Mar 47 H. Marquand
2 Jul 48 Vt Addison
1 Apr 49 Ld Macdonald
30 Oct 51 Ld Cherwell
11 Nov 53 E of Selkirk
20 Dec 55 (*office vacant*)
18 Oct 56 Sir W. Monckton
16 Jan 57 R. Maudling
14 Oct 59 Ld Mills

Minister of Pensions

10 Dec 16 G. Barnes
17 Aug 17 J. Hodge
10 Jan 19 Sir L. Worthington-Evans
2 Apr 20 I. Macpherson
31 Oct 22 G. Tryon
23 Jan 24 F. Roberts
11 Nov 24 G. Tryon
7 Jun 29 F. Roberts
3 Sep 31 G. Tryon
18 Jun 35 R. Hudson
30 Jul 36 H. Ramsbotham
7 Jun 39 Sir W. Womersley

3 Aug 45 W. Paling
17 Apr 47 J. Hynd
7 Oct 47 G. Buchanan
2 Jul 48 H. Marquand
17 Jan 51 G. Isaacs
5 Nov 51 D. Heathcoat Amory

(Minister of Pensions and National Insurance)

3 Sep 53 O. Peake
20 Dec 55 J. Boyd-Carpenter

Minister of Social Insurance

8 Oct 44 Sir W. Jowitt

(Minister of National Insurance)

8 Nov 44 Sir W. Jowitt
25 May 45 L. Hore-Belisha
4 Aug 45 J. Griffiths
28 Feb 50 Edith Summerskill
31 Oct 51 O. Peake
(3 *Sep* 53 *combined with Ministry of Pensions*)

Minister without Portfolio

25 May 15–5 Dec 16 M of Lansdowne
10 Dec 16–12 Aug 17 A. Henderson
10 Dec 16–18 Apr 18 Vt Milner
17 Jul 17–21 Jan 18 Sir E. Carson
29 May 17–27 Jan 20 G. Barnes
22 Jun 17–10 Jan 19 J. Smuts
18 Apr 18–10 Jan 19 A. Chamberlain
2 Apr 20–13 Feb 21 Sir L. Worthington-Evans
1 Apr 21–14 Jul 21 C. Addison
10 Jan 19–19 May 19 Sir E. Geddes
7 Jun 35–22 Dec 35 A. Eden
7 Jun 35–31 Mar 36 Ld E. Percy
21 Apr 39–14 Jul 39 L. Burgin
3 Sep 39–10 May 40 Ld Hankey
11 May 40–22 Feb 42 A. Greenwood
30 Dec 42–8 Oct 44 Sir W. Jowitt
4 Oct 46–20 Dec 46 A. Alexander
17 Apr 47–29 Sep 47 A. Greenwood
18 Oct 54–11 Jun 57 E of Munster
11 Jun 57–23 Oct 58 Ld Mancroft
23 Oct 58– E of Dundee

Postmaster-General

1900 D of Norfolk
2 Apr 00 M of Londonderry
8 Aug 02 A. Chamberlain
6 Oct 03 Ld Stanley
10 Dec 05 S. Buxton
14 Feb 10 H. Samuel
11 Feb 14 C. Hobhouse
26 May 15 H. Samuel
18 Jan 16 J. Pease
10 Dec 16 A. Illingworth
1 Apr 21 F. Kellaway
31 Oct 22 N. Chamberlain
7 Mar 23 Sir W. Joynson-Hicks
28 May 23 Sir L. Worthington-Evans
22 Jan 24 V. Hartshorn
11 Nov 24 Sir W. Mitchell-Thomson
7 Jun 29 H. Lees-Smith
2 Mar 31 C. Attlee
3 Sep 31 W. Ormsby-Gore
10 Nov 31 Sir K. Wood
7 Jun 35 G. Tryon
3 Apr 40 W. Morrison
30 Dec 42 H. Crookshank
4 Aug 45 E of Listowel
17 Apr 47 W. Paling
28 Feb 50 N. Edwards
5 Nov 51 Earl De La Warr
7 Apr 55 C. Hill
16 Jan 57 E. Marples
22 Oct 59 J. Bevins

Minister of Reconstruction

17 Jul 17–10 Jan 19 C. Addison
11 Nov 43–23 May 45 Ld Woolton

Minister for Science

14 Oct 59 Vt Hailsham

Secretary for Scotland

1900 Ld Balfour
6 Oct 03 A. Murray
2 Feb 05 M of Linlithgow
10 Dec 05 J. Sinclair (Ld Pentland)
13 Feb 12 T. M'Kinnon Wood
9 Jul 16 H. Tennant
10 Dec 16 R. Munro
24 Oct 22 Vt Novar
22 Jan 24 W. Adamson
6 Nov 24 Sir J. Gilmour

(Secretary of State for Scotland)

15 Jul 26 Sir J. Gilmour
7 Jun 29 W. Adamson
25 Aug 31 Sir A. Sinclair
28 Sep 32 Sir G. Collins
29 Oct 36 W. Elliot
16 May 38 J. Colville
14 May 40 E. Brown
8 Feb 41 T. Johnston
25 May 45 Ld Rosebery
3 Aug 45 J. Westwood
7 Oct 47 A. Woodburn
28 Feb 50 H. McNeil
30 Oct 51 J. Stuart
13 Jan 57 J. Maclay

Minister of Shipping

10 Dec 16 Sir J. Maclay (Ld)
(*office abolished* 31 *Mar* 21)
13 Oct 39 Sir J. Gilmour
3 Apr 40 R. Hudson
14 May 40 R. Cross
(1 *May* 41 *combined with Ministry of Transport to form Ministry of War Transport*)

Minister of Supply

14 Jul 39 L. Burgin
12 May 40 H. Morrison
3 Oct 40 Sir A. Duncan
29 Jun 41 Ld Beaverbrook
4 Feb 42 Sir A. Duncan
3 Aug 45 J. Wilmot
7 Oct 47 G. Strauss
31 Oct 51 D. Sandys
18 Oct 54 S. Lloyd
7 Apr 55 R. Maudling
16 Jan 57 A. Jones
(*office wound up* 22 *Oct* 59)

Minister of Town and Country Planning

30 Dec 42 W. Morrison
4 Aug 45 L. Silkin
28 Feb 50 H. Dalton
(*recast as Local Government and Planning* 31 *Jan* 51)

President of the Board of Trade

1900 C. Ritchie
7 Nov 00 G. Balfour
12 Mar 05 M of Salisbury
10 Dec 05 D. Lloyd George
12 Apr 08 W. Churchill
14 Feb 10 S. Buxton
11 Feb 14 J. Burns
5 Aug 14 W. Runciman
10 Dec 16 Sir A. Stanley
26 May 19 Sir A. Geddes
19 Mar 20 Sir R. Horne
1 Apr 21 S. Baldwin
24 Oct 22 Sir P. Lloyd-Greame
22 Jan 24 S. Webb
6 Nov 24 Sir P. Lloyd-Greame (changed name to Cunliffe-Lister 27 Nov 24)

7 Jun 29 W. Graham
25 Aug 31 Sir P. Cunliffe-Lister
5 Nov 31 W. Runciman (Ld)
28 May 37 O. Stanley
5 Jan 40 Sir A. Duncan
3 Oct 40 O. Lyttelton
29 Jun 41 Sir A. Duncan
4 Feb 42 J. Llewellin
22 Feb 42 H. Dalton
25 May 45 O. Lyttelton
27 Jul 45 Sir S. Cripps
29 Sep 47 H. Wilson
24 Apr 51 Sir H. Shawcross
30 Oct 51 P. Thorneycroft
13 Jan 57 Sir D. Eccles
14 Oct 59 R. Maudling

Minister of Transport

17 Aug 19 Sir E. Geddes
7 Nov 21 Vt Peel
12 Apr 22 E of Crawford
31 Oct 22 Sir J. Baird
24 Jan 24 H. Gosling
11 Nov 24 W. Ashley
7 Jun 29 H. Morrison
3 Sep 31 J. Pybus
22 Feb 33 O. Stanley
29 Jun 34 L. Hore-Belisha
28 May 37 L. Burgin
21 Apr 39 E. Wallace
14 May 40 Sir J. Reith
3 Oct 40 J. Moore-Brabazon

(Minister of War Transport)

1 May 41 Ld Leathers

(Minister of Transport)

3 Aug 45 A. Barnes
31 Oct 51 J. Maclay
7 May 52 A. Lennox-Boyd

(Minister of Transport and Civil Aviation)

1 Oct 53 A. Lennox-Boyd
28 Jul 54 J. Boyd-Carpenter
20 Dec 55 H. Watkinson

(Minister of Transport)

14 Oct 59 E. Marples

Secretary of State for War

1900 M of Lansdowne
1 Nov 00 St J. Brodrick
6 Oct 03 H. Arnold-Forster
10 Dec 05 R. Haldane (Vt)
12 Jun 12 J. Seely
30 Mar 14 H. Asquith
5 Aug 14 Earl Kitchener
6 Jul 16 D. Lloyd George
10 Dec 16 E of Derby
18 Apr 18 Vt Milner
10 Jan 19 W. Churchill
13 Feb 21 Sir L. Worthington-Evans
24 Oct 22 E of Derby
22 Jan 24 S. Walsh
6 Nov 24 Sir L. Worthington-Evans
7 Jun 29 T. Shaw
26 Aug 31 M of Crewe
5 Nov 31 Vt Hailsham
7 Jun 35 Vt Halifax
22 Nov 35 A. Duff Cooper
28 May 37 L. Hore-Belisha
5 Jan 40 O. Stanley
11 May 40 A. Eden
22 Dec 40 D. Margesson
22 Feb 42 Sir J. Grigg
3 Aug 45 J. Lawson
4 Oct 46 F. Bellenger
7 Oct 47 E. Shinwell
28 Feb 50 J. Strachey
31 Oct 51 A. Head
18 Oct 56 J. Hare
6 Jan 58 C. Soames
27 Jul 60 J. Profumo

Minister for Welsh Affairs

28 Oct 51 Sir D. Maxwell Fyfe
18 Oct 54 G. Lloyd-George
13 Jan 57 H. Brooke

First Commissioner of Works

1900 A. Akers-Douglas
8 Aug 02 Ld Windsor
10 Dec 05 L. Harcourt
3 Nov 10 Earl Beauchamp
6 Aug 14 Ld Emmott
25 May 15 Ld Harcourt (Vt)
10 Dec 16 Sir A. Mond
1 Apr 21 E of Crawford
31 Oct 22 Sir J. Baird
22 Jan 24 F. Jowett
10 Nov 24 Vt Peel
18 Oct 28 M of Londonderry
7 Jun 29 G. Lansbury
25 Aug 31 M of Londonderry
5 Nov 31 W. Ormsby-Gore
16 Jun 36 Earl Stanhope
28 May 37 Sir P. Sassoon
7 Jun 39 H. Ramsbotham
3 Apr 40 Earl De La Warr
18 May 40 Ld Tryon
3 Oct 40 Sir J. Reith (Ld)

(Minister of Works & Buildings and First Commissioner of Works)

23 Oct 40 Ld Reith

(Minister of Works and Planning)

11 Feb 42 Ld Reith
21 Feb 42 Ld Portal

(Minister of Works)

Feb 43 Ld Portal
21 Nov 44 D. Sandys
4 Aug 45 G. Tomlinson
10 Feb 47 C. Key
28 Feb 50 R. Stokes
26 Apr 51 G. Brown
1 Nov 51 D. Eccles
18 Oct 54 N. Birch
20 Dec 55 P. Buchan-Hepburn
16 Jan 57 H. Molson
22 Oct 59 Ld J. Hope

Ministers of State, 1943–1960

The office of Minister of State was created in 1943 at the Foreign Office, as a war-time measure to deal with the increased burden of work on the Foreign Secretary. Since then Ministers of State have been created where a Minister is particularly overworked, or where it is necessary (as in the case of the Scottish Office) for the Minister to spend a considerable amount of time away from London. At the end of 1960, there were eight Ministers of State: at the Foreign Office (2), the Home Office, the Colonial Office, the Commonwealth Relations Office, the Scottish Office, and the Board of Trade, and a Minister for Welsh Affairs.

Leaders of the House of Commons

1900	A. Balfour
5 Dec 05	Sir H. Campbell-Bannerman
5 Apr 08	H. Asquith
10 Dec 16	A. Bonar Law
23 Mar 21	A. Chamberlain
23 Oct 22	A. Bonar Law
22 May 23	S. Baldwin
22 Jan 24	J. R. MacDonald
4 Nov 24	S. Baldwin
5 Jun 29	J. R. MacDonald
7 Jun 35	S. Baldwin
28 May 37	N. Chamberlain
11 May 40	C. Attlee [2]
19 Feb 42	Sir S. Cripps
22 Nov 42	A. Eden
27 Jul 45	H. Morrison
30 Oct 51	H. Crookshank
7 Apr 55	R. Butler

Leaders of the House of Lords

1900	3rd M of Salisbury
12 Jul 02	D of Devonshire
13 Oct 03	M of Lansdowne
10 Dec 05	M of Ripon
14 Apr 08	E of Crewe (M) [1]
10 Dec 16	Earl Curzon (M)
22 Jan 24	Vt Haldane
6 Nov 24	Marquess Curzon
27 Apr 25	4th M of Salisbury
7 Jun 29	Ld Parmoor
5 Nov 31	1st Vt Hailsham
7 Jun 35	M of Londonderry
22 Nov 35	Vt Halifax
27 Oct 38	Earl Stanhope
14 May 40	Vt Caldecote
3 Oct 40	Vt Halifax
22 Dec 40	Ld Lloyd
8 Feb 41	Ld Moyne
21 Feb 42	Vt Cranborne (5th M of Salisbury)
3 Aug 45	Vt Addison
28 Oct 51	5th M of Salisbury
29 Mar 57	E of Home
27 Jul 60	2nd Vt Hailsham

[1] During the critical summer of 1911 Vt Morley was temporarily Leader of the House of Lords in place of the M of Crewe.

[2] Although Mr. Attlee fulfilled the role of Leader of the House of Commons during this period, he was technically only Deputy Leader.

Ministerial Resignations

Resignations from ministerial office are not easy to classify. A retirement on the ground of ill-health may always conceal a protest or a dismissal. However, there are some cases where ministers have unquestionably left office because they were not willing to continue to accept collective responsibility for some part of Government policy and some cases where the individual actions of ministers have been thought impolitic or unworthy. The list of cases involving individual responsibility has been taken directly from Professor S. E. Finer's article 'The Individual Responsibility of Ministers', *Public Administration*, Winter 1956, pp. 377-96. There is inevitably considerable arbitrariness in the list of the cases involving collective responsibility.

Collective Responsibility

9–16 Sep 03	J. Chamberlain (*Imperial preference*)
4–15 Sep 03	C. Ritchie, Ld Balfour of Burleigh, Ld G. Hamilton, D of Devonshire (*Free trade*)
2 Aug 14	Vt Morley, J. Burns (*Entry into war*)
5 Aug 14	C. Trevelyan (*Entry into war*)
31 Dec 15	Sir J. Simon (*Compulsory National Service*)
14 Jul 21	C. Addison (*Housing*)
28 Aug 27	Vt Cecil (*Disarmament*)

19 May 30	Sir O. Mosley (*Unemployment*)
2 Mar 31	Sir C. Trevelyan (*Education*)
28 Sep 32	Sir H. Samuel, Sir A. Sinclair, Vt Snowden, M of Lothian (*Free trade*)
20 Feb 38	A. Eden, Vt Cranborne (*Negotiations with Mussolini*)
16 May 38	Ld Harlech (*Partition of Palestine*)
1 Oct 38	A. Duff Cooper (*Munich*)
1 Mar 45	H. Strauss (*Treatment of Poles by Yalta Conference*)
16 Apr 50	S. Evans (*Agricultural subsidies*)
23–24 Apr 51	A. Bevan, H. Wilson, J. Freeman (*Budget proposals*)
31 Oct 56	A. Nutting (*Suez*)
5 Nov 56	Sir E. Boyle (*Suez*)
29 Mar 57	M of Salisbury (*Release of Archbishop Makarios*)
6 Jan 58	P. Thorneycroft, E. Powell, N. Birch (*Economic policy*)

Individual Responsibility

6 Mar 05	G. Wyndham (*Ireland*)
30 Mar 14	J. Seely (*Curragh mutiny*)
3 May 16	A. Birrell (*Irish rebellion*)
12 Jul 17	A. Chamberlain (*Campaign in Mesopotamia*)
8 Aug 17	N. Chamberlain (*Ministry of National Service*)
25 Apr 18	Ld Rothermere (*Air Force*)
9 Mar 22	E. Montagu (*Turkey*)
18 Dec 35	Sir S. Hoare (*Laval Pact*)
22 May 36	J. Thomas (*Budget leak*)
12–16 May 38	Earl Winterton, Vt Swinton (*Criticism of air strength*)
21 Jan 41	R. Boothby (*Blocked Czechoslovakian assets*)
26 May 46	B. Smith (*Overwork and criticism*)
13 Nov 47	H. Dalton (*Budget leak*)
3 Feb 49	J. Belcher (*Lynskey tribunal*)
20 Jul 54	Sir T. Dugdale (*Crichel Down*)

SOURCES.—R. C. K. Ensor, *England 1870–1914*, (1936); C. L. Mowat, *Britain Between the Wars* (1955); *The Annual Register, 1900–1960*; *Keesing's Archives, 1931–1960*.

Biographical Notes

Prime Ministers, Chancellors of the Exchequer, and Foreign Secretaries.[1]

Anderson, John (Sir). 1st Vt Waverley (1952)
b. 1882. *Educ.* George Watson's Coll., Edin.; Edinburgh and Leipzig Univs. Entered Col. O., 1905. Sec. to Min. of Shipping, 1917–19. K.C.B., 1919. Addit. Sec. to Loc. Govt. Bd., 1919. 2nd Sec. to Min. of Health, 1919. Ch. of Bd. of Inland Revenue, 1919–22. Joint U.-S. to Ld. Lieut. of Ireland, 1920–22. P.U.-S. Home O., 1922–32. Gov. of Bengal, 1932–37. M.P. (Nat.) for Scottish Univs., 1938–50. Ld. Privy S., 1938–39. Home Sec. and Min. of Home Security, 1939–40. Ld. Pres. of Council, 1940–43. Chanc. of Exch., 1943–45. d. 1958.

Asquith, Herbert Henry. 1st E of Oxford and Asquith (1925)
b. 1852. *Educ.* City of London School; Oxford. Barrister, 1876, practised. M.P. (Lib.) for E. Fife, 1886–1918. M.P. for Paisley, 1920–24. Home Sec., 1892–95. Chanc. of Exch., 1905–8. P.M. and Leader of Lib. party, 1908–1916. Sec. for War, 1914. Formed Coalition Govt., 1915. Resigned as P.M.

[1] Virtually all the most eminent politicians of this century held one of these three offices. But, common sense being more important than consistency, we have added biographies of the two most outstanding exceptions — Joseph Chamberlain and Aneurin Bevan.

became Leader of Opposition, 1916. Resigned Leadership of Lib. party, 1926. d. 1928.

Attlee, Clement Richard. 1st Earl Attlee (1955)
b. 1883. *Educ.* Haileybury; Oxford. Barrister, 1906; practised, 1906–9. Lecturer at L.S.E., 1913–23. M.P. (Lab.) for Limehouse, Stepney, 1922–50. M.P. for W. Walthamstow, 1950–55. P.P.S. to J. R. MacDonald, 1922–24. U.-S. for War, 1924. Chanc. of D. of Lanc., 1930–31. Postm.-Gen., 1931. Dep. Leader of Lab. party in Commons, 1931–35. Leader of Lab. party, 1935–55. Leader of Opposition, 1935–40. Ld. Privy S., 1940–42. Sec. for Dominions, 1942–43. Ld. Pres. of Council, 1943–45. Dep. P.M., 1942–45. P.M., 1945–51. Min. of Def., 1945–46. Leader of Opposition, 1951–55.

Baldwin, Stanley. 1st Earl Baldwin of Bewdley (1937)
b. 1867. *Educ.* Harrow; Cambridge. Family business. M.P. (Con.) for Bewdley div. of Worcs., 1908–37. Joint F.S. to Treas., 1917–21; Pres. of Bd. of Trade, 1921–22; Chanc. of Exch., 1922–23. Leader of Con. party, 1923–37. P.M., 1923–24 and 1924–29. Leader of Opposition, 1924, 1929–31. Ld. Pres. of Council, 1931–35. P.M., 1935–37. d. 1947.

Balfour, Arthur James. 1st Earl of Balfour (1922)
b. 1848. *Educ.* Eton; Cambridge. M.P. (Con.) for Hertford, 1874–85. M.P. for E. Manchester, 1885–1906. M.P. for City of London, 1906–22. P.P.S. to Ld. Salisbury, 1878–80. Pres. of Loc. Govt. Bd., 1885. Sec. for Scotland, 1886. (Member of Cabinet, Nov. 1886.) Ch. Sec. for Ireland, 1887–91. Leader of Commons and 1st Ld. of Treas., 1891–92 and 1895–1902. P.M., 1902–5. Leader of Con. party, 1902–11. Member of Committee of Imperial Defence, 1914. Attended war cabinet meetings, 1914–15. 1st Ld. of Admir., 1915–16. For. Sec., 1916–19. Ld. Pres. of Council, 1919–22 and 1925–29. d. 1930.

Bevan, Aneurin
b. 1897. *Educ.* Elem.; Central Labour College. Miner. M.P. (Lab.) for Ebbw Vale, 1929–60. Treasurer of Lab. party, 1956–60. Deputy Leader of Lab. party, 1959–60. Min. of Health, 1945–51. Min. of Lab. and Nat. Service, 1951. Resigned, 1951. d. 1960.

Bevin, Ernest
b. 1881. *Educ.* Elem. National Organiser of Dockers' Union, 1910–21. Gen. Sec. of T.&G.W.U., 1921–40. Member of General Council of T.U.C., 1925–40, M.P. (Lab.) for C. Wandsworth, 1940–50. M.P. for E. Woolwich, 1950–51. Min. of Lab. and Nat. Service, 1940–45. For. Sec., 1945–51. Ld. Privy S., Mar–Apr 1951. d. 1951.

Bonar Law, Andrew
b. 1858. *Educ.* Canada and Glasgow H.S. Family business. M.P. (Con.) for Blackfriars, Glasgow, 1900–6. M.P. for Dulwich, 1906–10. M.P. for Bootle, 1911–18. M.P. for C. Glasgow, 1918–23. P.S. to Bd. of Trade, 1902–5. Leader of Con. party in Commons, 1911–21. Col. Sec., 1915–16. Chanc. of Exch., 1916–18. Ld. Privy S. and Leader of Commons, 1919–21. Resigned, 1921. P.M. and Leader of Con. party, 1922–23. Resigned, 1923. d. 1923.

Butler, Richard Austen
b. 1902. *Educ.* Marlborough; Cambridge. M.P. (Con.) for Saffron Walden since 1929. U.-S. India O., 1932–37. P.S. Min. of Lab., 1937–38. U.-S. For. O., 1938–41. Pres. Bd. of Educ., 1941–44. Min. of Educ., 1944–45. Min. of Lab., 1945. Chanc. of Exch., 1951–55. Ch. of N.U.C.A., 1945–56. Pres. of N.U.C.A., 1956. Leader of Commons, 1955–61. Ld. Privy S., 1955–59. Home Sec., 1957–62. Ch. of Con. party organisation, 1959–61.

Campbell-Bannerman, Henry (Sir)
b. 1836. *Educ.* Glasgow H.S.; Glasgow Univ. and Cambridge. Family business. M.P. (Lib.) for Stirling Burghs, 1868–1908. F.S. to War O., 1871–74 and 1880–82. Sec. to Admir., 1882–84. Ch. Sec. for Ireland (without seat in cabinet), 1884–85. Sec. for War, 1886 and 1892–95. G.C.B., 1895. Leader of Lib. party in Commons, 1899–1908. P.M., 1905–8. Resigned, 1908. d. 1908.

Chamberlain, (Arthur) Neville

b. 1869. *Educ.* Rugby; Birmingham Coll. Birmingham and business career. Ld. Mayor of Birmingham, 1915–16. Dir.-Gen. of Nat. Service, 1916–17. M.P. (Con.) for Ladywood, Birmingham, 1918–29. M.P. for Edgbaston, Birmingham, 1929–40. Postm.-Gen., 1922–23. Paym.-Gen., 1923. Min. of Health, 1923. Chanc. of Exch., 1923–24. Min. of Health, 1924–29 and 1931. Ch. of Con. party organisation, 1930–31. Chanc. of Exch., 1931–37. P.M. and Leader of Con. party, 1937–40. Ld. Pres. of Council, 1940. Resigned, 1940. d. 1940.

Chamberlain, Joseph

b. 1836. *Educ.* University College School. Family business. Mayor of Birmingham, 1873–75. M.P. (Lib.) for Birmingham, 1876–85. M.P. for Birmingham W., 1885–86. M.P. (Lib. U.) for Birmingham W., 1886–1914. Pres. of Bd. of Trade, 1880–85. Pres. of Loc. Govt. Bd., 1886. Col. Sec., 1895–1903. d. 1914.

Chamberlain, (Joseph) Austen (Sir)

b. 1863. *Educ.* Rugby; Cambridge. M.P. (Con.) for E. Worcs., 1892–1914. M.P. for W. Birmingham, 1914–37. Lib. U. Whip, 1892. Civil Ld. of Admir., 1895–1900. F.S. to Treas., 1900–2. Postm.-Gen., 1902–3. Chanc. of Exch., 1903–5. Sec. for India, 1915–17. Resigned, 1917. Min. without Portfolio in war cabinet, 1918–19. Chanc. of Exch., 1919–21. Ld. Privy S. and Leader of Con. party in Commons, 1921–22. For. Sec., 1924–29. K.G., 1925. 1st Ld. of Admir., 1931. d. 1937.

Churchill, Winston Leonard Spencer (Sir)

b. 1874. *Educ.* Harrow; Sandhurst. Army, 1895–1916. M.P. (Con.) for Oldham, 1900–6. M.P. (Lib.) for N.W. Manchester, 1906–8. M.P. (Lib.) for Dundee, 1908–22. M.P. (Con.) for Epping, 1924–45. M.P. for Woodford since 1945. U.-S. for Col. O., 1906–8. Pres. of Bd. of Trade, 1908–10. Home Sec., 1910–11. 1st Ld. of Admir., 1911–15. Chanc. of D. of Lanc., 1915. Min. of Munitions, 1917–19. Sec. for War and Air, 1919–21. Sec. for Air and Col., 1921. Col. Sec., 1921–22. Chanc. of Exch., 1924–29. 1st Ld. of Admir., 1939–40. P.M. and Min. of Def., 1940–45. Leader of Con. party, 1940–55. Leader of Opposition, 1945–51. Min. of Def., 1951–52. P.M., 1951–55. K.G., 1953.

Cripps, (Richard) Stafford (Sir)

b. 1889. *Educ.* Winchester; London. Barrister, 1913. M.P. (Lab.) for E. Bristol, 1931–50. M.P. for S.E. Bristol, 1950. Kt., 1930. Sol. Gen., 1930–31. Brit. Amb. to U.S.S.R., 1940–42. Ld. Privy S. and Leader of Commons, 1942. Min. of Aircraft Prod., 1942–45. Pres. of Bd. of Trade, 1945–47. Min. for Econ. Affairs, 1947. Chanc. of Exch., 1947–50. d. 1952.

Curzon, George Nathaniel. Ld Curzon (1898), 1st Earl (1911), 1st Marquess Curzon of Kedleston (1921)

b. 1859. *Educ.* Eton; Oxford. M.P. (Con.) for Southport, 1886–98. U.-S. India O., 1891–92. U.-S. For. O., 1895–98. Viceroy of India, 1899–1905. Entered House of Lords as Irish representative peer, 1908. Ld. Privy S., 1915–16. Pres. of Air Bd., 1916. Ld. Pres. of Council, 1916–19. Member of war cabinet. Leader of Lords, 1916–24. For. Sec., 1919–24. Ld. Pres. of Council, 1924–25. d. 1925.

Dalton, (Edward) Hugh John Neale. (Life Peer, 1960)

b. 1887. *Educ.* Eton; Cambridge, L.S.E. Barrister, 1914. Univ. Lecturer, London, 1919–36. M.P. (Lab.) for Camberwell, 1924–29. M.P. Bishop Auckland, 1929–31 and 1935–59. U.-S. For. O., 1929–31. Min. of Econ. Warfare, 1940–42. Pres. of Bd. of Trade, 1942–45. Chanc. of Exch., 1945–47. Chanc. of D. of Lanc., 1948–50. Min. of Town and Country Planning, 1950–51. Min. of Loc. Govt. and Planning, 1951. d. 1962.

Eden, (Robert) Anthony (Sir). 1st E of Avon (1961)

b. 1897. *Educ.* Eton; Oxford. M.P. (Con.) for Warwick and Leamington, 1923–57. P.P.S. to Sir A. Chamberlain (For. Sec.), 1926–29. U.-S. For. O., 1931–33. Ld. Privy S., 1934–35. Min. without Portfolio for League of Nations Affairs, 1935. For. Sec., 1935–38. Resigned, 1938. Sec. for Dominions,

1939–40. Sec. for War, 1940. For. Sec., 1940–45. Leader of Commons, 1942–45. Dep. Leader of Opposition, 1945–51. For. Sec., 1951–55. K.G., 1954. P.M. and Leader of Con. party, 1955–57.

Gaitskell, Hugh Todd Naylor

b. 1906. *Educ.* Winchester; Oxford. M.P. (Lab.) for S. Leeds since 1945. Princ. Private Sec. to Min. of Econ. Warfare, 1940–42. Princ. Asst. Sec. Bd. of Trade, 1942–45. P.S. Min. of Fuel and Power, 1946–47. Min. of Fuel and Power, 1947–50. Min. of State for Econ. Affairs, 1950. Chanc. of Exch., 1950–51. Leader of Lab. party, 1955-63. d. 1963.

Grey, Edward (Sir). 1st Vt Grey of Fallodon (1916)

b. 1862. *Educ.* Winchester; Oxford. Succ. to Btcy., 1882. M.P. (Lib.) for Berwick-on-Tweed, 1885–1916. U.-S. For. O., 1892–95. For. Sec., 1905–16. (For. Sec. in House of Lords, 1916.) d. 1933.

Halifax, 3rd Vt (1934), Edward Frederick Lindley Wood. 1st Ld Irwin (1925), 1st E of (1944)

b. 1881. *Educ.* Eton; Oxford. M.P. (Con.) for Ripon, 1910–25. U.-S. Col. O., 1921–22. Pres. of Bd. of Educ., 1922–24. Min. of Agric., 1924–25. Viceroy of India, 1926–31. Pres. of Bd. of Educ., 1932–35. Sec. for War, 1935. Ld. Privy S., 1935–37. Leader of Lords, 1935–38. Ld. Pres. of Council, 1937–38. For. Sec., 1938–40. Leader of Lords, 1940. Brit. Amb. to U.S.A., 1941–46. d. 1959.

Heathcoat Amory, Derick. 1st Vt Amory (1960)

b. 1899. *Educ.* Eton; Oxford. M.P. (Con.) for Tiverton, 1945–60. Min. of Pensions, 1951–53. Min. of State for Bd. of Trade, 1953–54. Min. of Ag., Fish. and Food, 1954–58. Chanc. of Exch., 1958–60.

Henderson, Arthur

b. 1863. *Educ.* Elem. M.P. (Lab.) for Barnard Castle, 1903–18. M.P. for Widnes, 1919–22. M.P. for Newcastle E., 1923. M.P. for Burnley, 1924–31. M.P. for Clay Cross, 1933–35. Sec. of Lab. party, 1911–34. Treasurer of Lab. party, 1930–35. Leader of Lab. party in Commons, 1908–10 and 1914–17. Chief Whip, 1914. Pres. Bd. of Educ., 1915–16. Paym.-Gen., 1916. Min. without portfolio and member of war cabinet, 1916–17. Resigned from cabinet, 1917. Chief Lab. party Whip, 1920–24 and 1925–27. Home Sec., 1924. For. Sec., 1929–31. Leader of Lab. Opposition, 1931–32. d. 1935.

Hicks-Beach, Michael Edward (Sir). 1st Vt St Aldwyn (1906), 1st Earl (1915)

b. 1837. *Educ.* Eton; Oxford. Succ. to Btcy., 1854. M.P. (Con.) for E. Gloucs., 1864–85. M.P. for W. Bristol, 1885–1906. Sec. of Poor Law Bd., 1868. U.-S. Home O., 1868. Ch. Sec. for Ireland, 1874–78. (Seat in cabinet, 1876.) Sec. for Col., 1878–80. Chanc. of Exch. and Leader of Commons, 1885–86. Leader of Opposition in Commons, 1886. Ch. Sec. for Ireland, 1886–87. Resigned 1887, but remained in cabinet without portfolio. Pres. of Bd. of Trade, 1888–92. Chanc. of Exch., 1895–1902. Resigned 1902. d. 1916.

Hoare, Samuel John Gurney (Sir). 1st Vt Templewood (1944)

b. 1880. *Educ.* Harrow; Oxford. M.P. (Con.) for Chelsea, 1910–44. Succ. to Btcy., 1915. Sec. for Air, 1922–24 and 1924–29. Sec. for India, 1931–35. For. Sec., 1935. 1st Ld. of Admir., 1936–37. Home Sec., 1937–39. Ld. Privy S., 1939–40. Sec. for Air, 1940. Brit. Amb. to Spain, 1940–44. d. 1959.

Home, 14th E of (1951–63). Sir Alexander Frederick Douglas-Home, Ld Dunglass (1918–51)

b. 1903. *Educ.* Eton; Oxford. M.P. (Con.) for S. Lanark, 1931–45. M.P. for Lanark, 1950–51. P.P.S. to N. Chamberlain, 1937–40. Joint U.-S. For. O., 1945. (Succ. to E. 1951.) Min. of State Scottish O., 1951–55. Sec. Commonwealth Relations, 1955–60. Dep. Leader of Lords, 1956–57. Ld. Pres. of Council, 1957 and 1959–60. Leader of Lords, 1957–60. For. Sec. 1960–63.

Horne, Robert Stevenson (Sir). 1st Vt Horne of Slamannan (1937)

b. 1871. *Educ.* George Watson's Coll., Edin.; Glasgow Univ. Member of Faculty of Advocates, 1896. K.B.E., 1918. M.P. (Con.) for Hillhead, Glasgow,

1918–37. Min. of Lab., 1919–20. Pres. of Bd. of Trade, 1920–21. Chanc. of Exch., 1921–22. d. 1940.

Lansdowne, 5th M of (1866). Henry Charles Keith Petty-Fitzmaurice, Vt Clanmaurice (1845–63), E of Kerry (1863–66)

b. 1845. *Educ.* Eton; Oxford. Succ. to M. 1866. Junior Ld. of Treas. (Lib.), 1869–72. U.-S. for War, 1872–74. U.-S. India O., 1880. Resigned and opposed Lib. Govt. in Lords, 1880. Gov.-Gen. of Canada, 1883–88. Viceroy of India, 1888–94. Sec. for War (Con.), 1895–1900. For. Sec., 1900–5. Leader of Con. party in Lords, 1903–16. Min. without portfolio, member of war cabinet, 1915–16. Left Con. party, 1917. d. 1927.

Lloyd, (John) Selwyn Brooke

b. 1904. *Educ.* Fettes; Cambridge. Barrister, 1930. M.P. (Con.) for Wirral since 1945. Min. of State For. O., 1951–54. Min. of Supply, 1954–55. Min. of Def., 1955. For. Sec., 1955–60. Chanc. of Exch., 1960–62.

Lloyd George, David. 1st Earl Lloyd George of Dwyfor (1945)

b. 1863. *Educ.* Church School. Solicitor, 1884. M.P. (Lib.) for Caernarvon Boroughs, 1890–1945 (Ind. L., 1931–45). Pres. of Bd. of Trade, 1905–8. Chanc. of Exch., 1908–15. Min. of Munitions, 1915–16. Sec. for War, 1916. Resigned, 1916. P.M., 1916–22. Leader of Lib. party, 1926–31. d. 1945.

MacDonald, James Ramsay

b. 1866. *Educ.* Drainie School. M.P. (Lab.) for Leicester, 1906–18. M.P. for Aberavon, Glamorganshire, 1922–29. M.P. for Seaham, 1929–35. (Nat. Lab., 1931–37.) M.P. for Scottish Univs., 1936–37. Sec. of L.R.C. and Lab. party, 1900–12. Treas. of Lab. party, 1912–24. Chairman of I.L.P., 1906–9. Ch. of Lab. party, 1911–14. Resigned Chairmanship, 1914. Ch. of P.L.P. and Leader of official Opposition, 1922. Leader of Lab. party, 1922–31. P.M. and For. Sec., 1924. P.M., 1929–31. P.M. of National Govt., 1931–35. Ld. Pres. of Council, 1935–37. d. 1937.

McKenna, Reginald

b. 1863. *Educ.* St. Malo, Ebersdorf and King's Coll. School; Cambridge. Barrister, 1887. M.P. (Lib.) for N. Monmouthshire, 1895–1918. F.S. to Treas., 1905–7. Pres. Bd. of Educ., 1907–8. 1st Ld. of Admir., 1908–11. Home Sec., 1911–15. Chanc. of Exch., 1915–16. Ch. of Midland Bank Ltd., 1919–43. d. 1943.

Macmillan, (Maurice) Harold

b. 1894. *Educ.* Eton; Oxford. M.P. (Con.) for Stockton-on-Tees, 1924–29 and 1931–45. M.P. for Bromley since 1945. P.S. Min. of Supply, 1940–42. U.-S. Col. O., 1942. Min. resident at Allied H.Q. in N.W. Africa, 1942–45. Sec. for Air, 1945. Min. of Housing and Loc. Govt., 1951–54. Min. of Def., 1954–55. For. Sec., 1955. Chanc. of Exch., 1955–57. P.M. and Leader of Con. party 1957–63.

Morrison, Herbert Stanley. Life Peer (1959), of Lambeth

b. 1888. *Educ.* Elem. Member of L.C.C., 1922–45. Leader of Council, 1934–40. M.P. (Lab.) for S. Hackney, 1923–24, 1929–31, 1935–45. M.P. for E. Lewisham, 1945–50. M.P. for S. Lewisham, 1950–59. Min. of Transport, 1929–31. Min. of Supply, 1940. Home Sec. and Min. of Home Security, 1940–45. Member of war cabinet, 1942–45. Dep. P.M., 1945–51. Ld. Pres. of Council and Leader of Commons, 1945–51. For. Sec., 1951. Dep. Leader of Opposition, 1951–55.

Reading, 1st M of (1926). Rufus Daniel Isaacs (Sir), 1st Ld (1914), 1st Vt (1916), 1st E of (1917)

b. 1860. *Educ.* Brussels, Anglo-Jewish Acad., London, University College Sch. Family business. Barrister, 1887. M.P. (Lib.) for Reading, 1904–13. Kt., 1910. Sol. Gen., 1910. Att. Gen., 1910–13 (seat in cabinet, 1912). Ld. Chief Justice, 1913–21. Brit. Amb. to U.S.A., 1918–19. Viceroy of India, 1921–26. For. Sec., 1931. d. 1935.

Ritchie, Charles Thomson. 1st Ld Ritchie of Dundee (1905)

b. 1838. *Educ.* City of London School. M.P. (Con.) for Tower Hamlets, 1874–85.

M.P. for St. George's in the East, 1885–92. M.P. for Croydon, 1895–1903. F.S. to Admir., 1885–86. Pres. of Loc. Govt. Bd., 1886–92. Pres. of Bd. of Trade, 1895–1900. Home Sec., 1900–2. Chanc. of Exch., 1902–3. Resigned, 1903. d. 1906.

Salisbury, 3rd M of (1868). Robert Arthur Talbot Gascoyne-Cecil, Vt Cranborne (1865–68)
b. 1830. *Educ.* Eton; Oxford. M.P. (Con.) for Stamford, 1853–68. Sec. for India, 1866. Resigned, 1867. Succ. to M. 1868. Sec. for India, 1874–76. For. Sec., 1878–80. Leader of Opposition in Lords, 1881–85. Leader of the Con. party, 1885–1902. P.M. and For. Sec., 1885–86. P.M. 1886. P.M. and For. Sec., 1887–92 and 1895–1900. P.M. and Ld. Privy S., 1900–2. d. 1903.

Simon, John Allsebrook (Sir). 1st Vt Simon (1940)
b. 1873. *Educ.* Fettes; Oxford. Barrister, 1899. M.P. (Lib.) for Walthamstow, 1906–18. M.P. for Spen Valley, 1922–31. M.P. (L. Nat.) for Spen Valley, 1931–40. Kt., 1910. Sol. Gen., 1910–13. Att. Gen. (with seat in cabinet), 1913–15. Home Sec., 1915–16. For. Sec., 1931–35. Leader of L. Nat. party, 1931–40. Home Sec. and Dep. Leader of Commons, 1935–37. Chanc. of Exch., 1937–40. Ld. Chanc., 1940–45. d. 1954.

Snowden, Philip. 1st Vt Snowden (1931)
b. 1864. *Educ.* Bd. School. M.P. (Lab.) for Blackburn, 1906–18. M.P. for Colne Valley, 1922–31. Ch. of ILP 1903–6 and 1917–20. Chanc. of Exch., 1924, 1929–31, and 1931. Ld. Privy S., 1931–32. Resigned, 1932. d. 1937.

Thorneycroft, (George Edward) Peter
b. 1909. *Educ.* Eton; Woolwich. Barrister, 1935. M.P. (Con.) for Stafford, 1938–45. M.P. for Monmouth since 1945. P.S. Min. of War Transport, 1945. Pres. of Bd. of Trade, 1951–57. Chanc. of Exch., 1957–58. Resigned, 1958. Min. of Aviation, 1960-62.

Wood, (Howard) Kingsley (Sir)
b. 1881. *Educ.* Central Foundation Boys' School. Solicitor, 1903. Kt., 1918. M.P. (Con.) for W. Woolwich, 1918–43. P.P.S. to Min. of Health, 1919–22. P.S. Min. of Health, 1924–29. P.S. Bd. of Educ., 1931. Postm. Gen., 1931–35 (seat in cabinet, 1933). Min. of Health, 1935–38. Sec. for Air, 1938–40. Ld. Privy S., 1940. Chanc. of Exch., 1940–43. d. 1943.

SOURCES.—*Dictionary of National Biography, 1900–1950; Who Was Who, 1900–1960; Who's Who.*

Index of Ministers

The educational information in this index is necessarily incomplete. It is not always possible to trace the name or status of an elementary or secondary school. When several schools are recorded, the last is normally named here. All schools that are unstarred are 'public schools' or, more precisely, members of the Headmasters' Conference. By courtesy, we have listed the Royal Military College (Sandhurst) and the Royal Military Academy (Woolwich) in the University column. In this index promotion from a knighthood to a higher order of chivalry or to a baronetcy is not recorded.

When an individual appears more than once on a page, the number is indicated.

Name	Born	School	Univ.	Died	Page references
Adamson, W. M.	1881	Elementary		1945	30
Addison, 1st Vt (1945). C. Addison	1869	Trinity Coll., Harrogate*	London	1951	5, 8, 9, 10, 11^2, 12, 18^2, 32, 33^3, 34, 35
Ailwyn, 1st Ld (1921). Sir A. E. Fellowes (K.C.V.O. 1911)	1855	Eton	Cambridge	1924	1, 3^2
Airlie, 12th E of (1900). D. L. G. W. Ogilvy	1893	Eton	..	..	18
Aitchison, Ld (Scot. judge 1933). C. M. Aitchison	1882	Falkirk H.S.*	Edinburgh	1941	19, 22
Akers-Douglas, A., 1st Vt Chilston (1911)	1851	Eton	Oxford	1926	1, 2
Albemarle, 8th E of (1894) A. A. C. Keppel	1858	Eton	..	1942	15
Aldington, 1st Ld (1962). Sir T. A. R. W. Low (K.C.M.G. 1957)	1914	Winchester	Oxford	..	37, 38, 41
Alexander, 1st E (1952). H. R. L. G. Alexander, 1st Vt (1946)	1891	Harrow	Sandhurst	..	37
Alexander of Hillsborough, 1st E (1963). A. V. Alexander, 1st Vt (1950)	1885	Elementary	..	..	16, 18, 27, 33^2, 34^2
Allan, R. A.	1914	Harrow	Cambridge	..	40, 41
Allendale, 1st Vt (1911). W. C. B. Beaumont, 2nd Ld Allendale (1907)	1860	Eton	Cambridge	1923	4, 5, 7^2, 9
Allendale, 2nd Vt (1923). W. H. C. Beaumont	1890	Eton	Cambridge	1956	22, 26, 31
Alness, 1st Ld (1934). R. Munro	1868	Aberdeen G.S.*	Edinburgh	1955	6, 8, 11
Alport, Ld (Life Peer 1961) C. J. Alport	1912	Haileybury	Cambridge	..	40^2, 42
Althorp, 1st Vt (1905). C. R. Spencer, Vt Althorp (1857). 6th Earl Spencer (1910)	1857	Harrow	Cambridge	1922	4, 7
Altrincham, 1st Ld (1945). Sir E. W. M. Grigg (K.C.V.O. 1920)	1879	Winchester	Oxford	1955	24, 25, 29, 30, 32
Alverstone, 1st Vt (1913). Sir R. E. Webster (G.C.M.G. 1893). 1st Ld Alverstone (1900)	1842	King's Coll. Sch. & Charterhouse	Cambridge	1915	3
Amery, J.	1919	Eton	Oxford	..	40, 42^2
Amery, L. S.	1873	Harrow	Oxford	1955	10^2, 14, 17^2, 28, 31
Ammon, 1st Ld (1944). C. G. Ammon	1875	Elementary	..	1960	15, 18, 36
Amory, 1st Vt (1960). D. Heathcoat Amory	1899	Eton	Oxford	..	37^3, 38, 39, 40
Amulree, 1st Ld (1929). Sir W. W. Mackenzie (K.B.E. 1918)	1860	Perth Academy*	Edinburgh & London	1942	19, 21
Amwell, 1st Ld (1947). F. Montague	1876	Elementary	..	..	19, 28, 30
Ancaster, 2nd E (1910). G. H. D.-Willoughby	1867	Eton	Cambridge	1951	10, 14
Anderson, Ld (Scot. judge 1913). A. M. Anderson	1862	Dundee H.S.*	Edinburgh	1936	6
Anderson, D. C.	1916	Trinity Coll. Glenalmond	Oxford & Edinburgh	..	43
Anderson, Sir J. (K.C.B. 1919). 1st Vt Waverley (1952)	1882	George Watson's Coll., Edin.	Edinburgh & Leipzig	1958	23^2, 26^2, 28^2, 31
Anson, Sir W. (3rd Bt. 1873)	1843	Eton	Oxford	1914	2
Anstruther, H. T.	1860	Eton	Edinburgh	1926	3
Anstruther-Gray, Sir W. J. (1st Bt. 1956)	1905	Eton	Oxford	..	32
Archibald, 1st Ld (1949). G. Archibald	1898	Allan Glen's H.S. Glasg.*	..	..	36

Name	Born	School	Univ.	Died	Page references
Arnold, 1st Ld (1924). S. Arnold	1878	Manchester G.S.	..	1945	16, 19
Arnold-Forster, H. O.	1855	Rugby	Oxford	1909	1, 2
Ashbourne, 1st Ld (1885). E. Gibson	1837		Dublin	1913	2
Ashby St Ledgers, 1st Ld (1910). I. C. Guest, 2nd Ld Wimborne (1914), 1st Vt Wimborne (1918)	1873	Eton	Cambridge	1939	6, 7, 11
Ashfield, 1st Ld (1920). Sir A. H. Stanley (Kt 1914)	1874	American Schs.	..	1948	11
Ashley, W. W. 1st Ld Mount Temple (1932)	1867	Harrow	Oxford	1939	14, 15, 18
Asquith, H. H. 1st E of Oxford & Asquith (1925)	1852	City of London	Oxford	1928	3, 5, 6, 7
Assheton, R. 1st Ld Clitheroe (1955)	1901	Eton	Oxford	..	24, 26, 27, 29
Astor, 2nd Vt (1919). W. Astor	1879	Eton	Oxford	1952	10, 12
Atholl, 8th D of (1917). J. G. Stewart-Murray, M of Tullibardine (1871)	1871	Eton	..	1942	13
Atholl, Duchess of. K. M.	1874	Wimbledon H.S.	..	1960	17
Atkinson, Ld (Ld of Appeal 1905). J. Atkinson	1844	Royal Belfast Academical Institution*	Queen's Coll., Galway	1932	3
Attlee, 1st E (1955). C. R. Attlee	1883	Haileybury	Oxford	..	16, 19^{2}, 26^{2}, 27, 28, 32, 33
Avon, 1st E of (1961). Sir (R.) A. Eden (K.G. 1954)	1897	Eton	Oxford	..	20^{2}, 21, 23^{2}, 24, 2 30, 31, 36, 39
Bagot, 4th Ld (1887). W. Bagot	1857	Eton	..	1932	3
Baird, Sir J. L. (2nd Bt. 1920). 1st Ld Stonehaven (1925), 1st Vt (1938)	1874	Eton	Oxford	1941	10, 11, 12, 15^{2}
Baker, H. T.	1877	Winchester	Oxford	1960	6
Balcarres, Ld (1880). D. A. E. Lindsay, 27th E of Crawford (1913)	1871	Eton	Oxford	1940	3, 8, 10, 11^{2}, 12^{3}
Baldwin of Bewdley, 1st E (1937). S. Baldwin	1867	Harrow	Cambridge	1947	9, 11, 13^{2}, 14, 16, 20^{2}, 22
Balfour, 1st E of (1922). A. J. Balfour	1848	Eton	Cambridge	1930	1^{3}, 7, 9, 10, 16
Balfour, 2nd E of (1930). G. W. Balfour	1853	Eton	Cambridge	1945	2^{3}
Balfour of Burleigh, 6th Ld (1869). A. H. Bruce	1849	Eton	Oxford	1921	2
Balfour of Inchrye, 1st Ld (1945). H. H. Balfour	1897	R.N. Coll., Osborne	..	..	23, 27, 29, 32
Barber, A. P. L.	1920	Secondary	Oxford	..	39, 43
Barnes, A.	1887	Northampton Institute*	..	..	19, 35
Barnes, G. N.	1859	Elementary	..	1940	9, 12
Barnston, Sir H. (1st Bt 1924)	1870	Private Schs.	Oxford	1929	13, 15, 18
Barrie, H. T.	1860	Secondary	..	1922	10
Barry, R.	1866	Secondary	Royal Univ. of Ireland	1913	4, 6, 7
Barton, Sir D. P. (1st Bt 1918)	1853	Harrow	Oxford	1937	3
Bath, 5th M of (1896). T. H. Thynne, Vt Weymouth (1862)	1862	Eton	Oxford	1946	2, 15
Bathurst, 8th E (1943). H. A. J. Bathurst	1927	Canada & Eton	Oxford	..	43
Bathurst, Sir C. (K.B.E. 1917). 1st Ld Bledisloe (1918). 1st Vt (1935)	1867	Sherborne & Eton	Oxford	1958	12, 17
Bayford, 1st Ld (1929). Sir R. A. Sanders (1st Bt 1920)	1867	Harrow	Oxford	1940	11, 13^{2}, 14
Beatty, 2nd E (1936). D. F. Beatty, Vt Borodale (1919)	1905	R. N. C. Osborne & Dartmouth	..	..	31

Name	Born	School	Univ.	Died	Page references
Beauchamp, 7th E (1891). W. Lygon	1872	Eton	Oxford	1938	4, 5^{3}, 6, 7
Beaumont, W. C. B. 2nd Ld Allendale (1907), 1st Vt (1911)	1860	Eton	Cambridge	1923	4, 5, 7^{2}, 9
Beaverbrook, 1st Ld (1917). Sir W. M. Aitken (Kt 1911)	1879	Elementary	..	1964	11, 26, 27^{3}, 28, 29^{3}, 31
Beck, Sir (A.) C. T. (Kt 1920)	1878	Haileybury	Cambridge	1932	7, 9^{2}, 13
Beechman, (N.) A.	1896	Westminster	Oxford	..	30, 32
Belcher, J. W.	1905	Latymer Upper	London	..	34
Bellenger, F. J.	1894	Elementary	..	..	35^{2}
Belper, 2nd Ld (1880). H. Strutt	1840	Harrow	Cambridge	1914	3
Benn, W. Wedgwood, 1st Vt Stansgate (1941)	1877	Secondary	London	1960	6, 19, 33
Bennett of Edgbaston, 1st Ld (1953), Sir P. F. Bennett (Kt 1941)	1880	King Edward's Birmingham	..	1957	37
Bennett, Sir E. N. (Kt 1930)	1868	Durham	Oxford	1947	20, 25
Bernays, R. H.	1902	Rossall	Oxford	1945	24^{2}
Beswick, F.	1912	Elementary	..	..	33
Betterton, Sir H. B. (1st Bt 1929). 1st Ld Rushcliffe (1935)	1872	Rugby	Oxford	1949	14, 17, 20, 21
Bevan, A.	1897	Elementary	..	1960	34^{2}
Bevin, E.	1881	Elementary	..	1951	27, 28, 33^{2}
Bevins, (J.) R.	1908	Liverpool Coll.	..	..	38, 40, 42^{2}
Bingley, 1st Ld (1933). G. R. Lane-Fox	1870	Eton	Oxford	1947	14, 17
Birch, (E.) N. C.	1906	Eton	..	..	37, 38^{2}, 39, 42^{2}
Birkenhead, 1st E of (1922). Sir F. E. Smith (Kt 1915), 1st Ld Birkenhead (1919), 1st Vt (1921)	1872	Birkenhead	Oxford	1930	8^{2}, 9, 12^{2}, 17
Birkenhead, 2nd E of (1930). F. W. F. Smith, Vt Furneaux (1922)	1907	Eton	Oxford	..	26, 39
Birnam, Ld (Scot. judge 1945). Sir (T.) D. K. Murray (Kt 1941)	1884	Hamilton Acad.* & Glasgow H.S.*	Glasgow	1955	30, 32
Birrell, A.	1850	Amersham Hall*	Cambridge	1933	4^{2}, 6, 8
Blades, Ld (Scot. judge 1947). D. P. Blades	1888	Berwickshire H.S.*	Edinburgh	1959	36
Bledisloe, 1st Vt (1935). Sir C. Bathurst (K.B.E. 1917), 1st Ld Bledisloe (1918)	1867	Sherborne & Eton	Oxford	1958	12, 17
Blenkinsop, A.	1911	Newcastle on Tyne Royal G.S.	..	..	34, 35, 36
Blindell, Sir J. (Kt 1936)	1884	St. Mary's, Hitchin*	..	1937	22, 25
Bondfield, Miss M. G.	1873	Elementary	..	1953	16, 19
Boothby, Ld (Life Peer 1958). Sir R. J. G. Boothby (K.B.E. 1953)	1900	Eton	Oxford	..	28
Bottomley, A. G.	1907	Elementary	..	..	33, 34
Boulton, Sir W. W. (1st Bt 1944)	1873	Privately	..	1949	26, 30, 31
Bowden, H. W.	1905	Secondary	..	..	36
Bowyer, Sir G. E. W. (Kt 1929). 1st Ld Denham (1937)	1886	Eton	Oxford	1948	18, 23, 26
Boyd, 1st Vt (1960). A. T. Lennox-Boyd	1904	Sherborne	Oxford	..	23, 24^{2}, 28, 32, 37^{2}, 38, 40
Boyd-Carpenter, Sir A. B. (Kt 1926)	1873	Harrow	Oxford	1937	14^{3}, 15
Boyd-Carpenter, J. A.	1908	Stowe	Oxford	..	36, 38, 41, 42^{2}
Boyle, Sir E. C. G. (3rd Bt 1945)	1923	Eton	Oxford	..	38, 39^{2}, 40
Brabazon, 1st Ld (1942). J. T. C. Moore-Brabazon	1884	Harrow	Cambridge	1964	15, 18, 27, 28, 31

Name	Born	School	Univ.	Died	Page references
Brabner, R. A.	1911	Felsted	Cambridge	1945	27
Brace, W.	1856	Elementary	..	1947	7, 10
Bracken, 1st Vt (1952). B. Bracken	1901	Sedbergh	..	1958	28, 31
Bradford, 5th E of (1915). O. Bridgeman, Vt Newport (1898)	1873	Harrow	Cambridge	1957	13, 15
Braine, B. R.	1914	Hendon C.S.*	..	..	42
Braithwaite, Sir J. G. (1st Bt 1954)	1895	Bootham	..	1958	38
Brecon, 1st Ld (1957). D. V. P. Lewis	1905	Monmouth*	..	..	40
Brentford, 1st Vt (1929). Sir W. Joynson-Hicks (1st Bt 1919)	1865	Merchant Taylors' Sch.	..	1932	14^4, 15^2, 17
Brentford, 3rd Vt (1958). L. W. Joynson-Hicks	1902	Winchester	Oxford	..	38, 42
Bridgeman, 1st Vt (1929). W. C. Bridgeman	1864	Eton	Cambridge	1935	8, 11^3, 13, 14, 17
Bridport, 1st Vt (1868). A. N. Hood	1814			1904	3
Bridport, 3rd Vt (1924). R. A. H. N. Hood	1911	R.N. Coll., Dartmouth	..	..	26
Brodrick, (W.) St. J. 9th Vt Midleton (1907), 1st E of (1920)	1856	Eton	Oxford	1942	1, 2^2
Bromley-Davenport, Sir W. (K.C.B. 1924)	1862	Eton	Oxford	1949	2
Brooke, H.	1903	Marlborough	Oxford	..	36, 39, 40
Brooman-White, R. C.	1912	Eton	Cambridge	1964	41, 43^2
Brown, E.	1881	Torquay*	..	1962	20,21,24,28^2,29,32
Brown, G. A.	1914	Secondary	..	..	33, 35
Brown, T. W.	1879	Campbell Coll., Belfast	Belfast	1944	13^2
Browne, J. N., Ld Craigton (Life Peer 1959)	1904	Cheltenham	..	..	41^3
Brownlow, 6th Ld (1927). P. F. A. Cust	1899	Eton	Sandhurst	..	26
Bruntisfield, 1st Ld (1942). Sir V. A. G. A. Warrender (8th Bt 1917)	1899	Eton	..	..	22^3, 23^2, 25, 27, 31
Bryan, P. E. O.	1913	St John's, Leatherhead	Cambridge	..	43
Bryce, 1st Vt (1914). J. Bryce	1838	Glasgow H.S.*	Glasgow & Oxford	1922	4
Buchan-Hepburn, P. G. T. 1st Ld Hailes (1957)	1901	Harrow	Cambridge	..	26, 30, 31, 32, 38, 41, 42^2
Buchanan, G.	1890	Elementary	..	1955	34, 35
Buchanan, T. R.	1846	Sherborne	Oxford	1911	4, 5
Buckley, A.	1877	Merchant Taylors' Sch., Crosby & Aldenham	..	..	14, 15
Buckmaster, 1st Vt (1933). Sir S. O. Buckmaster (Kt 1913), 1st Ld (1915)	1861	Aldenham	Oxford	1934	6, 7
Burden, 1st Ld (1950). T. W. Burden	1885	Elementary	London Sch. of Economics	..	36
Burgin, (E.) L.	1887	Christ's Coll., Finchley*	Lausanne & Paris	1945	21, 24^3, 25
Burke, W. A.	1890	Secondary	..	..	35
Burns, J.	1858	Elementary	..	1943	4, 6^2
Butcher, Sir H. W. (Kt 1953)	1901	Hastings G.S.*	..	..	38
Butler, R. A.	1902	Marlborough	Cambridge	..	20, 23, 24^2, 26, 28, 31, 36, 39^2, 40
Buxton, 1st E (1920). S. C. Buxton, 1st Vt (1914)	1853	Clifton	Cambridge	1934	4, 6^2
Buxton, N. E. N. 1st Ld Noel-Buxton (1930)	1869	Harrow	Cambridge	1948	15, 18

Name	Born	School	Univ.	Died	Page references
Cadogan, 5th E (1873). Vt Chelsea (1864)	1840	Eton	Oxford	1915	2
Caldecote, 1st Vt (1939). Sir T. W. H. Inskip (Kt 1922)	1876	Clifton	Cambridge	1947	15, 17, 18^2, 22^2, 23^3, 25, 28
Callaghan, (L.) J.	1912	Portsmouth Nn*	..	..	34, 35
Campbell, Sir J. H. M. (1st Bt 1916). 1st Ld Glenavy (1921)	1851	Kingstown*	Dublin	1931	3, 8, 12, 13
Campbell-Bannerman, Sir H. (G.C.B. 1895)	1836	Glasgow H.S.*	Glasgow	1908	3
Carr, R.	1916	Westminster	Cambridge	..	40
Carrington, 1st E (1895). C. R. Wynn-Carrington, 3rd Ld Carrington (1868), 1st M of Lincolnshire (1912)	1843	Eton	Cambridge	1928	4, 5^2
Carrington, 6th Ld (1938). P. A. R. Carington	1919	Eton	Sandhurst	..	37^2, 40, 41
Carson, 1st Ld (1921). Sir E. H. Carson (Kt 1900)	1854	Portarlington*	Dublin	1935	3, 8, 9, 10
Cary, Sir R. A. (1st Bt 1955)	1898	Ardingly	Sandhurst	..	32
Casey, Ld (Life Peer 1960). R. G. Casey	1890	Melbourne G.S.	Melbourne & Cambridge	..	27
Causton, R. K. 1st Ld Southwark (1910)	1843	Privately	..	1929	4, 6^2
Cavan, 10th E of (1900). F. R. Lambart	1865	Eton	Sandhurst	1946	20, 22
Cave, 1st Vt (1918). Sir G. Cave (Kt 1915)	1856	Merchant Taylors'	Oxford	1928	8, 10, 13, 16
Cawdor, 3rd E (1898). F. A. V. Campbell, Vt Emlyn (1847)	1847	Eton	Oxford	1911	1
Cawley, 1st Ld (1918). Sir F. Cawley (1st Bt 1906)	1850	Secondary	..	1937	11
Cazalet-Keir, Mrs T.	1899			..	32
Cecil of Chelwood, 1st Vt (1923). Ld R. Cecil	1864	Eton	Oxford	1958	7, 10, 12, 13, 17
Chadwick, Sir R. Burton (Kt 1920)	1869	Birkenhead & Privately	..	1951	17,
Chamberlain, (A.) N.	1869	Rugby	Birmingham	1940	9, 14^2, 15^2, 17, 20^2, 22, 23, 26
Chamberlain, J.	1836	University Coll. Sch.	..	1914	2
Chamberlain, Sir (J.) A. (K.G. 1925)	1863	Rugby	Cambridge	1937	1^3, 2, 8, 9^2, 10^2, 17, 21
Chambers, J.	1863	Royal Academical Institution	Queen's Coll., Belfast	1917	13
Champion, Ld (Life Peer 1962). A. J. Champion	1897	St. John's, Glastonbury*	..	..	33
Chandos, 1st Vt (1954). O. Lyttelton	1893	Eton	Cambridge	..	26, 27^2, 29, 31^2, 37
Chaplin, 1st Vt (1916). H. Chaplin	1840	Harrow	Oxford	1923	2
Chapman, A.	1897		Cambridge	..	29^2, 31
Charleton, H. C.	1870	Elementary	..	1959	19
Chatfield, 1st Ld (1937). Sir A. E. M. Chatfield (K.C.M.G. 1919)	1873	H.M.S. Britannia*	..	..	23
Chelmsford, 1st Vt (1921). F. J. N. Thesiger, 3rd Ld Chelmsford (1905)	1868	Winchester	Oxford	1933	15
Cherry, R. R.	1859	Secondary	Dublin	1923	4, 6
Cherwell, 1st Vt (1956). F. A. Lindemann, 1st Ld Cherwell (1941)	1886	Blair Lodge* & Darmstadt	Berlin	1957	29, 32, 37
Chesham, 3rd Ld (1882)	1850	Eton	..	1907	3
Chesham, 5th Ld (1952). J. C. C. Cavendish	1916	Eton	Cambridge	..	39, 41, 43
Chesterfield, 10th E of (1887). E. F. S-Stanhope	1854	Eton	Oxford	1933	7, 9, 13

Name	Born	School	Univ.	Died	Page references
Chichester-Clark, R.	1928	R.N. College*	Cambridge	..	43
Chilston, 1st Vt (1911). A. Akers-Douglas	1851	Eton	Oxford	1926	1, 2
Chorley, 1st Ld (1945). R. S. T. Chorley	1895	Kendall*	Oxford	..	36
Churchill, 1st Vt (1902). V. A. F. S. Churchill, Ld (1886)	1864	Eton	Sandhurst	1934	3
Churchill, Sir W. L. S. (K.G. 1953)	1874	Harrow	Sandhurst	..	4, 5^2, 6, 8, 10, 11^2 12, 17, 23, 26 27, 31^2, 36, 37
Cilcennin, 1st Vt (1955). J. P. L. Thomas	1903	Rugby	Oxford	1960	27, 30, 31, 37, 41^2
Clarendon, 5th E of (1870). E. H. Villiers	1846	Harrow	Cambridge	1914	3^2
Clarendon, 6th E of (1914). G. H. H. Villiers, Ld Hyde (1877)	1877	Eton	..	1955	13, 15, 17, 18
Clifden, 7th Vt (1930). F. G. Agar-Robartes	1883	Eton	Oxford	..	31
Clinton, 21st Ld (1904). C. J. R. H.-S-F.-Trefusis	1863	Eton	..	1957	10
Clitheroe, 1st Ld (1955). R. Assheton	1901	Eton	Oxford	..	24, 26, 27, 29
Clyde, Ld (Scot. judge 1920). J. A. Clyde	1863	Edinburgh Academy	Edinburgh	1944	3, 13
Clyde, Ld (Scot. judge 1954). J. L. M. Clyde	1898	Edinburgh Academy	Oxford & Edinburgh	..	39
Clydesmuir, 1st Ld (1947). Sir D. J. Colville (G.C.I.E. 1943)	1894	Charterhouse	Cambridge	1954	21, 23, 24^3
Clynes, J. R.	1869	Elementary	..	1949	12^2, 15, 18
Cobham, 9th Vt (1922). J. C. Lyttelton	1881	Eton	..	1949	25
Cochrane of Cults, 1st Ld (1919). T. H. A. E. Cochrane	1857	Eton	..	1951	1
Colebrooke, 1st Ld (1906). Sir E. A. Colebrooke (5th Bt 1890)	1861	Eton		1939	4, 7^2, 9, 13, 22, 26
Coleraine, 1st Ld (1954). R. K. Law	1901	Shrewsbury	Oxford	..	26^2, 30, 32
Collick, P. H.	1897	Elementary	..	..	33
Collindridge, F.	1890	Elementary	..	1951	36^2
Collings, J.	1831	Plymouth*	..	1920	1
Collins, Sir G. P. (K.B.E. 1919)	1875	H.M.S. Britannia*	..	1936	13, 21, 24
Colville, Sir D. J. (G.C.I.E. 1943). 1st Ld Clydesmuir (1947)	1894	Charterhouse	Cambridge	1954	21, 23, 24^3
Colyton, 1st Ld (1955). H. L. D. Hopkinson	1902	Eton	Cambridge	..	37^2, 40
Compton-Rickett, Sir J. (Kt 1907)	1847	K. Edward VI, Bath* & privately	..	1919	12
Conant, Sir R. J. E. (1st Bt 1954)	1899	Eton	Sandhurst	..	39
Conesford, 1st Ld (1955). H. G. Strauss	1892	Rugby	Oxford	..	29, 30, 37
Constable, Ld (Scot judge 1922). A. H. B. Constable	1865	Dollar*	Edinburgh	1928	13
Cook, T. F.	1908	Cardenden*	..	1952	33
Cooper of Culross, 1st Ld (1954). T. M. Cooper	1892	George Watson's Coll., Edin.	Edinburgh	1955	22, 25^2, 30
Cope, 1st Ld (1945). Sir W. Cope (1st Bt 1928)	1870	Repton	Cambridge	1946	15, 18^2
Cornwall, Sir E. (Kt 1905)	1863	Elementary		1953	13
Coventry, 9th E of (1843)	1838	Eton	Oxford	1930	3
Craig, C. C.	1869	Clifton	..	1960	15

Name	Born	School	Univ.	Died	Page references
Craig, Sir J. (Bt 1918). 1st Vt Craigavon (1927)	1871	Merchiston Castle	..	1940	10, 12, 13
Craigavon, 1st Vt (1927). Sir J. Craig (1st Bt 1918)	1871	Merchiston Castle	..	1940	10, 12, 13
Craigmyle, 1st Ld (1929). T. Shaw. Ld Shaw (Ld of Appeal 1909)	1850	Dunfermline H.S.*	Edinburgh	1937	4, 6
Craigton, Ld (Life Peer 1959). J. N. Browne	1904	Cheltenham	..	..	41^{3}
Cranborne, Vt (1865). R. A. T. Gascoyne-Cecil, 3rd M of Salisbury (1868)	1830	Eton	Oxford	1903	1^{3}
Cranborne, Vt (1868). J. E. H. Gascoyne-Cecil, 4th M of Salisbury (1903)	1861	Eton	Oxford	1947	1^{2}, 2, 13, 14, 16
Cranborne, Vt (1903). R. A. J. Gascoyne-Cecil, 5th M of Salisbury (1947)	1893	Eton	Oxford	..	23, 26, 27, 28^{3}, 29^{2}, 31, 36^{2}, 37, 39
Crathorne, 1st Ld (1959). Sir T. L. Dugdale (1st Bt 1945)	1897	Eton	Sandhurst	..	25, 30, 37, 38
Craven, 4th E of (1883). W. G. R. Craven	1868	Eton	..	1921	7
Crawford, 27th E of (1913). D. A. E. Lindsay, Ld Balcarres (1880)	1871	Eton	Oxford	1940	3, 8, 10, 11^{2}, 12^{3}
Crawley, A. M.	1908	Harrow	Oxford	..	34
Crewe, 1st M of (1911). R. O. A. Crewe-Milnes, 2nd Ld Houghton (1885), 1st E of Crewe (1895)	1858	Harrow	Cambridge	1945	3, 5^{5}, 7, 8, 21
Cripps, Sir (R.) S. (Kt. 1930)	1889	Winchester	London	1952	19, 26, 28, 33, 34
Croft, 1st Ld (1940). Sir H. Page-Croft (1st Bt 1924)	1881	Eton & Shrewsbury	Cambridge	1947	30^{2}, 32
Cromer, 2nd E of (1917). R. T. Baring, Vt Errington (1901)	1877	Eton	..	1953	15
Crookshank, 1st Vt (1956). H. F. C. Crookshank	1893	Eton	Oxford	1961	20, 23, 24, 26, 29, 32, 36, 37, 39
Cross, 1st Vt (1886). R. Cross	1823	Rugby	Cambridge	1914	1
Cross, Sir R. H. (1st Bt 1941)	1896	Eton	..	..	24, 25^{2}, 26, 29
Crossley, Sir S. B. (2nd Bt 1872). 1st Ld Somerleyton (1916)	1857	Eton	Oxford	1935	2, 13, 15
Cunliffe-Lister, Sir P. (K.B.E. 1920). *Born Lloyd-Greame, changed surname to Cunliffe-Lister in* 1924. 1st Vt Swinton (1935), 1st E of Swinton (1955)	1884	Winchester	Oxford	..	11^{2}, 14, 17^{2}, 20, 21, 23^{2}, 28, 29, 32, 37, 38^{2}
Curzon, 1st M (1921). G. N. Curzon. 1st Ld Curzon of Kedleston (1898), 1st E (1911)	1859	Eton	Oxford	1925	7, 9, 10, 14, 16
Curzon, Vt (1876). R. G. P. Curzon. 4th E of Howe (1900)	1861	Eton	Oxford	1929	3^{2}
Curzon, Vt (1900). F. R. H. P. Curzon, 5th E of Howe (1929)	1884	Eton	Oxford	..	18
Cushendun, 1st Ld (1927). R. J. McNeill	1861	Harrow	Oxford	1936	14, 17^{4}
Dalton, Ld (Life Peer 1960). (E.) H. J. N. Dalton	1887	Eton	Cambridge	1962	18, 28, 29, 33, 34^{2}, 35
Darwen, 1st Ld (1946). J. P. Davies	1885	Bootham	..	1950	36
Daryngton, 1st Ld (1923). H. Pike Pease	1867	Brighton Coll.	Cambridge	1949	8, 12

Name	Born	School	Univ.	Died	Page references
Davidson, 1st Vt (1937). Sir J. C. C. Davidson (G.C.V.O. 1935)	1889	Westminster	Cambridge	..	14^{2}, 17, 21, 25
Davies, E. A. J.	1902	Wycliffe Coll.	London	..	33
Davies, Sir G. F. (Kt 1936)	1875	Uppingham	Cambridge	1950	22, 25, 26^{2}
Davies, R. J.	1877	Elementary	..	1954	15
Davison, J. E.	1870	Elementary	..	1927	16
Deedes, W. F.	1913	Harrow	..	..	37, 40^{2}
de Freitas, Sir G. S. (K.C.M.G. 1961)	1913	Haileybury	Cambridge	..	33, 34
De La Warr, 9th E (1915). H. E. D. B. Sackville, Ld Buckhurst (1900)	1900	Eton	Oxford	..	16, 18, 19^{2}, 20, 23^{5}, 25, 38
De L'Isle, 1st Vt (1956). W. P. Sidney, 6th Ld De L'Isle & Dudley (1945)	1909	Eton	Cambridge	..	32, 38, 42
Denbigh, 9th E of (1892). R. B. A. A. Fielding	1859	Oscott Coll., Birmingham*	Woolwich	1939	3
Denham, 1st Ld (1937). Sir G. E. W. Bowyer (Kt 1929)	1886	Eton	Oxford	1948	18, 23, 26
Denman, 3rd Ld (1894). T. Denman	1874		Sandhurst	1954	4, 5, 7
Derby, 17th E of (1908). E. G. V. Stanley, Ld Stanley (1893)	1865	Wellington	..	1948	8, 11, 14
Desborough, 1st Ld (1905). W. H. Grenfell	1855	Harrow	Oxford	1955	18
Devonport, 1st Vt (1917). Sir H. E. Kearley (1st Bt 1908), 1st Ld Devonport (1910)	1856	Surrey C.S.*	..	1934	4, 6, 12
Devonshire, 8th D of (1891). S. C. Cavendish, M of Hartington (1858)	1833	Privately	Cambridge	1908	1, 2
Devonshire, 9th D of (1908). V. C. W. Cavendish, M of Hartington (1891)	1868	Eton	Cambridge	1938	1, 3, 7, 14
Devonshire, 10th D of (1938). E. W. S. Cavendish, M of Hartington (1908)	1895	Eton	Cambridge	1950	23^{2}, 28^{2}, 31
Devonshire, 11th D of (1950). A. R. B. Cavendish, M of Hartington (1944)	1920	Eton	Cambridge	..	40
Dewar, Ld (Scot. judge 1910). A. Dewar	1860	Perth Academy*	Edinburgh	1917	6
Dickson, Ld (Scot. judge 1915). S. Dickson	1850		Glasgow & Edinburgh	1922	3^{2}
Digby, (K.) S. D. W.	1910	Harrow	Cambridge	..	38, 41
Dilhorne, 1st Ld (1962). Sir R. E. Manningham-Buller (Kt 1951)	1905	Eton	Oxford	..	32, 38^{2}, 42
Dodds-Parker, A. D.	1909	Winchester	Oxford	..	36, 37, 39, 40
Donoughmore, 6th E of (1900). R. W. J. Hely-Hutchinson	1875	Eton	Oxford	1948	2
Dorman-Smith, Sir R. H. (Kt 1937)	1899	Harrow	Sandhurst	..	23
Doverdale, 2nd Ld (1925). O. Partington	1872	Rossall	..	1935	6
Downham, 1st Ld (1919). W. Hayes Fisher	1853	Haileybury	Oxford	1920	1, 3, 8, 10, 11^{2}
Drewe, Sir C. (K.C.V.O. 1953)	1896	Eton	Woolwich	..	30, 32, 39, 43
Dudley, 2nd E (1885). W. H. Ward, Vt Ednam (1867)	1867	Eton	..	1932	2^{2}
Duff Cooper, A. 1st Vt Norwich (1952)	1890	Eton	Oxford	1954	17, 20, 21, 23^{2}, 25, 28^{2}
Dufferin & Ava, 4th M of (1930). B. S. H.-T.-Blackwood, E of Ava (1918)	1909	Eton	Oxford	1945	23, 26
Dugdale, J.	1905	Wellington	Oxford	1963	33, 34

Name	Born	School	Univ.	Died	Page references
Dugdale, Sir T. L. (1st Bt 1945). 1st Ld Crathorne (1959)	1897	Eton	Sandhurst	..	25, 30, 37, 38
Duke, Sir H. E. (Kt 1918). 1st Ld Merrivale (1925)	1855	Secondary	Glasgow	1939	8, 10
Duncan, Sir A. R. (Kt 1921)	1884			1952	24, 27, 29[4], 32
Dundas, Ld (Scot. judge 1905). D. Dundas	1854	Edinburgh Academy	Oxford & Edinburgh	1922	3
Dundee, 11th E of (1953). H. J. Scrymgeour-Wedderburn, Vt Dudhope (1952)	1902	Winchester	Oxford	..	24, 29, 42
Dunedin, 1st Vt (1926) A. G. Murray, 1st Ld Dunedin (1905)	1849	Harrow	Cambridge	1942	2, 3
Dunglass, Ld (1918) A. F. Douglas-Home. 14th E of Home (1951)	1903	Eton	Oxford	..	31, 37, 39[3], 40
Dunmore, 8th E of (1907). A. E. Murray, Vt Fincastle (1871)	1871			1962	16, 22, 28
Dunrossil, 1st Vt (1959). W. S. Morrison	1893	George Watson's Coll., Edin.	Edinburgh	1961	23[2], 24, 25, 29[2], 32
Durbin, E. F. M.	1906	Taunton	Oxford	1948	35
Ebury, 5th Ld (1932). R. E. Grosvenor	1914	Harrow	..	1957	26
Eccles, 1st Ld (1962). 1st Vt (1963) Sir D. M. Eccles (K.C.V.O.) 1953	1904	Winchester	Oxford	..	37, 38, 40[2], 41
Ede, J. C.	1882	Dorking H.S.*	Cambridge	..	28, 33
Eden, Sir (R.) A. (K.G. 1954). 1st E of Avon (1961)	1897	Eton	Oxford	..	20[2], 21, 23[2], 24, 26, 30, 31, 36, 39
Edmondson, Sir A. J. (Kt 1934). 1st Ld Sandford (1945)	1887	University Coll. Sch.	..	1959	26[2], 31[2], 32
Edwards, Sir C. (Kt 1935)	1867	Elementary	..	1954	19, 30
Edwards, (L.) J.	1904	Aylesbury G.S.*	Leeds	1959	33, 34[2]
Edwards, N.	1897	Elementary	..	..	34, 35
Edwards, W. J.	1900	Secondary	..	..	34
Eldon, 4th E of (1926). J. Scott, Vt Encombe (1900)	1899	Ampleforth	Oxford	..	26, 31
Elgin, 9th E of (1863). V. A. Bruce	1849	Eton	Oxford	1917	4
Elibank, Master of (1st Ld 1912). A. W. C. O. Murray	1870	Cheltenham	..	1920	4, 5, 6, 7
Elliot, W. E.	1888	Glasgow Academy	Glasgow	1958	14, 17[2], 20[2], 23, 24[2]
Elliott, A.	1846	Privately	Edinburgh & Cambridge	1923	1
Ellis, J. E.	1841	Friends' Schs.*	..	1910	4
Elphinstone, 16th Ld (1893). S. H. Elphinstone	1869	Marlborough	..	1955	13
Emmott, 1st Ld (1911). A. Emmott	1858	Grove House, Tottenham*	London	1926	5, 6
Emrys-Evans, P. V.	1894	Harrow	Cambridge	..	28, 31
Erne, 5th E of (1914). J. H. G. Crichton	1907	Eton	Sandhurst	1940	26
Ernle, 1st Ld (1919). R. E. Prothero	1851	Marlborough	Oxford	1937	10[2]
Erroll, 19th E of (1891). C. G. Hay	1852	Harrow	..	1927	3
Erroll, F. J.	1914	Oundle	Cambridge	..	39, 41[2], 42
Evans, S. N.	1898	Elementary	..	..	35
Evans, Sir S. T. (G.C.B. 1916)	1859	Secondary	London	1918	4, 6
Eyres-Monsell, Sir B. M. (G.B.E. 1929). 1st Vt Monsell (1935)	1881	H.M.S. Britannia*	..	..	10, 13, 14, 15, 18 20, 21, 22, 23[2]
Fairfax, 13th Ld (1939). T. B. M. Fairfax	1923	Eton	..	1964	39, 43

Name	Born	School	Univ.	Died	Page references
Guest, I. C. 1st Ld Ashby St Ledgers (1910), 2nd Ld Wimborne (1914), 1st Vt 1918)	1873	Eton	Cambridge	1939	6, 7, 11
Guinness, W. E. 1st Ld Moyne (1932)	1880	Eton	..	1944	14³, 17², 27², 28, 29
Gulland, J. W.	1864	Edinburgh H.S.*	Edinburgh	1920	6², 8
Gwynne, R. S.	1873	Shrewsbury	Cambridge	1924	14
Hacking, 1st Ld (1945). Sir D. H. Hacking (1st Bt 1938)	1884	Giggleswick	Manchester	1950	15, 17², 18, 20, 21, 23, 25
Haden-Guest, 1st Ld (1950). L. H. Haden-Guest	1877	Hulme's G.S.*,	Manchester	1960	36
Hailes, 1st Ld (1957). P. G. T. Buchan-Hepburn	1901	Harrow	Cambridge	..	26, 30, 31, 32, 38, 41, 42²
Hailsham, 1st Vt (1929). Sir D. M. Hogg (Kt 1922), 1st Ld Hailsham (1928)	1872	Eton	..	1950	15, 16, 17², 21², 22²
Hailsham, 2nd Vt (1950–63). Q. M. Hogg	1907	Eton	Oxford	..	39³, 40, 41
Haldane, 1st Vt (1911). R. B. Haldane	1856	Edinburgh Academy	Edinburgh & Göttingen	1928	4, 5, 6, 15
Halifax, 1st E of (1944). E. F. L. Wood. 1st Ld Irwin (1925), 3rd Vt Halifax (1934)	1881	Eton	Oxford	1959	10, 14, 17, 20², 22, 23², 25, 26
Hall, 1st Vt (1946). G. H. Hall	1881	Elementary	..	..	18, 26, 27, 28, 33, 34
Hall, F.	1855	Elementary	..	1933	16
Hall, W. G.	1887	Ellesmere	..	1962	33
Halsbury, 1st E (1898). H. S. Giffard, 1st Ld Halsbury (1885)	1823	Privately	Oxford	1921	1
Hamilton, M of (1885). J. A. E. Hamilton, 3rd D of Abercorn (1913)	1869	Eton	..	1953	3
Hamilton, Ld G.	1845	Harrow	..	1927	2
Hamilton of Dalzell, 2nd Ld (1900). G. G. Hamilton	1872	Eton	Sandhurst	1952	4, 7
Hamilton, Sir R. W. (Kt 1918)	1867	St Paul's	Cambridge	1946	20
Hampden, 3rd Vt (1906). T. W. Brand	1869	Eton	Cambridge	1958	22, 26
Hanbury, R.	1845	Rugby	Oxford	1903	1²
Hankey, 1st Ld (1939). M. P. A. Hankey	1877	Rugby	..	1963	24, 28, 29
Hannan, W.	1906	N. Kelvinside S.S.*	..	..	36
Hanworth, 1st Vt (1936). Sir E. M. Pollock (K.B.E. 1917), 1st Ld Hanworth (1926)	1861	Charterhouse	Cambridge	1936	10, 12, 13
Harcourt, 1st Vt (1916). L. Harcourt	1863	Eton	..	1922	4², 5, 6, 8
Hardman, D. R.	1901	Coleraine Acad. Inst.*	Cambridge	..	33
Hardwicke, 6th E (1897). A. E. P. H. Yorke. Vt Royston (1873)	1867	Eton	..	1904	2³
Hare, J. H. 1st Ld Blakenham (1963).	1911	Eton	..	..	40³, 42
Harlech, 4th Ld (1938). W. G. A. Ormsby-Gore	1885	Eton	Oxford	1964	14, 17, 21³, 23, 25
Harmsworth, 1st Ld (1939). C. B. Harmsworth	1869	Marylebone G.S.*	Dublin	1948	5, 10
Harris, 4th Ld (1872). G. R. C. Harris	1851	Eton	Oxford	1932	3
Harris, F. L.	1886	Winchester	Cambridge	1926	12
Harrison, Sir (J.) H. (1st Bt 1961)	1907	Northampton G.S.*	Oxford	..	43²
Hartington, M of (1908). E. W. S. Cavendish, 10th D of Devonshire (1938)	1895	Eton	Cambridge	1950	23², 28², 31

Name	Born	School	Univ.	Died	Page references
Hartshorn, V.	1872	..	..	1931	16, 18
Harvey, I. D.	1914	Fettes	Oxford	..	40, 42
Hastings, Sir P. (Kt 1924)	1880	Charterhouse	..	1952	16
Hawke, 9th Ld (1939). B. W. Hawke	1901	Winchester	Cambridge	..	39, 43
Hawkesbury, 1st Ld (1893) C. G. S. Foljambe, 1st E of Liverpool (1905)	1846	Eton	..	1907	4
Haworth, Sir A. A. (1st Bt 1911)	1865	Rugby	..	1944	6
Hay, J. A.	1919	Hove & Sussex G.S.*	..	..	41
Hayes, J. H.	1889	Secondary	..	1941	20
Hayes Fisher, W. 1st Ld Downham (1919)	1853	Haileybury	Oxford	1920	1, 3, 8, 10, 11³
Head, 1st Vt (1960). A. H. Head	1906	Eton	Sandhurst	..	38, 40, 42
Headlam, Sir C. M. (1st Bt 1935)	1876	King's Sch., Canterbury	Oxford	1964	17, 21²
Heald, Sir L. F. (Kt 1951)	1897	Charterhouse	Oxford	..	38
Heath, E. R. G.	1916	Chatham House*	Oxford	..	38, 39, 40, 42, 43
Heathcoat Amory, D. 1st Vt Amory (1960)	1899	Eton	Oxford	..	37³, 38, 39, 40
Henderson, 1st Ld (1945). W. W. Henderson	1891	Q. Elizabeth G.S., Darlington*	..	..	33, 36
Henderson of Ardwick, 1st Ld (1950). J. Henderson	1884	Elementary	..	1950	35
Henderson, A.	1863	Elementary	..	1935	8², 9, 15, 18
Henderson, A.	1893	Queen's Coll., Taunton*	Cambridge	..	30², 33, 34²
Henderson, T.	1867	Elementary	..	1960	20
Henderson, Sir V. L. (Kt 1927)	1884	Uppingham	Sandhurst	..	17
Henderson-Stewart, Sir J. (1st Bt 1957)	1897	Morrison's Acad., Crieff*	Edinburgh	1961	37, 41
Hennessy, Sir G. R. J. (1st Bt 1927). 1st Ld Windlesham (1937)	1877	Eton	..	1953	15, 18³, 22
Henry, Sir D. S. (1st Bt 1922)	1864	Mount St Mary's Coll.	Belfast	1925	13²
Herbison, Miss M. M.	1907	Bellshill Acad.*	Glasgow	..	34
Herschell, 2nd Ld (1899). R. F. Herschell	1878	Eton	Oxford	1929	5, 7, 9, 13
Hewart, 1st Vt (1940). Sir G. Hewart (Kt 1916), 1st Ld (1922)	1870	Manchester G.S.	Oxford	1943	10, 12, 13
Hewins, W. A. S.	1865	Wolverhampton G.S.	Oxford	1931	10
Hicks, (E.) G.	1879	Elementary	..	1954	30
Hicks-Beach, M. E. Vt St Aldwyn (1906), 1st E (1914)	1837	Eton	Oxford	1916	1
Hill, Ld (Life Peer 1963) C. Hill	1904	St Olave's	Cambridge	..	37, 41, 42
Hill, J. E. B.	1912	Charterhouse	Oxford	..	43
Hills, J. W.	1867	Eton	Oxford	1938	14
Hoare, Sir S. J. G. (2nd Bt 1915). 1st Vt Templewood (1944)	1880	Harrow	Oxford	1959	14², 17, 20, 23⁵
Hobhouse, Sir C. E. H. (4th Bt 1916)	1862	Eton	Oxford	1941	4, 5, 6²
Hobson, Ld (Life Peer 1963) C. R. Hobson	1904	Elementary	..	..	35
Hodge, J.	1855	Hutchesontown G.S.*	..	1937	11, 12
Hodges, F.	1887	Elementary	..	1947	15
Hogg, Sir D. M (Kt 1922). 1st Ld Hailsham (1928), 1st Vt (1929)	1872	Eton	..	1950	15, 16, 17², 21², 22²
Hogg, Q. M. 2nd Vt Hailsham (1950–63)	1907	Eton	Oxford	..	27, 31, 39³, 40, 41

Name	Born	School	Univ.	Died	Page references
Holden, 3rd Ld (1937). A. W. E. Holden	1898	Eton	Oxford	1951	33
Home, 14th E of (1951–63). A. F. Douglas-Home, Ld Dunglass (1918)	1903	Eton	Oxford	..	31, 37, 39³, 40
Hope, Ld J. A. 1st Ld Glendevon (1964)	1912	Eton	Oxford	..	36, 39, 40, 41, 42
Hope, J. F. 1st Ld Rankeillour (1932)	1870	Oratory Sch.	Oxford	1949	9, 11, 13
Hope, A. O. J. 2nd Ld Rankeillour (1949)	1897	Oratory Sch.	Sandhurst	1958	25, 26²
Hopkinson, H. L. D. 1st Ld Colyton (1955)	1902	Eton	Cambridge	..	37², 40
Hore-Belisha, 1st Ld (1954). L. Hore-Belisha	1893	Clifton	Paris, Heidelberg & Oxford	1957	20, 21², 24, 25², 32
Horne, 1st Vt (1937). Sir R. S. Horne (K.B.E. 1918)	1871	George Watson's Coll., Edin.	Glasgow	1940	9, 11²
Hornsby-Smith, Dame (M.) P. (D.B.E. 1961)	1914	Richmond*	..	..	37, 40, 42²
Horobin, Sir I. M. (Kt 1955)	1899	Highgate	Cambridge	..	42
Horsburgh, Lady (Life Peeress 1959). Miss F. Horsburgh	1889	St Hilda's, Folkestone*	..	..	24, 28, 32 37, 38,
Howard, G. W. A.	1877		Cambridge	1935	7, 8, 13
Howe, 4th E (1900). R. G. P. Curzon, Vt Curzon (1876)	1861	Eton	Oxford	1929	3³
Howe, 5th E (1929). F. R. H. P. Curzon, Vt Curzon (1900)	1884	Eton	Oxford	1964	18
Hudson, 1st Vt (1952). R. S. Hudson	1886	Eton	Oxford	1957	20, 24³, 25, 27, 31
Hudson, Sir A. U. M. (1st Bt 1942)	1897	Eton	Sandhurst	1956	21, 22, 23, 24, 27, 32
Hughes-Young, M. H. C.	1912	Harrow	Sandhurst	..	43
Hunter, Ld (Scot. judge 1911). W. Hunter	1865			1957	6
Huntingdon, 15th E of (1939). F. J. C. W. P. Hastings, Vt Hastings (1901)	1901	Eton	Oxford	..	33
Hutchison, 1st Ld (1932) R. Hutchison	1873			1950	25
Hutchison, Sir J. R. H. (1st Bt 1956)	1893	Harrow	..	..	38
Hylton, 3rd Ld (1899). H. G. H. Joliffe	1862	Eton	Oxford	1945	9, 13², 15
Hylton-Foster, Sir H. B. H. (Kt 1954)	1905	Eton	Oxford	..	38, 43
Hynd, J. B.	1902	Secondary	..	..	35²
Illingworth, 1st Ld (1921). A. H. Illingworth	1865	London International Coll.* & Switzerland	..	1942	12
Illingworth, P. H.	1869		Cambridge	1915	6²
Ingleby, 1st Vt (1955). O. Peake	1897	Eton	Sandhurst & Oxford	..	23, 26², 31, 37, 38², 41
Inman, 1st Ld (1946). P. A. Inman	1892	Harrogate*	Leeds	..	33
Inskip, Sir T. W. H. (Kt 1922). 1st Vt Caldecote (1939)	1876	Clifton	Cambridge	1947	15, 17, 18², 22², 23, 25, 28
Inverforth, 1st Ld (1919). A. Weir	1865	Secondary	..	1955	11
Irwin, 1st Ld (1925). E. F. L. Wood. 3rd Vt Halifax (1934). 1st E of (1944)	1881	Eton	Oxford	1959	10, 14, 17, 20², 22, 23², 25, 26
Isaacs, G. A.	1883	Elementary	..	..	34, 35
Isaacs, Sir R. D. (Kt 1910). 1st Ld Reading (1914), 1st Vt (1916), 1st E of (1917), 1st M of (1926)	1860	University Coll. Sch.	..	1935	5, 6², 20

Name	Born	School	Univ.	Died	Page references
Kitchener of Khartoum, 1st E (1914). H. H. Kitchener, 1st Ld (1898), 1st Vt (1902)	1850	France	Woolwich	1916	6, 8
Lambert, 1st Vt (1945). G. Lambert	1866	Privately	..	1958	4, 5
Lane-Fox, G. R. 1st Ld Bingley (1933)	1870	Eton	Oxford	1947	14, 17
Lansbury, G.	1859	Elementary	..	1940	19
Lansdowne, 5th M of (1866). H. C. K. Petty-Fitzmaurice, Vt Clanmaurice (1845). E of Kerry (1863)	1845	Eton	Oxford	1927	1, 2, 8
Lansdowne, 8th M of (1944). G. J. C. M. N. Petty-Fitzmaurice	1912	Eton	Oxford	..	40, 43
Law, A. Bonar	1858	Glasgow H.S.*	..	1923	2, 8, 9, 10, 13
Law, R. K. 1st Ld Coleraine (1954)	1901	Shrewsbury	Oxford	..	26^{2}, 30, 32
Lawrence, 2nd Ld (1879). J. H. Lawrence	1846	Wellington	Cambridge	1913	3
Lawrence, Miss (A.) S.	1871		Cambridge	1947	19
Lawson, 1st Ld (1950). J. J. Lawson	1881	Elementary	..	..	16, 19, 34
Lawson, Sir J. G. (1st Bt 1905)	1856	Harrow	Oxford	1919	2
Leach, W.	1870	Bradford G.S.	..	1949	16
Leathers, 1st Vt (1954). F. J. Leathers, 1st Ld (1941)	1883			..	30, 32, 37
Leburn, (W.) G.	1913	Strathallan*	..	1963	41
Lee of Fareham, 1st Vt (1922). Sir A. Lee (K.C.B. 1916). 1st Ld (1918)	1868	Cheltenham	Woolwich	1947	1, 8, 10^{2}
Lee, F.	1906	Langworthy Rd.*	..	..	34
Lees-Smith, H. B.	1878	Aldenham	..	1941	19^{2}
Legh, P. R. 4th Ld Newton (1960)	1915	Eton	Oxford	..	43^{4}
Lennox-Boyd, A. T. 1st Vt Boyd (1960)	1904	Sherborne	Oxford	..	23, 24^{2}, 28, 32, 37^{2}, 38, 40
Leonard, W.	1887	Elementary	..	..	35
Lever, Sir (S.) H. (K.C.B. 1917)	1869	Merchant Taylors' Sch., Crosby	..	1947	9
Lewis, Sir (J.) H. (G.B.E. 1922)	1858	Secondary	McGill & Oxford	1933	4, 6^{2}, 8, 10
Lewis, T. A.	1881		Cardiff	1923	13
Lincolnshire, 1st M of (1912). C. R. Wynn-Carrington, 3rd Ld Carrington (1868), 1st E (1895)	1843	Eton	Cambridge	1928	4, 5^{2}
Lindgren, Ld (Life Peer 1961). G. S. Lindgren	1900	Elementary	..	..	33, 34, 35
Lindsay, K.	1897	St Olave's	Oxford	..	23^{2}
Linlithgow, 1st M of (1902). J. A. L. Hope, 7th E of Hopetoun (1873)	1860	Eton	..	1908	2, 3
Linlithgow, 2nd M of (1908). V. A. J. Hope, E of Hopetoun (1902)	1887	Eton	..	1952	14
Listowel, 5th E of (1931). W. F. Hare, Vt Ennismore (1924)	1906	Eton	Oxford	..	28, 33^{2}, 34, 35
Liverpool, 1st E of (1905). C. G. S. Foljambe, 1st Ld Hawkesbury (1893)	1846	Eton	..	1907	4
Liverpool, 2nd E of (1907). A. W. D. S. Foljambe, Vt Hawkesbury (1905)	1870	Eton	Sandhurst	1941	7
Llewellin, 1st Ld (1945). J. J. Llewellin	1893	Eton	Oxford	1957	23, 24, 28^{3}, 29^{2}, 30^{2}, 32

Name	Born	School	Univ.	Died	Page references
Llewellyn, Sir D. T. (Kt 1960)	1916	Eton	Cambridge	..	36
Lloyd, 1st Ld (1925). Sir G. A. Lloyd (G.C.I.E. 1918)	1879	Eton	Cambridge	1941	28
Lloyd, 2nd Ld (1941). A. D. F. Lloyd	1912	Eton	Cambridge	..	37^2, 39, 40
Lloyd, G.	1902	Harrow	Cambridge	..	23, 24, 28, 30, 32, 38, 40, 42
Lloyd, (J.) S. B.	1904	Fettes	Cambridge	..	36, 38, 39^2, 40
Lloyd George of Dwyfor, 1st E (1945). D. Lloyd George	1863	Llanystumdwy Church Sch.*	..	1945	4, 5, 8^2, 9
Lloyd-George, G. 1st Vt Tenby (1957)	1894	Eastbourne	Cambridge	..	21, 24, 28^2, 29, 32, 37^2, 38, 40
Lloyd-Greame, Sir P. (K.B.E. 1920). *Changed name to Sir P. Cunliffe-Lister in* 1924, 1st Vt Swinton (1935). 1st E of Swinton (1955)	1884	Winchester	Oxford	..	11^2, 14, 17^2, 20, 21, 23^2, 28, 29, 32, 37, 38^2
Loch, 2nd Ld (1900). E. D. Loch	1873	Winchester		1942	7, 16, 20, 22
Lochee of Gowrie, 1st Ld (1908) E. Robertson	1846		St Andrew's & Oxford	1911	4
Locker-Lampson, G. L. T.	1875	Eton	Cambridge	1946	14, 17^2
Londonderry, 6th M of (1884). C. S. Vane-Tempest-Stewart. Vt Castlereagh (1872)	1852	Eton	Oxford	1915	1, 2^3
Londonderry, 7th M of (1915). C. S. H. Vane-Tempest-Stewart. Vt Castlereagh (1884)	1878	Eton	Sandhurst	1949	12, 17, 20, 21^2, 23
Long, 1st Vt (1921). W. H. Long	1854	Harrow	Oxford	1924	1, 2^2, 8, 10^2
Longford, 7th E of (1961). F. A. Pakenham, 1st Ld Pakenham (1945)	1905	Eton	Oxford	..	33, 34^3, 35^2, 36
Loreburn, 1st E (1911). Sir R. T. Reid (Kt 1894), 1st Ld Loreburn (1906)	1846	Cheltenham	Oxford	1923	3, 5
Lothian, 11th M of (1930). P. H. Kerr	1882	Oratory Sch.	Oxford	1940	20, 21
Lough, T.	1850	Wesleyan Sch., Dublin*	..	1922	4
Lovat, 16th Ld (1887). S. J. Fraser	1871	Fort Augustus Abbey	Oxford	1933	17
Lovat, 17th Ld (1933). S. C. J. Fraser	1911	Ampleforth	Oxford	..	31
Low, Sir T. A. R. W. (K.C.M.G. 1957), 1st Ld Aldington (1962)	1914	Winchester	Oxford	..	37, 38, 41
Lucan, 5th E of (1914). G. C. Bingham, Ld Bingham (1888)	1860	Harrow	Sandhurst	1949	13, 15, 18^2, 22, 26
Lucan, 6th E of (1949). G. C. P. Bingham, Ld Bingham (1914)	1898	Eton	Sandhurst	..	33, 36
Lucas of Chilworth, 1st Ld (1946). G. W. Lucas	1896	Elementary	..	..	35, 36^2
Lucas & Dingwall, 8th & 11th Ld (1905). A. T. Herbert	1876	Bedford G.S.*	Oxford	1916	5^3, 6
Lucas-Tooth, Sir H. V. H. D. (1st Bt 1920)	1903	Eton	Oxford	..	36, 40
Lunn, W.	1872	Elementary	..	1942	16, 19^2
Lyttelton, A.	1857	Eton	Cambridge	1913	2
Lyttelton, O. 1st Vt Chandos (1954)	1893	Eton	Cambridge	..	26, 27^2, 29, 31^2, 37
Lytton, 2nd E of (1891). V. A. G. R. Lytton	1876	Eton	Cambridge	1947	7, 10^3

Name	Born	School	Univ.	Died	Page references
Mabane, 1st Ld 1962, Sir W. Mabane (K.B.E. 1954)	1895	Woodhouse Grove*	Cambridge	..	23, 25, 26, 28, 31
Macartney, Sir W. (K.C.M.G. 1913)	1852	Eton	Oxford	1924	1
McCorquodale, 1st Ld (1955). M. S. McCorquodale	1901	Harrow	Oxford	..	27, 31
McCurdy, C. A.	1870	Loughboro' G.S.*	Cambridge	1941	12^3
Macdonald, of Gwaenysgor, 1st Ld (1949). G. Macdonald	1888	Elementary	..	..	34, 35
MacDonald, J. Ramsay	1866	Elementary	..	1937	15^2, 18, 20, 22
MacDonald, M. J.	1901	Bedales*	Oxford	..	20, 23^4, 28
McEwen, Sir J. H. F. (1st Bt 1953)	1894	Eton	Oxford	1962	24, 30
McKenna, R.	1863	Privately	London	1943	3, 4, 5^2, 7
Mackeson, Sir H. R. (1st Bt 1954)	1905	Rugby	Sandhurst	..	37, 38
Maclay, 1st Ld (1922). Sir J. P. Maclay (1st Bt 1914)	1857	Glasgow H.S.*	..	1951	12
Maclay, J. S. 1st Vt Muirshiel (1964)	1905	Winchester	Cambridge	..	31, 38, 40, 41
Maclean, Sir D. (K.B.E. 1917)	1864	Secondary	..	1932	20, 21
Maclean, Sir F. (1st Bt 1957)	1911	Eton	Cambridge	..	38, 42
Macleod, I. N.	1913	Fettes	Cambridge	..	38, 40^2, 42
Macmillan, Ld (Ld of Appeal 1930). H. P. Macmillan	1873		Edinburgh & Glasgow	1952	16, 24
Macmillan, (M.) H.	1894	Eton	Oxford	..	28^2, 29, 31, 37^2, 39^3
Macnamara, T. J.	1861	St Thomas', Exeter*	..	1931	4, 5, 7, 10, 11
McNeil, H.	1907	Woodside, Glasg.*	Glasgow	1955	33^2, 34
McNeill, R. J. 1st Ld Cushendun (1927)	1861	Harrow	Oxford	1936	14, 17^4
Macpherson, Sir I. (1st Bt 1933). 1st Ld Strathcarron (1936)	1880	George Watson's Coll., Edin.	Edinburgh	1937	10, 11, 12
Macpherson, N. M. S. 1st Ld Drumalbyn (1963)	1908	Fettes	Oxford	..	41^2
MacRobert, A. M.	1873	Paisley G.S. & Acad.*	Glasgow & Edinburgh	1930	18^2
Mallet, Sir C. E. (Kt 1917)	1862	Harrow	Oxford	1947	6
Malmesbury, 5th E of (1899). J. E. Harris	1872		Oxford	1950	15
Manchester, 9th D of (1892). W. A. D. Montagu	1877	Eton	Cambridge	1947	5
Mancroft, 1st Ld (1937). Sir A. M. Samuel (1st Bt, 1932)	1872	Secondary	..	1942	17^2
Mancroft, 2nd Ld (1942). S. M. S. Mancroft	1914	Winchester	Oxford	..	37, 39, 40^2, 42
Manningham-Buller, Sir R. E. (Kt 1951), 1st Ld Dilhorne (1962)	1905	Eton	Oxford	..	32, 38^2, 42
Marchamley, 1st Ld (1908). G. Whiteley	1855	Abroad	Zürich	1925	4, 6
Marchwood, 1st Vt (1945). Sir F. G. Penny (Kt 1929), 1st Ld Marchwood (1937)	1876	K. Edward VI G.S., Southampton*	..	1955	18, 22^4, 26
Margesson, 1st Vt (1942). (H.) D. R. Margesson	1890	Harrow	Cambridge	..	18, 22^2, 25, 30^2
Marlborough, 9th D of (1892). C. R. J. Spencer-Churchill, M of Blandford (1883)	1871	Winchester	Cambridge	1934	2^2, 10
Marley, 1st Ld (1930). D. L. Aman	1884	Marlborough & R.N.C. Greenwich	..	1952	19, 20
Marples, E.	1907	Stretford G.S.*	..	..	37, 38, 41, 42^2
Marquand, H. A.	1901	Cardiff H.S.*	Cardiff	..	34^3, 35^3
Marshall, F.	1883	Elementary	..	1962	34
Masterman, C. F. G.	1873	Weymouth*	Cambridge	1927	5^2, 6^2
Mathers, 1st Ld (1951). G. Mathers	1886	Elementary	..	..	31, 36

Name	Born	School	Univ.	Died	Page references
Mott-Radclyffe, Sir C. E. (Kt 1957)	1911	Eton	Oxford	..	32
Mount Temple, 1st Ld (1932). W. W. Ashley	1867	Harrow	Oxford	1939	14, 15, 18
Moyne, 1st Ld (1932). W. E. Guinness	1880	Eton	..	1944	14^3, 17^2, 27^2, 28, 29
Muir, J. W.	1879		..	1931	16
Muir-Mackenzie, 1st Ld (1915). Sir K. A. Muir-Mackenzie (K.C.B. 1898)	1845	Charterhouse	Oxford	1930	16, 20
Muirhead, A. J.	1890	Eton	Oxford	1939	23, 24^2
Munro, P.	1883	Leeds G.S.	Oxford	1942	25, 30
Munro, R. 1st Ld Alness (1934)	1868	Aberdeen G.S.*	Edinburgh	1955	6, 8, 11
Munster, 5th E of (1928). G. W. R. H. FitzClarence	1906	Charterhouse	..	..	22, 25^2, 26^2, 28, 31, 37, 38, 42
Murray, Ld (Scot. judge 1922). C. D. Murray	1866	Edinburgh Academy	Edinburgh	1936	13^2
Murray, A. G. 1st Ld Dunedin (1905). 1st Vt (1926)	1849	Harrow	Cambridge	1942	2, 3
Murray, Sir (T.) D. K. (Kt 1941). Ld Birnam (Scot. judge 1945)	1884	Hamilton Acad.* & Glasgow H.S.*	Glasgow	1955	30, 32
Nathan, 1st Ld (1940). H. L. Nathan	1889	St Paul's	..	1964	34, 35
Neal, A.	1862	Wesley Coll., Sheffield*	..	1933	11
Neal, H.	1897	Elementary	..	..	35
Neave, A. M. S.	1916	Eton	Oxford	..	41, 42
Newton, 2nd Ld (1899). T. W. Legh	1857	Eton	Oxford	1942	7, 8, 10
Newton, 4th Ld (1960). P. R. Legh	1915	Eton	Oxford	..	43^4
Nicholls, Sir H. (1st Bt 1960)	1912	Q. Mary's G.S., Walsall*	..	..	40, 42
Nicolson, Sir H. G. (K.C.V.O. 1953)	1886	Wellington	Oxford	..	28
Noble, Sir A. H. P. (K.C.M.G. 1959)	1908	Radley	..	..	38, 39, 40, 41
Noel-Baker, P. J.	1889	Bootham	Cambridge	..	30, 33^2, 34, 35
Noel-Buxton, 1st Ld (1930). N. E. N. Buxton	1869	Harrow	Cambridge	1948	15, 18
Norfolk, 15th D of (1860). H. FitzAlan-Howard, E of Arundel (1847)	1847	Oratory Sch.	..	1917	2
Norfolk, 16th D of (1917). B. M. FitzAlan-Howard, E of Arundel (1908)	1908	Oratory Sch.	..	..	27, 31
Norman, Sir H. (Kt 1906)	1858	Privately	Harvard & Leipzig	1939	6
Normanby, 4th M of (1932). O. C. J. Phipps, E of Mulgrave (1912)	1912	Eton	Oxford	..	31, 32
Normand, Ld (Ld of Appeal 1947). W. G. Normand	1884	Fettes	Oxford, Paris & Edinburgh	1962	18, 22^2
Northumberland, 10th D of (1940). H. A. Percy	1914	Eton	Oxford	..	32
Norton, C. W. 1st Ld Rathcreedan (1916)	1845	Abroad	Dublin & Sandhurst	1930	4, 6^2
Norwich, 1st Vt (1952). A. Duff Cooper	1890	Eton	Oxford	1954	17, 20, 21, 23^2, 25, 28^2
Novar, 1st Vt (1920). Sir R. C. Munro-Ferguson (G.C.M.G. 1914)	1860	Privately	Sandhurst	1934	14
Nugent, Sir (G.) R. H. (1st Bt 1960)	1907	Imperial Service Coll.	Woolwich	..	37, 40, 41
Nutting, (H.) A.	1920	Eton	Cambridge	..	36^2, 39

Name	Born	School	Univ.	Died	Page references
)akshott, Ld (Life Peer 1964) Sir H.D. Oakshott(1st Bt 1959)	1904	Rugby	Cambridge	..	39, 43^3
)'Brien, Sir I. J. (1st Bt 1916). 1st Ld Shandon (1918)	1857	Secondary & Privately	Univ. of Ireland	1930	6, 7, 12
)'Connor, C. A.	1854	St Stanislaus Coll.*	Dublin	1928	6, 7
)'Connor, Sir J. (Kt 1925)	1872	Blackrock Coll.		1931	7, 8, 13
)'Connor, Sir T. J. (Kt 1936)	1891			1940	25
)gmore, 1st Ld (1950). D. R. Rees-Williams	1903	Mill Hill	Wales	..	33^2, 34
)'Hagan, 3rd Ld (1900). M. H. T. Townley-O'Hagan	1882	Marlborough	Cambridge	1961	5, 7
)liver, G. H.	1888	Bolton*	..	..	33
)livier, 1st Ld (1924). S. Olivier	1859	Lausanne & Tonbridge	Oxford	1943	16
)'Neill, Sir (R. W.) H. (1st Bt 1929). 1st Ld Rathcavan (1953)	1883	Eton	Oxford	..	24
)nslow, 4th E of (1870). W. H. Onslow. Vt Cranley (1855)	1853	Eton	Oxford	1911	1, 2^2
)nslow, 5th E of (1911). R. W. A. Onslow, Vt Cranley (1876)	1876	Eton	Oxford	1945	10^3, 13, 14^2, 17^2
)nslow, 6th E of (1945). W. A. B. Onslow. Vt Cranley (1913)	1913	Winchester	Sandhurst	..	39, 43
)rmsby-Gore, W. G. A. 4th Ld Harlech (1938)	1885	Eton	Oxford	..	14, 17, 21^3, 23, 25
)rmsby-Gore, Sir (W.) D. (K.C.M.G. 1961) 5th Ld Harlech (1964)	1918	Eton	Oxford	..	39^2
)rr Ewing, C. I.	1912	Harrow	Oxford	..	41^2, 42
)wen, Sir G. (Kt 1944)	1881	Ardwyn G.S.*	Aberystwyth	1963	22
)xford & Asquith, 1st E of (1925). H. H. Asquith	1852	City of London	Oxford	1928	3, 5, 6, 7
'age-Croft, Sir H. (1st Bt 1924). 1st Ld Croft (1940)	1881	Eton & Shrewsbury	Oxford	1947	30^2, 32
'akenham, 1st Ld (1945). F. A. Pakenham, 7th E of Longford (1961)	1905	Eton	Oxford	..	33, 34^3, 35^2, 36
'aling, W.	1883	Elementary		..	19, 29, 30, 35^2
'arker, J.	1863	Wesleyan Sch.*	..	1948	13
'arker, J.	1906	Marlborough	Oxford	..	33
'arkinson, J. A.	1870	Elementary	..	1941	16, 19^2
'armoor, 1st Ld (1914). Sir C. A. Cripps (K.C.V.O. 1908)	1852	Winchester	Oxford	1941	15, 18
'artington, O. 2nd Ld Doverdale (1925)	1872	Rossall	..	1935	6
'assfield, 1st Ld (1929). S. J. Webb	1859	Switzerland & Secondary	..	1947	16, 19^2
'eake, O. 1st Vt Ingleby (1955)	1897	Eton	Sandhurst & Oxford	..	23, 26^2, 31, 37, 38^2, 41
'earson, A.	1898	Elementary	..	..	36^2
'ease, Sir A. F. (1st Bt 1920)	1866	Brighton	Cambridge	1927	10
'ease, J. A. 1st Ld Gainford (1917)	1860	Tottenham*	Cambridge	1943	4, 5, 6^3, 8
'eat, C. U.	1892	Sedbergh	Oxford	..	29^2, 32
'eel, 1st E (1929). W. R. W. Peel, 2nd Vt (1912)	1867	Harrow	Oxford	1937	9, 10, 11^2, 12^2, 14, 17^2, 21
'embroke & Montgomery, 14th E of (1895). S. Herbert	1853	Eton	Oxford	1913	3
'enny, Sir F. G. (Kt 1929), 1st Ld Marchwood (1937), 1st Vt (1945)	1876	K. Edward VI G.S., Southampton*	..	1955	18, 22^4, 26
'entland, 1st Ld (1909). J. Sinclair	1860	Edinburgh Academy & Wellington	Sandhurst	1925	4, 6^2
'ercy, Earl (1871). H. A. G. Percy	1871	Eton	Oxford	1909	1, 2

Name	Born	School	Univ.	Died	Page references
Percy of Newcastle, 1st Ld (1953). Ld E. Percy	1887	Eton	Oxford	1958	14[2], 17, 24
Perkins, Sir R. D. (Kt 1954)	1903	Eton	Cambridge	..	28, 32
Perth, 17th E of (1951) Vt Strathallan (1937)	1907	Downside	Cambridge	..	40
Pethick-Lawrence, 1st Ld (1945). F. W. Pethick-Lawrence	1871	Eton	Cambridge	1961	18, 34
Pickthorn, Sir K. W. M. (1st Bt 1959)	1892	Aldenham	Cambridge	..	37
Pike, Miss M.	1918	Hunmanby Hall	Reading	..	42
Pike Pease, H. 1st Ld Daryngton (1923)	1867	Brighton Coll.	Cambridge	1949	8, 12
Pilkington, Sir R. A. (K.B.E. 1961)	1908	Charterhouse	Oxford	..	27, 31
Pim, J.	1858		Dublin	1949	7[2]
Pitt, Dame E. M. (D.B.E.) 1962	1906	Bordesley Green, Birmingham*	..	..	42[2]
Plymouth, 2nd E of (1923). I. M. Windsor-Clive	1889	Eton	Cambridge	1943	17, 18, 20, 21, 23
Plunkett, Sir H.	1854	Eton	Oxford	1932	2, 4
Pollock, Sir E. M. (K.B.E. 1917). 1st Ld Hanworth (1926), 1st Vt (1936)	1861	Charterhouse	Cambridge	1936	10, 12, 13
Ponsonby, 1st Ld (1930). A. A. W. H. Ponsonby	1871	Eton	Oxford	1946	15, 19[3]
Popplewell, E.	1899	Elementary	..	..	36
Portal, 1st Vt (1945). Sir W. R. Portal (3rd Bt 1931). 1st Ld (1935)	1885	Eton	Oxford	1949	29, 30
Portland, 6th D of (1879). W. J. A. C. J. Cavendish-Bentinck	1857	Eton	..	1943	3
Portland, 7th D of (1943). W. A. Cavendish-Bentinck, M of Titchfield (1893)	1893	Eton	Sandhurst	..	18, 22
Portsmouth, 6th E of (1891). N. Wallop, Vt Lymington (1856)	1856	Eton	Oxford	1917	4
Powell, J. B.	1862			1923	13
Powell, (J.) E.	1912	King Edward's, Birmingham	Cambridge	..	39, 40, 42
Pratt, Sir J. W. (Kt 1922)	1873	S. Shields*	Glasgow	1952	11, 13
Pretyman, E. G.	1860	Eton	Woolwich	1931	1[2], 8, 10
Primrose, N. J. A.	1882	Eton	Oxford	1917	5, 12
Profumo, J. D.	1915	Harrow	Oxford	..	38, 39, 40[2], 41, 42
Prothero, R. E. 1st Ld Ernle	1851	Marlborough	Oxford	1937	10
Pybus, Sir (P.) J. (1st Bt 1934)	1880		..	1935	21
Pym, L. R.	1884	Bedford	Cambridge	1945	30, 32
Raglan, 3rd Ld (1884). G. F. H. Somerset	1857	Eton	Sandhurst	1921	2
Ramsbotham, H. 1st Ld Soulbury (1941), 1st Vt (1954)	1887	Uppingham	Oxford	..	20, 23[3], 25[2], 28
Ramsden, J. E.	1923	Eton	Oxford	..	42
Rankeillour, 1st Ld (1932). J. F. Hope	1870	Oratory Sch.	Oxford	1949	9, 11, 13
Rankeillour, 2nd Ld (1949). A. O. J. Hope	1897	Oratory Sch.	Sandhurst	1958	25, 26[2]
Ranksborough, 1st Ld (1914). J. F. Brocklehurst	1852	Rugby	Cambridge	1921	7, 9, 13
Rathcavan, 1st Ld (1953). Sir (R. W.) H. O'Neill (1st Bt 1929)	1883	Eton	Oxford	..	24
Rathcreedan, 1st Ld (1916). C. W. Norton	1845	Abroad	Dublin & Sandhurst	1930	4, 6[2]
Rea, 1st Ld (1937). Sir W. R. Rea (1st Bt 1935)	1873	University Coll. Sch.	..	1948	7, 8, 13, 22

Name	Born	School	Univ.	Died	Page references
Reading, 1st M of (1926). Sir R. D. Isaacs (Kt 1910), 1st Ld Reading (1914), 1st Vt (1916), 1st E of (1917)	1860	University Coll. Sch	..	1935	5, 6^2, 20
Reading, 2nd M of (1935). G. R. Isaacs, Vt Erleigh (1917)	1889	Rugby	Oxford	1960	36^2, 39
Redmayne, M.	1910	Radley	..	..	39, 43^2
Rees-Williams, D. R. 1st Ld Ogmore (1950)	1903	Mill Hill	Wales	..	33^2, 34
Reid, Ld (Ld of Appeal 1948). J. S. C. Reid	1890	Edinburgh Academy	Cambridge	..	25, 30^2, 32
Reid, Sir R. T. (Kt 1894). 1st Ld Loreburn (1906), 1st E (1911)	1846	Cheltenham	Oxford	1923	3, 5
Reith, 1st Ld (1940). Sir J. C. W. (Kt 1927)	1889	Glasgow Academy & Gresham's	..	..	24, 30^2
Renton, D. L.	1908	Oundle	Oxford	..	40, 42
Rhodes, H.	1895	Elementary	..	..	34
Rhondda, 1st Vt (1917). D. A. Thomas	1856	Privately	Cambridge	1918	11, 12
Richards, R.	1884	Elementary	..	1954	16
Ridley, 1st Vt (1900). Sir M. White Ridley (5th Bt 1877)	1842	Harrow	Oxford	1904	1
Ripon, 1st M of (1871). G. F. S. Robinson, Vt Goderich (1833), 1st E of Ripon (1859)	1827	Privately	..	1909	3, 5
Rippon, (A.) G. F.	1924	King's Coll., Taunton	Oxford	..	40
Ritchie, 1st Ld (1905). C. T. Ritchie	1838	City of London	..	1906	1^2, 2
Robens, Ld (Life Peer 1961). A. Robens	1910	Secondary	..	..	34, 35
Roberts, C. H.	1865	Marlborough	Oxford	1959	5, 9
Roberts, F. O.	1876	Elementary	..	1941	16, 19
Roberts, G. H.	1869	Elementary	..	1928	8, 11^2, 12, 13
Robertson, E. 1st Ld Lochee of Gowrie (1908)	1846		St Andrew's & Oxford	1911	4
Robertson, J.	1867	Elementary	..	1926	6
Robertson, J. J.	1898	Elementary	..	1955	34
Robertson, J. M.	1856	Stirling*	..	1933	16
Robson, Ld (Ld of Appeal 1910) Sir W .S. Robson (Kt 1905)	1852	Privately	Cambridge	1918	4^2, 6
Rochester, 1st Ld (1931). Sir E. H. Lamb (Kt 1914)	1876	Dulwich & Wycliffe Coll.	..	1955	21, 25
Rodgers, J. C.	1906	St Peter's, York	Oxford	..	41
Rosebery, 6th E of (1929). A. E. H. M. A. Primrose, Ld Dalmeny (1882)	1882	Eton	Sandhurst	..	31
Ross, Sir J. (1st Bt 1919)	1854	Foyle Coll.*	Dublin	1935	12
Rothermere, 1st Vt (1919). Sir H. S. Harmsworth (1st Bt 1910), 1st Ld Rothermere (1914)	1868	Secondary	..	1940	12
Rothschild, J. A. de	1878	Lycée Louis le Grand*	Cambridge	1957	29
Royle, C.	1896	Stockport G.S.*	..	..	36
Runciman, of Doxford 1st Vt (1937). W. Runciman, 2nd Ld Runciman (1933)	1870	S. Shields H.S* & Privately	Cambridge	1949	3, 4, 5^2, 6, 8, 21, 22, 24
Rushcliffe, 1st Ld (1935). Sir H. B. Betterton (1st Bt 1929)	1872	Rugby	Oxford	1949	14, 17, 20, 21
Russell, 2nd E (1878). J. F. S. Russell	1865	Winchester	Oxford	1931	19^2

Name	Born	School	Univ.	Died	Page references
Russell, Ld (Scot. judge 1936) A. Russell	1884	Glasgow Academy	Glasgow	..	25
Russell, Sir T. W. (1st Bt 1917)	1841	Madras Acad., Fife*	..	1920	2, 4, 6, 8, 10
St Aldwyn, 1st E (1914). M. E. Hicks-Beach, 1st Vt St Aldwyn (1906)	1837	Eton	Oxford	1916	1
St Aldwyn, 2nd E (1916). M. J. Hicks-Beach	1912	Eton	Oxford	..	37, 40, 43
St Audries, 1st Ld (1911). Sir A. F. Acland Hood (4th Bt 1892)	1853	Eton	Oxford	1917	3^2
St Oswald, 4th Ld (1957). R. D. G. Winn	1916	Stowe	Bonn & Freiburg	..	43
Salisbury, 3rd M of (1868). R. A. T. Gascoyne-Cecil, Vt Cranborne (1865)	1830	Eton	Oxford	1903	1^3
Salisbury, 4th M of (1903). J. E. H. Gascoyne-Cecil, Vt Cranborne (1868)	1861	Eton	Oxford	1947	1^2, 2, 13, 14, 16
Salisbury, 5th M of (1947). R. A. J. Gascoyne-Cecil, Vt Cranborne (1903)	1893	Eton	Oxford	..	23, 26, 27, 28^3, 29^2, 31, 36^2, 37, 39
Salter, 1st Ld (1953). Sir (J.) (A. Salter K.C.B. 1922)	1881	Oxford H.S.*	Oxford	..	24, 29, 30, 32, 36, 38
Salvesen, Ld (Scot. judge 1905). E. Salvesen	1857	Collegiate Sch., Edin.*	Edinburgh	1942	3
Samuel, 1st Vt (1937). Sir H. L. Samuel (G.B.E. 1920)	1870	University Coll. Sch.	Oxford	1963	4, 5, 6^3, 7, 8^2, 20
Samuel, Sir A. M. (1st Bt 1932). 1st Ld Mancroft (1937)	1872	Norwich G.S.*	..	1942	17^2
Samuels, A. W.	1852	Royal Sch., Dungannon*	Dublin	1925	13^2
Sanders, Sir R. A. (1st Bt 1920). 1st Ld Bayford (1929)	1867	Harrow	Oxford	1940 1959	11, 13^2, 14
Sanders, W. S.	1871	Elementary	Berlin	1941	19
Sandford, 1st Ld (1945). Sir A. J. Edmondson (Kt 1934)	1887	University Coll. Sch.	..	1959	26^2, 31^2, 32
Sandhurst, 1st Vt (1917). W. Mansfield, 2nd Ld Sandhurst (1876)	1855	Rugby	..	1921	7, 9, 13
Sandys, D.	1908	Eton	Oxford	..	29, 30^2, 32, 37, 38, 40^4
Sankey, 1st Vt (1932). Sir J. Sankey (Kt 1914), 1st Ld (1929)	1866	Lancing	Oxford	1948	18, 20
Sassoon, Sir P. A. G. D. (3rd Bt 1912)	1888	Eton	Oxford	1939	17, 20, 23, 25^2
Saye & Sele, 18th Ld (1907). G. C. T.- W.-Fiennes	1858	Eton		1937	7
Scarbrough, 11th E of (1945). L. R. Lumley	1896	Eton	Sandhurst & Oxford	..	31
Scott, Sir L. F. (Kt 1922)	1869	Rugby	Oxford	1950	13
Scott, Sir (R.) D. (Kt 1955)	1901	Mill Hill	Cambridge	..	31
Seely, J. E. B. 1st Ld Mottistone (1933)	1868	Harrow	Cambridge	1947	5, 6^2, 11, 12
Sefton, 6th E of (1901). O. C. Molyneux	1871			1930	5
Sefton, 7th E of (1930). H. W. O. Molyneux	1898	Harrow	Sandhurst	..	26
Selborne, 2nd E of (1895). W. W. Palmer, Vt Wolmer (1882)	1859	Winchester	Oxford	1942	1, 2, 8
Selborne, 3rd E of (1942). R. C. Palmer, Vt Wolmer (1895)	1887	Winchester	Oxford	..	14, 18, 28^2

Name	Born	School	Univ.	Died	Page references
Ward, Sir (A.) L. (1st Bt 1929)	1875	St Paul's	Paris & Darmstadt	1956	22², 26³
Ward, W. D.	1877	Eton	Cambridge	1946	7, 13
Wardle, G. J.	1865	Elementary	..	1947	11²
Warne, G. H.	1881	Elementary	..	1928	16
Warrender, Sir V. A. G. A. (8th Bt 1917). 1st Ld Bruntisfield (1942)	1899	Eton	..	..	22³, 23², 25, 27, 31
Waterhouse, C.	1893	Cheltenham	Cambridge	..	25², 26², 29², 31
Watkinson, 1st Vt (1964), H. A. Watkinson	1910	Queen's Coll., Taunton*	London	..	37, 40², 41, 42
Watson, Sir J. C. (Kt 1931)	1883	Neilson Instit., Paisley*	Glasgow & Edinburgh	1944	19, 22
Watson, W., Ld Thankerton (Ld of Appeal 1929)	1873	Winchester	Cambridge	1948	13, 15, 18
Waverley, 1st Vt (1952). Sir J. Anderson (K.C.B. 1919)	1882	George Watson's Coll., Edin.	Edin. & Leipzig	1958	23², 26², 28², 31
Webb, Sir H. (1st Bt 1916)	1866	Privately	..	1940	6
Webb, M.	1904	Christ Ch., Lancaster*	..	1956	35
Webb, S. J. 1st Ld Passfield (1929)	1859	Switzerland & Secondary	..	1947	16, 19²
Webster, Sir R. E. (G.C.M.G. 1893). 1st Ld Alverstone (1900). 1st Vt. (1913)	1842	King's Coll. Sch. & Charterhouse	Cambridge	1915	3
Wedderburn, H. J. S., 13th Vt Dudhope (1952). 11th E of Dundee (1953)	1902	Winchester	Oxford	..	24, 29, 42
Wedgwood, 1st Ld (1942). J. C. Wedgwood	1872	Clifton & R.N.C. Greenwich	..	1943	16
Weir, 1st Vt (1938). Sir W. D. Weir (Kt 1917), 1st Ld (1918)	1877	Glasgow H.S.*	..	1959	12
Westwood, 1st Ld (1944). W. Westwood	1880	Elementary	..	1953	36
Westwood, J.	1884	Elementary	..	1948	19, 29, 34
Wheatley, Ld (Scot. judge 1954). J. Wheatley	1908	Mount St Mary's Coll.	Glasgow	..	36²
Wheatley, J.	1869	Elementary	..	1930	16
White, (H.) G.	1880	Birkenhead	Liverpool	..	20
Whiteley, G. 1st Ld Marchamley (1908)	1855	Abroad	Zürich	1925	4, 6
Whiteley, W.	1882	Elementary	..	1955	19, 30, 31, 35
Whitley, J. H.	1866	Clifton	London	1935	4, 6
Wilkins, W. A.	1899	Elementary	..	..	36
Wilkinson, Miss E. C.	1891	Stretford Rd.*	Manchester	1947	27, 29, 33
Willey, F. T.	1910	Johnston Sch.*	Cambridge	..	35
Williams, Sir E. J. (K.C.M.G. 1952)	1890	Elementary	..	1963	35
Williams, Sir H. G. (Kt 1939)	1884	Privately	Liverpool	1954	17
Williams, J. P.	1840	Elementary	..	1904	2
Williams, Sir R. R. (1st Bt 1918)	1865	Eton	Oxford	1955	11
Williams, 1st Ld (Life Peer 1961), T. Williams	1888	Elementary	..	..	27, 33
Williamson, Sir A. (Bt 1909) 1st Ld Forres (1922)	1860	Craigmont*	Edinburgh	1931	11
Willingdon, 1st M of (1936). F. Freeman-Thomas, 1st Ld Willingdon (1910). 1st Vt (1924), 1st E (1931)	1866	Eton	Cambridge	1941	4, 7
Willink, Sir H. U. (1st Bt 1957)	1894	Eton	Cambridge	..	28, 32
Wills, Sir G. (Kt 1958)	1905	Privately	Cambridge	..	39, 43²
Wilmot, 1st Ld (1950). J. Wilmot	1895	Secondary	London	..	29, 35

II
PARTIES

Conservative Party

Party Leaders, 1900–1960

1900	M of Salisbury	28 May 23	S. Baldwin
14 Jul 02	A. Balfour	31 May 37	N. Chamberlain [2]
13 Nov 11	A. Bonar Law [1]	9 Oct 40	(Sir) W. Churchill
21 Mar 21	A. Chamberlain [1]	21 Apr 55	Sir A. Eden
23 Oct 22	A. Bonar Law [1]	22 Jan 57	H. Macmillan

Leaders in the House of Lords

1900	3rd M of Salisbury	1940	Vt Caldecote
1902	D of Devonshire	1940	Vt Halifax
1903	M of Lansdowne	1941	Ld Lloyd
1916	Earl Curzon	1941	Ld Moyne
1925	4th M of Salisbury	1942	Vt Cranborne (5th M of Salisbury)
1931	1st Vt Hailsham	1957	E of Home
1935	M of Londonderry	1960	2nd Vt Hailsham
1935	Vt Halifax		
1938	Earl Stanhope		

Principal Office-Holders

Chairmen of the Party Organisation		*Principal Agents*	
1911–16	A. Steel-Maitland	Mar 1885–Jul 03	R. Middleton
1916–23	Sir G. Younger	Jul 03–Nov 05	L. Wells
Mar 23–Nov 26	S. Jackson	Nov 05–Dec 06	A. Haig
Nov 26–May 30	J. Davidson	Dec 06–Jan 12	P. Hughes
Jun 30–Apr 31	N. Chamberlain	May 12–Jun 15	J. Boraston
Apr 31–Mar 36	Ld Stonehaven	Jun 15–Apr 20	(Sir) J. Boraston & W. Jenkins
Mar 36–Mar 42	(Sir) D. Hacking		
Mar 42–Sep 44	T. Dugdale	Apr 20–Dec 20	W. Jenkins
Oct 44–Jul 46	R. Assheton	Dec 20–Mar 23	Sir M. Fraser
Jul 46–Jul 55	Ld Woolton (Vt)	Mar 23–Feb 24	Sir R. Hall
Nov 55–Sep 57	O. Poole	Mar 24–Jan 27	(Sir) H. Blain
Sep 57–Oct 59	Vt Hailsham	Jan 27–Feb 28	Sir L. Maclachlan
Oct 59–	R. Butler	Feb 28–Feb 31	R. Topping

Deputy Chairmen		*General Directors*	
Sep 57–Oct 59	O. Poole (Ld)	Feb 31–Sep 45	(Sir) R. Topping
Oct 59–	Sir T. Low	Oct 45–Aug 57	(Sir) S. Pierssené
		Sep 57–	(Sir) W. Urton

[1] A. Bonar Law, 1911–21, and A. Chamberlain, 1921–22, were Leaders of the Conservative Party in the House of Commons. The title 'Leader of the Party' is only given to those who are already Conservative Prime Ministers. The only occasion in the century that the title 'Leader of the Party' was conferred on a Conservative before he was Prime Minister was in 1922 to Mr. A. Bonar Law.

[2] N. Chamberlain remained Leader of the Conservative party until 4 Oct 40, though he was succeeded as Prime Minister by W. Churchill on 10 May 40, and resigned from the Government on 30 Sep 40.

Conservative Research Department 1929–1960

Directors		*Chairman*	
1930–39	(Sir) J. Ball	1929	N. Chamberlain
1939–45	*vacant*	1940	Sir K. Wood
1945–51	D. Clarke	1943	Sir J. Bell (*Acting Hon. Chairman*)
1948–50	H. Hopkinson	1945	R. Butler
1948–59	P. Cohen		
1951–	(Sir) M. Fraser		

SOURCES.—*1958–60 Annual Conference Reports of the National Union of Conservative and Unionist Associations*, and information from the Conservative Research Department.

Chief Whips in the House of Commons

1900	Sir W. Walrond
1902	Sir A. Acland Hood
1911	Ld Balcarres
1912	Ld E. Talbot
1921	L. Wilson
1923	(Sir) B. Eyres-Monsell
1931	D. Margesson
1941	J. Stuart
1948	P. Buchan-Hepburn
1955	E. Heath
1959	M. Redmayne

Chief Whips in the House of Lords

1900	Earl Waldegrave
1911	D of Devonshire
1916	Ld Hylton
1922	E of Clarendon
1925	E of Plymouth
1929	E of Lucan (5th)
1940	Ld Templemore
1945	Earl Fortescue
1958	Earl St Aldwyn

SOURCE.—*Dod's Parliamentary Companion, 1900–61.*

Chairmen of 1922 Committee [1]

Jan 23–Nov 32	(Sir) G. Rentoul	Dec 40–Dec 44	A. Erskine Hill
Dec 32–Dec 35	W. Morrison	Dec 44–Jun 45	J. McEwen
Dec 35–Jul 39	Sir H. O'Neill	Aug 45–Nov 51	Sir A. Gridley
Sep 39–Nov 39	Sir A. Somerville	Nov 51–Nov 55	D. Walker-Smith
Dec 39–Dec 40	W. Spens	Nov 55–	J. Morrison

SOURCE.—*The Times Index, 1923–60*, information from the 1922 Committee, R. T. McKenzie, *British Political Parties* (1955), pp. 57-61.

National Union of Conservative and Unionist Associations — Annual Conferences, 1900–1960 [2]

Date	*Place*	*President*	*Chairman*
19 Dec 00	London	M of Zetland	Ld Windsor
26–27 Nov 01	Wolverhampton	Ld Llangattock	Sir A. Hickman
14–15 Oct 02	Manchester	E of Dartmouth	Sir C. Cave
1–2 Oct 03	Sheffield	E of Derby	F. Lowe
28–29 Oct 04	Southampton	D of Norfolk	H. Bowles
14–15 Nov 05	Newcastle-upon-Tyne	Ld Montagu of Beaulieu	Sir W. Plummer
27 Jul 06	London	D of Northumberland	H. Imbert-Terry
14–15 Nov 07	Birmingham	,,	D of Rutland
19–20 Nov 08	Cardiff	E of Plymouth	Sir R. Hodge
17–18 Nov 09	Manchester	E of Cawdor	Sir T. Wrightson
17 Nov 10	Nottingham	E of Derby	H. Chaplin
16–17 Nov 11	Leeds	D of Portland	Ld Kenyon

[1] Or the Conservative (Private) Members Committee. This is an organisation of the entire back-bench membership of the Conservative Party in the Commons. It acts as a sounding-board of Conservative opinion in the House, but is not authorised to formulate policy.

[2] 1900–12, National Union of Conservative and Constitutional Associations, 1912–17 National Union Association of Conservative and Liberal-Unionist Associations, 1917–24 National Unionist Association, 1924– National Union of Conservative and Unionist Associations.

Date	Place	President	Chairman
14–15 Nov 12	London	Ld Faber	Sir W. Crump
12–14 Nov 13	Norwich	Ld Farquhar	A. Salvidge
1914–16	*No conference held*	Sir A. Fellowes	Sir H. Samuel
1917	London	,,	,,
1918–19	*No conference held*	,,	,,
10–11 Jun 20	Birmingham	,,	J. Williams
17–18 Nov 21	Liverpool	A. Chamberlain	Sir A. Benn
15–16 Dec 22	London	E of Derby	Sir A. Leith
25–26 Oct 23	Plymouth	Ld Mildmay of Flete	Sir H. Nield
2–3 Oct 24	Newcastle-upon-Tyne	D of Northumberland	E of Selborne
8–9 Oct 25	Brighton	G. Loder	Sir P. Woodhouse
7–8 Oct 26	Scarborough	G. Lane-Fox	Dame C. Bridgeman
6–7 Oct 27	Cardiff	Vt Tredegar	Sir R. Sanders
27–28 Sep 28	Great Yarmouth	Ld Queenborough	J. Gretton
21–22 Nov 29	London	Ld Faringdon	G. Rowlands
1 Jul 30	London	N. Chamberlain	Countess of Iveagh
1931	*No conference held*	,,	G. Herbert
6–7 Oct 32	Blackpool	Ld Stanley	Earl Howe
5–6 Oct 33	Birmingham	E of Plymouth	Sir G. Ellis
4–5 Oct 34	Bristol	Ld Bayford	Miss R. Evans
3–4 Oct 35	Bournemouth	G. Herbert	Sir W. Cope
1–2 Oct 36	Margate	Ld Ebbisham	Sir L. Brassey
7–8 Oct 37	Scarborough	Ld Bingley	Mrs C. Fyfe
1938	*No conference held*	M. of Londonderry	Sir E. Ramsden
1939	,,	,,	N. Colman
1940	,,	Ld Queenborough	Lady Hillingdon
1941	,,	,,	Sir C. Headlam
1942	,,	M of Salisbury	R. Catterall
20–21 May 43	London	,,	,,
1944	*No conference held*	,,	Mrs L. Whitehead
14–15 Mar 45	London	Ld Courthope	R. Butler
3–5 Oct 46	Blackpool	O. Stanley	R. Proby
2–4 Oct 47	Brighton	H. Macmillan	Mrs Hornyold-Strickland
7–9 Oct 48	Llandudno	G. Summers	Sir H. Williams
12–14 Oct 49	London	Vt Swinton	D. Graham
12–14 Oct 50	Blackpool	Sir D. Maxwell Fyfe	A. Nutting
1951	*No conference held*	Ld Ramsden	Mrs L. Sayers
9–11 Oct 52	Scarborough	Sir T. Dugdale	C. Waterhouse
8–10 Oct 53	Margate	M of Salisbury	Mrs J. Warde
7–9 Oct 54	Blackpool	A. Eden	Sir G. Llewellyn
6–8 Oct 55	Bournemouth	Mrs L. Sayers	Mrs E. Emmet
11–13 Oct 56	Llandudno	R. Butler	Sir E. Edwards
10–12 Oct 57	Brighton	E of Woolton	Mrs W. Elliot
8–11 Oct 58	Blackpool	Sir R. Proby	Sir S. Bell
1959	*No conference held*	H. Brooke	E. Brown
12–15 Oct 60	Scarborough	,,	,,

SOURCES.—*National Union Gleanings 1900–12, Gleanings and Memoranda 1912-33, Politics in Review 1934–60*, all published by the National Union of Conservative Associations; *National Union of Conservative and Unionist Associations, Annual Conference Reports, 1958 and 1960.*

Conservative Party Policy Statements and Manifestos

The fullest bibliography on the Conservative Party is to be found in G. D. M. Black, *A Source Book of Conservatism* (1964).

Labour Party

Party Leaders and Deputy Leaders

Year	*Chairman of the Parliamentary Party*[1]	*Vice-Chairman*[1]
1906	J. K. Hardie	D. Shackleton
1907	"	"
1908	A. Henderson	G. Barnes
1909	"	"
1910	G. Barnes	J. Clynes
1911	J. R. MacDonald	W. Brace
1912	"	J. Parker
1913	"	"
1914	A. Henderson	A. Gill
1915	"	J. Hodge } *Acting*
1916	"	G. Wardle } *Chairmen*
1917	W. Adamson	"
1918	"	J. Clynes
1919	"	"
1920	"	"
1921	J. Clynes	J. Thomas & S. Walsh
1922	J. R. MacDonald	S. Walsh & J. Wedgwood
1923	"	J. Clynes
1924	" [2]	"
1925	"	"
1926	"	"
1927	"	"
1928	"	"
1929	" [2]	..
1930	"	..
1931	A. Henderson [3]	C. Attlee
1932	G. Lansbury	"
1933	"	"
1934	"	"
1935	C. Attlee	A. Greenwood
1936	"	"
1937	"	"
1938	"	"
1939	"	"
1940	" [2]	"
1941	"	"
1942	"	"
1943	"	"
1944	"	"
1945	" [2]	H. Morrison
1946	"	"
1947	"	"
1948	"	"
1949	"	"
1950	"	"
1951	"	"
1952	"	"
1953	"	"
1954	"	"
1955	H. Gaitskell	J. Griffiths
1956	"	"
1957	"	"
1958	"	"
1959	"	A. Bevan
1960	"	G. Brown

[1] In 1922 the designation was changed from 'Chairman' to 'Chairman and Leader', and 'Vice-Chairman' to 'Deputy Leader'.

[2] When the Labour Party was in power in 1924, 1929–31, 1940–45, & 1945–51, a Liaison Committee was set up. The Chairmen of these committees are listed on p. 96.

[3] A. Henderson lost his seat in the 1931 election. The acting leader of the Labour Parliamentary Party in 1931 was G. Lansbury.

SOURCES.—*Labour Party Annual Conference Reports, Labour Year Books;* H. Pelling, *A Short History of the Labour Party* (1961), p. 130.

Leaders in the House of Lords

1924	Ld Parmoor & Vt Haldane[1]	1935	Ld Snell
1924	Vt Haldane	1940	Ld (Vt) Addison
1928	Ld Parmoor	1951	Earl Jowitt
1931	Ld Ponsonby	1955	Vt Alexander of Hillsborough

Labour Representation Committee — Executive Officers 1900–1905

Year	*Chairman*	*Treasurer*	*Secretary*
1900	F. Rogers		J. R. MacDonald
1901	,,		,,
1902	R. Bell	F. Rogers	,,
1903	,,	A. Gee	,,
1904	D. Shackleton	A. Henderson	,,
1905	,,	,,	,,

Labour Party — National Executive Committee, 1906–1960

Year	*Chairman*	*Treasurer*	*Secretary*
1906	J. Stephenson	A. Henderson	J. R. MacDonald
1907	W. Hudson	,,	,,
1908	J. Clynes	,,	,,
1909	J. Keir Hardie	,,	,,
1910	W. Robinson	,,	,,
1911	B. Turner	,,	,,
1912	G. Roberts	J. R. MacDonald	A. Henderson
1913	T. Fox	,,	,,
1914	W. Anderson	,,	,,
1915	,,	,,	,,
	G. Wardle	,,	,,
1916	F. Purdy	,,	,,
1917	J. McGurk	,,	,,
1918	W. Hutchinson	,,	,,
1919	A. Cameron	,,	,,
1920	F. Jowett	,,	,,
1921	S. Webb	,,	,,
1922	J. R. MacDonald	,,	,,
1923	C. Cramp	,,	,,
1924	R. Williams	,,	,,
1925	F. Roberts	,,	,,
1926	G. Lansbury	,,	,,
1927	H. Morrison	,,	,,
1928	Susan Lawrence	,,	,,
1929		*Hon. Secretary & Treasurer*	
1930	S. Hirst	A. Henderson	..
1931	G. Lathan	,,	..
1932	J. Compton	,,	..
1933	W. Smith	,,	..
1934	W. Robinson	,,	..
		Treasurer	
1935	Jennie Adamson	A. Henderson	J. Middleton
1936	H. Dalton	G. Lathan	,,
1937	G. Dallas	,,	,,
1938	,,	,,	,,
1939	Barbara Gould	,,	,,
1940	J. Walker	,,	,,
1941	W. Green	,,	,,
1942	A. Dobbs	,,	,,
1943	G. Ridley	A. Greenwood	,,
1944	Ellen Wilkinson	,,	M. Phillips
1945	H. Laski	,,	,,
1946	P. Noel-Baker	,,	,,
1947	E. Shinwell	,,	,,
1948	J. Griffiths	,,	,,
1949	S. Watson	,,	,,
1950	Alice Bacon	,,	,,

[1] Ld Parmoor and Vt Haldane were joint spokesmen for the Labour Government of 1924 in the House of Lords.

Year	Chairman	Treasurer	Secretary
1951	H. Earnshaw	A. Greenwood	M. Phillips
1952	A. Greenwood	"	"
1953	W. Burke	"	"
1954	Edith Summerskill	H. Gaitskell	"
1955	E. Gooch	"	"
1956	Margaret Herbison	A. Bevan	"
1957	T. Driberg	"	"
1958	Barbara Castle	"	"
1959	G. Brinham	"	"
1960	R. Crossman	H. Nicholas	"

SOURCES.—*Labour Representation Committee Annual Conference Reports, 1900–5,* and *Labour Party Annual Conference Reports, 1906–60.*

Chief Whips in the House of Commons

1906	D. Shackleton	1916	G. Roberts	1925	A. Henderson
1906	A. Henderson	1916	J. Parker	1927	T. Kennedy
1907	G. Roberts	1919	W. Tyson Wilson	1931	(Sir) C. Edwards
1914	A. Henderson	1920	A. Henderson	1942	W. Whiteley
1914	F. Goldstone	1924	B. Spoor	1955	H. Bowden

Chief Whips in the House of Lords

1924	Ld Muir-Mackenzie	1944	Ld Southwood
1924	E de la Warr	1945	Ld Ammon
1930	Ld Marley	1949	Ld Shepherd
1937	Ld Strabolgi	1954	E of Lucan (6th)
1942	E of Listowel		

SOURCES.—*Dod's Parliamentary Companion, 1900–61, Labour Party Annual Conference Reports.*

Parliamentary Labour Party — Parliamentary Committee

This committee was originally known as the Executive Committee of the Parliamentary Labour Party. Its name was changed in 1951 to avoid confusion with the N.E.C. The committee was first elected in 1923 to take the place of the Policy Committee of the P.L.P. It consists of twelve Commons' members, elected at the opening of every session of Parliament by members of the P.L.P. with seats in the House of Commons. There are six *ex-officio* members: the Leader and Deputy Leader of the Party, the Chief Whip in the House of Commons, the Leader of the Labour Peers, the Chief Whip of the Labour Peers and their elected representative. The elected Commons' members of the Parliamentary Committee sit on the Front Bench with the Party's Leader, Deputy Leader, Chief Whip and the Assistant Whips. Ex-Labour Ministers have the right, by custom of the House, to sit on the Front Bench, but usually prefer a place on the Back Benches. The officers and the elected twelve are joined on the Front Benches by a number of other members who have been allotted the responsibility of looking after particular subjects. Since 1955 it has become the practice of the Leader of the P.L.P. to invite members to take charge of particular subjects, and these members will include some who are not members of the Parliamentary Committee. In 1924 and 1929 when the Labour Party was in office a Consultative Committee of twelve was appointed representative of both Front and Back Benches. During the war-time coalition the P.L.P. elected an Administrative Committee of twelve, with Peers' representation, all of whom were non-Ministers. When the Labour Party was in office from 1945–51, the P.L.P. set up a small Liaison Committee of three elected Back Bench M.P.s, the Leader of the House, the Government Chief Whip and an elected Back Bench Labour Peer.

Parliamentary Labour Party — Executive Committee

The figures denote the order of successful candidates in the ballot.

	Feb 1923	Dec 1924	Dec 1925	Dec 1926	Dec 1927	1928
W. Adamson	9	..	11	11	8	There is no record of an Executive Committee election in 1928
H. Dalton	..	..	12	3	7	
R. Davies	12	..	..	..	..	
W. Graham	..	8	2	2	3	
A. Henderson	..	10	..	12	2	
T. Johnston	3	..	..	4	4	
F. Jowett	6	..	..	..	..	
G. Lansbury	2	1	10	9	10	
H. Lees-Smith	..	11	4	6	6	
J. Maxton	..	6	..	..	..	
E. Morel	5	..	..	..	..	
F. Roberts	..	12	..	..	..	
T. Shaw	11	..	7	..	12	
E. Shinwell	7	..	..	..	..	
R. Smillie	..	2	5	7	..	
P. Snowden	1	3	1	1	1	
J. Thomas	4	4	3	5	5	
C. Trevelyan	..	7	6	8	11	
S. Walsh	..	..	8	..	..	
S. Webb	10	..	9	10	9	
J. Wedgwood	..	9	..	..	..	
J. Wheatley	8	5	..	..	..	

	Nov 1931	Nov 1932	Nov 1933	Nov 1934
Sir S. Cripps	1	1	2	1
D. Grenfell	2	2	1	2
G. Hicks	4	3	3	5
M. Jones	7	7	4	6
W. Lunn	5	4	6	4
N. Maclean	6	6	7	7
T. Williams	3	5	5	3

	Nov 1935	Nov 1936	Nov 1937	Nov 1938	Nov 1939
A. Alexander	6	5	2	2	1
W. Wedgwood Benn	..	..	7	5	2
J. Clynes	1	6	..	..	..
H. Dalton	2	3	5	3	10
D. Grenfell	5	4	4	4	4
G. Hall	..	..	..	..	7
T. Johnston	3	2	3	6	..
M. Jones	10	8	11	12	..
J. Lawson	..	..	..	..	12
H. Lees-Smith	9	11	8	8	5
W. Lunn	11	..	..	..	..
N. Maclean	12	..	..	..	..
H. Morrison	4	1	1	1	8
P. Noel-Baker	..	10	12	10	11
F. Pethick-Lawrence	8	9	9	9	6
D. Pritt	..	12	..	..	..
E. Shinwell	..	..	10	11	9
T. Williams	7	7	6	7	3

Parliamentary Labour Party — Parliamentary Committee

	Nov 1951	Nov 1952	Nov 1953	Nov 1954	Jun 1955	Nov 1956	Nov 1957	Nov 1958	Nov 1959	Nov 1960
A. Bevan	..	12	9[a]	..	7	3	3	1	..	..
A. Bottomley	..	..	..	..	..	..	12	9	..	..
G. Brown	..	..	..	..	8	10	9	..	8	..
J. Callaghan	7	6	4	10	3	5	5	5	2	1
R. Crossman	..	..	..	..	..	..	..	..	13[d]	..
H. Dalton	8	5	5	4	..	..	..	..	..	..
J. Chuter Ede	5	2	6	9	..	..	..	..	..	..
T. Fraser	..	..	..	..	14[c]	12	8	12	7	6
H. Gaitskell	3	3	2	1[b]	2[c]	..	..	..	..	..
P. Gordon Walker	..	..	..	..	..	..	11	6	9	8
A. Greenwood	12	..	..	..	10	6	7	8	6[d]	..
J. Griffiths	1	1	1	1[b]	1[c]	..	..	..	..	..
R. Gunter	..	..	..	..	..	..	..	..	..	7
W. Glenvil Hall	2	9	12	11	..	..	..	..	..	..
D. Healey	..	..	..	..	..	..	..	..	12	5
D. Houghton	..	..	..	..	..	..	..	..	..	10
F. Lee	..	..	..	..	..	..	..	..	5	12
G. Mitchison	..	..	..	..	12	4	2	3	10	3
P. Noel-Baker	9	8	10	8	9	8	10	10	..	..
A. Robens	4	4	7	6	4	2	6	7	4	..
E. Shinwell	11	11	11	7	..	..	..	..	..	..
Sir F. Soskice	..	7	3	3	..	7	4	4	3	2
M. Stewart	..	..	..	..	..	..	..	..	..	4
R. Stokes	6	..	..	..	11	..	..	..	..	..
E. Summerskill	10	10	8	5	6	9	..	11	..	..
F. Willey	..	..	..	..	..	..	..	..	11	11
H. Wilson	..	..	13[a]	12	5	1	1	2	1	9
K. Younger	..	..	..	..	13[c]	11	..	..	..	..

[a] A. Bevan resigned from the Parliamentary Committee on 14 Apr 54, H. Wilson, who was 13th in order of votes obtained, took his place on the Committee on 28 Apr 54.

[b] H. Gaitskell and J. Griffiths both obtained 170 votes and tied for first place.

[c] H. Gaitskell and J. Griffiths were elected Leader and Deputy Leader of the Parliamentary Labour Party on 14 Dec 55 and 2 Feb 56, K. Younger and T. Fraser as runners-up filled the vacant places on the Parliamentary Committee.

[d] A. Greenwood resigned from the Parliamentary Committee on 13 Oct 60. R. Crossman, who was 13th in order of votes obtained, took his place on the Committee for a few weeks until the 1960–61 sessional elections in November.

Chairmen of Parliamentary Committees when Labour has been in power

1924 R. Smillie

1929–31 *Consultative Committee*

1929 H. Snell
1930 J. Barr

1940–45 *Administrative Committee*

1940 H. Lees-Smith
1941 H. Lees-Smith
1942 A. Greenwood
1943 A. Greenwood
1944 A. Greenwood

1945–51 *Liaison Committee*

1945 N. Maclean
1946 M. Webb
1947 M. Webb
1948 M. Webb
1949 M. Webb
1950 W. Glenvil Hall

SOURCES.—1923–29, *Daily Herald* and *Directory for National Council of Labour, TUC General Council, Labour Party and the Parliamentary Labour Party* (published annually by the Labour Party); 1931–1960, *Labour Party Annual Conference Reports*; *The Times*; and *Labour Party Directory*.

Labour Representation Committee — Annual Conferences, 1900–1905

Date	*Place*	*Chairman*
27–28 Feb 00	London	W. Steadman
1 Feb 01	Manchester	J. Hodge
20–22 Feb 02	Birmingham	W. Davis
19–21 Feb 03	Newcastle-upon-Tyne	J. Bell
4–5 Feb 04	Bradford	J. Hodge
26–29 Jan 05	Liverpool	A. Henderson

Labour Party — Annual Conferences, 1906–1960

15–17 Feb 06	London	A. Henderson
24–26 Jan 07	Belfast	J. Stephenson
20–22 Jan 08	Hull	W. Hudson
27–29 Jan 09	Portsmouth	J. Clynes
9–11 Feb 10	Newport	J. Keir Hardie
1–3 Feb 11	Leicester	W. Robinson
24–26 Jan 12	Birmingham	B. Turner
29–31 Jan 13	London	G. Roberts
27–30 Jan 14	Glasgow	T. Fox
1915	*No conference held*	
26–28 Jan 16	Bristol	W. Anderson
23–26 Jan 17	Manchester	G. Wardle
23–25 Jan 18	Nottingham	W. Purdy
26–28 Jun 18	London	W. Purdy
25–27 Jun 19	Southport	J. McGurk
22–25 Jun 20	Scarborough	W. Hutchinson
21–24 Jun 21	Brighton	A. Cameron
27–30 Jun 22	Edinburgh	F. Jowett
26–29 Jun 23	London	S. Webb
7–10 Oct 24	London	J. Ramsay MacDonald
29 Sep–2 Oct 25	Liverpool	C. Cramp
11–15 Oct 26	Margate	R. Williams
3–7 Oct 27	Blackpool	F. Roberts
1–5 Oct 28	Birmingham	G. Lansbury
30 Sep–4 Oct 29	Brighton	H. Morrison
6–10 Oct 30	Llandudno	Susan Lawrence
5–8 Oct 31	Scarborough	S. Hirst
3–7 Oct 32	Leicester	G. Lathan
2–6 Oct 33	Hastings	J. Compton
1–5 Oct 34	Southport	W. Smith
30 Sep–4 Oct 35	Brighton	W. Robinson
5–9 Oct 36	Edinburgh	Jennie Adamson
4–8 Oct 37	Bournemouth	H. Dalton
1938	*No conference held*	
29 May–2 Jun 39	Southport	G. Dallas
13–16 May 40	Bournemouth	Barbara Gould
2–4 Jun 41	London	J. Walker
25–28 May 42	London	W. Green
14–18 Jun 43	London	A. Dobbs
11–15 Dec 44	London	H. Laski
21–25 May 45	Blackpool	Ellen Wilkinson
10–14 Jun 46	Bournemouth	H. Laski
26–30 May 47	Margate	P. Noel-Baker
17–21 May 48	Scarborough	E. Shinwell
6–10 Jun 49	Blackpool	J. Griffiths
2–6 Oct 50	Margate	S. Watson
1–3 Oct 51	Scarborough	Alice Bacon
29 Sep–3 Oct 52	Morecambe	H. Earnshaw
28 Sep–2 Oct 53	Margate	A. Greenwood
27 Sep–1 Oct 54	Scarborough	W. Burke
10–14 Oct 55	Margate	Edith Summerskill
1–5 Oct 56	Blackpool	E. Gooch
30 Sep–4 Oct 57	Brighton	Margaret Herbison
29 Sep–3 Oct 58	Scarborough	T. Driberg
28–29 Nov 59	Blackpool	Barbara Castle
3–7 Oct 60	Scarborough	G. Brinham

SOURCES.—*1900–5 Reports of the Labour Representation Committee Annual Conferences, 1961 Report of the Labour Party Annual Conference*, pp. 272–3.

Labour Party Policy Statements and Manifestos

There is a full chronological list of Labour Party Programmes, Reports, Pamphlets, etc., from 1914 to 1947, in G. D. H. Cole, *History of the Labour Party from 1914* (1948), pp. 488-500. Since 1918 complete lists of Labour Party publications have been given in the *Labour Party Annual Conference Reports*.

Labour Party—Membership Statistics, 1900–1960

Year	No. Constit. & Central Parties	Total Indiv. Members ('000s)	T.U.s		Soc. & Co-op. Socs.		Total Membership ('000s)
			No.	Members ('000s)	No.	Members ('000s)	
1900–01	7	..	41	353	3	23	376
1901–02	21	..	65	455	2	14	469
1902–03	49	..	127	847	2	14	861
1903–04	76	..	165	956	2	14	970
1904–05	73	..	158	855	2	15	900
1905–06	73	..	158	904	2	17	921
1906–07	83	..	176	975	2	21	998
1907	92	..	181	1,050	2	22	1,072
1908	133	..	176	1,127	2	27	1,159
1909	155	..	172	1,451	2	31	1,486
1910	148	..	151	1,394	2	31	1,431
1911	149	..	141	1,502	2	31	1,539
1912	146	..	130	1,858	2	31	1,895
1913	158	..	[a]	[a]	2	33	[a]
1914	179	..	101	1,572	2	33	1,612
1915	177	..	111	2,054	2	33	2,093
1916	199	..	119	2,171	3	42	2,220
1917	239	..	123	2,415	3	47	2,465
1918	389	[b]	131	2,960	4	53	3,013
1919	418	..	126	3,464	7	47	3,511
1920	492	..	122	4,318	5	42	4,360
1921	456	..	116	3,974	5	37	4,010
1922	482	..	102	3,279	5	32	3,311
1923	503	..	106	3,120	6	36	3,156
1924	529	..	108	3,158	7	36	3,194
1925	549	..	106	3,338	8	36	3,374
1926	551	..	104	3,352	8	36	3,388
1927	532	..	97	3,239	6	55[c]	3,294
1928	535	215	91	2,025[d]	7	52	2,292[d]
1929	578	228	91	2,044	6	59	2,331
1930	607	277	89	2,011	7	58	2,347
1931	608	297	80	2,024	7	37	2,358
1932	608	372	75	1,960	9	40	2,372
1933	612	366	75	1,899	9	40	2,305
1934	614	381	72	1,858	8	40	2,278
1935	614	419	72	1,913	9	45	2,378
1936	614	431	73	1,969	9	45	2,444
1937	614	447	70	2,037	8	43	2,528
1938	614	429	70	2,158	9	43	2,630
1939	614	409	72	2,214	6	40	2,663
1940	614	304	73	2,227	6	40	2,571
1941	585	227	68	2,231	6	28	2,485
1942	581	219	69	2,206	6	29	2,454
1943	586	236	69	2,237	6	30	2,503
1944	598	266	68	2,375	6	32	2,673
1945	649	487	69	2,510	6	41	3,039
1946	649	645	70	2,635[d]	6	42	3,322[d]
1947	649	608	73	4,386	6	46	5,040
1948	656	629	80	4,751	6	42	5,422
1949	660	730	80	4,946	5	41	5,717
1950	661	908	83	4,972	5	40	5,920

[a] Owing to the operation of the Osborne Judgement it was made impossible to compile membership statistics for 1913.

[b] Individual membership statistics were not compiled 1918–27.

[c] The Royal Arsenal Cooperative Society, through its Political Purposes Committee, continued its affiliation with the Labour Party; its membership is included in the 1927–60 totals.

[d] From 1928–46 inclusive, trade unionist members of the Labour Party had to 'contract in' to payment to party political funds.

Year	No. Constit. & Central Parties	Total Indiv. Members ('000s)	T.U.s No.	T.U.s Members ('000s)	Soc. & Co-op. Socs. No.	Soc. & Co-op. Socs. Members ('000s)	Total Member-ship ('000s)
1951	667	876	82	4,937	5	35	5,849
1952	667	1,015	84	5,072	5	21	6,108
1953	667	1,005	84	5,057	5	34	6,096
1954	667	934	84	5,530	5	35	6,498
1955	667	843	87	5,606	5	35	6,484
1956	667	845	88	5,658	5	34	6,537
1957	667	913	87	5,644	5	26	6,583
1958	667	889	87	5,628	5	26	6,542
1959	667	848	87	5,564	5	25	6,437
1960	667	790	86	5,513	5	25	6,328

SOURCE.—*1961 Labour Party Annual Conference Report*, p. 37.

The Labour Party — Organisation and Constitutions

The Labour Representation Committee was formed on 27 Feb 1900 to promote a distinct Labour group in Parliament, representing the affiliated trade unions and socialist societies. After the general election of 1906 the L.R.C. group of M.P.s decided to assume the title of 'Labour Party' and elected their first officers and whips. Policy was determined by the Labour Party through the annual conference and its executive authority, the National Executive Committee. There was no official party leader, but an annually elected chairman of the parliamentary party. There were scarcely any official Labour Party constituency organisations (except for those provided by local trades councils, groups of miners' lodges, and local branches of the I.L.P.). In 1914 there were only two constituency associations with individual members: Woolwich and Barnard Castle, which Will Crooks and Arthur Henderson had built up on their own.

The Reorganisation of the Labour Party, 1918

The reorganisation of the Labour Party was projected by Arthur Henderson in collaboration with Sidney Webb. Their main aims were to provide local Labour Parties in every constituency or group of constituencies. These local Labour Parties were to be based fundamentally on individual subscribing membership, though representation was provided for trades councils, trade union branches, and socialist societies. The members of the N.E.C. were to be elected by the annual conference as a whole (though eleven were to be elected from candidates nominated by the trade unions and socialist societies as a single group, five were to represent the local Labour Parties, and four were to be women). The scheme also involved an increase in affiliation fees.

The original plan was amended, so that the N.E.C. was increased to a membership of 23 (adding two to the number specified for affiliated organisations). It was agreed that the election programme should be produced by the N.E.C. and P.L.P. jointly — subject to the aims of the Party and the decisions of the annual conferences. The object of the pre-war Party had

Trades Union Sponsored M.P.s, 1918–1959

No figures for Trades Union sponsored M.P.s are available before 1918. Unions are here listed under their 1960 titles. M.P.s from 1918–24 sponsored by Unions which subsequently amalgamated with other Unions and adopted other titles are listed under their present titles.

Trades Unions	1918	1922	1923	1924	1929	1931	1935	1945	1950	1951	1955	1959
National Union of Mineworkers (Miners' Federation of Great Britain, 1918–45)	25	41	43	40	42	26	32	34	37	36	34	31
Transport and General Workers' Union	3	7	10	10	13	1	7	17	16	14	14	14
National Union of Railwaymen	1	3	4	3	8	..	5	12	10	9	8	5
Transport Salaried Staffs Association (Railway Clerks' Association, 1918–50)	..	..	..	..	7	..	6	9	7	7	5	5
National Union of General and Municipal Workers	4	5	5	4	6	2	6	10	6	6	4	4
Associated Society of Woodworkers	1	1	3	2	6	1	2	3	3	3	2	1
Union of Shop, Distributive and Allied Workers	..	1	4	4	4	1	6	8	8	9	9	9
British Iron, Steel and Kindred Trades Association	..	2	1	3	4	1	1	2	2	2	2	2
United Textile Factory Workers' Association	4	3	3	2	4	..	..	3	2	1	1	1
Amalgamated Engineering Union (Amalgamated Society of Engineers, 1918–20)	1	7	4	4	3	2	3	4	8	8	6	8
National Union of Boot and Shoe Operatives	1	2	1	..	2	..	..	4	1	1	..	..
Associated Society of Locomotive Engineers and Firemen	..	..	..	1	1	..	1	2	2	2	2	3
United Society of Boilermakers, etc.	1	1	2	2	1	1	1	..	..	..	..	..
Union of Post Office Workers	..	2	3	2	..	..	..	1	1	2	1	2
National Union of Agricultural Workers	..	..	1	..	..	..	..	1	1	1	1	2
Electrical Trades Union	..	..	..	..	..	..	..	1	1	1	..	..
Others	8	11	18	11	13	..	8	9	6	6	6	5
Total T.U. M.P.s	49	86	102	88	114	35	78	120	111	108	95	92
Co-operative Party M.P.s	1	4	6	5	9	1	9	23	18	16	18	16
Total unsponsored M.P.s	7	52	83	58	164	10	67	250	186	171	164	150
Total Labour M.P.s	57	142	191	151	287	46	154	393	315	295	277	258

Sources.—1918–24, *Labour Party Annual Conference Reports*; 1929–59, *Trade Unions and the Labour Party since 1945*, by M. Harrison (1960) (these figures are also based on the Labour Party Conference Reports but modified by examination of union accounts); J. Bailey, *The British Co-operative Movement* (1955).

been to 'organise and maintain in Parliament and in the country a political Labour Party'. In 1918 this was changed to a new formula: 'to secure for the producers by hand and by brain the full fruits of their industry, and the most equitable distribution thereof that may be possible, upon the basis of the common ownership of the means of production and the best obtainable system of popular administration and control of each industry and service'.[1]

The 1918 constitution was modified in 1937 in favour of the local constituency Labour Parties, which had repeatedly demanded a greater share in the control of party affairs. Representation of the constituency parties on the N.E.C. was increased from five to seven. The seven were to be elected by the vote of the constituency delegates alone. The twelve trade union representatives and one representative of the socialist societies were to be elected separately by their respective conference delegations. The five women members may be nominated by any affiliated organisation and are elected by a vote of the whole party conference. The Leader (since 1929) and the Deputy Leader (since 1953) are *ex officio* members of the N.E.C. The Treasurer of the Party may be nominated by any affiliated organisation, and is elected by the vote of the whole party conference.

SOURCES.—H. Pelling, *The Origins of the Labour Party, 1880–1900* (1954); F. Bealey and H. Pelling, *Labour and Politics, 1900–1906* (1958); P. P. Poirier, *The Advent of the Labour Party* (1958); G. D. H. Cole, *British Working-Class Politics, 1832–1914* (1941); G. D. H. Cole, *A History of the Labour Party from 1914* (1948); R. T. McKenzie, *British Political Parties* (1955).

Other Sponsored M.P.s

M.P.s are also sponsored by organisations which are not members of the Trades Union Congress. The two major instances of this are the National Union of Teachers and the National Farmers' Union.

National Union of Teachers

The N.U.T. has sponsored and assisted parliamentary candidates since 1895. The number of sponsored candidates has varied, but a strict parity between the parties has always been maintained. The executive may now sponsor up to a total of four candidates from each of the Conservative, Labour and Liberal parties.

National Farmers' Union

In 1909 the N.F.U. set up a Parliamentary Fund with the object of sending two sponsored M.P.s to Parliament from each side of the House. Although sometimes 'independent on agricultural questions' all N.F.U. M.P.s have been Conservatives. Since 1945 the N.F.U. has not sponsored any candidates and has adopted a position of strict neutrality between the political parties.

[1] The 1914 and 1918 Labour Party constitutions are set out and compared in G. D. H. Cole, *A History of the Labour Party from 1914* (1948), pp. 71–81.

N.U.T. adopted and supported M.P.s, 1900–1960

Election	Total	Con.	Lab.	Lib.
1900	3	1	..	2
1906	2	..	..	2
1910 (Jan)	1	..	..	1
1910 (Dec)	2	..	1	1
1918	1	1	..	..
1922	3	1	2	..
1923	3	..	3	..
1924	4	1	3	..
1929	5	..	5	..
1931	3	1	2	..
1935	5	1	4	..
1945	2	..	2	..
1950	4	..	4	..
1951	4	..	4	..
1955	6	2	4	..
1959	6	2	4	..

SOURCE.—Information received from the National Union of Teachers. J. D. Stewart, *British Pressure Groups* (1958).

N.F.U. sponsored M.P.s, 1922–1945

Election	No. of M.P.s
1922	4
1923	3
1924	2
1929	No candidates
1931	,,
1935	2

SOURCES.—*National Farmers' Union Yearbooks, 1900–60*; P. Self and H. Storing, *The State and the Farmer* (1962), pp. 42–7, 204; J. D. Stewart, *British Pressure Groups* (1958), pp 173–4.

Liberal Party

Party Leaders, 1900–1960[1]

1900	Sir H. Campbell-Bannerman	4 Nov 31	Sir H. Samuel[2]
5 Apr 08	H. Asquith (E of Oxford and Asquith)	25 Nov 35	Sir A. Sinclair
14 Oct 26	D. Lloyd George	1 Aug 45	C. Davies
		5 Nov 56	J. Grimond

Leaders in the House of Lords

1900	Earl of Kimberley	1924	Earl Beauchamp
1902	Earl Spencer	1931	M of Reading
1905	M of Ripon	1936	M of Crewe
1908	E (M) of Crewe	1944	Vt Samuel
1916	Vt Grey	1955	Ld Rea

[1] All were Liberal 'Leaders in the House of Commons'. Sir H. Campbell-Bannerman from 1905–8, and H. Asquith 1908–16 were the only 'Leaders of the Liberal Party' from 1900–60.

[2] At the General Election in 1931 there were three Liberal groups in the House of Commons. Sir H. Samuel led the main group of Liberal M.P.s. D. Lloyd George led a small family group of Independent Liberals, and Sir J. Simon (Ld) led what was to become in 1932 the Liberal National Group (see *Minor Parties*). On 25 Nov 35 D. Lloyd George and the other Independent Liberals rejoined the Liberal Party in the House of Commons.

Principal Office-Holders
Liberal Central Association, 1900–1936

Secretary

1893 (Sir) R. Hudson
1927 Ld Stanmore
1935 Ld Stanmore & Sir W. Rea (Ld)

National Liberal Federation, 1900–1936

Chairman of Committee

1900 (Sir) E. Evans
1918 Sir G. Lunn
1920 A. Brampton
1931 R. Muir
1933 R. Walker
1934 M. Gray

Treasurer

1900 J. Massie
1905 R. Bird
1909 F. Wright
1922 Sir R. Hudson
1926 Sir F. Layland-Barratt
1932 P. Heffer

Secretary

1893 (Sir) R. Hudson
1922 F. Barter
1925 H. Oldman
1930 H. Oldman & W. Davies
1931 W. Davies

Liberal Party Organisation, 1936–1960

Secretary

1936 W. Davies
1952 H. Harris (*General Director*)
1960 D. Robinson (*Directing Secretary*)

Chairman of Executive Committee

1936 M. Gray
1946 P. Fothergill
1949 Ld Moynihan
1950 F. Byers
1952 P. Fothergill
1954 G. Acland
1957 D. Abel
1959 L. Behrens

SOURCES.—*Liberal Magazine 1900–1950*; *Liberal Year Book 1900–1939*; *Dod's Parliamentary Companion 1950–1960.*

Chief Whips in House of Commons

1900 H. Gladstone
1905 G. Whiteley
1908 J. Pease
1910 Master of Elibank
1912 P. Illingworth
1915 J. Gulland
1916 N. Primrose
1917 F. Guest
1921 C. McCurdy
1919–23 G. Thorne (*Ind. Lib.*)
1923 V. Phillipps
1924 Sir G. Collins
1926 Sir R. Hutchinson
1930 Sir A. Sinclair
1931 G. Owen
1932 W. Rea (*Opposition Liberal*)
1935 Sir P. Harris
1945 T. Horabin
1946 F. Byers
1950 J. Grimond
1956 D. Wade

Chief Whips in House of Lords[1]

1896 Ld Ribblesdale
1907 Ld Denman
1911-22 Ld Colebrooke
1919 Ld Denman (*Ind. Lib.*)
1924 Ld Stanmore
1944 Vt Mersey
1949 M of Willingdon
1950 Ld Rea
1955 Ld Amulree

SOURCE.—*Dod's Parliamentary Companion 1900–1961.*

National Liberal Federation — Annual Conferences, 1900–1935

Date	*Place*	*President*
27–28 Mar 00	Nottingham	R. Spence Watson
14–15 May 01	Bradford	,,
13–14 May 02	Bristol	A. Birrell
14–15 May 03	Scarborough	,,

[1] Before 1905 there was scarcely any formal allotment of the office of Whip in the House of Lords.

Date	*Place*	*President*
12–13 May 04	Manchester	A. Birrell
18–19 May 05	Newcastle-upon-Tyne	,,
23–24 May 06	Liverpool	A. Acland
6–7 Jun 07	Plymouth	,,
18–19 Jun 08	Birmingham	Sir W. Angus
1–2 Jul 09	Southport	,,
25 Nov 10	Hull	,,
23–24 Nov 11	Bath	Sir J. Brunner
21–22 Nov 12	Nottingham	,,
26–27 Nov 13	Leeds	,,
1914–1918	*No conference held*	
27–28 Nov 19	Birmingham	Sir G. Lunn
25–26 Nov 20	Bradford	J. Robertson
24–25 Nov 21	Newcastle-upon-Tyne	,,
17–18 May 22	Blackpool	,,
30 May–1 Jun 23	Buxton	Sir D. Maclean
22–23 May 24	Brighton	,,
14–15 May 25	Scarborough	,,
17–18 Jun 26	Weston-super-Mare	J. Spender
26–27 May 27	Margate	Sir C. Hobhouse
11–12 Oct 28	Great Yarmouth	,,
3–4 Oct 29	Nottingham	,,
16–17 Oct 30	Torquay	A. Brampton
14–15 May 31	Buxton	,,
28–29 Apr 32	Clacton-on-Sea	,,
18–19 May 33	Scarborough	R. Muir
2–5 May 34	Bournemouth	,,
23–25 May 35	Blackpool	,,

Liberal Party—Annual Assemblies, 1936–1960

Date	*Place*	*President*
18–19 Jun 36	London	Ld Meston
27–31 May 37	Buxton	,,
19–20 May 38	Bath	,,
11–12 May 39	Scarborough	,,
1940	*No assembly held*	
18–19 Jul 41	London	,,
4–5 Sep 42	London	,,
15–17 Jul 43	London	,,
1944	*No assembly held*	
1– 3 Feb 45	London	Lady V. Bonham-Carter
9–11 May 46	London	,,
24–26 Apr 47	Bournemouth	I. Foot
22–24 Apr 48	Blackpool	E. Dodds
24–26 Mar 49	Hastings	Sir A. MacFadyean
27–28 Jan 50	London	,,
29–30 Sep 50	Scarborough	P. Fothergill
1951	*No assembly held*	
15–17 May 52	Hastings	R. Walker
9–11 Apr 53	Ilfracombe	L. Robson
22–24 Apr 54	Buxton	H. Graham White
14–16 Apr 55	Llandudno	Ld Rea
27–29 Sep 56	Folkestone	L. Behrens (*acting*)
19–21 Sep 57	Southport	,,
18–21 Sep 58	Torquay	N. Micklem
1959	*No assembly held*	Sir A. Comyns Carr
29 Sep–1 Oct 60	Eastbourne	Sir A. Murray

SOURCES.—*Liberal Year Book 1902–1939*; *The Liberal Magazine 1900–1950*; *National Liberal Federation, Annual Reports 1900–1936*; *Keesing's Archives 1939–60*.

Liberal Party Policy Statements and Manifestos

The Liberal Publication Department published miscellaneous collections of *Pamphlets and Leaflets, 1908–30*. The *Liberal Magazine* was published from 1893 until 1950.

Minor Parties

Common Wealth

This party was founded in 1942 by Sir Richard Acland (Liberal M.P. for Barnstaple) during the war-time electoral truce. Its immediate aim was to contest all by-elections where a 'reactionary' candidate was in the field, and was not opposed by a Labour or other 'progressive' candidate. Seats were won at Eddisbury (1943), Skipton (1944), and Chelmsford (1945). In 1943 membership of Common Wealth was proscribed by the Labour party. In the 1945 General Election Common Wealth put up twenty-three candidates but were only successful in Chelmsford where no Labour candidate stood: the victor there, E. Millington, joined the Labour Party. Sir R. Acland joined the Labour Party as soon as the 1945 results were known. Common Wealth survived as an organisation but contested no further parliamentary elections.

Communist Party

The Communist Party of Great Britain was founded in July 1920. In its early years it sought to affiliate to the Labour Party but was rebuffed. In 1922 J. T. W. Newbold (Motherwell) was elected to Parliament; S. Saklatvala (N. Battersea) was also elected in 1922 as a Labour M.P. (although a member of the Communist Party). After defeat in 1923, he was elected again in 1924 as a Communist. Since 1924 the Labour Party has ruled that no member of the Communist Party could be an individual member of the Labour Party and in 1935, 1943, and 1946 the Labour Party turned down further Communist requests for affiliation. In 1935 and again in 1945 W. Gallacher was elected as a Communist for W. Fife; and in 1945 P. Piratin was elected for the Mile End division of Stepney.

Secretaries of the Communist Party: 1920–29 A. Inkpin, 1929–56 H. Pollitt, 1956– J. Gollan.

Communist Candidates

1922	5	1931	26	1951	10
1923	8	1935	2	1955	17
1924	8	1945	21	1959	18
1929	25	1950	100		

SOURCES.—H. Pelling, *The British Communist Party* (1958).

Co-operative Party

In 1917 the Co-operative Congress agreed to organise as a political party. In the 1918 General Election one Co-operative M.P. was elected; he joined with the Labour Party in the House of Commons. Labour and Co-operative candidates never opposed each other at elections but it was not till 1926 that a formal understanding was reached and Co-operative Parties were made eligible for affiliation to divisional Labour Parties. In 1938 the Co-operative Party adopted a written constitution and in 1941 its representatives were invited to attend meetings of the National Council of Labour on equal terms with the Labour Party and the T.U.C. In 1946, the 1926 agreement with the Labour Party was replaced; Co-operative candidates were to run formally as Co-operative and Labour Candidates,[1] and after the General Election of 1959 it was agreed that the number of Co-operative candidates should be limited to 30.[2]

In 1951 the Co-operative Party adopted a new constitution to prevent its members from joining organisations proscribed by the Labour Party.

Co-operative M.P.s and Candidates

Year	M.P.s (Candidates)	Year	M.P.s (Candidates)
1918	1 (10)	1935	9 (21)
1922	4 (11)	1945	23 (33)
1923	6 (10)	1950	18 (33)
1924	5 (10)	1951	16 (37)
1929	9 (12)	1955	18 (38)
1931	1 (18)	1959	16 (30)

SOURCES.—J. Bailey, *The British Co-operative Movement* (1955), *Reports of the Annual Co-operative Congress 1900–60*, *The People's Year Book 1932*.

Independent Labour Party

The Independent Labour Party, formed in 1893, was one of the founding bodies of the Labour Representation Committee in 1900. The I.L.P. was affiliated to the Labour Party but it held its own conferences, sponsored its own parliamentary candidates, and maintained its own policies, even after the 1918 revision of the Labour Party constitution. Differences with the Labour Party grew in the late 1920's and the 37 I.L.P. Members among the 288 Labour M.P.s elected in 1929 provided some of the second Labour Government's strongest critics. At the 1930 conference of the I.L.P., it was agreed that I.L.P. members should vote against the Labour government when its actions conflicted with I.L.P. policy. The I.L.P. was disaffiliated by the 1932 Labour Party Conference. In 1935 17 I.L.P. candidates stood, all against Labour candidates, and four (all in Glasgow) were successful. In 1945 three of the five I.L.P. candidates won but, after the death of the party's leader, James Maxton in 1946, the I.L.P. M.P.s one by one rejoined the Labour Party. In the elections of 1950 and 1951 there were three I.L.P. candidates and in 1955 and 1959 two candidates. All lost their deposits.

Irish Nationalist Party

From the days of Parnell until the First World War between 80 and 86 Irish Nationalists sat in the House of Commons — at times divided by internal frictions but with a safe control of more than three-quarters of the seats in Ireland. Divisions over support for the war and the Easter Rebellion broke the party's hold and in 1918 only 7 of its 58 candidates were elected. After partition the party only fought two or three of the twelve seats in Northern Ireland but from 1922 to 1924, and 1929 to 1955, it held one or both of the two Fermanagh and Tyrone seats. T. P. O'Connor, from 1885 the solitary Irish Nationalist Member representing an English constituency, continued to be returned unopposed for the Scotland Division of Liverpool until his death in 1929.

Chairmen of the Irish Parliamentary Party

1900 J. Redmond | 1917 J. Dillon

SOURCE.—F. S. L. Lyons, *The Irish Parliamentary Party 1890–1910* (1951).

[1] L.P. Annual Report, 1946, pp. 229-31.

[2] L.P. Annual Report, 1960, p. 24.

Liberal National Party (National Liberal Party since 1948)

In June 1931 Sir J. Simon, W. Runciman, and about 23 other M.P.s rejected the Liberal Whip over Free Trade policy. In the October 1931 election 41 candidates stood as Liberal Nationals, 35 successfully. In October 1932 when the 'Samuelite' Liberals left the government over the Ottawa agreements, the 'Simonite' Liberal Nationals remained. They fought the 1935 election in alliance with the Conservatives and 33 of their 44 candidates were returned. In 1945 13 of the 51 Liberal National Candidates were returned although E. Brown, who had succeeded Sir J. Simon as leader on 4 December 1940 was defeated. In May 1947 the Woolton-Teviot agreement was signed which urged the combination of Conservative and Liberal National Constituency Associations and in 1948 the party was renamed the National Liberal Party. By 1959 one M.P. still styled himself National Liberal, six styled themselves Conservative and National Liberal, and four National Liberal and Conservative.

Chairmen of the Parliamentary Party		*Chief Whips*	
1931	Sir J. Simon	1937	C. Kerr
1940	E. Brown	1940	H. Holdsworth
1945	(Sir) J. Henderson-Stewart	1942	N. Beechman
1946	Sir S. Holmes	1945	(Sir) H. Butcher
1947	J. Maclay		
1956	(Sir) J. Duncan		
1959	Sir J. Henderson-Stewart		
1961	Sir C. Thornton Kemsley		

SOURCES.—Information from the National Liberal Party, and *Dod's Parliamentary Companion, 1931–61.*

National Labour Party

The party was formed in 1931 from the small group of Labour M.P.s who supported the National Government under Ramsay MacDonald. In the 1931 General Election 13 of its 20 candidates were elected. In 1935 8 of its 20 candidates were elected. The party wound itself up in 1940 and in 1945 of the 7 surviving National Labour members 3 retired, 2 stood unsuccessfully as National candidates, and 2 as Independents (one K. Lindsay successfully — but in a new constituency, English Universities).

New Party, British Union of Fascists, Union Movement

Sir Oswald Mosley (Conservative, then Independent M.P. 1918–24, Labour M.P. 1926–31) resigned from the Labour Government in May 1930 after his *Memorandum* for dealing with unemployment had been rejected by the Cabinet. In October 1930 a resolution calling upon the National Executive to consider the Memorandum was narrowly defeated at the Labour Party Conference. On 6 December 1930 the *Mosley Manifesto* summarising the main proposals in the Memorandum was published, signed by 17 Labour M.P.s. Six of the 17 signatories of the Manifesto resigned from the Labour Party to form the New Party in March 1931 (Sir Oswald and Lady Cynthia Mosley, O. Baldwin, W. J. Brown, R. Forgan, and J.

Strachey), but Baldwin and Brown remained members for only one day and Strachey resigned in June. The New Party received two further recruits before the 1931 General Election, W. E. D. Allen (Conservative) and R. Dudgeon (Liberal). In the Election the New Party contested 24 seats but failed to win a single one, the 4 New Party M.P.s all losing their seats.

In 1932 the New Party was renamed the British Union of Fascists after Mosley had been to Italy to study the 'modern movements'. The Director of Organisation and Deputy Leader was R. Forgan. In the 1935 General Election, the B.U.F. put up no candidates and, with the slogan 'Fascism next Time', advised their supporters not to vote. The B.U.F. fought a number of by-elections in 1937 and 1940, before it was dissolved by the Government on 30 May 1940.

In 1948, Sir Oswald Mosley formed the Union Movement. Its only Parliamentary contest was in the 1959 General Election, when he fought North Kensington, losing his deposit.

SOURCE.—Colin Cross, *The Fascists in Britain*, (1961).

Scottish National Party

The party was founded in 1928 and has fought every subsequent General Election. Its only success was in the Motherwell by-election of April 1945. But the victor, Dr. R. D. McIntyre, was defeated in the General Election three months later.

Scottish National Candidates

1929	2	1950	4
1931	4	1951	1
1935	6	1955	2
1945	8	1959	5

Sinn Fein

The Sinn Fein Party, founded during the war-time troubles, won 73 of the 103 Irish seats it contested in 1918: these candidates never took their seats at Westminster. In 1922 and 1923, C. Healy, successful in Fermanagh and Tyrone, was the only Sinn Fein candidate. The party reappeared in 1955 and 1959, contesting all twelve Northern Ireland seats. In 1955 it won seats in Mid-Ulster, and in Fermanagh and South Tyrone, but its candidates were disqualified as felons.

Welsh Nationalist Party — Plaid Cymru

The party was founded in 1925 and has fought elections consistently since then — but without any success at the parliamentary level.

Welsh Nationalist Candidates

1929	1	1950	7
1931	2	1951	4
1935	1	1955	11
1945	8	1959	20

Minor Parties — Representation in the House of Commons

	Total	Ir. Nat.	Comm.	I.L.P.	Ind. Con.	Other
1900	82	82	..	..	..	..
1906	83	83	..	..	..	..
1910	82	82	..	..	..	..
1910	84	84	..	..	..	..
1918	83	80[a]	..	..	..	3
1922	12	3	1	..	3	5
1923	7	3	..	..	..	4
1924	5	1	1	..	..	3
1929	8	3	..	..	1	4
1931	5	2	..	..	..	2
1935	9	2	1	4	..	2
1945	22	2	2	3	2	13
1950	3	2	..	..	..	1[b]
1951	3	2	..	..	..	1
1955	3	2	..	..	..	1[b]
1959	1	..	..	..	1	..

[a] There were 73 Sinn Fein candidates elected in Ireland who never took their seats. There were also 7 Nationalists elected.

[b] The 'other' candidate listed in 1950 and 1955 was, in fact, the Speaker.

SOURCES.—*The Constitutional Year Book, 1919*; D. E. Butler, *The Electoral System in Britain since 1918* (1963).

III
PARLIAMENT

House of Commons

Speaker of the House of Commons

1895	W. Gully (Vt Selby)
20 Jun 05	J. Lowther (Vt Ullswater)
28 Apr 21	J. Whitley
21 Jun 28	E. Fitzroy
9 Mar 43	D. Clifton Brown (Vt Ruffside)
1 Nov 51	W. Morrison (Vt Dunrossil)
21 Oct 59	Sir H. Hylton-Foster

Chairman of Ways and Means Committee

1900	J. Lowther
1905	G. Lawson
1906	A. Emmott
1911	J. Whitley
1922	J. Hope
1924	R. Young
1931	Sir D. Herbert
1942	D. Clifton Brown
1943	J. Milner
1945	C. Williams
1945	J. Milner
1951	Sir C. MacAndrew
1959	Sir G. Touche

Deputy Chairman of Ways and Means Committee

(*office created* 1902)

1902	A. Jeffreys
1905	L. Hardy
1906	J. Caldwell
1910	J. Whitley
1911	D. Maclean
1919	Sir E. Cornwall
1922	E. Fitzroy
1924	C. Entwistle
1924	E. Fitzroy
1928	D. Herbert
1929	H. Dunnico
1931	R. Bourne
1938	D. Clifton Brown
1942	J. Milner
1943	C. Williams
1945	Sir C. MacAndrew
1945	H. Beaumont
1948	F. Bowles
1950	Sir C. MacAndrew
1951	R. Morris
1956	Sir G. Touche
1959	Sir W. Anstruther-Gray

Officers of the House of Commons

Clerk

1900	(Sir) A. Milman
1902	Sir C. Ilbert
1921	(Sir) T. Webster
1930	Sir H. Dawkins
1937	(Sir) G. Campion
1948	(Sir) F. Metcalfe
1954	(Sir) E. Fellowes

Librarian

1887	R. Walpole
1908	A. Smyth
1937	V. Kitto
1946	H. Saunders
1950	S. Gordon

Parliament, 1900–1960

Sessions		Allocation of Parliamentary Time		Parliamentary Bills		Questions to Ministers		
						Daily Average		
?arliament Met	Parliament Prorogued	Total Days on which House sat	Days on which Private Members had Precedence [a]	Total Bills Intro-duced	Total Bills Receiving Royal Assent	Starred Questions	Unstarred Questions	Sessional Total of all Questions
3 Dec 00	15 Dec 00	11	3	..	..	..	..	314
3 Jan 01	25 Jan 01	3	..	..	..		..	
4 Feb 01	17 Aug 01	118	14	303	127	69 [b]	..	6,448[b]
6 Jan 02	18 Dec 02	181	17	300	121	..	..	7,168
7 Feb 03	14 Aug 03	115	14	311	128	28	18	4,536
2 Feb 04	15 Aug 04	124	13	308	121	38	18	5,933
4 Feb 05	11 Aug 05	114	12	309	86	47	19	6,244
)ate of Dissolution 8 Jan 06. Duration of Parliament 5 yrs, 2 mths, 7 days.								
3 Feb 06	21 Dec 06	156	16	346	121	70	22	11,865
2 Feb 07	28 Aug 07	131	13	294	116	72	21	10,147
9 Jan 08	19 Dec 08	171	18	364	129	75	21	13,811
6 Feb 09	3 Dec 09	179	14	325	110	62	19	12,251
)ate of Dissolution 10 Jan 10. Duration of Parliament 3 yrs, 10 mths, 28 days.								
5 Feb 10	28 Nov 10	103	9	289	101	81	24	8,201
)ate of Dissolution 28 Nov 10. Duration of Parliament 9 mths, 3 days.								
1 Jan 11	16 Dec 11	172	11	373	134	87	21	15,439
4 Feb 12	7 Mar 13	206	14	343	101	97	19	19,913
o Mar 13	15 Aug 13	102	10	315	108	88	18	8,936
o Feb 14	18 Sep 14	130	16	391	168	55	16	7,705
1 Nov 14	27 Jan 16	155	..	162	152	72	16	12,976
5 Feb 16	22 Dec 16	127	..	112	105	108	20	15,743
7 Feb 17	6 Feb 18	181	..	102	91	92	16	19,146
2 Feb 18	21 Nov 18	119	..	99	86	89	15	12,025
)ate of Dissolution 25 Nov 18. Duration of Parliament 7 yrs, 9 mths, 25 days.								
4 Feb 19	23 Dec 19	163	16	203	152	126	27	20,523
o Feb 20	23 Dec 20	167	17¼	215	138	110	22	18,652
5 Feb 21	10 Nov 21	141	11¾	202	125	101 [c]	19 [c]	14,133[c]
4 Dec 21	19 Dec 21	4	..	..	..			
7 Feb 22	4 Aug 22	113	11	196	105	.. [d]	.. [d]	.. [d]
)ate of Dissolution 26 Oct 22. Duration of Parliament 3 yrs, 9 mths, 5 days.								
o Nov 22	15 Dec 22	20	..	10	10	103 [d]	18 [d]	12,860[d]
3 Feb 23	16 Nov 23	114	17¼	181	78	107	21	12,370
)ate of Dissolution 16 Nov 23. Duration of Parliament 11 mths, 27 days.								
8 Jan 24	9 Oct 24	129	21½	248	79	101	25	13,092
)ate of Dissolution 9 Oct 24. Duration of Parliament 9 mths, 1 day.								
2 Dec 24	22 Dec 25	148	22½	247	145	91	23	14,035
2 Feb 26	15 Dec 26	151	21	180	105	71	17	10,713
8 Feb 27	22 Dec 27	144	19¾	195	91	74	14	10,536
7 Feb 28	3 Aug 28	115	24½	168	79	67	13	7,559
6 Nov 28	10 May 29	100	..	115	64	68	17	7,074
Date of Dissolution 10 May 29. Duration of Parliament 4 yrs, 7 mths, 2 days.								

[a] Excluding Private Members' Bills and Motions taken in Government time; Adjournment Debates initiated by Private nbers; Motions on first going into Committee of Supply, etc.
[b] For both sessions in 1901. [c] For both sessions in 1921. [d] For both sessions in 1922

Parliament, 1900–1960 (continued)

Sessions		Allocation of Parliamentary time		Parliamentary Bills		Questions to Ministers		
Parliament met	Parliament Prorogued	Total Days on which House sat	Days on which Private Members had Precedence [a]	Total Bills Introduced	Total Bills Receiving Royal Assent	Daily Average: Starred Questions	Daily Average: Unstarred Questions	Sessional Total of all Questions
25 Jun 29	1 Aug 30	189	31	237	132	93	24	18,327
28 Oct 30	7 Oct 31	187	21¼	212	106	78	15	14,373
Date of Dissolution 8 Oct 31. Duration of Parliament 2 yrs, 4 mths, 28 days.								
3 Nov 31	17 Nov 32	155	1	125	103	69	10	9,667
22 Nov 32	17 Nov 33	143	26½	147	92	58	8	7,559
21 Nov 33	16 Nov 34	156	22¼	173	111	58	9	8,768
20 Nov 34	25 Oct 35	151	..	116	98	59	9	8,449
Date of Dissolution 25 Oct 35. Duration of Parliament 3 yrs, 11 mths, 21 days.								
26 Nov 35	30 Oct 36	137	19½	149	111	82	13	10,215
3 Nov 36	22 Oct 37	157	24	170	126	79	11	11,769
26 Oct 37	4 Nov 38	168	26¼	179	113	85	14	13,787
8 Nov 38	23 Nov 39	200	14	227	171	92	17	18,460
28 Nov 39	20 Nov 40	127	..	80	73	84	27	13,536
21 Nov 40	11 Nov 41	113	..	55	54	77	23	10,825
12 Nov 41	10 Nov 42	116	..	46	46	80	23	11,592
11 Nov 42	23 Nov 43	122	..	59	58	83	22	11,911
24 Nov 43	28 Nov 44	153	..	55	52	77	17	11,498
29 Nov 44	15 Jun 45	95	..	57	48	91	18	7,856
Date of Dissolution 15 Jun 45. Duration of Parliament 9 yrs, 5 mths, 20 days.								
1 Aug 45	6 Nov 46	212	..	106	104	128	30	27,313
12 Nov 46	20 Oct 47	164	..	73	71	108	22	17,310
21 Oct 47	13 Sep 48	171	..	92	89	97	21	16,303
14 Sep 48	25 Oct 48	10	..	..	..	132	41	853
26 Oct 48	16 Dec 49	208	10½	146	125	86	18	17,334
Date of Dissolution 3 Feb 50. Duration of Parliament 4 yrs, 4 mths, 15 days.								
1 Mar 50	26 Oct 50	105	5	58	57	105	19	9,861
31 Oct 50	4 Oct 51	153	19	107	81	108	18	15,720
Date of Dissolution 5 Oct 51. Duration of Parliament 1 yr, 6 mths, 4 days.								
31 Oct 51	30 Oct 52	157	18⅓	113	88	99	17	14,192
4 Nov 52	29 Oct 53	162	20	78	62	91	16	13,878
3 Nov 53	25 Nov 54	187	18¾	113	95	89	15	15,990
30 Nov 54	6 May 55	84	10	72	33	90	17	7,262
Date of Dissolution 6 May 55. Duration of Parliament 3 yrs, 6 mths, 6 days.								
7 Jun 55	5 Nov 56	219	25¼	126	101	86	16	18,285
6 Nov 56	1 Nov 57	159	19¾	93	75	90	20	14,259
5 Nov 57	23 Oct 58	156	19¾	112	89	84	18	12,734
28 Oct 58	18 Sep 59	159	20	113	89	89	21	14,518
Date of Dissolution 18 Sep 59. Duration of Parliament 4 yrs, 3 mths, 11 days.								
20 Oct 59	27 Oct 60	160	22	103	80	81	21	13,471

[a] Excluding Private Members' Bills and Motions taken in Government time; Adjournment Debates initiated by Priv Members; Motions on first going into Committee of Supply, etc.

SOURCES.—Information from the '*Black Book*', a compilation of Parliamentary statistics at the House of Commons, a the *Sessional Returns of the House of Commons*. Questions to Ministers taken from D. N. Chester and N. Bowring, *Question Parliament* (1962), pp. 87-8, and 316.

Parliamentary Sessions

In 1900 sessions of Parliament lasted from February to July or August. Occasionally Parliament sat through the summer. In 1930 both Houses agreed that they should adjourn between July and October, and that the session should last from September or October to the September or October of the following year. During the summer recess the Speaker or the Lord Chancellor has the power to give notice of an earlier meeting of Parliament if it is in the national interest.

Parliamentary Hours of Sitting

In 1902 the House of Commons met from 2 until 11.30 p.m., but this was altered in 1906 to 2.45 until 11.30, to allow more time for lunch. During the 1939–45 war the time for rising in the evening was changed to 10.30 p.m. Since the war this has not been altered. Since 1945 the normal hours for sitting have been 2.30 until 10.30 p.m. on every weekday except Friday. From 1900–39 the House met on Fridays from 12 a.m. to 5.30 p.m. Since 1939 the House meets on Fridays at 11 a.m. and adjourns for the week-end at 4.30 p.m.

Government and Private Members' Time

Until 1939 Government business had precedence at every sitting of the House of Commons except certain Wednesdays and Fridays and Tuesday evenings after 8.15 p.m. until Easter. This generally gave Private Members about 8 Wednesdays and 13 Fridays on which they had precedence. This was always subject to the possibility that the House, or Government, might direct that the time was needed for Government business. Between 1914–18 and 1939–48 Private Members' time was abolished completely. When Private Members' time was restored, the Government retained precedence on all days except for 20 Fridays. Since 22 February 1960 four extra half-days (two Mondays and two Wednesdays) have been allotted for consideration of Private Members' motions, in addition to the 20 Fridays. Friday sittings are generally considered as half-days. The Government therefore retained ninety per cent of the House's time.

SOURCES.—Sir I. Jennings, *Parliament* (2nd ed., 1957), pp. 95–9, 121–2; Sir T. Erskine May, *Parliamentary Practice* (1950); Sir G. Campion, *An Introduction to the Procedure of the House of Commons* (1950); *Report of the Select Committee on the Hours of Meeting and Rising of the House*, H.C. 126 of 1930.

Regnal Years

Until 1962 the dates of Acts of Parliament were recorded in terms of the regnal years during the session in which they were passed. Regnal years date from the accession of the sovereign. Thus the act listed as *11 & 12 Geo. 6, ch. 65* was passed in the parliamentary session during the eleventh and twelfth regnal year of George VI (1948). The parliamentary session of 1948–49 covered three regnal years, and its acts appear under the style *12, 13 & 14 Geo. 6.*

Sovereign	Regnal Year	Date
Victoria	63	20 Jun 1899–19 Jun 1900
	64	20 Jun 1900–22 Jan 01
Edward VII	1	22 Jan 01–21 Jan 02
	10	22 Jan 10–6 May 10
George V	1	6 May 10–5 May 11
	26	6 May 35–20 Jan 36
Edward VIII	1	20 Jan 36–11 Dec 36
George VI	1	11 Dec 36–10 Dec 37
	16	11 Dec 51–6 Feb 52
Elizabeth II	1	6 Feb 52–5 Feb 53
	10	6 Feb 61–5 Feb 62

Regnal years from 1154–1945 are listed in *Handbook of Dates*, ed. C. R. Cheney (1945), pp. 18-31.

Main Select Committees

Public Accounts, 1862

Chairmen

1896	A. O'Connor	1938	F. Pethick-Lawrence
1901	Sir A. Hayter	1941	W. Elliot
1906	V. Cavendish	1943	Sir A. Pownall
1908	(Sir) R. Williams	1945	O. Peake
1919	F. Acland	1948	R. Assheton
1921	A. Williams	1950	Sir R. Cross
1923	F. Jowett	1950	C. Waterhouse
1924	W. Guinness	1951	J. Edwards
1924	W. Graham	1952	(Sir) G. Benson
1929	A. Samuel	1959	H. Wilson
1931	M. Jones		

The Committee is made up of 15 members, including the Chairman, and meets on about 30 days each session. The Chairman is usually a member of the Opposition.

Terms of Reference: 'for the examination of the accounts showing the appropriation of the sums granted by parliament to meet the public expenditure', 'and of such other accounts laid before parliament as the committee may think fit' (*added 15 Nov 34*). 'The Committee shall have power to send for persons, papers and records, and to report from time to time' (*added 14 Nov 33*).

Sources.—*Reports of the Select Committee on Public Accounts*; *Select Committee Returns, 1900–1960*; L. A. Abraham and S. C. Hawtrey, *A Parliamentary Dictionary* (1956); B. Chubb, *The Control of Public Expenditure* (1952).

Estimates, 1912

Chairmen

1912	Sir F. Banbury	1931	Sir V. Henderson
1914	(*suspended*)	1935	Sir I. Salmon
1917	(*see National Expenditure Committee*)	1939	(*see National Expenditure Committee*)
1920	Sir F. Banbury	1945	B. Kirby
1924	Sir J. Marriott	1950	A. Anderson
1926	(Sir) V. Henderson	1951	Sir R. Glyn
1927	A. Bennett	1953	C. Waterhouse
1929	H. Charleton	1957	R. Turton
1930	H. Romeril		

The Committee originally consisted of 15 members. In 1921 this was increased to 24, in 1924 to 28, in 1948 to 36 and in 1960 to 43 members. It sits an average of 16 days each session. The Chairman is usually a Government supporter.

Terms of Reference: 'to examine and report upon such of the Estimates presented to the Committee as may seem fit to the Committee', (*7 Apr 12 original terms*) 'and to suggest the form in which the Estimates shall be presented for examination, and to report what if any economies consistent with the policy implied in those Estimates may be effected therein' (*added in 1921*). In 1924 power was also given to appoint sub-committees. In 1956 the wording of the terms of reference was re-arranged but the substance remained unchanged.

In 1960 the terms were altered to read: 'to examine such of the Estimates presented to this House as may seem fit to the committee and report how, if at all, the policy implied in those Estimates may be carried out more economically and, if the committee think fit, to consider the principal variations between the Estimates and those relating to the previous financial year, and the form in which the Estimates are presented to the House', 'the committee shall have power to send for persons, papers and records, and sit notwithstanding any adjournment of the House, to adjourn from place to place, and to report from time to time: to appoint sub-committees and to refer to such sub-committees any of the matters referred to the committee [each sub-committee has the same powers of sending for persons, etc., sitting and adjourning as the main committee], the committee shall have power to report from time to time the minutes of evidence taken before sub-committees and reported by them to the committee'.

National Expenditure, 1917–1920 and 1939–1945

Chairmen

1917	H. Samuel	1939–45	Sir J. Wardlaw-Milne
1919–20	Sir F. Banbury		

No Estimates were presented to Parliament during the two wars, and the Committee on Estimates lapsed. A Committee on National Expenditure was established each year. It consisted of 26 members 1917–20, and 32 members 1939–45. It met about 13 days a session between 1917–20, and about 19 days a session between 1939–45.

1939–45 Terms of Reference: 'to examine the current expenditure defrayed out of moneys provided by Parliament for the Defence Services, for Civil Defence, and for other services directly connected with the war, and to report what, if any, economies, consistent with the execution of the policy decided by the Government, may be effected therein'.

SOURCES.—*Reports of the Select Committee on Estimates*; *Select Committee Returns, 1900–1960*; Sir I. Jennings, *Parliament* (2nd ed., 1957), pp. 303-16.

Nationalised Industries (Reports and Accounts), 1956 [1]

Chairmen

1956	Sir P. Spens	1957	Sir T. Low

The Committee is appointed on a sessional basis and consists of 13 members. It has met on about 25 days each session.

Terms of Reference: 'to examine the reports and accounts of the nationalised industries established by statute, whose controlling boards are wholly appointed by Ministers of the Crown and whose annual receipts are not

[1] Select Committees were set up each session from 1951–56, under the Chairmanship of R. Assheton (1951–54) and Sir P. Spens (1954–56).

wholly or mainly derived from moneys provided by Parliament or advanced by the Exchequer'.

SOURCES.—*Reports of the Select Committee on Nationalised Industries (Reports and Accounts), 1957–1960; Select Committee Returns, 1957–1960.*

Statutory Instruments, 1944
(1944–1947 Statutory Rules and Orders)

Chairmen

1944 Sir C. MacAndrew　　1951 E. Fletcher
1950 G. Nicholson

The Committee consists of 11 members, and meets on about 16 days each session.

Terms of Reference: the original terms of 21 Jun 44 have been considerably enlarged by additional powers conferred over the last fifteen years. The Committee now has power to consider all S.I.s, drafts of S.I.s, and all schemes requiring approval by S.I. and to draw the attention of the House to them on any of the following grounds: (i) that they involve public money, (ii) that they are immune from challenge in the courts, (iii) that they have effect retrospectively, (iv) that there seems to have been an unjustifiable delay in publication of the S.I., laying it before Parliament, or sending notification to the Speaker, and (v) if elucidation is considered necessary. The Committee has the same powers as the Estimates Committee to sit when it wishes, to report from time to time, and to call for witnesses. It is obliged to give any government department an opportunity to explain an S.I. or document before drawing it to the attention of the House.

Since 1890 the Statutory Rules and Orders have been published in annual volumes. The average annual total of Orders made between 1894–1900 was just over 1,000.[1]

Statutory Instruments

Year	Annual Total	General	Local
1900	995	174	821
1910	1,368	218	1,150
1920	2,475	916	1,559
1929	1,262	391	871
1940	2,222	1,626	596
1950	2,144	1,211	933
1958	2,280	685	1,595

The distinction between 'General' and 'Local' follows that adopted between public Acts and local and personal Acts of Parliament. The lists do *not* include 'provisional rules', rules of an executive character (most of which are local), rules made by other bodies (e.g. local authorities) but confirmed by a government department (mostly local and very numerous). The list also excludes some rules made by statutory authorities which are not government departments.

The figures were given by Sir. C. Carr in evidence before the *Committee*

[1] From C. K. Allen, *Law and Orders* (2nd ed. 1956), p. 31.

on Ministers' Powers: Minutes of Evidence, II, p. 205; the *Select Committee on Procedure* (H.C. 189 of 1945–46, p. 243); and the *Select Committee on Delegated Legislation* (H.C. 301 of 1953, p. 2). The figures for 1950 and 1958 are based on J. E. Kersell, *Parliamentary Supervision of Delegated Legislation* (1960).

SOURCES.—*Select Committee Returns, 1944–60*; *Select Committee on Statutory Instruments (Rules and Orders, 1944–47) Minutes of Proceedings* (published after each Session); Sir I. Jennings, *Parliament* (2nd ed. 1957), pp. 489-516 (quotes Sir C. Carr's figures); Ld Hewart, *The New Despotism* (1929); C. K. Allen, *Law and Orders* (1944); G. W. Keeton, *The Passing of Parliament* (1952); L. A. Abraham and S. C. Hawtrey, *A Parliamentary Dictionary* (1956) and information from the Committee Office of the House of Commons.

Payment of M.P.s

In 1900 M.P.s were unpaid. From the beginning of 1912 a salary of £400 per year was paid to all members not receiving salaries as Ministers or officers of the House. From 1913 to 1954 £100 of M.P.s' salaries was made tax-exempt in respect of parliamentary expenses. In 1924 M.P.s were allowed free railway travel between London and their constituencies. In 1931 the £400 salary was cut to £360, as an economy measure; in 1934 it was restored to £380 and then to £400. In June 1937 the salary was increased to £600. In May 1946 it was increased again to £1,000 and salaries of £500 were authorised for M.P.s who, as Ministers or Leaders of the Opposition, had an official salary of less than £5,000. Free travel was granted between M.P.s' homes and Westminster as well as to their constituencies. In 1953 a sessional allowance was introduced of £2 per day for every day (except Friday) on which the House sat: this was payable to all M.P.s — including Ministers. In 1957 the sessional allowance (usually amounting to about £280 p.a.) was replaced by an annual £750 to cover parliamentary expenses. The whole £1,750 which ordinary M.P.s have drawn since 1957 is subject to tax but M.P.s may claim, as tax free, any expenses up to £1,750 incurred in respect of parliamentary duties.

SOURCES.—H.C. 255 of 1920, *Report of the Select Committee on Members' Expenses*; Cmd. 5624, 1937–38, *Report of the Departmental Committee on an M.P.s' Pension Scheme*; H.C. 93 of 1945–46, *Report of the Select Committee on Members' Expenses*; H.C. 72 of 1954, *Report of the Select Committee on Members' Expenses, etc.*; *Ministerial Salaries Act, 1957* (17 Jul).

House of Lords

Lord Chairmen of Committees

(*Deputy Speaker of the House of Lords. The Lord Chancellor is the Speaker.*)

1889	E of Morley	1944	Ld Stanmore
1905	4th E of Onslow	1946	E of Drogheda
1911	E of Donoughmore	1957	Ld Merthyr
1931	5th E of Onslow		

Officers of the House of Lords

Clerk		*Librarian*	
1885	(Sir) H. Graham	1897	A. Strong
1917	Sir A. Thring	1904	E. Gosse
1930	Sir E. Alderson	1914	A. Butler
1934	(Sir) H. Badeley	1922	C. Clay
1949	(Sir) R. Overbury	1956	C. Dobson
1953	(Sir) F. Lascelles		
1959	(Sir) V. Goodman		

SOURCES.—*Dod's Parliamentary Companion*; *Whitaker's Almanack*; *Hansard*.

Life Peerages Act, 1958

By this Act, life peers were to be appointed by the Sovereign on the recommendation of the Prime Minister. For the first time women were allowed to sit and vote in the House of Lords, as life peeresses. One of the aims of the Act was to provide for more balanced party representation in the House of Lords.[1]

Composition of the House of Lords
(including minors)

Year	Dukes[a]	Marquesses	Earls	Viscounts	Barons	Life Peers[b]	Law Lords[c]	Repres. Scotland[d]	Repres. Ireland[d]	Archbps. and Bishops	Total
1901	32	34	165	38	248	..	4	16	28	26	591
1910	31	35	161	50	272	..	4	16	28	26	623
1919	28	40	165	71	319	..	6	16	27	26	698
1930	30	38	166	82	370	..	7	16	18	26	753
1939	30	38	159	96	389	..	7	16	13	26	781
1950	30	38	168	99	444	..	9	16	6	26	847
1960	26	26	132	111	538	24	8	16	1	26	908

[a] Including Royal Dukes.
[b] Created by the Life Peers Act, 1958, and including 5 baronesses.
[c] Lords of Appeal in Ordinary.
[d] Scottish and Irish peers sitting by virtue of other titles are listed under their superior title.

SOURCES.—*Constitutional Year Books, 1900–39*; *Dod's Parliamentary Companion, 1940–61*.

Creation of Peerages, 1900–1960

Administration		New Creations	Advanced in Rank	Total	Duration of Ministry (Yrs.)	Average Annual Creations[a]
Salisbury	1895–02	44	n.a.	44	7	6
Balfour	1902–05	18	5	23	3½	7
Campbell-Bannerman	1905–08	21	..	21	2⅓	9
Asquith	1908–15	67	13	80	7	11
Asquith	1915–16	17	2	19	1½	13
Lloyd George	1916–22	91	25	116	5¾	20
Bonar Law	1922–23	3	..	3	½	6
Baldwin	1923–24	8	1	9	⅔	14
MacDonald	1924	4	1	5	¾	7
Baldwin	1924–29	42	10	52	4½	12
MacDonald	1929–31	20	..	20	2¼	9
MacDonald	1931–35	44	6	50	3¾	13
Baldwin	1935–37	29	5	34	2	17
Chamberlain	1937–40	20	4	24	3	8
Churchill	1940–45	62	9	71	5¼	14
Attlee	1945–51	86	8	94	6¼	15
Churchill	1951–55	33	6	39	3½	11
Eden	1955–57	19	3	22	1¾	13
Macmillan	1957–60	60 [b]	1	61 [b]	4	15

[a] New creations only.
[b] Including 19 life peers and 5 life peeresses created under the *Life Peerages Act, 1958*.

SOURCES.—*Constitutional Year Books, 1900–39*; *Dod's Parliamentary Companion, 1900–61*; *Debrett's Peerage*; *Burke's Peerage*.

[1] At the end of 1960, 24 life peers had been created under this act, including 5 life peeresses. These comprise 7 members of the Labour Party, 6 Conservatives, and 11 whose politics are not stated.

State of Parties in the House of Lords

Year	Con.	Lab.	Lib.	Ind.	Other	Politics not stated	Minors
1900	466	..	69	..	..	39	15
1905	462	..	77	..	..	41	11
1910	472	..	105	..	..	40	13
1914	471	..	112	..	..	58	13
1919	481	..	130	..	..	66	21
1925	512	10	109	..	..	88	20
1930	490	17	79	..	..	140	27
1935	545	16	57	3	..	130	23
1940	277	10	48	1	1	427	23
1945	457	30	79	5	..	218	27
1950	439	48	57	13	..	283	23
1955	393	41	38	16	..	356	23
1960	349	39	32	14	..	474	8

SOURCES.—*Constitutional Year Books*, 1900–39; *Dod's Parliamentary Companion*, 1940–60.

These figures for the state of parties in the House of Lords should be treated with extreme caution. The considerable difference between the strength of parties in 1935 and 1940 is due to the different systems of compilation of the two reference books: the Constitutional Year Books and Dod. Attendance at the House of Lords is often irregular and party allegiance obscure. Since 1958 when official leave of absence was instituted for peers (on the recommendation of the 'Swinton Committee' reporting in Jan 1956),[1] the potential effective size of the House of Lords was reduced to approximately 625 peers. The figures (from the attendance records) for the session 1957/58 show that 518 peers attended at least once, and that approximately 100 attended at least 50 per cent of the time.

Powers

Until 1911 the legislative powers of the House of Lords were in theory co-equal with those of the House of Commons, except for the convention that financial measures must originate in the Lower House. The *Parliament Act, 1911* provided (a) that bills certified by the Speaker as money bills would become law one month after being sent to the House of Lords, even without the latter's consent; and (b) that any other public bill (except one to extend the Life of Parliament), passed by the House of Commons in three successive sessions and rejected by the House of Lords, nevertheless would become law, provided that two years had elapsed between the second reading in the first session and the third reading in the third session of the House of Commons. The *Parliament Act, 1949* reduced the delaying powers to two sessions and one year.

[1] *Report by the Select Committee on the Powers of the House in Relation to the Attendance of its Members* (H.M.S.O.: 24 Jan 56) (Chairman: E of Swinton).

Pay

On 21 May 1946 it was agreed that regular attenders at the House of Lords should be reimbursed their travelling expenses. In practice, this was made to apply only to peers attending at least one-third of the sittings of the House. From July 1957 peers were entitled to claim a maximum of three guineas per day for expenses incurred in attendance at the House. This was additional to travelling expenses and claims were not subject to any minimum number of attendances.

SOURCES.—1908 (H.L. 234), *Select Committee Report on the House of Lords*; Cd. 9038/1918, *The Reform of the Second Chamber* (Conference: Vt Bryce); Cmd. 7380/1948, *Report of the Inter Party Conference on the Parliament Bill*; H.M.S.O. (24 Jan 56), *Report of the Select Committee on the Power of the House in Relation to the Attendance of its Members.*

Sir T. Erskine May, *Parliamentary Practice* (16th edition, 1957); Sir G. Campion, *An Introduction to the Procedure of the House of Commons* (1950); J. Redlich, *Procedure of the House of Commons* (3 vols., 1908); P. A. Bromhead, *The House of Lords and Contemporary Politics, 1911–1957* (1958); Sir I. Jennings, *Parliament* (2nd ed., 1957).

IV
ELECTIONS

General Election Statistics

IT is impossible to present election statistics in any finally authoritative way. British law makes no acknowledgement of the existence of political parties, and in most general elections the precise allegiance of at least a few of the candidates is in doubt. This, far more than arithmetic error, explains the discrepancies between the figures provided in various works of reference.

Such discrepancies, however, are seldom on a serious scale (except, perhaps, for 1918). Election figures suffer much more from being inherently confusing than from being inaccurately reported. The complications that arise from unopposed returns, from plural voting, from two-member seats, and, above all, from variations in the number of candidates put up by each party are the really serious hazards in psephological interpretation.

In the figures which follow an attempt is made to allow for these factors by a column which shows the average vote won by each opposed candidate (with the vote in two-member seats halved, and with University seats excluded). This still gives a distorted picture, especially when, as in 1900 or 1931, there were many unopposed candidates or when, as in 1929, 1931, or 1950 there was a sharp change in the number of Liberals standing; in 1918 the situation was so complicated that any such statistics are omitted, as they are likely to confuse more than to clarify; for other elections they should be regarded as corrective supplements to the cruder percentages in the previous column rather than as substitutes for them.

The turn-out percentages are modified to allow for the distorting effect of the two-member seats which existed up to 1950.

To simplify classification, some arbitrary decisions have been made. Before 1918 candidates have been classified as Conservative, Liberal, or Irish Nationalist, even if their designation had a prefix such as Tariff Reform, or Independent. From 1918 onwards candidates not officially recognised by their party have been classified with 'Others' (except that in 1935 Ind. Lib. are placed with Lib.). Liberal Unionists have been listed as Conservatives throughout. Liberal National, National Labour, and National candidates are listed with Conservatives except in 1931.

General Election Results, 1900–1918

	Total Votes	M.P.s Elected	Candi-dates	Unopposed Returns	% Share of Total Vote	Average % Vote per Opposed Candidate
1900. 28 Sep–24 Oct						
Conservative	1,797,444	402	579	163	51·1	52·5
Liberal	1,568,141	184	406	22	44·6	48·2
Labour	63,304	2	15	..	1·8	26·6
Irish Nationalist	90,076	82	100	58	2·5	80·0
Others	544	..	2	..	·0	2·2
Elec. 6,730,935 Turnout 74·6%	3,519,509	670	1,102	243	100·0	..
1906. 12 Jan–7 Feb						
Conservative	2,451,454	157	574	13	43·6	44·1
Liberal	2,757,883	400	539	27	49·0	52·6
Labour	329,748	30	51	..	5·9	39·9
Irish Nationalist	35,031	83	87	74	0·6	63·1
Others	52,387	..	22	..	0·9	18·8
Elec. 7,264,608 Turnout 82·6%	5,626,503	670	1,273	114	100·0	..
1910. 14 Jan–9 Feb						
Conservative	3,127,887	273	600	19	46·9	47·5
Liberal	2,880,581	275	516	1	43·2	49·2
Labour	511,392	40	81	..	7·7	38·4
Irish Nationalist	124,586	82	104	55	1·9	77·7
Others	22,958	..	14	..	0·3	15·4
Elec. 7,694,741 Turnout 86·6%	6,667,404	670	1,315	75	100·0	..
1910. 2–19 Dec						
Conservative	2,424,566	272	550	72	46·3	47·9
Liberal	2,293,686	272	467	35	43·8	49·5
Labour	376,581	42	59	3	7·2	42·8
Irish Nationalist	131,721	84	106	53	2·5	81·9
Others	8,768	..	9	..	0·2	9·1
Elec. 7,709,981 Turnout 81·1%	5,235,322	670	1,191	163	100·0	..
1918. Sat., 14 Dec						
Coalition Unionist	3,504,198	335	374	42	32·6	
Coalition Liberal	1,455,640	133	158	27	13·5	
Coalition Labour	161,521	10	18	..	1·5	
(Coalition)	(5,121,359)	(478)	(550)	(69)	(47·6)	
Conservative	370,375	23	37	..	3·4	
Irish Unionist	292,722	25	38	..	2·7	
Liberal	1,298,808	28	253	..	12·1	
Labour	2,385,472	63	388	12	22·2	
Irish Nationalist	238,477	7	60	1	2·2	
Sinn Fein	486,867	73	102	25	4·5	
Others	572,503	10	197	..	5·3	
Elec. 21,392,322 Turnout 58·9%	10,766,583	707	1,625	107	100·0	

General Election Results, 1922–1931

	Total Votes	M.P.s Elected	Candi-dates	Unopposed Returns	% Share of Total Vote	Average % Vote per Opposed Candidate
1922. Wed., 15 Nov						
Conservative	5,500,382	345	483	42	38·2	48·6
National Liberal	1,673,240	62	162	5	11·6	39·3
Liberal	2,516,287	54	328	5	17·5	30·9
Labour	4,241,383	142	411	4	29·5	40·0
Others	462,340	12	59	1	3·2	28·3
Elec. 21,127,663 Turnout 71·3%	14,393,632	615	1,443	57	100·0	..
1923. Thu., 6 Dec						
Conservative	5,538,824	258	540	35	38·1	42·6
Liberal	4,311,147	159	453	11	29·6	37·8
Labour	4,438,508	191	422	3	30·5	41·0
Others	260,042	7	31	1	1·8	27·6
Elec. 21,281,232 Turnout 70·8%	14,548,521	615	1,446	50	100·0	..
1924. Wed., 29 Oct						
Conservative	8,039,598	419	552	16	48·3	51·9
Liberal	2,928,747	40	340	6	17·6	30·9
Labour	5,489,077	151	512	9	33·0	38·2
Communist	55,346	1	8	..	0·3	25·0
Others	126,511	4	16	1	0·8	29·1
Elec. 21,731,320 Turnout 76·6%	16,639,279	615	1,428	32	100·0	..
1929. Thu., 30 May						
Conservative	8,656,473	260	590	4	38·2	39·4
Liberal	5,308,510	59	513	..	23·4	27·7
Labour	8,389,512	288	571	..	37·1	39·3
Communist	50,614	..	25	..	0·3	5·3
Others	243,266	8	31	3	1·0	21·2
Elec. 28,850,870 Turnout 76·1%	22,648,375	615	1,730	7	100·0	..
1931. Tue., 27 Oct						
Conservative	11,978,745	473	523	56	55·2	62·9 (Conservative, National Labour, Liberal National)
National Labour	341,370	13	20	..	1·6	
Liberal National	809,302	35	41	..	3·7	
Liberal	1,403,102	33	112	5	6·5	28·8
(National Government)	(14,532,519)	(554)	(696)	(61)	(67·0)	..
Independent Liberal	106,106	4	7	..	0·5	35·8
Labour	6,649,630	52	515	6	30·6	33·0
Communist	74,824	..	26	..	0·3	7·5
New Party	36,377	..	24	..	0·2	3·9
Others	256,917	5	24	..	1·2	21·9
Elec. 29,960,071 Turnout 76·3%	21,656,373	615	1,292	67	100·0	..

General Election Results, 1935–1959

	Total Votes	M.P.s Elected	Candi-dates	Unopposed Returns	% Share of Total Vote	Average % Vote per Opposed Candidate
1935. Thu., 14 Nov						
Conservative	11,810,158	432	585	26	53·7	54·8
Liberal	1,422,116	20	161	..	6·4	23·9
Labour	8,325,491	154	552	13	37·9	40·3
Independent Labour Party	139,577	4	17	..	0·7	22·2
Communist	27,117	1	2	..	0·1	38·0
Others	272,595	4	31	1	1·2	21·3
Elec. 31,379,050 Turnout 71·2%	21,997,054	615	1,348	40	100·0	..
1945. Thu., 5 Jul [a]						
Conservative	9,988,306	213	624	2	39·8	40·1
Liberal	2,248,226	12	306	..	9·0	18·6
Labour	11,995,152	393	604	1	47·8	50·4
Communist	102,780	2	21	..	0·4	12·7
Common Wealth	110,634	1	23	..	0·4	12·6
Others	640,880	19	104	..	2·0	15·4
Elec. 33,240,391 Turnout 72·7%	25,085,978	640	1,682	3	100·0	..
1950. Thu., 23 Feb						
Conservative	12,502,567	298	620	2	43·5	43·7
Liberal	2,621,548	9	475	..	9·1	11·8
Labour	13,266,592	315	617	..	46·1	46·7
Communist	91,746	..	100	..	0·3	2·0
Others	290,218	3	56	..	1·0	12·6
Elec. 33,269,770 Turnout 84·0%	28,772,671	625	1,868	2	100·0	..
1951. Thu., 25 Oct						
Conservative	13,717,538	321	617	4	48·0	48·6
Liberal	730,556	6	109	..	2·5	14·7
Labour	13,948,605	295	617	..	48·8	49·2
Communist	21,640	..	10	..	0·1	4·4
Others	177,329	3	23	..	0·6	16·8
Elec. 34,645,573 Turnout 82·5%	28,595,668	625	1,376	4	100·0	..
1955. Thu., 26 May						
Conservative	13,286,569	344	623	..	49·7	50·2
Liberal	722,405	6	110	..	2·7	15·1
Labour	12,404,970	277	620	..	46·4	47·3
Communist	33,144	..	17	..	0·1	4·2
Others	313,410	3	39	..	1·1	20·8
Elec. 34,858,263 Turnout 76·7%	26,760,498	630	1,409	..	100·0	..
1959. Thu., 8 Oct						
Conservative	13,749,830	365	625	..	49·4	49·6
Liberal	1,638,571	6	216	..	5·9	16·9
Labour	12,215,538	258	621	..	43·8	44·5
Communist	30,897	..	18	..	0·1	4·1
Others	224,405	1	56	..	0·8	10·0
Elec. 35,397,080 Turnout 78·8%	27,859,241	630	1,536	..	100·0	..

[a] Result announced 26 July 1945

General Election Results by Regions

	1900	1906	Jan 1910	Dec 1910	1918[a]	1922	1923	1924	1929	1931	1 5	1945	1950	1951	1955	1959
County of London																
Conservative	51	19	33	30	Coal.	43	29	39	24	53	39	12	12	14	15	18
Liberal	8	38	25	26	53	9	11	3	2	4	1	..	..	..	..	..
Labour	..	2	1	3	Op.	9	22	19	36	5	22	48	31	29	27	24
Others	..	..	..	..	9	1	..	1	..	..	..	2	..	..	..	..
Rest of S. England																
Conservative	123	45	107	104	Coal.	130	89	150	111	156	147	88	144	153	163	171
Liberal	32	107	46	49	149	23	48	5	18	4	3	3	1	..	..	1
Labour	..	3	2	2	Op.	9	27	10	35	5	15	91	54	46	42	34
Others	..	..	..	..	16	3	1	..	1	..	..	3	..	..	1	..
Midlands																
Conservative	60	27	49	50	Coal.	53	45	64	35	80	67	24	35	35	39	49
Liberal	27	59	31	30	67	17	17	2	5	3	1	..	..	..	..	..
Labour	1	2	8	8	Op.	17	25	21	47	4	19	64	59	59	57	47
Others	..	..	..	..	20	..	..	..	..	..	..	2	..	..	..	..
Northern England																
Conservative	98	31	45	50	Coal.	82	57	101	51	146	106	43	61	69	75	77
Liberal	55	102	86	82	121	27	48	9	10	9	5	2	1	2	2	2
Labour	..	20	22	21	Op.	60	64	59	108	15	60	128	107	99	90	88
Others	1	1	1	1	50	2	2	2	2	1	..	..	..	..	..	..
Wales																
Conservative	6	..	2	3	Coal.	6	4	9	1	11	11	4	4	6	6	7
Liberal	27	33	27	26	20	10	12	10	9	8	6	6	5	3	3	2
Labour	1	1	5	5	Op.	18	19	16	25	16	18	25	27	27	27	27
Others	..	..	..	..	15	1	..	..	..	..	..	..	..	..	..	..
Scotland																
Conservative	36	10	9	9	Coal.	13	14	36	20	57	43	29	32	35	36	31
Liberal	34	58	59	58	54	27	22	8	13	7	3	..	2	1	1	1
Labour	..	2	2	3	Op.	29	34	26	37	7	20	37	37	35	34	38
Others	..	..	..	..	17	2	1	1	1	..	5	5	..	..	..	1
Ireland																
Conservative	19	16	19	17	Coal.	10	10	12	10	10	10	9	10	9	10	12
Liberal	1	3	1	1	1	..	..	..	..	..	..	..	..	..	..	..
Labour	..	..	..	..	Op.	..	..	..	..	..	..	..	..	..	..	..
Others	81	82	81	83	100	2	2	..	2	2	2	3	2	3	2	..
Universities																
Conservative	9	9	9	9	Coal.	8	9	8	8	8	9	4	..	..	..	..
Liberal	..	..	..	..	13	3	2	3	2	2	1	1	..	..	..	..
Labour	..	..	..	..	Op.	..	..	..	..	..	..	..	..	..	..	..
Others	..	..	..	..	2	1	1	1	2	2	2	7	..	..	..	..
Totals																
Conservative	402	157	273	272	Coal.	345	258	419	260	521	432	213	298	321	344	365
Liberal	184	400	275	272	478	116	159	40	59	37	20	12	9	6	6	6
Labour	2	30	40	42	Op.	142	191	151	288	52	154	394	315	295	277	258
Others	82	83	82	84	229	12	7	5	8	5	9	22	3	3	3	1
Total seats	670	670	670	670	707	615	615	615	615	615	615	640	625	625	630	630

The heavy vertical lines indicate redistributions of seats.
Northern England includes Cheshire, Lancashire, Yorkshire, and all counties to their north.
Midlands includes Hereford, Worcs., Warwickshire, Northants, Lincs., Notts., Leics., Staffs., Salop, Derbyshire.
Southern England includes the rest of England, except for the County of London.

[a] In 1918 all Coalition and all non-Coalition candidates are listed together. In fact a substantial number of the 48 Conservatives who were elected without the Coupon worked with the Government. Virtually no Coupons were issued to Irish candidates but 23 of the 101 non-University seats in Ireland went to Unionists.

Party Changes between Elections

The party composition of the House of Commons changes continuously partly owing to Members changing their allegiance and partly owing to by-election results. The following table shows the net change due to both causes during the life of each Parliament. (Seats vacant at dissolution are included under the last incumbent's party.)

		Con.	Lib.	Lab.	Others
1895–1900	Dissolution	399	189	..	82
1900–05	Election Dissolution	402 369	184 215	2 4	82 82
1906–09	Election Dissolution	157 168	400 373	30 46	83 83
1910	Election Dissolution	273 274	275 274	40 40	82 82
1910–18	Election Dissolution	272 281	272 260	42 39	84 90
1918–22 [a]	Election Dissolution	383 378	161 155	73 87	90 87
1922–23	Election Dissolution	345 344	116 117	142 144	12 10
1923–24	Election Dissolution	258 259	159 158	191 193	7 5
1924–29	Election Dissolution	419 400	40 46	151 162	5 7
1929–31	Election Dissolution	260 263	59 57	288 281 [b]	8 14
1931–35	Election Dissolution	521 512	37 34	52 59	5 10
1935–45	Election Dissolution	432 398	20 18	154 166	9 33
1945–50	Election Dissolution	213 218	12 10	393 391	22 21
1950–51	Election Dissolution	298 298	9 9	315 314	3 4
1951–55	Election Dissolution	321 322	6 6	295 294	3 3
1955–59	Election Dissolution	344 340	6 6	277 281	3 3
1959–	Election	365	6	258	1

[a] In this form the 1918–22 figures are highly misleading. This amplification may help:

	Co. U.	Con.	Co. Lib.	Lib.	Co. Lab.	Lab.	O.
Election . .	335	48	133	28	10	63	90
Dissolution . .	313	65	120	35	11	76	87

[b] This figure includes 15 National Labour M.P.s.

By-elections

	Total[a] By-elections	Changes	Con. +	Con. −	Lib. +	Lib. −	Lab. +	Lab. −	Others +	Others −
1900–05	113	32	2	26	20	6	5	..	5	..
1906–09	101	20	12	..	..	18	5	..	3	2
1910	20	..	..	..	..	..	..	..	..	..
1911–18	245	31	16	4	4	16	2	4	10	8
1918–22	109	27	4	13	5[b]	11[b]	14	1	4	2
1922–23	16	6	1	4	3	1	2	..	..	1
1923–24	10	3	2	1	..	1	1	1	..	..
1924–29	64	20	1	16	6	3	13	1	..	..
1929–31	36	7	4	1	..	1	2	4	1	1
1931–35	64	10	..	9	..	1	10	..	..	..
1935–45	219	28	..	27	..	..	11	1	17	..
1945–50	52	3	3	..	..	..	..	..	..	3
1950–51	16	..	..	..	..	..	..	..	..	..
1951–55	48	1	1	..	..	..	..	1	..	..
1955–59	52	6	1	4	1	1	4	..	..	1

[a] Up to 1918, and to a lesser extent to 1926, the number of by-elections is inflated by the necessity for Ministers to stand for re-election on appointment. In 53 such cases the returns were unopposed.

[b] In 1918–22 Opposition Liberals won 5 seats and lost 2. Coalition Liberals lost 9.

Seats Changing Hands at By-elections

Date	Constituency	General Election	By-election
6 Sep 01	N.E. Lanark.	Lib.	Con.
1 Nov 01	Galway	Con.	Nat.
0 May 02	Bury	Con.	Lib.
9 Jul 02	Leeds N.	Con.	Lib.
1 Aug 02	N.E. Lancs.	Lib.	Lab.
8 Aug 02	S. Belfast	Con.	Ind. U.
2 Oct 02	Devonport	Lib.	Con.
9 Nov 02	Orkney & Shetland	Con.	Ind. Lib.
2 Jan 03	E. Cambs.	Con.	Lib.
1 Mar 03	Woolwich	Con.	Lab.
7 Mar 03	E. Sussex	Con.	Lib.
0 Mar 03	N. Fermanagh	Con.	Ind. Con.
4 Jul 03	Barnard Castle	Lib.	Lab.
6 Aug 03	Argyll	Con.	Lib.
7 Sep 03	St. Andrews	Con.	Lib.
5 Jan 04	Norwich	Con.	Lib.
0 Jan 04	Gateshead	Lib.	Lab.
0 Jan 04	Ayr	Con.	Lib.
2 Feb 04	Mid-Herts.	Con.	Lib.
7 Mar 04	E. Dorset	Con.	Lib.
6 Apr 04	Isle of Wight	Con.	Ind. Con.
0 Jun 04	Devonport	Con. 02 / Lib. 00	Lib.
6 Jul 04	W. Shropshire	Con.	Lib.
0 Aug 04	N.E. Lanark.	Con. 01 / Lib. 00	Lib.
7 Jan 05	Stalybridge	Con.	Lib.
6 Jan 05	N. Dorset	Con.	Lib.
3 Mar 05	Bute	Con.	Lib.
5 Apr 05	Brighton	Con.	Lib.
1 Jun 05	Whitby	Con.	Lib.
9 Jun 05	Finsbury E.	Con.	Lib.
3 Oct 05	Barkston Ash	Con.	Lib.
7 Nov 05	Normanton	Lib.	Lab.
3 Aug 06	Cockermouth	Lib.	Con.
31 Dec 06	Mid-Cork	Nat.	I. Nat.
30 Jan 07	N.E. Derbyshire[a]	Lib.	Lab.
26 Feb 07	Brigg	Lib.	Con.
4 Jul 07	Jarrow	Lib.	Lab.
16 Jul 07	Colne Valley	Lib.	I. Lab.
31 Jul 07	N.W. Staffs.[a]	Lib.	Lab.
17 Jan 08	Mid-Devon	Lib.	Con.
31 Jan 08	S. Hereford	Lib.	Con.
24 Mar 08	Peckham	Lib.	Con.
24 Apr 08	Manchester N.W.	Lib.	Con.
20 Jun 08	Pudsey	Lib.	Con.
1 Aug 08	Haggerston	Lib.	Con.
24 Sep 08	Newcastle-o-T.	Lib.	Con.
2 Mar 09	Glasgow C.	Lib.	Con.
1 May 09	Cork City	Nat.	I. Nat.
4 May 09	Attercliffe	Lib.	Lab.
4 May 09	S.W. Warwicks.	Lib.	Con.
15 Jul 09	Mid-Derbyshire	Lib.	Lab.
28 Oct 09	Bermondsey	Lib.	Con.
1910—no change			
28 Apr 11	Cheltenham	Lib.	Con.
13 Nov 11	Oldham	Lib.	Con.
21 Nov 11	S. Somerset	Lib.	Con.
20 Dec 11	N. Ayrshire	Lib.	Con.
5 Mar 12	Manchester S.	Lib.	Con.
13 Jul 12	Hanley	Lab.	Lib.
26 Jul 12	Crewe	Lib.	Con.
8 Aug 12	Manchester N.W.	Lib.	Con.
10 Sep 12	Edinburgh	Lib.	Con.
26 Nov 12	Bow & Bromley	Lab.	Con.
30 Jan 13	Londonderry	Con.	Lib.
18 Mar 13	S. Westmorland	Con.	Ind. Con.
16 May 13	E. Cambs.	Lib.	Con.

[a] Miners candidates standing as Lib-Lab, who only joined the Labour Party in 1909.

Date		Constituency	General Election	By-election
20 Aug	13	Chesterfield	Lab.	Lib.
8 Nov	13	Reading	Lib.	Con.
12 Dec	13	S. Lanarkshire	Lib.	Con.
19 Feb	14	Bethnal Green S.W.	Lib.	Con.
26 Feb	14	Leith	Lib.	Con.
20 May	14	N.E. Derbyshire	Lab.	Con.
23 May	14	Ipswich	Lib.	Con.
9 Dec	14	Tullamore	Nat.	I. Nat.
9 Mar	16	E. Herts.	Con.	Ind.
15 Nov	16	W. Cork	I. Nat.	Nat.
23 Dec	16	Ashton-u-Lyne	Con.	Lib. (Unop.)
3 Feb	17	N. Roscommon	Nat.	S.F.
10 May	17	S. Longford	Nat.	S.F.
10 Jul	17	E. Clare	Nat.	S.F.
10 Aug	17	Kilkenny	Nat.	S.F.
2 Nov	17	Salford N.	Lib.	Lab.
19 Apr	18	Tullamore	{ I. Nat. 14 Nat. 10	S.F.
20 Jun	18	E. Cavan	Nat.	S.F.
1 Mar	19	Leyton W.	Co. U.	Lib.
29 Mar	19	Hull C.	Co. U.	Lib.
16 Apr	19	C. Aberdeen & Kincardine	Co. U.	Lib.
27 May	19	E. Antrim	Con.	Ind. U.
16 Jul	19	Bothwell	Co. U.	Lab.
30 Aug	19	Widnes	Co. U.	Lab.
20 Dec	19	Spen Valley	Co. Lib.	Lab.
7 Feb	20	Wrekin	Co. Lib.	Ind.
27 Mar	20	Dartford	Co. Lib.	Lab.
27 Mar	20	Stockport	Co. Lab.	Co. U.
3 Jun	20	Louth	Co. U.	Lib.
27 Jul	20	S. Norfolk	Lib.	Lab.
12 Jan	21	Dover	Co. U.	Ind.
2 Mar	21	Woolwich E.	Lab.	Co. U.
3 Mar	21	Dudley	Co. U.	Lab.
4 Mar	21	Kirkcaldy	Co. Lib.	Lab.
5 Mar	21	Penistone	Lib.	Lab.
7 Jun	21	Westminster, St. G.	Co. U.	Ind.
8 Jun	21	Heywood & Radcliffe	Co. Lib.	Lab.
14 Dec	21	Southwark, S.E.	Co. Lib.	Lab.
18 Feb	22	Manchester, Clayton	Con.	Lab.
20 Feb	22	Camberwell N.	Co. U.	Lab.
24 Feb	22	Bodmin	Co. U.	Lib.
30 Mar	22	Leicester E.	Co. Lib.	Lab.
25 Jul	22	Pontypridd	Co. Lib.	Lab.
18 Aug	22	Hackney S.	Ind.	Co. U.
18 Oct	22	Newport	Co. Lib.	Con.
3 Mar	23	Mitcham	Con.	Lab.
3 Mar	23	Willesden E.	Con.	Lib.
6 Mar	23	Liverpool, Edge Hill	Con.	Lab.
7 Apr	23	Anglesey	Ind.	Lib.
31 May	23	Berwick on Tweed	Nat. Lib.	Con.
21 Jun	23	Tiverton	Con.	Lib.
22 May	24	Liverpool, W. Toxteth	Con.	Lab.
5 Jun	24	Oxford	Lib.	Con.
31 Jul	24	Holland with Boston	Lab.	Con.
17 Sep	25	Stockport	Con.	Lab.
17 Feb	26	Darlington	Con.	Lab.
12 Mar	26	English Univs.	Lib.	Con.
29 Apr	26	East Ham N.	Con.	Lab.
28 May	26	Hammersmith N.	Con.	Lab.
29 Nov	26	Hull C.	Lib.	Lab.
23 Feb	27	Stourbridge	Con.	Lab.
28 Mar	27	Southwark N.	Lab.	Lib.
1 Jun	27	Bosworth	Con.	Lib.
9 Jan	28	Northampton	Con.	Lab.
9 Feb	28	Lancaster	Con.	Lib.
6 Mar	28	St. Ives	Con.	Lib.
4 Apr	28	Linlithgow	Con.	Lab.
13 Jul	28	Halifax	Lib.	Lab.
29 Oct	28	Ashton-u-Lyne	Con.	Lab.
29 Jan	29	W. Midlothian	Con.	Lab.
7 Feb	29	Battersea S.	Con.	Lab.
20 Mar	29	Eddisbury	Con.	Lib.
21 Mar	29	N. Lanark	Con.	Lab.
21 Mar	29	Holland	Con.	Lib.
31 Jul	29	Preston	Lib.	Lab.
14 Dec	29	Liverpool, Scotland	I. Nat.	Lab. (Unop.)
6 May	30	Fulham W.	Lab.	Con.
30 Oct	30	Paddington S.	Con.	Ind.
6 Nov	30	Shipley	Lab.	Con.
26 Mar	31	Sunderland	Lab.	Con.
30 Apr	31	Ashton-u-Lyne	Lab.	Con.
21 Apr	32	Wakefield	Con.	Lab.
26 Jul	32	Wednesbury	Con.	Lab.
27 Feb	33	Rotherham	Con.	Lab.
25 Oct	33	Fulham E.	Con.	Lab.
24 Apr	34	Hammersmith N.	Con.	Lab.
14 May	34	West Ham, Upton	Con.	Lab.
23 Oct	34	Lambeth N.	Lib.	Lab.
25 Oct	34	Swindon	Con.	Lab.
6 Feb	35	Liverpool, Wavertree	Con.	Lab.
16 Jul	35	Liverpool, W. Toxteth	Con.	Lab.
6 May	36	Camberwell, Peckham	Con.	Lab.
9 Jul	36	Derby	Con.	Lab.
26 Nov	36	Greenock	Con.	Lab.
27 Feb	37	Oxford Univ.	Con.	Ind. Con
19 Mar	37	English Univs.	Con.	Ind.
29 Apr	37	Wandsworth C.	Con.	Lab.
22 Jun	37	Cheltenham	Con.	Ind. Con
13 Oct	37	Islington N.	Con.	Lab.
16 Feb	38	Ipswich	Con.	Lab.
6 Apr	38	Fulham W.	Con.	Lab.
5 May	38	Lichfield	Con.	Lab.
7 Nov	38	Dartford	Con.	Lab.
18 Nov	38	Bridgwater	Con.	Ind.
24 May	39	Lambeth, Kennington	Con.	Lab.
1 Aug	39	Brecon & Radnor	Con.	Lab.
24 Feb	40	Cambridge Univ.	Con.	Ind. Con
8 Jun	40	Newcastle N.	Con.	Ind. Con
25 Mar	42	Grantham	Con.	Ind.
29 Apr	42	Rugby	Con.	Ind.
29 Apr	42	Wallasey	Con.	Ind.

Date	Constituency	General Election	By-election
5 Jun 42	Maldon	Con.	Ind.
9 Feb 43	Belfast W.	U.	Eire Lab.
7 Apr 43	Eddisbury	Con.	C.W.
7 Jan 44	Skipton	Con.	C.W.
7 Feb 44	W. Derbyshire	Con.	Ind.
2 Apr 45	Motherwell	Lab.	S. Nat.
3 Apr 45	Scottish Univs.	Con.	Ind.
6 Apr 45	Chelmsford	Con.	C.W.
8 Mar 46	English Univs.	Ind.	Con.
6 Jun 46	Down	Ind. U.	U.
9 Nov 46	Scottish Univs.	Ind.	Con.
8 Jan 48	Glasgow, Camlachie	I.L.P.	Con.

Date	Constituency	General Election	By-election
	1950–51—no change		
13 May 53	Sunderland, S.	Lab.	Con.
8 May 56	Mid-Ulster	S.F.	Ind. U.
14 Feb 57	Lewisham N.	Con.	Lab.
28 Feb 57	Carmarthen	Lib.	Lab.
12 Feb 58	Rochdale	Con.	Lab.
13 Mar 58	Glasgow, Kelvingrove	Con.	Lab.
27 Mar 58	Torrington	Con.	Lib.
17 Mar 60	Brighouse & Spenborough	Lab.	Con.

Electoral Administration

From 1900 to 1918 electoral arrangements were governed primarily by the *Representation of the People Act, 1867* as modified by the *Ballot Act, 1872*, the *Corrupt Practices Act, 1883*, the *Franchise Act, 1884*, the *Registration Act, 1885*, and the *Redistribution of Seats Act, 1885*. The *Representation of the People Act, 1918*, the *Equal Franchise Act, 1928*, and the *Representation of the People Act, 1948* (consolidated in 1949) constitute the only major legislation in the century.

The Franchise. From 1885 the United Kingdom had a system of fairly widespread male franchise, limited however by a year's residence qualification and some other restrictions. Voting in more than one constituency was permitted to owners of land, to occupiers of business permises, and to university graduates. The *Representation of the People Act, 1918* reduced the residence qualification to six months and enfranchised some categories of men who had not previously had the vote. It also enfranchised women over 30. In 1928 the *Equal Franchise Act* lowered the voting age for women to 21. In 1948 the *Representation of the People Act* abolished the business and university votes for parliamentary elections; it also abolished the six months' residence qualification.

Electorate 1900-1960

Year	Population	Population over 21	Electorate	Electorate as % of Adult Population [a]	
				Male	Total
1900	41,155,000	22,675,000	6,730,935	58	27
1910	44,915,000	26,134,000	7,694,741	58	28
1919	44,599,000	27,364,000	21,755,583	..	78
1929	46,679,000	31,711,000	28,850,870	..	90
1939	47,762,000	32,855,000	32,403,559	..	97
1949	50,363,000	35,042,000	34,269,770	..	98
1959	52,157,000	35,911,000	35,397,080	..	99

[a] This percentage makes allowance for plural voting. In the period before 1914 this amounted to about 500,000. After 1918 the business vote reached its peak in 1929 at 370,000. The university electorate rose from 39,101 in 1900 to 217,363 in 1945.

Redistribution. The *Redistribution of Seats Act, 1885* left the House of Commons with 670 members. The 1885 Act, while removing the worst anomalies, specifically rejected the principle that constituencies should be approximately equal in size. This principle was, however, substantially accepted in the *Representation of the People Act, 1918*, on the recommendation of the Speaker's Conference of 1917, although Wales, Scotland and Ireland were allowed to retain disproportionate numbers of seats. The 1918 Act increased the size of the House of Commons to 707 but this fell to 615 in 1922 on the creation of the Irish Free State. Population movements produced substantial anomalies in representation and the *Redistribution of Seats Act, 1944* authorised the immediate subdivision of constituencies with more than 100,000 electors, which led to 25 new seats being created at the 1945 election and raised the size of Parliament to 640. It also provided for the establishment of Permanent Boundary Commissioners to report every three to seven years. The Boundary Commissioners' first recommendations were enacted in the *Representation of the People Act, 1948* (with the controversial addition by the Government of 17 extra seats as well as the abolition of the 12 University seats) and the 1950 Parliament had 625 members. The next reports of the Boundary Commissioners, given effect by resolutions of the House in December 1954 and January 1955, increased the number of constituencies to 630. The controversy caused by these changes led to the *Redistribution of Seats Act, 1958*, which modified the rules governing the Boundary Commissioners' decisions and asked them to report only every 10 to 15 years.

Election Expenses

Candidates' expenses were restricted by the *Corrupt Practices Act, 1883* on a formula based on the number of electors. Candidates still had to bear the administrative costs of the election. The *Representation of the People Act, 1918* removed from the candidates responsibility for the Returning Officers' fees and lowered the maximum limits on expenditure. This limit was further reduced by the *Representation of the People Act, 1948*. In the following table the effect of variations in the number of unopposed

General Election Expenses

Year	Total Expenditure £	Candidates	Average per Candidate £	Con.	Lib.	Lab.
1900	777,429	1,002	776	..	..	..
1906	1,166,858	1,273	917	..	..	..
1910 Jan	1,295,782	1,315	985	..	..	..
1910 Dec	978,312	1,191	821	..	..	..
1918	No pub. returns	1,625	..	..	..	..
1922	1,018,196	1,442	706	..	..	..
1923	982,340	1,446	685	845	789	464
1924	921,165	1,428	645	..	..	..
1929	1,213,507	1,730	701	905	782	452
1931	654,103	1,292	510	..	..	..
1935	722,093	1,349	530	777	495	365
1945	1,073,216	1,468	645	780	532	595
1950	1,170,114	1,868	728	777	459	694
1951	946,013	1,376	688	773	488	658
1955	904,677	1,409	641	692	599	531
1959	1,051,217	1,536	684	761	532	705

candidates should be borne in mind (unopposed candidates seldom spent as much as £200). It is notable how the modifications in the law have kept electioneering costs stable despite a fivefold depreciation in the value of money and a fivefold increase in the size of the electorate.

Sources

Official returns, listing candidates' votes and expenses, have been published as Parliamentary Papers about one year after every General Election, except 1918: *1901 (352) lix, 145; 1906 (302) xcvi, 19; 1910 (259) lxxiii, 705; 1911 (272) lxii, 701; 1924 (2) xviii, 681; 1924–5 (151) xviii, 775; 1926 (1) xxii, 523; 1929–30 (114) xxiv, 755; 1931–2 (109) xx, 1; 1935–6 (150) xx, 217; 1945–6 (128) xix, 539; 1950 (146) xviii, 311; 1951–2 (210) xxi, 841; 1955 (141) xxxii, 913;* 1959-60 (173) *xxiv*, 1031.

More usable returns, identifying candidates by party and supplying supplementary data, are to be found in the following works:

Dod's Parliamentary Companion, *Vacher's Parliamentary Guide*, and *Whitaker's Almanack*, all issued annually (or more often).

Parliamentary Poll Book, by F. H. McCalmont (7th ed. 1910). This gives all returns from 1832 to 1910 (Jan).

Pall Mall Gazette House of Commons, issued in paperback form after each election from 1892 to 1910 (Dec).

The Times House of Commons, issued after the elections of January 1910 and December 1910 and 1918 and after every election since 1929.

The Constitutional Year Book, issued annually from 1885 to 1939. Up to 1920 it gives all results from 1885. Up to 1930 it gives the results for all post-1918 contests. Thereafter it records the latest four elections.

From 1945, the results of each election have been analysed in statistical appendices to the Nuffield College series of studies, *The British General Election of 1945* (1947), by R. B. McCallum and Alison Readman, *The British General Election of 1950* (1951), by H. G. Nicholas, *The British General Election of 1951* (1952), by D. E. Butler, *The British General Election of 1955* (1955), by D. E. Butler, and *The British General Eelection of 1959* (1960), by D. E. Butler and Richard Rose.

Further data is to be found in *The Electoral System in Britain, 1918–62*, by D. E. Butler (2nd ed. 1963), *Parliamentary Representation*, by J. F. S. Ross (2nd ed. 1948), and *Elections and Electors*, by J. F. S. Ross (1955). See also the *Report of the Royal Commission on Electoral Systems* (*Cd.* 5163/1910; evidence *Cd.* 5352/1910).

The problems of electoral administration are also dealt with in the reports of the Speakers' Conferences on Electoral Reform of 1917 and 1944 and the Ullswater Conference of 1930 (*Cd. 8463/1917*; *Cmd. 3636/1930*; *Cmd. 6534/1944*; and *Cmd. 6543/1944*), and in the reports of the Boundary Commissioners (*Cmd. 7260, 7274, 7270, 7231 of 1947*, and *Cmd. 9311–4 of 1954*). See also H. L. Morris, *Parliamentary Franchise Reform in England from 1885 to 1918* (New York 1921), and *The Redistribution of Seats*, by D. E. Butler, *Public Administration*, Summer 1955, pp. 125-47.

Public Opinion Polls

The British Institute of Public Opinion was established in 1938. Its name was changed in 1952 to Social Surveys (Gallup Poll) Ltd. Its poll findings were published exclusively in the *News Chronicle* until October 1960. As the years advanced, its questions on politics became increasingly systematic and detailed. Some of its early findings are collected in *Public Opinion, 1935–1946*, edited by H. Cantril (Princeton University Press, 1951). Others may be found in the *News Chronicle*, in occasional pamphlets, and in the 1959 *Gallup Election Handbook*, and in the monthly *Gallup Political Index* available since 1960 from Social Surveys (Gallup Poll) Ltd. (211 Regent Street, London, W.1.).[1]

The following tables show in summary form the answers to the question 'If there were a General Election tomorrow, how would you vote?':

Voting Intention (Gallup Poll)

	Government %	Opposition %	Don't Know %
1939 Feb	50	44	6
1939 Dec	54	30	16
1940 Feb	51	27	22

[1] The only other regularly published newspaper polls have appeared in the *Daily Express* (which runs its own polling organisation but is reticent about its methods) and the *Daily Mail*. The *Daily Mail*, employing National Opinion Polls Ltd., began in the late 1950's to supply valuable information about electoral trends.

Voting Intention (Gallup Poll)

	Con. %	Lab. %	Lib. %	Other %	Don't Know %	Con. lead over Lab. %
1943 Jun	31	38	9	8	14	−7
Jul	27	39	9	9	16	−12
Dec	27	40	10	9	14	−13
1944 Feb	23	37	10	14	16	−14
1945 Feb	24	42	11	11	12	−18
Jun	32	45	15	7	..	−13
1946 Jan	30	49	10	4	7	−19
May	37	40	12	3	8	−3
1947 Jan	38	41	11	2	8	−3
—						
Mar	38	38	9	2	13	..
—						
—						
Jun	38	38	11	2	11	..
Jul	38	38	11	2	11	..
Aug	37	34	9	3	17	3
Sep	39	35	10	4	12	4
—						
Nov	44	33	8	2	13	11
—						
1948 Jan	38	37	9	1	15	1
Feb	38	35	7	3	17	3
Mar	38	36	7	2	17	2
Apr	36	35	9	5	15	1
May	37	34	9	2	18	3
—						
Jul	42	35	8	3	12	7
Aug	40	34	7	2	17	6
Sep	38	33	8	1	20	5
Oct	38	34	8	2	18	4
Nov	38	36	7	2	17	2
—						
1949 Jan	38	35	11	2	14	3
Feb	38	37	8	2	15	1
Mar	36	37	11	2	14	−1
Apr	36	37	11	1	15	−1
May	39	35	9	2	15	4
Jun	37	34	10	1	18	3
Jul	38	36	10	2	14	2
Aug	38	36	10	2	14	2
Sep	40	34	9	2	15	6
Oct	43	34	8	1	14	9
Nov	40	32	11	1	16	8
—						
1950 Jan	38	38	10	2	12	..
Feb	40	41	10	1	8	−1
Mar	41	43	6	1	9	−2
—						
May	40	42	8	1	9	−2
Jun	39	42	8	2	9	−3
Jul	38	39	10	3	10	−1
Aug	40	42	8	1	9	−2
Sep	38	41	10	2	9	−3
Oct	40	42	8	..	10	−2
—						
Dec	41	39	9	1	10	2

Voting Intention (Gallup Poll)

		Con. %	Lab. %	Lib. %	Other %	Don't Know %	Con. lead over Lab. %
1951	Jan	44	33	9	1	13	11
	Feb	46	34	8	2	10	12
	Mar	44	33	8	1	14	11
	Apr	45	34	7	2	12	11
	May	42	34	9	2	13	8
	Jun	42	36	9	1	12	6
	Jul	43	34	9	1	13	9
	Aug	44	34	10	1	11	10
	Sep	47	36	5	1	11	11
	Oct	45	39	5	..	11	6
	—						
	Dec	43	41	6	1	9	2
1952	Jan	40	43	5	2	10	−3
	Feb	35	40	10	1	14	−5
	Mar	38	43	9	1	9	−5
	—						
	May	40	44	6	1	9	−4
	Jun	38	46	9	1	6	−8
	Jul	36	45	8	2	9	−9
	—						
	Sep	37	44	8	2	9	−7
	Oct	37	43	8	1	11	−6
	Nov	38	40	8	1	13	−2
	Dec	39	40	9	1	11	−1
1953	Jan	38	41	9	1	11	−3
	Feb	38	41	9	1	11	−3
	Mar	41	39	7	1	12	2
	Apr	41	39	7	..	13	2
	May	41	39	7	1	12	2
	Jun	41	41	6	1	11	..
	—						
	Aug	39	40	7	1	13	−1
	Sep	39	42	6	1	12	−3
	Oct	39	42	7	1	11	−3
	—						
	Dec	39	41	6	1	13	−2
1954	Jan	39	40	6	1	14	−1
	Feb	39	40	7	1	13	−1
	Mar	41	40	6	1	12	1
	Apr	40	40	6	1	13	..
	May	40	41	6	1	12	−1
	Jun	39	40	7	1	13	−1
	—						
	Aug	38	43	7	1	11	−5
	Sep	38	43	7	1	11	−5
	Oct	38	38	7	1	16	..
	Nov	39	40	5	1	15	−1
	Dec	42	43	2	..	13	−1
1955	Jan	40	39	6	1	14	1
	Feb	40	39	7	1	13	1
	Mar	40	39	7	1	13	1
	Apr	41	40	4	1	14	1
	May	43	40	2	1	14	3
	Jun	42	39	2	1	16	3
	Jul	42	38	8	1	11	4
	Aug	38	41	6	1	14	−3
	Sep	43	40	6	1	10	3
	Oct	40	39	7	1	13	1
	Nov	39	40	8	1	12	−1
	Dec	40	41	6	1	12	−1

Voting Intention (Gallup Poll)

		Con. %	Lab. %	Lib. %	Other %	Don't Know %	Con. lead over Lab. %
1956	Jan	40	41	6	1	12	−1
	Feb	39	40	8	1	12	−1
	Mar	36	38	6	1	19	−2
	Apr	36	40	6	1	17	−4
	May	37	40	7	1	15	−3
	—						
	Jul	36	42	7	1	14	−6
	Aug	36	42	5	1	16	−6
	Sep	40	42	1	1	16	−2
	Oct	36	40	8	1	15	−4
	Nov	38	38	7	..	17	..
	Dec	38	39	7	1	15	−1
1957	Jan	39	44	6	1	10	−5
	Feb	34	39	7	1	19	−5
	Mar	31	41	6	1	21	−10
	Apr	36	43	5	1	15	−7
	May	35	42	6	1	16	−7
	—						
	Jul	35	42	6	1	16	−7
	Aug	36	42	4	1	17	−6
	Sep	26	39	10	..	25	−13
	Oct	31	41	11	1	16	−10
	Nov	31	40	9	1	19	−9
	Dec	35	40	8	1	16	−5
1958	Jan	33	39	10	1	17	−6
	Feb	29	36	15	1	19	−7
	—						
	Apr	31	38	12	1	18	−7
	May	28	38	15	..	19	−10
	Jun	34	37	13	1	15	−3
	—						
	Aug	36	36	13	1	14	..
	Sep	37	35	11	..	17	2
	Oct	38	35	10	1	16	3
	Nov	39	36	9	1	15	3
	Dec	40	36	8	1	15	4
1959	Jan	37	36½	7	½	19	½
	Feb	33½	36½	6½	1	22½	−3
	Mar	35½	36	5	1	22	−½
	Apr	38	38	8½	1½	14	..
	May	38½	37½	8½	1	14½	1
	Jun	38½	37	9½	½	14½	1½
	Jul	38½	35	10½	½	15½	3½
	Aug	41	36	8½	1	13½	5
	Sep	41½	36	8	½	14	5½
	Oct	40½	39	4	½	16	1½
	Nov	43	39	6	1	11	4
	Dec	40½	37½	6	1	15	3
1960	Jan	39	35	8	1	17	4
	Feb	39½	36½	7½	½	16	3
	Mar	39	35	8½	½	17	4
	Apr	37½	35½	9½	½	17	2
	May	38½	36	9	1	15½	2½
	Jun	39	36½	9	1	14½	2½
	Jul	39	35	8	1	17	4
	Aug	40	35	8	½	16½	5
	Sep	40	34	9	1	16	6
	Oct	40½	30	10	½	19	10½
	Nov	39½	35	11½	..	14	4½
	Dec	40½	32	11½	1	15	8½

V
MAJOR SOCIAL LEGISLATION

Education

Education Act, 1902. This abolished school boards, gave powers to local authorities to provide secondary education, and made provisions for rate aid to voluntary schools (see Local Government section).

Education (Provision of Meals) Act, 1906. By this Act cheap school meals for children attending public elementary schools were given statutory recognition. Local authorities were to use voluntary organisations, contributing only to the cost of administration. In 1914 half the cost of the meals was provided by the Exchequer.

Education (Administrative Provisions) Act, 1907. This provided for medical inspection for elementary schools. In 1912 the Board of Education made grants to Local Education Authorities to make the treatment of children possible.

Education Act, 1918. Compulsory attendance was made universal until the age of 14. Day continuation (part-time compulsory) education was introduced for children between school-leaving age and 18. This almost disappeared under the economies proposed by Geddes but was revived in 1944.

Free milk was supplied to children in need in 1921. In 1934 it was subsidised by the Milk Marketing Board. Since 1946 it has been free to all.

Education Act, 1936. Provision was made for the school-leaving age to be raised to 15 in Sep 1939 but this was not implemented. 1940–1, the school meal service was expanded and subsidised to meet war-time needs. These provisions were continued after the war, by the *Education Act, 1944.*

Education Act, 1944. This Act changed the title of the President of the Board of Education to the Minister of Education. Primary and secondary education was divided at '11 plus', and secondary education was generally provided under this Act in three types of schools, grammar, technical, and modern. Some local authorities preferred to use their powers to amalgamate these into comprehensive schools. Provision was made for compulsory part-time education between the school-leaving age and 18 in county colleges, but this has not been implemented. The minimum school-leaving age was raised to 15 (in 1947) and provision (not yet implemented) was made for raising it to 16. Powers were granted under this Act, which led to a great expansion of technical colleges. No fees were to be charged in schools which were publicly provided or aided by grants from the local authority.

Health

National Insurance Act, 1911 (National Health Insurance, Pt. I). This was the first part of an act providing insurance against both ill-health and unemployment. The Act covered all those between the ages of 16 and 70 who were manual workers or earning less than £160 p.a. (This income limit was raised in 1920 and 1942.) The self-employed, non-employed, and those already provided for by other health insurance schemes were not insurable under this Act. The scheme was administered through independent units, or 'approved societies'. Local insurance committees were set up. The insurance included benefits for sickness, maternity, and medical needs. A weekly contribution was made by the insured person, his employer, and the government. The basic weekly sickness benefit was 10s. for men, 7s. 6d. for women.

Public Health Act, 1936. This replaced the 1875 Act, and consolidated the existing legislation.

National Health Service Act, 1946. By this Act, hospitals were transferred from local authorities and voluntary bodies and were to be administered by the Minister through regional hospital boards, general medical and dental services through executive councils, and other health services by county and county borough councils. Health centres were to be provided by local authorities for general, mental, dental, and pharmaceutical services, but were not in fact built. Almost all services under the Act were to be free.

National Health Service (Amendment) Act, 1949; National Health Service Acts, 1951 and 1952, and *National Health Service Contributions Acts, 1957–1958.* These made modifications in the original scheme by imposing charges for certain parts of the scheme (prescriptions, dental treatment, etc.).

Mental Health Act, 1959. The Board of Control was abolished and its functions passed to the new Mental Health Review Tribunals, local authorities, and the Minister of Health. The Act redefined the classifications of mental disorders, provided for further safeguards against improper detention, and extended the provisions for voluntary and informal treatment of patients.

Housing

(a) *Housing Acts*

Housing and Town Planning Act, 1909. This amended the law relating to the housing of the working classes, and provided for town-planning schemes. It also provided for the establishment of public health and housing committees of county councils.

Housing Acts, 1919, 1923, and *1924.* These Acts provided for varying subsidies to encourage the building of new houses for the working classes.

Housing Act, 1930. This Act extended subsidies and provided wider powers for slum clearance.

Housing (Financial Provisions) Act, 1933. This reduced the general subsidies, but increased subsidies for slum clearance.

Housing (Financial Provisions) Act, 1938. This Act regulated subsidies to housing.

Housing (Financial Provisions) Act, 1958. This Act provided grants for improvements to private houses.

House Purchase and Housing Act, 1959. This extended grants for improvements.

(b) *Rent and Mortgage Interest Restriction Acts*

Increase of Rent and Mortgage Interest (Restrictions) Acts, 1914 and *1920.* These acts established a limit to the rent of small houses, and protected tenants from eviction.

Rent Acts, 1919–39. These altered the exact limits on rents.

Rent Act, 1939. This extended rent restriction and security of tenure to houses which had become decontrolled and to new houses.

Furnished House Rent Control Act, 1946. This Act created rent tribunals to fix the prices of furnished lettings.

Landlord and Tenant Rent Control Act, 1949. Rent tribunals were authorised to determine 'reasonable' rents, on the application of the tenants, who could also apply for the recovery of premiums. The Act applied to unfurnished houses and flats.

Housing Repairs and Rents Act, 1954. This Act authorised landlords to increase rents where sufficient repairs to their property had been carried out. Rent could also be increased to cover the increase in cost since 1939 of other services provided by the landlord.

Rent Act, 1957. This decontrolled many houses in 1958 and permitted substantial increases on controlled rents.

Legal Aid

Poor Prisoners' Defence Act, 1903. This was the first Act which made provision for legal aid, which was limited to trials on indictment.

Poor Prisoners' Defence Act, 1930. This Act provided a comprehensive system of legal aid, extending aid to preliminary inquiries and to cases heard summarily before magistrates' courts.

Summary Jurisdiction (Appeals) Act, 1933. This Act made provision for free legal aid for criminal cases, payable out of county or borough funds at the discretion of the magistrates.

Legal Aid and Advice Act, 1949. This introduced a new system of aid for civil cases. It provided for the establishment of a network of local committees, composed of solicitors and some barristers to grant legal aid under regulations made by the Lord Chancellor. By this Act, aid was extended to cover all proceedings in civil courts and civil proceedings in magistrates' courts, except for certain types of action (of which defamation and breach of promise were the most important).

Cost in Criminal Cases Act, 1952. This Act empowered the courts, in the case of an indictable offence, to order reasonable defence costs to be paid out of public funds, when the accused was discharged or acquitted.

Mothers and Children

Midwives Act, 1902. This Act sought to improve the standards of midwifery. It only became fully operative in 1910. Further Acts were passed in 1936 and 1951.

Notification of Births Act, 1907. This gave powers to local authorities to insist on compulsory notification of births.

Notification of Births Extension Act, 1915. This made notification universally compulsory.

Children Act, 1908. This Act consolidated the existing law and recognised the need for legal protection of children. It provided legislation covering negligence to children. Imprisonment of children was abolished, and remand homes were set up for children awaiting trial. This was to be only in special juvenile courts.

Education (Choice of Employment) Act, 1910. This empowered authorities to set up their own juvenile employment bureaus.

National Insurance Act, 1911 (National Health Insurance Pt. I). This Act introduced maternity benefits.

Maternity and Child Welfare Act, 1918. This empowered authorities to set up 'home help' schemes and clinics.

Children and Young Persons Act, 1933. This extended responsibility for children until the age of 17 and included a careful definition of the meaning of the need for care and protection. It established approved schools, and made detailed regulations about juvenile court procedure.

Family Allowances Act, 1945. This granted a non-contributory allowance, to be paid to the mother, for each child other than the first.

Children Act, 1948. This gave local authorities new responsibilities, with children's officers to administer the children's service (see *Local Government section*).

Pensions

Old Age Pensions Act, 1908. This granted non-contributory pensions ranging from one to five shillings a week to be paid from national funds, subject to a means test, at the age of 70, where income was under £31 p.a. The weekly pension was raised in 1911, 1919, 1924, 1936 (when it stood at a maximum rate of 10s.), and in 1946 it was raised to 26s. a week for single persons, and 42s. for a married couple. The pension was raised again in 1952, and in 1957 the basic rate was 50s. plus 30s. for a dependent wife.

Widows', Orphans, and Old Age Contributory Pensions Act, 1925. This provided for a contributory scheme, covering almost the same field as the National Health Insurance scheme. Payment was made between the ages of 65 and 70 to insured persons and their wives. Special pensions were provided by the Exchequer on a non-contributory basis to all those who would have been entitled to a contributory pension, if the scheme had been in force earlier. The weekly rates were 10s. for widows, 7s. 6d. for orphans, and 10s. for old age pensioners.

Widows', Orphans' and Old Age Contributory Pensions Act, 1929. This extended the scope of the 1925 Act to widows very considerably.

Widows', Orphans', and Old Age Contributory Pensions (Voluntary Contributors) Act, 1937. This paid old age, widows' and orphans' benefits to special voluntary contributors, who entered the scheme by paying at a flat rate, related to a low entry age.

Old Age and Widows' Pensions Act, 1940. A pension at a basic rate of 10s. a week was paid at the age of 60 to insured women, and to the wife of an insured man who is himself 65. The Act also introduced supplementary pensions for old age pensioners and widow pensioners over the age of 60. In cases of need these pensioners were now the responsibility of the Assistance Board.

In 1942, the income limit for pensioners was raised to £420 p.a. to bring the scheme in line with the health and insurance schemes.

Blind Persons' Act, 1920. This established a non-contributory old age pension payable at the age of 60 to blind people, and made local authorities responsible for their welfare.

Blind Persons' Act, 1938. This reduced the age-limit to 40, and provided that all assistance by local authorities to the blind should be made exclusively by virtue of the Blind Persons Act, and not as poor relief.

Unemployment

Unemployed Workmen Act, 1905. This established 'Distress Committees' to investigate needs and to provide employment or assistance. Funds were to be partly voluntary, and partly from the local rates.

Labour Exchanges Act, 1909. These were established in 1909 and renamed Employment Exchanges in 1919.

National Insurance Act, 1911. This Act covered all those between the ages of 16 and 70 years, but was limited to manual workers in industries known to be subject to severe and recurrent unemployment. (The Act covered about 2¼ million men.) Within these limits it was compulsory, and financed by a triple weekly levy, from the workman, the employer, and the government. Payment of benefit continued only for a limited period, after which responsibility for the unemployed person lapsed to the poor law. In 1916 the Act was extended to include munitions workers.

Unemployment Insurance Act, 1920. The scheme was extended to cover the same field as the National Health Insurance scheme, and included non-manual workers with an income of under £250 p.a. Workers in agriculture or domestic service were excluded from the insurance scheme until 1936–37. It was administered through the local employment exchanges of the Ministry of Labour. The basic unemployment benefit was 7s. in 1911, increased to 15s. in 1920. It was increased in 1921, and in 1924 was 18s. It was reduced in 1928 and 1931. Additional allowances for dependants were introduced in 1921.

Unemployment Insurance Act, 1927. By this Act the original scheme was completely revised in accordance with the recommendations of the Blanesburgh Committee Report. The new scheme was to provide unlimited benefits after the insured person had satisfied certain qualifying contribution conditions.

Local Government Act, 1929. This Act abolished the Poor Law Guardians, and their responsibilities passed to county councils and county borough councils, who were so far as possible to administer the specialised branches through separate committees.

Poor Law Act, 1930. By this Act poor law was renamed Public Assistance. The existing law was consolidated.

Unemployment Insurance Act, 1930. This made qualification easier for transitional benefit, and abolished the requirement that the unemployed receiving benefits should be 'genuinely seeking work'. Transitional benefits were made to claimants in need of assistance, but unable to fulfil the usual qualifying conditions. Responsibility for the long-term unemployed was placed directly on the Exchequer in 1931, though receipt of benefit was made subject to a 'means test'. Dependents' benefits were increased.

Unemployment Act, 1934. An amended scheme was introduced distinguishing between 'unemployed benefit' paid from the Fund (at the basic rate of 17s. a week) for a limited period to those satisfying contribution conditions, and 'unemployment assistance' which was paid, subject to a 'means test', to those still needing assistance after exhausting their title to benefit, or those who were not entitled. These long-term unemployed were paid directly by the Exchequer through the newly created *Unemployment Assistance Board* (known as Assistance Board from 1940 and since 1948 as National Assistance Board). In 1937 juveniles between the ages of 14 and 16 were brought into the scheme for medical benefits only.

Unemployment Insurance (Agriculture) Act, 1936. A separate insurance scheme was set up for agricultural workers granting lower rates of benefit than the general scheme. In 1937, the benefits of voluntary insurance for widows, orphans, etc. (see *Contributory Pensions Act, 1925*), were extended to those with small incomes, without the qualifications of insurable employment essential to insurance under the main scheme. For the first time married women could become voluntary contributors for pensions.

Determination of Needs Act, 1941. This abolished the household 'means test'.

National Insurance (Industrial Injuries) Act, 1946. This covered all those in insurable employment against injuries and industrial diseases arising from their employment. It was financed by contributions from the insured person, his employer, and the government.

National Insurance Act, 1946. This Act covered all contributors between school-leaving age and pensionable age, for benefits for unemployment, sickness, maternity, retirement, widow's pensions, guardians' allowances, and death grants. The self-employed and non-employed were entitled to fewer benefits. The basic weekly rate for unemployment benefit was raised to 26s.

The national insurance scheme was amended by Acts in 1949, 1951, 1953, 1954, 1955, 1956, 1957, and 1959. In 1960 the basic weekly rate for unemployment benefit stood at 50s.

National Assistance Act, 1948. This Act repealed all the poor law still in existence and it established a comprehensive scheme to be financed from government funds, to cover all the arrangements for assistance then in force. Provision was also made for those not qualified for benefits under national insurance schemes, or where the benefits were insufficient.

Sources

Some of the major parliamentary papers connected with social legislation are: *The Royal Commission Report on the Poor Laws and the Relief of Distressed Areas* (Hamilton), Cd. 4499/1909; *Departmental Committee Report on Unemployment Insurance* (Blanesburgh), Vols. I and II, 1927; *Interdepartmental Committee Report on Social Insurance and Allied Services* (Beveridge), Cmd. 6404, 6405/1942–43; *Educational Reconstruction*, Cmd. 6458/1942–43; *A National Health Service*, Cmd. 6502/1943–44; *Employment Policy*, Cmd. 6527/1944; *Committee Report on Legal Aid and Advice in England and Wales* (Rushcliffe), Cmd. 6641/1944–45; *Committee Report on the Care of Children* (Curtis), Cmd. 6760 and 6922/1945–46; *Committee Report on the Cost of the National Health Service* (Guillebaud), Cmd. 9663/1955–56; *15–18: Report on the Central Advisory Council for Education, England* (Crowther), 1959; *Committee Report on the Youth Service in England and Wales* (Albemarle), Cmnd. 929/1960; *Committee Report on Children and Young Persons* (Ingleby), Cmnd. 1191/1960; *Working Party Report on Social Workers* (Younghusband), 1960. Details of these and other reports can be found in P. and G. Ford, *A Breviate of Parliamentary Papers 1900–1916* (1957); *1917–1939* (1951); *1940–1954* (1961).

Some of the chief studies of British social legislation since 1900 are: M. P. Hall, *The Social Services of Modern England* (1960); M. Bruce, *The Coming of the Welfare State* (1961); H. and M. Wickwar, *The Social Services, an historical survey* (1949); Political and Economic Planning, *The British Social Services* (1937); R. M. Titmuss, *Essays on the Welfare State* (1958); for a brief summary of the position in 1960, see: The Central Office of Information, *Social Services in Britain* (1960).

VI
NATIONALISATION

Main Landmarks

The Port of London Authority was set up in 1909 by the *Port of London Act, 1908*.

The Central Electricity Board was set up by the *Electricity (Supply) Act, 1926* to regulate central distribution of electricity.

The British Broadcasting Corporation was granted its first charter in 1926 as a public corporation.

The London Passenger Transport Board was established in 1933.

The Bank of England was nationalised, and received a charter in 1946.

The Coal Industry was nationalised by the *Coal Industry Nationalisation Act, 1946*, which set up the National Coal Board.

Civil Aviation was formally nationalised by the *Civil Aviation Act, 1946*. This covered the British Overseas Airways Corporation (set up in 1939), and two new corporations, British European Airways and British South American Airways.

Public Transport (and some private transport) was nationalised by the *Transport Act, 1947*. The British Transport Commission was established, and the Docks and Inland Waterways, Hotels, Railways, London Transport, Road Haulage, and Road Passenger Transport were administered by six executive boards. The *Transport Act, 1953*, denationalised Road Haulage.

Electricity was nationalised by the *Electricity Act, 1947*, which set up the British Electricity Authority in place of the Central Electricity Board. The *Electricity Act, 1957*, set up the Electricity Council and the Central Electricity Generating Board. The twelve area boards became financially autonomous.

Gas was nationalised by the *Gas Act, 1948*, which established the Gas Council and twelve Area Gas Boards.

Iron and Steel were nationalised by the *Iron and Steel Act, 1949*, and the Iron and Steel Corporation of Great Britain was established. The vesting date of the act was 1 Jan 51. The *Iron and Steel Act, 1953*, denationalised the industry, and set up the Iron and Steel Board.

The U.K. Atomic Energy Authority was established by the *U.K. Atomic Energy Authority Act, 1954*.

The board members of public corporations (including the Chairman and Deputy Chairman) are usually appointed by the Minister of the appropriate department. The exceptions are the B.B.C. and the Bank of England whose governors are appointed by the Crown.

Sources

For an analysis of the statutory provisions of the nationalised industries, see D. N. Chester, *The Nationalised Industries* (1951). Other studies of the nationalised industries include: The Acton Society Trust, *Twelve Studies on Nationalised Industries* (1950–53); H. A. Clegg and T. E. Chester, *The Future of Nationalisation* (1953); W. A. Robson, ed. *Problems of Nationalised Industries* (1952); W. A. Robson, *Nationalised Industry and Public Ownership* (1960).

See also the *Annual Reports and Accounts* of the nationalised industries and the Reports of the *Select Committee on Nationalised Industries*, October 1952, July 1953, and since 1957. The *Committee Report on the Coal Industry* (Reid), Cmd 6610/1945; the *Committee Report on the Gas Industry* (Heyworth), Cmd 6699/1945–6; the *Report of the Advisory Committee on the Organisation of the National Coal Board* (Fleck), N.C.B. 18 Jan 1955; the *Report of the Committee of Inquiry into the Electricity Supply Industry* (Herbert), Cmd 9672/1956.

Nationalised Industries — Board Chairmen and Members

United Kingdom Atomic Energy Authority 1954

The Chairman and members of the A.E.A. are appointed by the Lord President of the Council

Chairman

1 Aug 54	Sir E. Plowden (Ld)
1 Jan 60	Sir R. Makins

Members of the Authority

1954–59	Sir J. Cockcroft [1]
1954–57	Sir C. Hinton
1954–	Sir W. Penney
1954–60	Sir D. Perrott
1954–57	Ld Cherwell [2]
1954–57	Sir L. Fawcett [2]
1954–59	Sir I. Stedeford [2]
1955–59	W. Strath
1955–60	Sir R. Smith [2]
1955–60	C. Kearton [2]
1957–	Sir J. Chadwick [2]
1958–	Ld Citrine [2]
1958–	Sir W. Cook
1959–	Sir A. Hitchman
1959–	Sir L. Owen
1959–	Sir C. Pelly
1960–	S. Pears [2]
1960–	R. Geddes [2]

[1] Part-time since 1959.

[2] Part-time.

SOURCE.—*United Kingdom Atomic Energy Authority Annual Reports 1954–60.*

Civil Aviation

The Chairman, Deputy Chairman and members of all three corporations are appointed by the appropriate Minister

British European Airways Corporation, 1946-

Chairman

1 Aug 46	Sir H. Hartley
1 Apr 47	G. d'Erlanger
14 Mar 49	Ld Douglas

Deputy Chairman

1 Aug 46	W. Straight
1 Apr 47	(Sir) J. Keeling [1]

Members of the Corporation

1946–47	G. d'Erlanger
1946–49	I. Hayward [1]
1946–51	A. Measures [1]
1946–60	Sir P. Dollan [1]
1946–	(Sir) W. Edmenson [1]
1947–49	J. Wood
1949–55	P. Masefield
1949–	A. Ping [1]
1951–	K. Davies [1]
1953–	Sir A. Overton [1]
1955–	Ld Balfour of Inchrye [1]
1956–	A. Milward
1959–	Sir G. Guthrie [1]
1959–	R. Weir [1]
1960–	B. Shenstone [1]

[1] Part-time.

SOURCE.—*B.E.A. Annual Reports and Accounts, 1947–61.*

British Overseas Airways Corporation, 1939–

This was established in 1939, and became one of the three corporations under the Civil Aviation Act, 1946

Chairman

26 May 43 Vt Knollys
1 Jul 47 Sir H. Hartley
1 Jul 49 Sir M. Thomas
1 May 56 (Sir) G. d'Erlanger
29 Jul 60 Sir M. Slattery

Deputy Chairman

1 Aug 46 Sir H. Howitt
1 Apr 48 Sir M. Thomas
1 Jul 49 W. Straight
(1 Aug 49–30 Apr 50, *additional Deputy Chairman*, J. Booth)
21 Nov 55 Ld Rennell [1]
1 May 56 Sir G. Cribbett
20 Jun 60 Sir W. Neden [1]

Members of the Corporation

1946–47 Ld Trefgarne [1]
1946–48 Ld Rothschild [1]
1946–54 Sir C. Jones [1]
1946–55 R. Thornton [1]
1946–56 Ld Burghley [1]
1946–58 R. McCrindle [1]
1946–60 H. Newlands [1]
1947–49 W. Straight
1948–49 Ld Douglas [1]
1949– J. Booth
1950–58 Sir F. Brake [1]
1950–60 Sir J. Stephenson [1]
1953– (Sir) B. Smallpeice
1954–55 & 1956– Ld Rennell [1]
1955– Ld Tweedsmuir [1]
1958–60 F. Taylor [1]
1958–60 Sir W. Neden [1]
1959– K. Granville
1960– J. Connel [1]
1960– L. Poole [1]
1960– Sir W. Worboys [1]

[1] Part-time.

SOURCE.—*B.O.A.C. Annual Reports and Accounts, 1947–61.*

British South American Airways Corporation, 1946–49

The B.S.A.A.C. was merged with B.O.A.C. by the Airways Incorporation Act, 1949

Chairman

1 Aug 46 J. Booth
1 May 50 Sir M. Thomas

Deputy Chairman

1 Aug 46 (Sir) J. Stephenson
1 Apr 49 Sir F. Brake

Members of the Corporation

1946–47 Sir E. Plowden [1]
1946–48 D. Bennett [1]
1946–49 G. Sheppard [1]
1947–49 Ld Kershaw [1]
1947–49 Sir F. Brake [1]
1948–49 H. Brackley [1]
1949–50 Sir J. Stephenson [1]
1949–50 W. Straight [1]
1950– J. Booth [1]
1950– Sir C. Jones [1]

1949–50 *B.S.A.A.C. only remained in existence for legal and formal purposes overseas*

[1] Part-time.

SOURCE.—*B.S.A.A.C. Annual Reports and Accounts, 1947–49.*

National Coal Board, 1946–

The Chairman, Deputy Chairman and members of the Board are all appointed by the Minister

Chairman

15 Jul 46 Ld Hyndley (Vt)
1 Aug 51 Sir H. Houldsworth
1 Feb 56 (Sir) J. Bowman

Deputy Chairman

15 Jul 46 Sir A. Street
1 Aug 51 W. Drummond & Sir E. Coates
21 Feb 55 J. Bowman
1 Feb 56 (Sir) J. Latham
1 Sep 60 E. Browne
1 Oct 60 A. Robens

Members of the Board

1946–47 Ld Citrine
1946–53 E. Edwards
1946–55 Sir C. Ellis
1946–48 J. Gridley
1946–51 L. Lowe
1946–48 Sir C. Reid
1946–51 (Sir) E. Young
1947–49 Sir J. Hallsworth
1948–49 Sir R. Burrows
1948–55 Sir G. Vickers
1949–55 J. Hambro [1]
1949–55 Sir G. Heyworth [1]
1949–52 S. Jones [1]
1949–55 G. Martin [1]
1949–52 Sir G. Mitchell [1]
1951–57 Sir A. Bryan
1952–55 W. Bayliss [1]
1953–57 W. Sales

[1] Part-time

Members of National Coal Board (Continued)

1955–56	J. Latham
1955–57	W. Reid
1955–60	R. Thomas
1955–	A. Wynn
1956–60	S. Chambers[1]
1956–	J. Crawford
1956–57	W. Heywood[1]
1956–60	Sir H. Wilson Smith[1]
1957–	H. Hembry
1957–	H. Collins
1957–59	J. Blair-Cunynghame
1958–	W. Webber[1]
1958–	J. Birch[1]
1960–	C. Roberts
1960–	J. Smith[1]
1960–	F. Wilkinson

[1] Part-time

SOURCE.—*National Coal Board Annual Reports and Statements of Accounts 1946–60.*

British Electricity Authority, 1947–55 (Central Electricity Authority, 1955–57)

The Chairman and from four to six other members are appointed by the Minister. Four other members are appointed by the Minister from among the Area Board chairmen, the appointments being made from the boards in rotation

Chairman

15 Aug 47– Ld Citrine
31 Dec 57

Deputy Chairman

15 Aug 47–31 Aug 57	Sir H. Self
15 Aug 47–16 Dec 53	Sir J. Hacking
1 Jan 54–31 Aug 57	J. Eccles

Members of the Authority

1947–52	E. Bussey
1947–56	Dame C. Haslett[1]
1947–52	Sir W. Walker[1]
1947–57	E. Woodward[1]
1948–50	H. Randall[1]
1948–50	W. Lewis[1]
1948–50	J. Eccles[1]
1948–50	J. Pickles[1]
1948–54	T. Johnston[1]
1950–51	Sir N. Duke[1]
1950–51	N. Elliot[1]
1950–51	L. Howles[1]
1950–51	C. King[1]
1951–53	C. Melling[1]
1951–53	H. Mullens[1]
1951–53	H. Nimmo[1]
1951–53	S. Steward[1]
1952–54	J. Sullivan[1]
1953–55	D. Bellamy[1]
1953–55	Sir J. Hallsworth[1]
1953–55	W. Lewis[1]
1953–55	H. Randall[1]
1955–	N. Elliot[1]
1955–57	L. Howles[1]
1955–	D. Kendon[1]
1955–57	C. King[1]
1956–	Sir L. Nicholls[1]
1956–	G. Nairn[1]
1957–57	C. Melling[1]
1957–	R. Brown[1]
1957–	T. Ayres[1]

The Central Electricity Authority ceased to exist on 1 Jan 53 and was succeeded by two new statutory corporations—the Electricity Council and the Central Electricity Generating Board

[1] Part-time.

Electricity Council, 1957–

The Council consists of a Chairman, Deputy Chairman, and two other independent members appointed by the Minister, together with the Chairman and two other members of the Generating Board, and the Chairmen of the 12 Area Boards ex officio

Chairman

1 Sep 57	Sir H. Self
1 Sep 59	C. King

Deputy Chairman

1 Sep 57	Sir J. Eccles
1 Sep 57	R. Edwards[1] (*whole-time 1 Oct 59*)

Members of the Council

1957–	C. Melling
1957–	Ld Citrine[1]
1957–	T. Ayres
1957–	D. Bellamy
1957–	R. Brown
1957–	T. Daniel
1957–	N. Elliot
1957–	W. Gallon
1957–	A. Irens
1957–	D. Irving
1957–	D. Kendon
1957–59	C. King
1957–	W. Lewis
1957–59	J. Mould
1957–	H. Pugh
1959–	N. Marsh
1957–	Sir C. Hinton[2]
1957–	E. Long[2]
1959–	F. Brown[2]

[1] Part-time. [2] Members from the Central Electricity Generating Board.

SOURCES.—*British (Central) Electricity Authority Annual Reports 1947–58; Electricity Council Annual Reports 1958–60.*

Gas Council, 1948–

The Chairman, Deputy Chairman and members (the Chairmen of the 12 Area Boards) are all appointed by the Minister.

Chairman

23 Nov 48	Sir E. Sylvester
1 Jan 52	(Sir) H. Smith
1 Jan 60	Sir H. Jones

Deputy Chairman

25 Nov 48	H. Smith
1 Feb 52	(Sir) H. Jones
1 Jan 60	W. Hutchison

Members of the Council

1948–56	Sir A. Clow
1948–	E. Crowther
1948–50	W. Carr
1948–	R. Edwards
1948–52	H. Jones
1948–	G. Diamond
1948–	T. Mervyn Jones
1948–59	Sir J. Stephenson
1948–	M. Milne-Watson
1948–60	W. Hutchison
1948–53	O. Guard
1948–	C. Chester
1950–	D. Welman
1952–	S. Smith
1953–56	A. McBain
1956–	C. Leach
1956–	R. Johnson
1959–	J. Dyde
1960–	R. Bruce

SOURCE.—*Gas Council Annual Reports and Accounts 1948–61.*

Iron and Steel Corporation, 1950–53

The Chairman, Deputy Chairman and members of the Corporation were all appointed by the Minister.

Chairman

2 Oct 50	S. Hardie
25 Feb 52	Sir J. Green

Deputy Chairman

2 Oct 50	Sir J. Green
25 Feb 52	(*vacant*)

Members of the Corporation

1950–53	Sir V. Berry
1950–53	Sir J. Steele
1950–53	W. Stokes
1950–53	J. Garton [1]
1950–53	A. McBain [1]
1952–53	R. Marshall [1]

[1] Part-time.

SOURCE.—*Iron and Steel Corporation Reports and Accounts 1951–52.*

British Transport Commission, 1947–

The Chairman, Deputy Chairman, Members of the Commission, and Chairmen of the Executives are all appointed by the Minister.

Chairman

8 Sep 47	Sir C. Hurcomb (Ld)
15 Sep 53	Sir B. Robertson

Deputy Chairman

1 Jan 49	(Sir) J. Benstead

Members of the Commission

1947–48	Ld Ashfield
1947–49	J. Benstead
1947–59	Ld Rusholme
1947–53	Sir W. Wood
1947–59	Sir I. Bolton [1]
1950–56	J. Ryan [1]
1950–50	S. Hardie [1]
1951–	H. Barker [1]
1951–58	F. Pope (*part-time* 1955–58)
1953–58	(Sir) J. Train
1953–	Sir R. Wilson
1953–56	Sir H. Methven [1]
1954–	D. Cameron of Lochiel [1]
1954–	A. Valentine
1955–	T. Summerson [1]
1955–60	Sir C. Weir [1]
1955–	R. Hanks [1]
1956–58	J. Watkins
1958–	J. Ratter
1958–	Sir L. Sinclair [1]
1958–	Sir P. Warter [1]
1959–	F. Donachy [1]
1959–	K. Grand
1959–	G. Russell

[1] Part-time.

Chairmen of Executives of BTC

Docks and Inland Waterways Executive[1]

1947–53 Sir R. Hill

Hotels Executive[1]

1948–51 Ld Inman (*part-time from* 1950)
1951–53 Sir H. Methven (*part-time*)

London Transport Executive

1947–53 Ld Latham
1953–59 (Sir) J. Elliot
1959– A. Valentine

Railway Executive[1]

1947–51 Sir E. Missenden
1951–53 J. Elliot

Road Haulage Executive[1]

1948–53 G. Russell

Road Passenger Executive

1948–52 G. Cardwell
(1 *Oct* 52, *executive abolished by British Transport Commission (Executives) Order* 1952.)

[1] By the British Transport Commission (Executives) Order made by the Minister on 19 Aug 1953 (coming into effect on 1 Oct 1953) the Railway, Road Haulage, Docks and Inland Waterways, and Hotels Executives were abolished and their functions became directly exercisable by the Commission.

SOURCE.—*British Transport Commission Reports and Accounts 1948–61.*

VII

MAJOR TREATIES AND INTERNATIONAL ORGANISATIONS

to which Britain has subscribed since 1900[1]

30 Jan 02	Anglo-Japanese Alliance
8 Apr 04	Anglo-French Entente
31 Aug 07	Anglo-Russian Entente
18 Mar 15	Anglo-Russian Agreement over Constantinople
25 Apr 15	Treaty of London (Italy)
May 16	Sykes-Picot Agreement (Middle East)
31 Oct 17	Balfour Declaration (Palestine)
28 Jun 19	Treaty of Versailles (Germany) and League of Nations Covenant[2]
10 Sep 19	Treaty of St Germain (Austria)
27 Nov 19	Treaty of Neuilly (Bulgaria)
4 Jun 20	Treaty of Trianon (Hungary)
10 Aug 20	Treaty of Sèvres (Turkey)
6 Dec 21	Articles of Agreement for an Irish Peace
13 Dec 21	Washington Four Power Treaty (Pacific)
6 Feb 22	Washington Nine Power Treaty (China)
6 Feb 22	Washington Five Power Treaty (Naval)
23 Aug 23	Treaty of Lausanne (Middle East and the Straits)
15 Oct 25	Locarno Pact
19 Nov 26	Report of Inter-Imperial Relations Committee
27 Aug 28	General Pact for the Renunciation of War (Briand-Kellogg)
22 Apr 30	London Naval Treaty
11 Dec 31	Statute of Westminster (Dominions)
18 Jun 35	Anglo-German Naval Agreement
25 Mar 36	London Naval Treaty
20 Jul 36	Montreux Agreement (Straits)
7 Aug 36	Non-Intervention Agreement (Spain)
26 Aug 36	Anglo-Egyptian Treaty
29 Sep 38	Munich Agreement
31 Mar 39	Franco-British Guarantee to Poland
13 Apr 39	British Guarantee to Roumania and Greece
12 May 39	British Guarantee to Turkey
25 Aug 39	Anglo-Polish Agreement of Mutual Assistance
14 Aug 41	Atlantic Charter
23 Feb 42	Anglo-American Mutual Aid Agreement (Lend Lease 'Master Agreement')
26 May 42	Anglo-Soviet Treaty
22 Jul 44	Bretton Woods Agreement (International Finance)
11 Feb 45	Yalta Agreement
26 Jun 45	United Nations Charter[3]
2 Aug 45	Potsdam Agreement
6 Dec 45	Anglo-American Financial Agreement
9 Feb 47	Peace Treaties with Italy, Hungary, Roumania, Bulgaria, and Finland
17 Mar 48	Brussels Treaty Organisation
16 Apr 48	Organisation for European Economic-Cooperation
6 Jul 48	Economic-Cooperation Agreement (Marshall Aid)
21 Dec 48	The Republic of Ireland Act
4 Apr 49	North Atlantic Treaty Organisation (Nato)
5 May 49	Council of Europe
28 Nov 50	Colombo Plan (South and South-East Asia)
8 Sep 51	Treaty of Peace with Japan
8 Sep 54	South-East Asia Defence Treaty (Seato)

[1] See also the section on the *Commonwealth* (pp. 166-8).

[2] The *International Labour Organisation* (I.L.O.) was created by the Treaty of Versailles, as a semi-autonomous organisation associated with the League of Nations. On 16 Dec 20 a statute was drawn up for the establishment of the *International Court of Justice* at the Hague. The Hague Court had its preliminary session on 30 Jan 22.

[3] The Charter made provision for the continuance of the International Court of Justice at the Hague. The I.L.O. continued to function as one of the subsidiary organisations of the United Nations. (Among the other subsidiary organisations were F.A.O., U.N.E.S.C.O., W.H.O., I.M.F., etc. See The *Statesman's Year-Book, 1960*, pp. 9-11, for a brief summary of the organisations and their member countries.)

3 Oct 54	London Nine Power Agreement (European security and integration)
23 Oct 54	Western European Union (formerly Brussels Treaty Organisation)
21 Dec 54	European Coal and Steel Community (Britain made an agreement of association). Community formed on 18 Apr 51
4 Apr 55	Special agreement whereby Britain joined the Baghdad Pact (defence). (Pact signed 24 Feb 55)
15 May 55	Austrian State Treaty (occupation ended and declaration of neutrality)
4 Feb 59	European Atomic Energy Community (Euratom). Britain made an agreement of association. (Euratom formed 1 Jan 58)
21 Aug 59	Central Treaty Organisation (Cento). Formerly the the Baghdad Pact
20 Nov 59	European Free Trade Association
14 Dec 60	Organisation for Economic Co-operation and Development (formerly Organisation for European Economic Co-operation)

League of Nations, 1919–1939

Between 1919 and 1922 the British Government kept in touch with the League through its cabinet secretariat. After 1922 the Foreign Office was responsible for British representation at the League. A member of the Government was generally deputed to act as British representative at meetings of the League. No permanent national delegation stayed at Geneva. A. Eden was the only Minister appointed officially for League of Nations Affairs (7 Jun–22 Dec 35). Vt Cranborne was Parliamentary Under-Secretary at the Foreign Office with special responsibility for League of Nations Affairs from 6 Aug 35 until 20 Feb 38.

United Nations, 1946–

Since 1946 the British Government has had a permanent representative at the United Nations in New York. In addition, a Minister of State at the Foreign Office has usually been given special responsibility for United Nations affairs.

Permanent Representatives to the United Nations

1946	Sir A. Cadogan	1954	Sir P. Dixon
1950	Sir G. Jebb	1960	Sir P. Dean

SOURCES.—League of Nations, Official Journals; *United Nations Yearbooks, 1946–60.*

Sources

Among the major works on international relations since 1900 are: A. J. P. Taylor, *Struggle for Mastery in Europe, 1848–1918* (1954); M. R. D. Foot, *British Foreign Policy since 1898* (1956); C. R. M. F. Cruttwell, *A History of the Great War, 1914–18* (1936); C. B. Falls, *The First World War* (1960); G. M. Gathorne-Hardy, *A Short History of International Affairs, 1920–39* (1950); E. H. Carr, *International Relations between the Two World Wars* (1947); E. H. Carr, *Twenty Years' Crisis* (1947); G. F. Hudson, *Far East in World Politics* (1939); W. M. Jordan, *Great Britain, France and the German Problem, 1919–39* (1943); W. N. Medlicott, *British Foreign Policy since Versailles* (1940); F. S. Northedge, *British Foreign Policy: The Process of Readjustment, 1945–1961* (1962); P. A. Reynolds, *British Foreign Policy in the Inter-war Years* (1954); A. J. P. Taylor, *Origins of the Second World War* (1961); J. W. Wheeler-Bennett, *Munich: Prologue to Tragedy* (1948); A. Wolfers, *Britain and France between the two Wars* (1940); Sir L. Woodward, *British Foreign Policy in the Second World War* (1962); C. M. Woodhouse, *British Foreign Policy since the Second World War* (1961).

Among the main works on Britain and the international organisations are: F. P. Walters, *History of the League of Nations* (2 vols., 1951); G. L. Goodwin, *Britain and the United Nations* (1957); and A. H. Robertson, *European Institutions* (1959).

The Royal Institute of International Affairs has published the *Survey of International Affairs* annually since 1920. The main British documents of the period are edited by G. P. Gooch and H. Temperley, *British Documents on the Origins of the War* (vols. xi, 1927–39), and edited by R. Butler and Sir E. L. Woodward (later J. P. T. Bury), *Documents on British Foreign Policy, 1919–39* (three series, still in course of publication).

Since 1915 the texts of major public documents have been printed in the *Annual Register*. For reference only, see *The Statesman's Year-Book*, and the *Year Book of International Organisations, 1951–60*.

VIII

CIVIL SERVICE

Heads of Departments and Public Offices[1]

Secretary to the Cabinet

1916 Sir M. Hankey
1938 Sir E. Bridges
1947 Sir N. Brook

Admiralty

1884 Sir E. MacGregor
1907 Sir I. Thomas
1911 Sir G. Greene
1917 Sir O. Murray
1936 Sir R. Carter
1940 Sir H. Markham
1947 (Sir) J. Lang

Agriculture & Fisheries

1892 (Sir) T. Elliott
1913 Sir S. Olivier
1917 (Sir) D. Hall
1920 Sir F. Floud
1927 Sir C. Thomas
1936 (Sir) D. Fergusson
1945 Sir D. Vandepeer
1952 Sir A. Hitchman

(Agriculture, Fisheries & Food)

1955 Sir A. Hitchman
1959 Sir J. Winnifrith

Air

1917 Sir A. Robinson
1920 (Sir) W. Nicholson
1931 (Sir) C. Bullock
1936 Sir D. Banks
1939 Sir A. Street
1945 Sir W. Brown
1947 Sir J. Barnes
1955 Sir M. Dean

Aircraft Production (Director-General)

1940 Sir A. Rowlands
1943 Sir H. Scott
1945–1945 Sir F. Tribe

Aviation

(see *Transport & Civil Aviation*)

1959 Sir W. Strath
1960 (Sir) H. Hardman

Burma

(see *India & Burma*)

Civil Aviation (Director-General)

1941 Sir W. Hildred
1946 Sir H. Self
1947 Sir A. Overton
1953 (see *Transport & Civil Aviation*)

Civil Service Commission (First Commissioner)

1892 W. Courthope
1907 Ld F. Hervey
1910 (Sir) S. Leathers
1928 (Sir) R. Meiklejohn
1939 (Sir) P. Waterfield
1951 P. Sinker
1954 (Sir) L. Helsby
1959 Sir G. Mallaby

Colonial Office

1897 (Sir) E. Wingfield
1900 (Sir) M. Ommaney
1907 Sir F. Hopwood
1911 Sir J. Anderson
1916 Sir G. Fiddes
1921 Sir J. Masterton-Smith
1925 Sir S. Wilson
1933 Sir J. Maffey
1937 Sir C. Parkinson
1940 Sir G. Gater
1940 Sir C. Parkinson
1942 Sir G. Gater
1947 Sir T. Lloyd
1956 Sir J. Macpherson
1959 Sir H. Poynton

Commonwealth Relations Office

1947 Sir E. Machtig / Sir A. Carter
1949 Sir P. Liesching
1955 Sir G. Laithwaite
1959 Sir A. Clutterbuck

Customs Establishment (Chairman)

1900 (Sir) G. Ryder
1903 (Sir) T. Pittar

(Board of Customs and Excise)

1909 (Sir) L. Guillemard
1919 Sir H. Hamilton
1927 Sir F. Floud
1930 J. Grigg
1930 (Sir) E. Forber
1934 Sir E. Murray
1941 Sir W. Eady
1942 Sir A. Carter
1947 Sir W. Croft
1955 Sir J. Crombie

Defence

1947 Sir H. Wilson Smith
1948 Sir H. Parker
1956 Sir R. Powell
1960 Sir E. Playfair

Dominions Office

1925 Sir C. Davies
1930 Sir E. Harding
1940 Sir C. Parkinson
1940–1947 Sir E. Machtig

Economic Warfare (Director-General)

1939 Sir F. Leith-Ross
1940 Sir F. Leith-Ross / E of Drogheda
1942–1945 E of Drogheda

Education

1900 Sir G. Kekewich
1903 Sir R. Morant
1911 Sir A. Selby-Bigge
1925 Sir A. Symonds
1931 Sir H. Pelham
1937 (Sir) M. Holmes
1945 Sir J. Maud
1952 (Sir) G. Flemming
1959 Dame M. Smieton

[1] Except where stated otherwise, all these had the title of Permanent Secretary or Permanent Under-Secretary.

Exchequer and Audit Department (Comptroller and Auditor-General)[1]

1896 R. Mills
1900 D. Richmond
1904 (Sir) J. Kempe
1911 (Sir) H. Gibson
1921 Sir M. Ramsay
1931 (Sir) G. Upcott
1946 Sir F. Tribe
1958 Sir E. Compton

Food (Director-General)

1918 Sir C. Fielding
1919–1921 F. Coller
1939 Sir H. French
1945 Sir F. Tribe
1946 Sir P. Liesching
1949 (Sir) F. Lee
1951 Sir H. Hancock
1955 (see *Agriculture, Fisheries & Food*)

Foreign Office

1894 Sir T. Sanderson (Ld)
1906 Sir C. Hardinge (Ld)
1910 Sir A. Nicolson
1916 Ld Hardinge
1920 Sir E. Crowe
1925 Sir W. Tyrrell
1928 Sir R. Lindsay
1930 Sir R. Vansittart
1938 Sir A. Cadogan
1946 Sir O. Sargent[2]
1949 Sir W. Strang[2]
1953 Sir I. Kirkpatrick
1957 Sir F. Hoyer Millar

Forestry Commission (Chairman)

1920 Ld Lovat
1927 Ld Clinton
1929 Sir J. Stirling-Maxwell
1932 Sir R. Robinson (Ld)
1952 E of Radnor

Fuel & Power

1942 Sir F. Tribe
1945 Sir D. Fergusson
1952 Sir J. Maud

(Power)

1957 Sir J. Maud
1958 (Sir) D. Proctor

Health

1919 Sir R. Morant
1920 Sir A. Robinson
1935 Sir G. Chrystal
1940 Sir J. Maude
1945 Sir W. Douglas
1951 (Sir) J. Hawton
1960 (Sir) B. Fraser

Home Office

1895 Sir K. Digby
1903 Sir M. Chalmers
1908 Sir E. Troup
1922 Sir J. Anderson
1932 Sir R. Scott
1938 Sir A. Maxwell
1948 Sir F. Newsam
1957 Sir C. Cunningham

Home Security

1939 Sir T. Gardiner / Sir G. Gater
1940 Sir G. Gater
1942 Sir H. Scott
1943–1945 Sir W. Brown

Housing & Local Government

(see *Town & Country Planning*, 1943–51)

1951 Sir T. Sheepshanks
1955 Dame E. Sharp

India

1883 Sir A. Godley
1909 Sir R. Ritchie
1912 Sir T. Holderness
1920 Sir W. Duke
1924 Sir A. Hirtzel
1930 Sir F. Stewart

India & Burma

1937 Sir F. Stewart
1941–1948 (Sir) D. Monteath

Information (Director of Propaganda)

1918–1919 A. Bennett

(Director-General)

1939 Sir K. Lee
1940 F. Pick
1941 Sir C. Radcliffe
1945–1946 E. Bamford

(Central Office of Information) (Director-General)

1946 Sir E. Bamford
1946 Sir R. Fraser
1954 T. Clark

Board of Inland Revenue (Chairman)

1899 Sir H. Primrose
1907 (Sir) R. Chalmers
1911 Sir M. Nathan
1914 Sir E. Nott-Bower
1918 W. Fisher
1919 Sir J. Anderson
1922 Sir R. Hopkins
1927 Sir E. Gowers
1930 (Sir) J. Grigg
1934 Sir E. Forber
1938 Sir G. Canny
1942 Sir C. Gregg
1948 Sir E. Bamford
1955 Sir H. Hancock
1958 Sir A. Johnston

Irish Office

1893 Sir D. Harrel
1902 Sir A. Macdonnell
1908 Sir J. Dougherty
1914 Sir M. Nathan
1916 Sir W. Byrne
1918 J. Macmahon
1920–1922 J. Macmahon / Sir J. Anderson

Labour

1916 (Sir) D. Shackleton
1920 Sir D. Shackleton / Sir J. Masterton-Smith
1921 Sir H. Wilson
1930 Sir F. Floud
1935 Sir T. Phillips

(Labour & National Service)

1939 Sir T. Phillips
1944 (Sir) G. Ince
1956 Sir H. Emmerson
1959 Sir L. Helsby

Materials

1951 A. Hitchman
1952 Sir J. Helmore
1953–1954 Sir E. Bowyer

Munitions

1915 Sir H. Llewellyn Smith
1916 E. Phipps
1917 Sir G. Greene
1920–1921 Sir S. Dannreuther / D. Neylan

Unemployment Assistance Board (Chairman)

1934 Sir H. Betterton (Ld Rushcliffe)

[1] The Comptroller and Auditor-General is appointed by the Crown by letters patent and is not in the ordinary sense a civil servant.

[2] Joint Permanent Under-Secretaries—Head of the German Section: 1947–9 Sir W. Strang, 1949–50 Sir I. Kirkpatrick, 1950–1 Sir D. Gainer.

(Assistance Board)

1940 Ld Rushcliffe
1941 Ld Soulbury

(National Assistance Board)

1948 G. Buchanan
1954 Sir G. Hutchinson

National Insurance

1944 Sir T. Phillips
1949 Sir H. Hancock
1951 Sir G. King
1953 (*see Pensions & National Insurance*)

National Service

1917 S. Fawcett
1918–1919 W. Vaughan

Pensions

1916 Sir M. Nathan
1919 Sir G. Chrystal
1935 Sir A. Hore
1941 (Sir) A. Cunnison
1946 Sir H. Parker
1948 Sir A. Wilson

(Pensions & National Insurance)

1953 Sir G. King
1955 Sir E. Bowyer

Post Office

1899 Sir G. Murray
1903 Sir H. Babington-Smith
1909 Sir M. Nathan
1911 Sir A. King
1914 (Sir) E. Murray

(Director-General)

1934 (Sir) D. Banks
1936 Sir T. Gardiner
1946 Sir R. Birchall
1949 (Sir) A. Little
1955 (Sir) G. Radley
1960 Sir R. German

Power (see *Fuel & Power*)

Privy Council (Clerk of the Council)

1899 (Sir) A. FitzRoy
1923 Sir M. Hankey
1938 Sir R. Howorth
1942 (Sir) E. Leadbitter
1951 F. Fernau
1953 W. Agnew

Production

1942 Sir H. Self
1943–1945 J. Woods

Reconstruction

1943–1945 N. Brook

General Register Office (Registrar-General for England and Wales)

1880 Sir B. Henniker
1900 R. MacLeod
1902 (Sir) W. Dunbar
1909 (Sir) B. Mallet
1921 (Sir) S. Vivian
1945 (Sir) G. North
1959 E. Firth

Department of Scientific and Industrial Research (Secretary)

1916 (Sir) F. Heath
1927 H. Tizard
1929 (Sir) F. Smith
1939 (Sir) E. Appleton
1949 Sir B. Lockspeiser
1956 (Sir) H. Melville

Scottish Office

1892 Sir C. Scott-Moncrieff
1902 Sir R. Macleod
1909 Sir J. Dodds
1921 Sir J. Lamb
1933 Sir J. Jeffrey
1937 J. Highton
1937 Sir H. Hamilton
1946 (Sir) D. Milne
1959 Sir W. Murie

Shipping

1917 (Sir) J. Anderson
1919–1920 T. Lodge
1939–1941 Sir C. Hurcomb

Supply

1939 Sir A. Robinson
1940 Sir G. Gater
1940 Sir W. Brown
1942 Sir W. Douglas
1945 O. Franks
1946 Sir A. Rowlands
1953 Sir J. Helmore
1956 Sir C. Musgrave
1959, 1959– Sir W. Strath

Town & Country Planning

1943 Sir G. Whiskard
1946 Sir T. Sheepshanks

(Local Government & Planning)

1951 Sir T. Sheepshanks
1951 (see *Housing & Local Government*)

Board of Trade

1893 Sir C. Boyle
1901 Sir F. Hopwood
1907 (Sir) H. Llewellyn Smith
1913 Sir G. Barnes; Sir H. Llewellyn Smith
1916 Sir H. Llewellyn Smith; (Sir) W. Marwood
1919 Sir S. Chapman; Sir W. Marwood
1919 Sir S. Chapman; Sir H. Payne
1920 Sir S. Chapman
1927 Sir H. Hamilton
1937 Sir W. Brown
1941 Sir A. Overton
1945 Sir J. Woods
1951 Sir F. Lee
1960 Sir R. Powell

Transport

1919 Sir F. Dunnell
1921 Sir W. Marwood
1923 Sir J. Brooke
1927 C. Hurcomb
1937 Sir L. Browett

(Director-General of War Transport)

1941 Sir C. Hurcomb

(Transport)

1946 Sir C. Hurcomb
1947 Sir G. Jenkins

(Transport & Civil) Aviation

1953 Sir G. Jenkins

(Transport) (and see *Aviation*)

1959 Sir J. Dunnett

Treasury

1894 Sir F. Mowatt
1902 Sir F. Mowatt; Sir E. Hamilton
1903 Sir E. Hamilton; Sir G. Murray
1908 Sir G. Murray
1911 Sir R. Chalmers
1913 Sir T. Heath; Sir J. Bradbury
1916 Sir T. Heath; Sir J. Bradbury; Sir R. Chalmers
1919 Sir W. Fisher
1939 Sir H. Wilson
1942 Sir R. Hopkins
1945 Sir E. Bridges
1956 Sir N. Brook; Sir R. Makins
1960 Sir N. Brook; Sir F. Lee

University Grants Committee (Chairman)

1919 Sir W. McCormick
1930 Sir W. Buchanan-Riddell
1935 Sir W. Moberly
1949 (Sir) A. Trueman
1953 (Sir) K. Murray

War Office

1897 Sir R. Knox
1901 Sir E. Ward
1914 Sir R. Brade
1920 Sir H. Creedy
1939 Sir J. Grigg
1942 { Sir F. Bovenschen / Sir E. Speed }
1945 Sir E. Speed
1949 Sir G. Turner
1956 Sir E. Playfair
1960 (Sir) R. Way

Works

1895 Sir R. Brett (Vt Esher)
1902 Sir S. McDonnell
1912 Sir L. Earle
1933 Sir P. Duff
1941 Sir G. Whiskard
1943 Sir P. Robinson
1946 Sir H. Emmerson
1956 Sir E. Muir

Bank of England[1] (Governor)

1899 S. Gladstone
1901 (Sir) A. Prevost
1903 S. Morley
1905 A. Wallace
1908 R. Johnston
1913 W. Cunliffe (Ld)
1918 Sir B. Cokayne (Ld Cullen of Ashbourne)
1920 M. Norman (Ld)
1944 Ld Catto
1949 C. Cobbold (Ld)

[1] Founded in 1694, the Bank of England only passed into public ownership in 1946.

British Ambassadors to Leading Powers, 1900–1960

Austria-Hungary (–1914)

1896 Sir H. Rumbold
9 Sep 00 Sir F. Plunkett
7 May 05 Sir W. Goschen
1 Nov 08 Sir F. Cartwright
1 Nov 13 Sir M. de Bunsen
12 *Aug* 14 *War declared by G.B. on Austria-Hungary*

France

1896 Sir E. Monson
1 Jan 05 Sir F. Bertie (Ld)
19 Apr 18 E of Derby
27 Nov 20 Ld Hardinge of Penshurst
31 Dec 22 M of Crewe
30 Jul 28 Sir W. Tyrrell (Ld)
17 Apr 34 Sir G. Clerk
24 Apr 37 Sir E. Phipps
1 Nov 39 Sir R. Campbell
24 *Jun* 40 *Diplomatic mission withdrawn*
23 Oct 44 A. Duff Cooper
9 Jan 48 Sir O. Harvey
13 Apr 54 Sir G. Jebb
11 Apr 60 Sir P. Dixon

Germany

1895 Sir F. Lascelles
1 Nov 08 Sir W. Goschen
4 *Aug* 14 *War declared by G.B. on Germany*
10 Jan 20 Ld Kilmarnock (*ch. d'aff.*)
29 Jun 20 Ld D'Abernon
12 Oct 26 Sir R. Lindsay
1 Aug 28 Sir H. Rumbold
2 Aug 33 Sir E. Phipps
29 Apr 37 Sir N. Henderson
3 *Sep* 39 *War declared by G.B. on Germany*

(*Military Governors*)

1945 Sir B. Montgomery
1946 Sir S. Douglas
1947 Sir B. Robertson

(*British High Commissioners*)

1949 Sir B. Robertson
1950 Sir I. Kirkpatrick
1953 Sir. F. Hoyer Millar

(*Ambassadors to West Germany*)

5 May 55 Sir F. Hoyer Millar
7 Feb 57 Sir C. Steel

Italy

1898 Sir P. Currie (Ld)
17 Jan 03 Sir F. Bertie
1 Jan 05 Sir E. Egerton
1 Dec 08 Sir J. Rennell Rodd
21 Oct 19 Sir G. Buchanan
25 Nov 21 Sir R. Graham
26 Oct 33 Sir E. Drummond (E of Perth)
1 May 39 Sir P. Loraine
11 *Jun* 40 *War declared by Italy on G.B.*
5 Apr 44 Sir N. Charles (1944, *High Commissioner*; 1945, *Representative of H.M. Government with the personal rank of Ambassador*)
9 Oct 47 Sir V. Mallet
12 Nov 53 Sir A. Clarke

Russia

1898 Sir C. Scott
28 Apr 04 Sir C. Hardinge (Ld)
10 Feb 06 Sir A. Nicolson
23 Nov 10 Sir G. Buchanan
1917 *Diplomatic mission withdrawn*
1 Feb 24 Sir R. Hodgson (*ch. d'aff.*)
3 *Jun* 27 *Suspension of diplomatic relations*
7 Dec 29 Sir E. Ovey
24 Oct 33 Vt Chilston
19 Jan 39 Sir W. Seeds
12 Jun 40 Sir S. Cripps
4 Feb 42 Sir A. Kerr (Ld Inverchapel)
17 May 46 Sir M. Peterson
22 Jun 49 Sir D. Kelly
18 Oct 51 Sir A. Gascoigne
1 Oct 53 Sir W. Hayter
19 Feb 57 Sir P. Reilly
29 Apr 60 Sir F. Roberts

Turkey

1898 Sir N. O'Conor
1 Apr 08 Sir G. Barclay (*Min. plen. ad. int.*)
1 Jul 08 Sir G. Lowther
10 Oct 13 Sir L. Mallet
5 *Nov* 14 *War declared by G.B. on Turkey*
1 Nov 20 Sir H. Rumbold
2 Feb 24 (Sir) R. Lindsay (*H.M. Representative*)
1 Mar 25 Sir R. Lindsay (*Ambassador*)
12 Nov 26 Sir G. Clerk
16 Dec 33 Sir P. Loraine
25 Feb 39 Sir H. Knatchbull-Hugessen
29 Sep 44 Sir M. Peterson
10 May 46 Sir D. Kelly
20 Apr 49 Sir N. Charles
6 Dec 51 Sir K. Helm
13 Jan 54 Sir J. Bowker
15 Nov 58 Sir B. Burrows

U.S.A.

Date	Ambassador
1893	Sir J. Pauncefote (Ld)
4 Jun 02	(Sir) M. Herbert
23 Oct 03	Sir M. Durand
3 Feb 07	J. Bryce
19 Apr 13	Sir A. Spring-Rice
1 Jan 18	E of Reading
25 Mar 20	Sir A. Geddes
2 Feb 24	Sir E. Howard
11 Mar 30	Sir R. Lindsay
29 Aug 39	M of Lothian
24 Jan 41	Vt Halifax (E of)
23 May 46	Ld Inverchapel
22 May 48	Sir O. Franks
31 Dec 52	Sir R. Makins
2 Nov 56	Sir H. Caccia

SOURCES.—*Foreign Office List, 1960* (for ambassadors appointed before 1902 see the Foreign Office Lists before 1955); *Whitaker's Almanack 1900-1961.*

Size of Civil Service

Adequate statistics of the number of civil servants engaged in each branch of government activity since 1900 are not readily available. Moreover, the transfer of functions between departments makes comparisons of one year with another potentially misleading. An analysis of civil service strength for certain years is to be found in *The Organisation of British Central Government, 1914–1956*, by D. N. Chester and F. M. G. Willson. The figures in heavy type in the following table are taken from the statement *Staffs Employed in Government Departments* which has been published annually, or more frequently, by the Treasury as a Command Paper since 1919 (with retrospective figures for 1914 included in the first issue). The other figures in the table are taken from the *Annual Estimates* presented to Parliament by the Civil Service and Revenue Departments, and the *East India Home Accounts*. These figures are liable to slight error as they are estimates and not reports of the actual staff employed. In each case they are estimates for the year ending March 31 of the following year (e.g. under the third column headed '1 Apr 1920' the estimates are for 1920–21). The figures in this table should be used with great caution because of the considerable differences in the sources.

[See Table on next page.]

Number of Civil Servants

	1900–01	1 Aug 1914	1 Apr 1920	1 Apr 1930	1 Apr 1938	1 Apr 1950	1 Apr 1960
Total Non-industrial Staff	n.a.	282,420	380,963	306,154	376,491	575,274	637,374
Total Industrial Staff	n.a.	497,100	n.a.	483,100	204,400	396,900	358,900
Total Civil Service Staff	n.a.	779,520	n.a.	789,254	580,891	972,174	996,274
Admiralty	n.a.	4,366	13,432	7,433	10,609	30,801	30,731
War Office	n.a.	1,636	7,434	3,872	7,323	33,493	47,244
Air	..	..	2,839	1,704	4,317	24,407	27,563
Aviation	..	..	..	..	..	5,271	24,756
Foreign Office [a]	142	187	885	730	902	6,195	5,992
Colonial Office	109	214	256	365	438	1,286	1,211
Dominions & C.R.O.	..	..	..	52	91	904	847
India Office	589	554	342	n.a.	539	..	..
Irish Office	559	1,007	829	..	..	..	..
Scottish Office	159	401	517	68	n.a.	749	887
Treasury [b]	120	140	291	299	344	1,396	1,322
Home Office	297	773	926	1,024	1,688	3,953	3,534
Agriculture	182	2,976	3,446	2,463	4,588	16,842	14,938
Education	864	2,187	1,522	1,041	1,435	3,280	2,738
Food	..	..	4,142	..	..	30,785	[c]
Fuel and Power	..	..	..	..	..	6,358	1,768
Health	[d]	[d]	5,820	6,711	6,771	5,893	4,993
Labour	..	4,428	17,835	18,076	26,934	29,902	21,394
(Housing and) Local Government	425	963	[d]	[d]	[d]	1,312	2,802
Munitions	..	1,250	11,440	..	..	..	..
National Insurance	..	1,957	2,263	n.a.	n.a.	35,539	[e]
Pensions	..	..	24,169	6,175	3,147	10,954	36,323
Post Office	79,482	208,889	209,269	194,933	224,374	249,869	254,919
Supply	..	..	..	..	..	13,312	..
Board of Trade	1,359	2,535	5,410	4,398	4,611	10,136	6,735
Transport	..	..	876	759	2,820	6,906	6,909
Works	140	679	580	2,054	3,584	17,573	10,693
Customs and Excise	3,792	10,256	12,602	11,659	14,669	14,236	15,338
Exchequer and Audit Department	230	269	269	331	369	501	532
Inland Revenue Board	5,345	9,753	19,446	21,059	24,342	49,740	56,026
National Assistance	..	..	..	..	8,105	8,516	10,509
Stationery Office	100	517	728	1,660	1,947	3,241	2,903

[a] Home civil servants only.
[b] Not including subordinate departments (e.g. Committee of Imperial Defence, University Grants Commission).
[c] Combined with Ministry of Agriculture and Fisheries.
[d] The functions of the Local Government Board passed to the Ministry of Health in 1919. In 1943 the Ministry of Town and Country Planning (later becoming the Ministry of Housing and Local Government) took back many of these functions from the Ministry of Health.
[e] National Insurance merged with the Ministry of Pensions.

SOURCES.—*Staffs Employed in Government Departments* (H.M.S.O., first published in 1919) figures in heavy type. *Civil Estimates, Estimates for Revenue Departments, Service Estimates,* and *East India* (*Home Accounts*) (H.M.S.O. annually), figures in light type.

IX

ARMED FORCES

Chiefs of the Three Services

Chief of Naval Staff

1899 Ld W. Kerr
1904 Sir J. Fisher (Ld)
1910 Sir A. Wilson
1911 Sir F. Bridgeman
1912 Prince Louis of Battenberg
1914 Ld Fisher
1915 Sir H. Jackson
1916 Sir J. Jellicoe
1917 Sir R. Wemyss
1919 Earl Beatty
1927 Sir C. Madden
1930 Sir F. Field
1933 Sir E. Chatfield (Ld)
1938 Sir R. Backhouse
1939 Sir D. Pound
1943 Sir A. Cunningham (Ld)
1946 Sir J. Cunningham
1948 Ld Fraser of North Cape
1951 Sir R. McGrigor
1955 Earl Mountbatten
1959 Sir C. Lambe
1960 Sir C. John

Chief of Imperial General Staff

1895 Vt Wolseley
1900 Ld Roberts (Earl)
1904 Sir N. Lyttelton
1908 Sir W. Nicholson
1912 Sir J. French
1914 Sir C. Douglas
1914 Sir J. Wolfe-Murray
1915 Sir W. Robertson
1918 Sir H. Wilson
1922 E of Cavan
1926 Sir G. Milne
1933 Sir A. Montgomery Massingberd
1936 Sir C. Deverell
1937 Vt Gort
1939 Sir E. Ironside
1940 Sir J. Dill
1941 Sir A. Brooke (Ld Alanbrooke)
1946 Vt Montgomery
1948 Sir W. Slim
1952 Sir J. Harding
1955 Sir G. Templer
1958 Sir F. Festing

Chief of Air Staff

1918 Sir H. Trenchard
1918 Sir F. Sykes
1919 Sir H. Trenchard
1930 Sir J. Salmond
1933 Sir G. Salmond
1933 Sir E. Ellington
1937 Sir C. Newall
1940 Sir C. Portal
1946 Sir A. Tedder (Ld)
1950 Sir J. Slessor
1953 Sir W. Dickson
1956 Sir D. Boyle
1960 Sir T. Pike

Committee of Imperial Defence, 1904–1946

The committee was first established in 1902 on a temporary basis to advise the Prime Minister, as a result of British experience in the Boer War of the need for planning and co-ordination of the Empire's defence forces. The C.I.D. was established permanently in 1904, as a small flexible advisory committee to the Prime Minister. Members were usually cabinet ministers concerned with defence, military leaders, and key civil servants. The Dominions also had representatives sitting on the committee occasionally. The Prime Minister was the chairman of the committee, which had no executive power, but exercised considerable influence. A secretariat was set up to assist the C.I.D., which was later adopted by the cabinet itself. During the two world wars the C.I.D. was suspended. Its functions between 1914–19 were taken over by the War Council (Nov 1914), the Dardanelles Committee (May 1915), the War Committee (Nov 1916), and finally the War Cabinet (Dec 1916–Nov 1919). The C.I.D. resumed plenary sessions in 1922. In the 'thirties the membership of the C.I.D. rose from about 11 to 18, and the committee became unwieldy. This led to the establishment of a Minister for the Co-ordination of Defence (1936–40), who was without a department, but worked through the Committee Secretariat. On the outbreak of the Second World World War the C.I.D. was again suspended, and its responsibilities taken over by the War Cabinet. In 1946 the decision to make the suspension permanent was published in a White Paper on the C.I.D. (Cmd. 6923). The committee was replaced by a cabinet defence committee, with executive power, and the Ministry of Defence was set up as a regular department.

Secretaries to the C.I.D.

1904	G. Clarke	1912	(Sir) M. Hankey [1]
1907	Sir C. Ottley	1938	H. Ismay

SOURCES.—F. A. Johnson, *Defence by Committee* (1960); D. N. Chester and F. M. G. Willson, *The Organisation of British Central Government* (1957); J. Ehrman, *Cabinet Government and War, 1890–1940* (1958).

Total Forces Serving [a] (year ending 31 March)

(to nearest '000)

	1900	1910	1920	1930	1940 [b]	1950 [b]	1960
Army	661	522	435	333	1,688	360	252
Royal Navy [d]	98	128	133	97	282	135	93
Royal Air Force	..	..	28	33	303	193	158
Total Forces	759 [c]	650	596	463	2,273 [e]	688	503

[a] Men locally enlisted abroad are excluded, except that the figures for the army include those whose documents are held in the U.K.

[b] Including Women's Auxiliaries. The figures for the war years include a number of casualties that had not been reported on the dates to which the figures relate. They also include men and women locally enlisted abroad.

[c] Including 278,000 non-regulars.

[d] Excluding the Royal Marine Police, except in 1940.

[e] The total strength of the Armed Forces reached its war-time peak in 1945 with 5,098,100 men and women serving.

Total Expenditure on Defence [a] (year ending 31 March)

(£ millions)

	1899–1900	1909–10	1919–20	1929–30	1939–40	1949–50	1959–60
War Office	43·6	27·2	395·0	40·5	81·9	291·8	428·2
Navy	26·0	35·8	156·5	55·8	69·4	186·8	364·6
Air Force	..	..	52·5	16·8	66·6	201·6	485·1
Defence Total [b]	69·8	63·0	604·0	113·1	626·4 [c]	740·7	1,475·7

[a] The figures refer to the Exchequer of the U.K. and include Northern Ireland only to the extent that services, taxes, etc., are reserved to the U.K. Parliament.

[b] The discrepancies between the service votes and the totals are due to the expenditures of the Ministries of Defence and Civil Aviation (1950 and 1960), and the Army Ordnance Factories.

[c] Including votes of credit of £408·5 m. Defence expenditure reached its war-time peak in 1944–5 at £5,125·0 m.

SOURCES.—*The Annual Abstract of Statistics, 1900–61*, for a brief summary of the statistics. The *Army*, *Navy* and *Air Estimates* giving the full figures, are published annually as government white papers.

[1] Sir M. Hankey (later Ld Hankey) became the Joint Secretary to the C.I.D. and the cabinet in 1916, and in 1923 he was also appointed Clerk to the Privy Council.

Conscription

After a long controversy about conscription, H. Asquith announced the introduction of the first *Military Service Bill* on 5 Jan 16. Military service lapsed in 1919. It was first introduced in peace time on 26 Apr 39. The period of compulsory service was to have been six months, but war intervened. Conscription was extended to women from Dec 1941 until Jan 1947, but few women were called up after Nov 1944. The *National Service Act, 1947* provided for the continuation of military service after the war. The period of service was twelve months. It was increased to eighteen months in Dec 1948, and to two years in Sep 1950. A government white paper published on 5 Apr 57 [1] announced a progressive reduction in the national service intake. No men were to be called up after the end of 1960, so that by the end of 1962 there should have been no national servicemen still in the forces. (This was slightly modified by the *Army Reserves Bill*, introduced in 1962.)

Principal Military Operations

Boer War, 1899–1902

Following the rejection by the British Government of the Boer ultimatum, the Transvaal and Orange Free State declared war on Britain in October 1899. Major operations against the Boers ended in the summer of 1900, but guerilla warfare continued. Peace was finally concluded at Vereeniging on 31 May 02.

First World War, 1914–1918

Britain declared war on Germany on 4 Aug 14, when German troops invaded Belgium and on Austria-Hungary on 12 Aug 14. Turkey joined the Central Powers in Nov 1914, and Bulgaria in May 1915. On 30 Oct 18 an armistice was agreed between the Allied Powers and the Ottoman Government. On 3 Nov 18 there was an armistice with Austria-Hungary, and on 11 Nov 18 with the German Government. The Treaty of Versailles was signed on 28 Jun 19.

Intervention in Russia, 1918–1919

British troops landed at Murmansk and Archangel in June and August of 1918. Troops also entered the Transcaucasus in August 1918. The withdrawal of troops from the Transcaucasus was completed by 5 Apr 19; and from Murmansk and Archangel by 28 Sep 19.[2]

Second World War, 1939–1945

Britain declared war on Germany on 3 Sep 39, following the German invasion of Poland. On 10 Jun 40 Italy declared war on Britain. In 1941 Bulgaria, Finland, Hungary, and Roumania joined the Axis powers. Britain declared war on Japan on 8 Dec 41. The declaration of the defeat of Germany

[1] Cmnd. 124/1957.

[2] C. H. Ellis, *Operations in Transcaspia, 1918–19* (St Antony's Papers, No. 6, 1959), and R. H. Ullman, *Anglo-Soviet Relations, 1917–21*: Vol. 1. *Intervention and the War* (Princeton, 1961).

was made on 8 May 45. On 14 Aug 45 the Japanese surrendered and the war in the Far East was officially ended. (The first atom bomb was dropped by the Americans on Hiroshima on 5 Aug 45, and the second on Nagasaki on 9 Aug 45.)

Korean War, 1950–1953

Britain declared her support for the United States' action in Korea on 28 Jun 50, following the invasion of South Korea by North Korean troops, and the call for a cease fire by an emergency session of the United Nations Security Council. The intervention of Chinese troops fighting with the North Koreans was confirmed on 6 Nov 50. An armistice was signed between the United Nations and the Communist forces on 27 Jul 53.

Suez, 1956

Following the Egyptian nationalisation of the Suez Canal on 26 Jul 56, tension grew in the Middle East. The Israeli army attacked the Egyptians on 29 Oct 56 in the Sinai peninsula. The rejection of a British and French ultimatum by Egypt resulted in a combined British and French attack on Egypt on 1 Nov 56. Operations were halted at midnight on 6-7 Nov 56. On 26 Jan 61 full diplomatic relations were resumed between Britain and Egypt.

BRITISH COSTS AND CASUALTIES IN THE MAJOR WARS[a]

War	Total Engaged ('000s)	Killed[b] ('000s)	Percentage, Col. 3 to Col. 2	Cost (£m.)
1899–1902 Boer War	448	22	4·9	217
1914–18 World War I	9,669	947	9·8	3,810
1939–45 World War II	5,896	265	4·5	34,423

[a] These figures, particularly for World War I, are open to dispute.
[b] Including those dying of wounds, of disease, and while prisoners of war.

SOURCE.—*Chambers's Encyclopaedia.*

British casualties in the Korean war were 749 killed.[1] Casualties in the Suez attack were 21 men killed.[2] The total expenditure incurred on the Korean War by Britain was about £50 m.[3] The military expenditure incurred by the Suez operation was about £30 m.[4]

[1] H. C. Deb., 1952–53, Vol. 518, Cols. *221-222.*
[2] H. C. Deb., 1956–57, Vol. 561, Col *36.*
[3] H. C. Deb., 1952–53, Vol. 517, Col. *1218.*
[4] H. C. Deb., 1956–57, Vol. 575, Col. *51.*

X
ROYALTY

British Kings and Queens, 1900–1960

Name	Accession	Coronation	Died	Age	Reigned
Victoria	20 Jun 1837	28 Jun 1838	22 Jan 1901	81	63 yrs
Edward VII	22 Jan 1901	9 Aug 1902	6 May 10	68	9 yrs
George V	6 May 10	22 Jun 11	20 Jan 36	70	25 yrs
Edward VIII	20 Jan 36	..	(Abdicated)	..	325 days
George VI	11 Dec 36	12 May 37	6 Feb 52	56	15 yrs
Elizabeth II	6 Feb 52	2 Jun 53	..	..	..

Use of Royal Power

Throughout this century great efforts have been made to avoid involving the Crown in politics. But there have been a few occasions when, unavoidably or deliberately, the Sovereign has been involved in decision making. No list of such occasions can be very satisfactory. It may omit times when in private audience the Sovereign expressed strong views to the Prime Minister. It may include times when, despite all the formality of consultation, the Sovereign had no real opportunity of affecting the outcome. The following list of incidents is compiled primarily from *Cabinet Government*, by Sir Ivor Jennings, *King George V*, by Harold Nicolson, and *King George VI*, by J. W. Wheeler-Bennett.

Dec 1909	Edward VII's refusal to promise to create peers until after a second general election.
Jul 1910	George V's sponsorship of the Constitutional Conference.
Nov 1910	George V's secret pledge to create peers, if necessary.
Jul 1914	George V's sponsorship of Buckingham Palace Home Rule Conference.
Mar 1917	George V's support for General Haig, when in danger of being dismissed.
May 1923	George V's summons of S. Baldwin as Prime Minister.
Jan 1924	George V's request to J. R. MacDonald to form government.
Aug 1931	George V's invitation to J. R. MacDonald to form National Government.
May 1940	George VI's invitation to W. Churchill to form Coalition Government.
Jul 1945	George VI's advice on switching appointment of Bevin and Dalton (a disputed allegation).
Jan 1957	Elizabeth II's summons of H. Macmillan as Prime Minister.

The Royal Family

Children of Queen Victoria

1. H.R.H. Princess Victoria (Princess Royal). Born 21 Nov 1840, married Prince Frederick of Prussia (1858), afterwards Kaiser Frederick III, died 5 Aug 1901.
2. **H.M. King Edward VII.** Born 9 Nov. 1841, married H.R.H. Princess Alexandra (eldest daughter of King Christian IX of Denmark), 10 Mar 1863, succeeded to the throne 22 Jan 1901, crowned at Westminster Abbey 9 Aug 1902, died 6 May 1910 (*for children, see below*).
3. H.R.H. Princess Alice. Born 25 Apr 1843, married Prince Louis (1862), afterwards Grand Duke of Hesse, died 14 Dec 1878.
4. H.R.H. Prince Alfred, D of Edinburgh. Born 6 Aug 1844, married Marie Alexandrovna (1874) only daughter of Alexander II, Emperor of Russia. Succeeded as D of Saxe-Coburg and Gotha 22 Aug 1893, died 30 Jul 1900.
5. H.R.H. Princess Helena. Born 25 May 1846, married H.R.H. Prince Christian of Schleswig-Holstein (1866), died 9 Jun 1923.
6. H.R.H. Princess Louise. Born 18 Mar 1848, married M of Lorne (1871), afterwards 9th D of Argyll, died 3 Dec 1939.
7. H.R.H. Prince Arthur, D of Connaught. Born 1 May 1850, married H.R.H. Princess Louisa of Prussia (1879), died 16 Jan 1942.
8. H.R.H. Prince Leopold, D of Albany. Born 7 Apr 1853, married Princess Helena of Waldeck (1882), died 28 Mar 1884.
9. H.R.H. Princess Beatrice. Born 14 Apr 1857, married H.R.H. Prince Henry of Battenberg (1885), died 26 Oct 1944.

Children of Edward VII

1. H.R.H. Prince Albert, D of Clarence and Avondale. Born 8 Jan 1864, died 14 Jan 1892.
2. **H.M. King George V.** Born 3 Jun 1865, married (6 Jul 1893) H.S.H. Princess Mary of Teck (Queen Mary, died 24 Mar 1953), succeeded to the throne 6 May 1910, crowned at Westminster Abbey 22 Jun 1911, assumed by Royal Proclamation (17 Jun 1917) the name of Windsor for his House and family, died 20 Jan 1936 (*for children, see below*).
3. H.R.H. Princess Louise (Princess Royal). Born 20 Feb 1867, married to 1st D of Fife (1889), died 4 Jan 1931. Children: (i) H.H. Princess Alexandra, Duchess of Fife. Born 17 May 1891, married H.R.H. Prince Arthur of Connaught (1913). Child: Alastair, D of Connaught, born 9 Aug 1914, died 26 Apr 1943. (ii) H.H. Princess Maud. Born 3 Apr 1893, married to 11th E of Southesk (1923), died 14 Dec 1945. Child: D of Fife, born 23 Sep 29, married (1956) Hon. Caroline Dewar.
4. H.R.H. Princess Victoria. Born 6 Jul 1868, died 2 Dec 1935.
5. H.R.H. Princess Maud. Born 26 Nov 1869, married Prince Charles of Denmark (1896), afterwards King Haakon VII of Norway, died 20 Nov 1938. Child: H.M. Olaf V, King of Norway. Born 2 Jul 1903, married (1929) H.R.H. Princess Marthe of Sweden. Children: (i) H.R.H.

Princess Ragnhild, born 9 Jun 1930, married (1953) to E. Lorentzen. (ii) H.R.H. Princess Astrid, born 12 Feb 1932. (iii) H.R.H. Harald, Crown Prince of Norway, born 21 Feb 1937.

Children of George V

1. H.R.H. D of Windsor. Born 23 Jun 1894, succeeded to the throne as **King Edward VIII** on 20 Jan 1936, abdicated 11 Dec 1936. Married Mrs W. Simpson on 3 Jun 1937.
2. **H.M. King George VI.** Born 14 Dec 1895, married Lady Elizabeth Bowes-Lyon, daughter of 14th E of Strathmore and Kinghorne on 26 Apr 1923, succeeded to the throne on 11 Dec 1936, crowned at Westminster Abbey 12 May 1937, died 6 Feb 1952 (*for children, see below*).
3. H.R.H. Princess Victoria (Princess Royal). Born 25 Apr 1897, married (1922) to 6th E of Harewood. Children: (i) George, 7th E of Harewood. Born 7 Feb 1923, married (1949) Marion, daughter of E. Stein. Children: David, Vt Lascelles, born 21 Oct 1950; J. Lascelles, born 5 Oct 1953; R. Lascelles, born 14 Feb 1955. (ii) G. Lascelles, born 21 Aug 1924, married (1952) Miss A. Dowding. Child: H. Lascelles, born 19 May 1953.
4. H.R.H. D of Gloucester. Born 31 Mar 1900, married (1935) Lady A. Montagu-Douglas-Scott, daughter of 7th D of Buccleuch. Children: (i) H.R.H. Prince William, born 18 Dec 1941. (ii) H.R.H. Prince Richard, born 26 Aug 1944.
5. H.R.H. D of Kent. Born 20 Dec 1902, married (1934) H.R.H. Princess Marina of Greece and Denmark, killed on active service 25 Aug 1942. Children: (i) H.R.H. Prince Edward, D of Kent, born 9 Oct 1935. (ii) H.R.H. Princess Alexandra, born 25 Dec 1936. (iii) H.R.H. Prince Michael, born 4 Jul 1942.
6. H.R.H. Prince John. Born 12 Jul 1905, died 18 Jan 1919.

Children of George VI

1. **H.M. Queen Elizabeth II.** Born 21 Apr 1926, married to Philip, D of Edinburgh on 20 Nov 1947, succeeded to the throne 6 Feb 1952, crowned at Westminster Abbey 2 Jun 1953. Children: (i) H.R.H. Prince Charles, Prince of Wales (26 Jun 1958), D of Cornwall, born 14 Nov 1948. (ii) H.R.H. Princess Anne, born 15 Aug 1950. (iii) Prince Andrew, born 19 Feb 1960.
2. H.R.H. Princess Margaret. Born 21 Aug 1930, married on 6 May 1960 to Antony Armstrong-Jones (created E of Snowdon, 1961). Child: David, Vt Linley, born 3 Nov 1961.

Private Secretaries to the Sovereign

1895–1901	Sir A. Bigge (Ld Stamfordham)	1936–43	Sir A. Hardinge
1901–13	Sir F. Knollys (Ld) (Vt)[1]	1943–52	Sir A. Lascelles
1910–31	Ld Stamfordham[1]	1953–	Sir M. Adeane
1931–36	Sir C. Wigram (Ld)		

[1] Ld Stamfordham and Ld Knollys were joint private secretaries 1910–13 to King George V.

Lord Chamberlains

1898	E of Hopetoun	1921	D of Atholl
1900	5th E of Clarendon	1922	E of Cromer
1905	Vt Althorp (Earl Spencer)	1938	6th E of Clarendon
1912	Ld Sandhurst (Vt)	1952	E of Scarbrough

SOURCES.—*Imperial Calendar*; *Whitaker's Almanack*; *Dictionary of National Biography*; *Who Was Who*; *Who's Who.*

XI
THE COMMONWEALTH

Major Commonwealth Changes

Independent Self-Governing Members of the Commonwealth

New Zealand [1] (1852)
Canada [1] (1867)
Australia [1] (1901)
South Africa [1] 1909–61
Newfoundland [1, 2] 1907–33
Ireland (Eire) 1922–48
India [3] 1947 (Republic 1950)
Pakistan 1947 (Republic 1956)
Ceylon 1948
Ghana 1957 (Republic 1960)
Malaya 1957 (Elective Monarchy)
Nigeria 1960
Cyprus 1961 (Republic 1960)
Sierra Leone 1961
Tanganyika 1961 (Republic 1962)
Jamaica 1962
Trinidad 1962
Uganda 1962

Central African Federation [4]

British Colonies and Protectorates

(All these were under British rule in 1900)

Aden
Ascension Island
Bahamas
Barbados—1958 [5]
Basutoland, Bechuanaland, Swaziland (High Commission Territories)
Bermudas
British Guiana
British Honduras
British Solomon Islands
British Somaliland—1960
Brunei
Ceylon—1948
Cyprus—1960
Falkland Islands
Fiji
Gambia
Gibraltar
Gilbert and Ellice Islands
Gold Coast—1957
Hong Kong
Jamaica—1958 [5]
Kenya
Leeward Islands—1958 [5]
Malay States—1957
Maldive Islands
Malta
Mauritius
Newfoundland—1907
Nigeria—1960
North Borneo
Northern Rhodesia [4]—1953
Nyasaland [4]—1953
Phoenix Islands
Pitcairn Islands
St. Helena
Sarawak
Seychelles
Sierra Leone—1961
Singapore
South African Colonies—1909 (Cape Colony, Natal, Orange Free State, Transvaal)
Southern Rhodesia [4]—1953
Tobago—1958 [5]
Tonga
Trinidad—1958
Tristan da Cunha
Uganda—1962
Virgin Islands
West Indies Federation 1958–62
Windward Islands
Zanzibar

Egypt was a British protectorate from 1914 until 1922

[1] These were recognised as having 'Dominion Status', in 1907.
[2] From 1933 to 1949 Newfoundland was governed by a U.K. Commission of Government. In 1949 Newfoundland joined the Canadian confederation as the tenth Province.
[3] Indian representatives have been invited to attend Imperial Conferences since 1917.
[4] Although the Central African Federation, set up in 1953, and composed of N. Rhodesia, S. Rhodesia and Nyasaland, is not a fully independent member of the Commonwealth, her Prime Ministers have been invited to the Prime Ministers' Conferences since 1955.
[5] Barbados, Jamaica, Trinidad, Tobago, the Leeward and the Windward Islands all formed the West Indies Federation between 1958 and 1962.

League of Nations Mandated Territories and United Nations Trusteeships

Cameroons 1919–60 (administered as part of Nigeria)[1]
Palestine 1917–48
Papua 1919—(mandated to Australia)
Samoa 1919—(mandated to New Zealand)
South West Africa 1919—(administered by South Africa)
Tanganyika 1919–61
Togo 1919–60 (administered as part of the Gold Coast, and then Ghana)

Condominiums

New Hebrides Islands (Britain and France)
Sudan—1956 (Britain and Egypt)

Other Territories under British Rule

Burma—1947
India—1947
Ireland—1922

SOURCES.—Brief histories of these territories can be found in the *Colonial Office List* and the *Commonwealth Relations Office List*. See also: K. C. Wheare, *The Constitutional Structure of the Commonwealth* (1960); W. K. Hancock and N. Mansergh, *Survey of British Commonwealth Affairs, 1918–52* (4 Vols. 1937, 1940, 1952, 1958).

Commonwealth Prime Ministers' Conferences, 1900–1960

Date	*Conference*	*Place*
30 Jun–11 Aug 02	Colonial Conference	London
15 Apr–9 May 07	Colonial Conference	"
23 May–20 Jun 11	Imperial Conference	"
Mar–May 17	Imperial War Conference	"
Jun–Aug 18	Imperial War Conference	"
1 Oct–8 Nov 23	Imperial Conference	"
19 Oct–23 Nov 26	Imperial Conference	"
1 Oct–14 Nov 30	Imperial Conference	"
14 May–15 Jun 37	Imperial Conference	"
1–16 May 44	Imperial Conference	"
23 Apr–23 May 46	Imperial Conference	"
11–22 Oct 48	Commonwealth Prime Ministers' Conference	"
21–28 Apr 49	Commonwealth Prime Ministers' Conference	"
4–12 Jan 51	Commonwealth Prime Ministers' Conference	"
3–9 Jun 53	Commonwealth Prime Ministers' Conference	"
31 Jan–8 Feb 55	Commonwealth Prime Ministers' Conference	"
27 Jun–6 Jul 56	Commonwealth Prime Ministers' Conference	"
26 Jun–5 Jul 57	Commonwealth Prime Ministers' Conference	"
3–13 May 60	Commonwealth Prime Ministers' Conference	"

SOURCES.—*Commonwealth Relations Office List 1951*, pp. 56–58, and *C.R.O. List 1960*; *Annual Register 1900–1961*; *Keesing's Archives 1945–61*.

Viceroys and Governors-General

Australia 1901–60

1 Jan	01	E of Hopetoun
9 Jan	03	Ld Tennyson
1 Jan	04	Ld Northcote
9 Sep	08	E of Dudley
1 Jun	11	Ld Denman
8 May	14	Sir R. Munro-Ferguson
6 Oct	20	Ld Forster
8 Oct	25	Ld Stonehaven
2 Jan	31	Sir I. Isaacs
3 Jan	36	Ld Gowrie
0 Jan	45	D of Gloucester
1 Mar	47	Sir W. McKell
8 May	53	Sir W. Slim
2 Feb	60	Vt Dunrossil

Canada 1900–60

	1898	E of Minto
10 Dec	04	Earl Grey
13 Oct	11	D of Connaught
11 Nov	16	D of Devonshire
11 Aug	21	Ld Byng
2 Oct	26	Vt Willingdon
4 Apr	31	E of Bessborough
2 Nov	35	Ld Tweedsmuir
21 Jun	40	E of Athlone
12 Apr	46	Vt Alexander
28 Feb	52	V. Massey
15 Sep	59	G. Vanier

Ceylon 1948–60

4 Feb	48	Sir H. Moore
6 Jul	49	Ld Soulbury
17 Jul	54	Sir O. Goonetilleke

Ghana 1957–60

24 Jun	57	E of Listowel

Viceroys of India 1900–47

	1899	Ld Curzon
30 Apr	04	Ld Ampthill (*officiating*)
13 Dec	04	Ld Curzon
18 Nov	05	E of Minto
23 Nov	10	Ld Hardinge of Penshurst
4 Apr	16	Ld Chelmsford
2 Apr	21	E of Reading

[1] In 1960, as the result of a plebiscite, the North Cameroons joined Nigeria and the South Cameroons became an ndependent republic.

10 Apr 25 E of Lytton (*officiating*)
3 Apr 26 Ld Irwin
29 Jun 29 Vt Goschen (*officiating*)
24 Oct 29 Ld Irwin
18 Apr 31 E of Willingdon
16 May 34 Sir G. Stanley (*officiating*)
18 Apr 36 M of Linlithgow
25 Jun 38 Ld Brabourne (*officiating*)
25 Oct 38 M of Linlithgow
20 Oct 43 Vt Wavell
24 Mar 47 Vt Mountbatten (Earl)

Dominion of India—Governors-General 1947–50

15 Aug 47 Earl Mountbatten
21 Jun 48 Chakravarty Rajagopalachari
26 Jan 50 Republic of India, with Indian presidents

Dominion of Pakistan—Governors-General 1947–56

15 Aug 47 M. Jinnah
14 Sep 48 Khwaja Nazimuddin
19 Oct 51 Ghulam Mohammed
6 Oct 55 Iskander Mirza
23 Mar 56 Republic of Pakistan with Pakistani presidents

Lord-Lieutenants of Ireland 1900–22

1895 Ld Cadogan
16 Aug 02 E of Dudley
3 Feb 06 E of Aberdeen
1 Jan 15 Ld Wimborne
6 May 18 Vt French
2 May 21 Vt FitzAlan

Governors of Northern Ireland 1922–60

11 Dec 22 D of Abercorn
7 Sep 45 Earl Granville
1 Dec 52 Ld Wakehurst

Governors-General New Zealand 1900–60

(*Governors*)

1897 E of Ranfurly
20 Jun 04 Ld Plunkett
22 Jun 10 Ld Islington
19 Dec 12 E of Liverpool

Governors-General

28 Jun 17 E of Liverpool
27 Sep 20 Earl Jellicoe
13 Dec 24 Sir C. Fergusson
18 Mar 30 Ld Bledisloe
12 Apr 35 Vt Galway
21 Feb 41 Ld Newall
16 Jun 46 Ld Freyberg
1 Dec 52 Sir C. Norrie (Ld)
3 Sep 57 Vt Cobham

Federation of Rhodesia & Nyasaland 1957–60

8 Oct 57 E of Dalhousie

South Africa 1910–61

31 May 10 Vt Gladstone
8 Sep 14 Vt Buxton
20 Nov 20 Prince Arthur of Connaught
21 Jan 24 E of Athlone
26 Jan 31 E of Clarendon
5 Apr 37 Sir P. Duncan
1 Jan 46 G. van Zyl
1 Jan 51 E. Jansen
25 Nov 59 C. Swart

The Union of South Africa became an independent republic outside the British Commonwealth on 31 May 61. C. Swart was sworn in as the first president.

West Indies 1957–60

10 May 57 Ld Hailes

SOURCES.—*Commonwealth Relations Office List 1960: Whitaker's Almanack 1900–1961:* The *Statesman's Year-Book 900–1960.*

XII
THE BRITISH ISLES

Scotland

UNTIL 1885, when the post of Secretary for Scotland was recreated (becoming Secretary of State for Scotland in 1926), the Lord Advocate was the principal Officer of State for Scotland, assisted by the Solicitor-General for Scotland. In 1900 there were Scottish boards for education, local government, agriculture, fisheries, and in 1919 health, but the majority were responsible to the Home Secretary, or another appropriate minister at Westminster. The Boards were recognised as an anachronism by the Reports of the Royal Commission on the Civil Service in 1914,[1] and the Haldane Committee on the Machinery of Government in 1918.[2] Both reports suggested that there was inadequate ministerial responsibility for the activities of these boards. In 1928 the Boards of Agriculture and Health and the Prison Commission for Scotland were abolished and their duties were assigned to statutory departments under the responsibility of the Secretary of State for Scotland. As the result of a general review of the Scottish administration by the Gilmour Committee,[3] the functions of the Departments of Agriculture, Education, Health, Prisons, and the Fisheries Board were vested directly in the Secretary of State for Scotland, by the *Reorganisation of Offices (Scotland) Act, 1939*. The Scottish Home Department was established at the same time. During and after the Second World War some additional administrative responsibilities were allocated to the Scottish Office. As a result of the Royal Commission Report on Scottish Affairs [4] published in 1954, there were further transfers to Scottish Departments of functions such as the responsibility for roads. The headquarters of the four Scottish Departments are in Edinburgh, with small liaison offices in Whitehall. Scottish Ministers divide their time between their Edinburgh headquarters and Whitehall, especially while Parliament is sitting. The Secretary of State, the Scottish Law officers, and the parliamentary under-secretaries have usually been members of the House of Commons, but since the appointment of the first Minister of State to the Scottish Office in 1951 this appointment has been held by members of the House of Lords.

Wales

The only significant devolution of administrative responsibility to Wales has taken place since 1950, and this to a much more limited extent than in

[1] Cd. 7338/1914. [2] Cd. 9320/1918. [3] Cmd. 5563/1936–37. [4] Cmd. 9212/1953–54

SOURCES.—Sir D. Milne, *The Scottish Office* (1957). Sir R. Coupland, *Welsh and Scottish Nationalism* (1954).

Scotland. A Welsh Board of Health was set up in 1919, but was only to exercise such powers in Wales as the Minister thought fit. A Welsh Office in the Ministry of Housing and Local Government was also established. In 1951 a Minister for Welsh Affairs was appointed, holding the office jointly with the Home Office from 1951 to 1957. From 1957 the Minister for Welsh Affairs has also been the Minister of Housing and Local Government. A second parliamentary secretary was appointed at the Home Office from 1951 to 1957 to be responsible for Welsh Affairs; since 1957 a Minister of State for Welsh Affairs has been appointed.

Ireland

From 1900–21 the Lord-Lieutenant[1] of Ireland was responsible for the administration of Irish affairs, with an office in Dublin. His Chief Secretary[2] was a member of the House of Commons, and assisted him in carrying on the parliamentary business of the department, for which he was the responsible minister. At the same time there were several departments in Dublin, working under the presidency of the Chief Secretary: the Department of Agriculture and Technical Instruction, the Irish Congested Districts Board, and the Local Government Board for Ireland. There were three boards of education commissioners, all of whom were appointed by the Lord-Lieutenant or the Government, and there was the Irish Land Commission. The Irish Public Works Board was controlled by the Treasury in London, and not by the Irish Government. There was scarcely any devolution of administrative authority to Ireland between 1900 and 1922.

The Irish Office remained in existence until 1924 after the partition of Ireland, though the posts of Chief Secretary and Lord-Lieutenant lapsed in 1922, with the recognition of the Irish Free State. The functions previously exercised by the Irish Office became the responsibility of the Home Office (for Northern Ireland) and the Colonial Office handled relations with Eire. When Ireland became a republic in 1949, the Commonwealth Relations Office continued to be the department responsible for relations with her.

The Northern Ireland Parliament was created by the *Government of Ireland Act, 1920*. The powers of the Crown are exercised by the Governor[1] who is appointed by the Crown. The parliament of Northern Ireland may legislate on all matters except those concerned with the succession to the Crown, making of peace or war, the armed forces of the Crown, the making of treaties, honours, naturalisation and aliens, post and telegraph services, civil aviation, and foreign trade. It was also prohibited from making laws which would interfere with religious freedom and from taking property without compensation. (The latter proviso was removed by statute in 1961.) Provision was made in the *Government of Ireland Act* for the continued representation of the Northern Ireland constituencies in the House of Commons of the United Kingdom. Twelve members are returned to Westminster. All United Kingdom bills apply to Northern Ireland, unless there is express provision to the contrary. The Treasury is responsible for financial relations with Northern Ireland, and other departments are concerned with trade,

[1] See p. 168 [2] See p. 48

commerce, and employment, but the Home Office retains the major responsibility for Northern Ireland.

SOURCES.—N. Mansergh, *The Government of Northern Ireland* (1936); T. Wilson (ed.), *Ulster under Home Rule* (1955); Sir F. Newsam, *The Home Office* (1954), pp. 167-70.

Prime Ministers of Northern Ireland, 1921–1960

7 Jun 21	Sir J. Craig (1927 Vt Craigavon)	6 May 43	Sir B. Brooke (1952 Vt Brookeborough)
26 Nov 40	J. Andrews		

Channel Islands

This is the only remaining part of the Dukedom of Normandy, and has been associated with England since 1066. The two bailiwicks of Jersey and Guernsey have their own local administration and legislative assemblies. Lieutenant-Governors to the two islands are appointed by the Crown for a period of five years. A Bailiff, also appointed by the Crown, presides over the *States* (the local legislatures) and over sittings of the Royal Court. Each bailiwick has an attorney-general and solicitor-general appointed by the Court. The islands have their own courts of law, but there remains leave to appeal to the Judicial Committee of the Privy Council. The island assemblies may initiate legislation but then must petition the Sovereign in Council to give these measures force of law. The bailiwick of Guernsey also includes seven smaller islands which are dependencies of Guernsey, though Alderney and Sark have their own legislatures.

SOURCE.—Sir F. Newsam, *The Home Office* (1954), pp. 170-6.

The Isle of Man

This island was successively under the rule of Norway, of Scotland, of the Stanley family and of the Dukes of Atholl before it became a Crown Colony in 1765. Since 1866 the internal affairs of the island have been regulated by the *Tynwald* and the *House of Keys*, and submitted to the Crown for confirmation by Order in Council. A Lieutenant-Governor is appointed by the Crown for seven years, and has executive authority, independent of the Tynwald, for some of the public services, such as police and prisons. The raising of revenue and expenditure needs the consent of the Tynwald, except for those reserved services for which the Lieutenant-Governor has responsibility. The finances of the island have been independent of the United Kingdom since 1866.

SOURCES.—Sir F. Newsam, *The Home Office* (1954), pp. 170-176; *Report of the Departmental Committee on the Constitution of the Isle of Man*, Cd. 5950/1911 (Minutes of Evidence, Cd. 6026/1912–13).

XIII
LAW

Principal Judges

Lord Chief Justice

1894 Ld Russell of Killowen
1900 Ld Alverstone
1913 Ld Reading (Vt) (E)
1921 Ld Trevethin
1922 Ld Hewart
1940 Vt Caldecote
1946 Ld Goddard
1958 Ld Parker of Waddington

Master of the Rolls

1897 Sir N. Lindley (Ld)
1900 Sir R. Webster (Ld Alverstone)
1900 Sir A. Smith
1901 Sir R. Collins
1907 Sir H. Cozens-Hardy (Ld)
1918 Sir C. Eady
1919 Ld Sterndale
1923 Sir E. Pollock (Ld Hanworth)
1935 Ld Wright
1937 Sir W. Greene (Ld)
1949 Sir R. Evershed (Ld)

President of the Probate, Divorce and Admiralty Division

1892 Sir F. Jeune
1905 Sir G. Barnes
1909 Sir J. Bigham
1910 Sir S. Evans
1918 Ld Sterndale
1919 Sir H. Duke (Ld Merrivale)
1933 Sir B. Merriman (Ld)

Lord President of the Court of Session

1899 Ld Kinross
1905 Ld Dunedin
1913 Ld Strathclyde
1920 Ld Clyde
1935 Ld Normand
1947 Ld Cooper
1955 Ld Clyde

Monopolies and Restrictive Practices Commission (Chairman)

1948 Sir A. Carter
1954 (Sir) D. Cairns

(Monopolies Commission)

1956 R. Levy

Lords of Appeal in Ordinary

1887–1910 Ld Macnaghten
1889–1900 Ld Morris
1894–1907 Ld Davey
1899–1909 Ld Robertson
1900–1905 Ld Lindley
1905–1928 Ld Atkinson
1907–1910 Ld Collins
1909–1929 Ld Shaw
1910–1912 Ld Robson
1912–1921 Ld Moulton
1913–1918 Ld Parker
1913–1930 Ld Sumner (Vt)
1913–1932 Ld Dunedin (Vt)
1918–1922 Vt Cave
1921–1929 Ld Carson
1923–1937 Ld Blanesburgh
1928–1944 Ld Atkin
1929–1935 Ld Tomlin
1929–1946 Ld Russell of Killowen
1929–1948 Ld Thankerton
1929–39 & 1941–47 Ld Macmillan
1932–35 & 1937–47 Ld Wright
1935–38 & 1939–41 Ld Maugham (Vt)
1935–1938 Ld Roche
1938–1944 Ld Romer
1938–1955 Ld Porter
1944–51 & 1954– Ld Simonds (Vt)
1944–1946 Ld Goddard
1946–1949 Ld Uthwatt

1946–1949	Ld du Parcq	1950–1954	Ld Asquith of Bishopstone
1947–1951	Ld MacDermott	1951–1960	Ld Cohen
1947–1953	Ld Normand	1953–	Ld Keith of Avonholm
1947–1957	Ld Oaksey	1954–1960	Ld Somervell of Harrow
1947–1959	Ld Morton of Henryton	1957–	Ld Denning
1948–	Ld Reid	1959–	Ld Jenkins
1949–1950	Ld Greene	1960–	Ld Morris of Borth-y-Gest
1949–	Ld Radcliffe		
1950–	Ld Tucker		

and such peers of Parliament as are holding, or have held, high judicial office.

Lords Justices of Appeal

1892–1900	Sir A. Levin Smith	1935–1948	Sir L. Scott
1894–1901	Sir J. Rigby	1937–1946	Sir F. MacKinnon
1897–1901	Sir R. Collins	1938–1942	Sir A. Clauson
1897–1914	Sir R. Williams	1938–1945	Vt Finlay
1899–1906	Sir R. Romer	1938–1944	Sir F. Luxmoore
1900–1906	Sir J. Stirling	1938–1944	Sir R. Goddard
1901–1906	Sir J. Mathew	1938–1946	Sir H. du Parcq
1901–1907	Sir H. Cozens-Hardy	1944–1947	Sir G. Lawrence
1906–1912	Sir J. Moulton	1944–1947	Sir F. Morton
1906–1913	Sir G. Farwell	1945–1950	Sir F. Tucker
1906–1915	Sir H. Buckley	1945–1951	Sir A. Bucknill
1907–1915	Sir W. Kennedy	1946–1954	Sir D. Somervell
1912–1913	Sir J. Hamilton	1946–1951	Sir L. Cohen
1913–1918	Sir C. Eady	1946–1951	Sir C. Asquith
1913–1916	Sir W. Phillimore	1947–1948	Sir F. Wrottesley
1914–1919	Sir W. Pickford	1947–1949	Sir R. Evershed
1915–1927	Sir J. Bankes	1948–1957	Sir J. Singleton
1915–1926	Sir T. Warrington	1948–1957	Sir A. Denning
1916–1934	Sir T. Scrutton	1949–1959	Sir D. Jenkins
1918–1919	Sir H. Duke	1950–1957	Sir N. Birkett
1919–1928	Sir J. Atkin	1951–1960	Sir F. Hodson
1919–1923	Sir R. Younger	1951–1960	Sir J. Morris
1923–1928	Sir C. Sargant	1951–1960	Sir C. Romer
1926–1934	Sir P. Lawrence	1954–1958	Sir H. Parker
1927–1938	Sir F. Greer	1957–	Sir F. Sellers
1928–1929	Sir J. Sankey	1957–	Sir B. Ormerod
1928–1929	F. Russell	1957–	Sir H. Pearce
1929–1940	Sir H. Slesser	1958–	Sir H. Willmer
1929–1938	Sir M. Romer	1959–	Sir C. Harman
1934–1935	Sir F. Maugham	1960–	Sir P. Devlin
1934–1935	Sir A. Roche	1960–	Sir G. Upjohn
1935–1937	Sir W. Greene	1960–	Sir T. Donovan

and ex officio *the Lord High Chancellor (President), the Lord Chief Justice, the Master of the Rolls, and the President of the Probate, Divorce and Admiralty Division.*

SOURCES.—*The Law List 1900–1961; Who Was Who 1900–1960, and Who's Who 1961; Whitaker's Almanack 1900–1960.*

Major Constitutional Cases

The Crown and the Royal Prerogative

Attorney-General v. *De Keyser's Royal Hotel Ltd.*, [1920] A.C. 508 (H.L.)

When an Act is passed covering the same ground, or part of the same ground, as the prerogative, the prerogative is to that extent by necessary implication superseded, at least so long as the statute remains in force; and the Crown must act under the statute. It was therefore held that the property in question, which had been taken compulsorily, had been taken under a statute, which provided also for compensation; and also that a right to compensation could be enforced by legal proceedings against the Crown. Whether there would have been a right to compensation even if the property had been taken under the prerogative was, in the circumstances, an academic question, which would probably have required an affirmative answer.

Rederiaktiebolaget 'Amphitrite' v. *The King*, [1921] 3 K.B. 500 (K.B.)

It is not competent for the government by contract to fetter its future executive action, which must necessarily be determined by the needs of the community when the question arises. Contracts hampering its freedom of action in matters which concern the welfare of the State do not bind the Crown, though the Crown can be made liable for what are in essence 'commercial' contracts.

China Navigation Co. Ltd. v. *Attorney-General*, [1932] 2 K.B. 197 (C.A.)

There is no legal duty on the Crown to afford by its military forces protection to British subjects in foreign parts. If, in the exercise of its discretion, the Crown decides to afford such protection, it may lawfully stipulate that it will do so only on the condition that the cost shall be borne by those asking for it. When Parliament has (now under the *Army Act, 1955*) sanctioned the raising and keeping of the army, the right of the Crown in time of peace as to the disposition and use of the forces so raised is a prerogative right the exercise of which cannot be controlled by the courts. (Also see *Glasbrook Bros. Ltd.* v. *Glamorgan County Council*, [1925] A.C. 270. Though the Crown may not without parliamentary sanction levy a charge in return for the performance of a public duty, the courts will enforce the payment for a service which cannot be demanded as of right, or for services asked in excess of those due.)

Duncan v. *Cammell Laird & Co. Ltd.*, [1942] A.C. 624 (H.L.)

The Crown, whether or not it is a party to a suit, may withhold any document or refuse to answer any question on the ground that such disclosure or answer would be injurious to the public interest, having regard to its contents; or on the ground that the document falls within a class which the public interest requires to be withheld for the proper functioning of the public service. (Viscount Simon's speech contains authoritative advice as to when disclosure should or should not be withheld.)

Tamlin v. *Hannaford*, [1950] 1 K.B. 18 (C.A.)

The British Transport Commission is not a servant or agent of the Crown, and it has none of the immunities and privileges of the Crown; its servants are not Civil servants; its property is not Crown property; and it is as much bound by Acts of Parliament as any other subject of the King.

R. v. *Casement*, [1917] 1 K.B. 98 (C.C.A.)

A subject may 'adhere to the King's enemies in his realm' and be found guilty of treason under the *Statute of Treasons, 1351*, whether the act complained of was committed within or outside the realm.

Joyce v. *Director of Public Prosecutions*, [1946] A.C. 347 (H.L.)

An alien abroad holding a British passport enjoys the protection of the Crown and consequently owes allegiance to the Crown. Therefore, if he adheres to the King's enemies elsewhere than in the realm, contrary to the *Treason Act, 1351*, he is guilty of treason, so long as he has not renounced that protection.

[See *Crown Proceedings Act, 1947* for responsibility and immunities of the Crown in tort.]

Parliamentary Sovereignty and Parliamentary Privilege

Vauxhall Estates, Ltd. v. *Liverpool Corporation*, [1932] 1 K.B. 733. (Divisional Court of K.B.D.)

It was held that Parliament could not bind its successors as to the subject matter of legislation. When an Act intends to govern the subject matter of future Acts, a future Act may expressly or impliedly repeal the relevant section of the earlier Act inconsistent with the latter.

[See *Ellen Street Estates Ltd.* v. *Minister of Health*, [1934] I K.B. 590, (C.A.) This affirmed the law as stated in the *Vauxhall Estates* case; and Maugham, L.J., went on to say 'The legislature cannot, according to our constitution, bind itself as to the *form* of subsequent legislation', although the question how far Parliament can bind future Parliaments as to the form of subsequent legislation was not relevant to the case.]

MacCormick v. *Lord Advocate* ('The Royal Numeral Case') [1953] S.L.T. 255

A Scottish case which challenged the doctrine of Parliamentary sovereignty as applied throughout the United Kingdom. Lord Cooper, President of the Court of Session, said 'The principle of the unlimited sovereignty of Parliament is a distinctively English principle which has no counterpart in Scottish constitutional law'. Though the case was decided on other, technical grounds, the Court suggested that the *Union Treaty* of 1707 was the fundamental law of Britain, and thus superior to Parliament. (The Court expressed considerable doubt whether in any case the Scottish Courts could treat the constitutionality of an Act of Parliament as a justiciable issue.)

Bowles v. *Bank of England*, [1913] 1 Ch. 57 (Ch.D.)

Up to 1912 it was the practice to anticipate the passing of financial legislation by collecting certain taxes on the authority of resolutions of the Committee of Ways and Means. In this case the practice was declared to be a violation of the *Bill of Rights*.

[To legalise within limits the provisional collection of revenue the *Provisional Collection of Taxes Act, 1913*, was passed. This Act gives statutory force under certain conditions for a period of four months to resolutions of the Committee of Ways and Means varying, renewing, or imposing customs or excise duties or income tax.]

R. v. *Graham-Campbell, ex parte Herbert*, [1935] 1 K.B. 594 (K.B.)

The Divisional Court upheld the refusal of the Chief Metropolitan Magistrate for want of jurisdiction to try alleged breaches of the *Licensing (Consolidation) Act, 1910*, by the Kitchen Committee of the House of Commons, on the principle that the House of Commons has the privilege of regulating its own internal affairs and procedures, including the sale, within the precincts of the House, of intoxicating liquor without a licence.

Bilston Corporation v. *Wolverhampton Corporation*, [1942] 1 Ch. 391 (Ch.D.)

The Court refused to grant an injunction to restrain a local authority from committing a breach of a contractual or statutory obligation not to oppose another local authority's application to Parliament for a private Bill, on the ground that this was a matter more properly within the cognisance of Parliament.

Re Parliamentary Privilege Act, 1770 [1958] A.C. 331 (P.C.) (*Strauss*' case)

The House of Commons would not be acting contrary to the Act of 1770 if it treated the issue of a writ against an M.P. in respect of a speech or proceeding by him in Parliament as a breach of its privileges. The House of Commons, in rejecting the recommendation of the Committee of Privileges that Mr. Strauss' letter to the Minister was a 'proceeding' in Parliament, held that not every communication between an M.P. and a Minister will be protected by Parliamentary privilege.

Viscountess Rhondda's Claim, [1922] A.C. 339

It was held by a majority of the House of Lords Committee of Privileges that a peeress in her own right is not entitled to a writ of summons to the House of Lords, in spite of the provision of Section I of the *Sex Disqualification (Removal) Act, 1919*, as a peeress in her own right before 1919 was disqualified at common law from sitting in the House, not by reason of her sex but because she held a dignity which by its nature did not entitle the holder (being a woman) to sit.

Re MacManaway, Re House of Commons (Clergy Disqualification) Act, 1801, [1951] A.C. 161 (P.C.)

Clergy of the Church of Ireland are disqualified from being elected to the Commons by Sec. 1 of the 1801 Act.

[This disqualification also attaches to the clergy of the Church of England, and the (Presbyterian) Church of Scotland; and the Roman Catholic Church (by the *Roman Catholic Relief Act, 1829*). Clergy of the Church in Wales are no longer disqualified since the *Welsh Church Act, 1914*.]

In re Parliamentary Election for Bristol South-East, [1961] 3 W.L.R. 577 (Election Court)

A person succeeding to the United Kingdom peerage is thereby disqualified from sitting in the House of Commons, whether or not a writ of summons has been issued by the Crown. Such disqualification derives from status, the attributes and disabilities of which the successor to an hereditary peerage is unable to divest himself, for it would be wholly inconsistent with the hereditary principle governing the House of Lords if such a successor could choose the House in which he wished to sit. Where votes have been given by persons knowing the facts which give rise to disqualification, such votes are void, even if the voters do not know the legal consequences of these facts.

Trade Unions

Taff Vale Railway Co. v. *Amalgamated Society of Railway Servants*, [1901] A.C. 426 (H.L.)

A trade union, registered under the *Trade Union Acts, 1871* and *1876*, may be sued in its registered name. Lord Hailsbury said, 'If the legislature has created a thing which can own property, which can employ servants, or which can inflict injury, it must be taken, I think, to have impliedly given the power to make it suable in a court of law, for injuries purposely done by its authority and procurement.'

[See *Trade Disputes Act*, 1906. Sec. 4 (1) reversed *Taff Vale*.]

Amalgamated Society of Railway Servants v. *Osborne*, [1910] A.C. 87 (H.L.)

There is nothing in the Trade Union Acts from which it can reasonably be inferred that trade unions as defined by Parliament were meant to have the power of collecting and administering funds for political purposes. Exercise of such powers is *ultra vires* and illegal.

[See *Trade Union Act*, 1913.]

Bonsor v. *Musicians' Union*, [1956] A.C. 104 (H.L.)

A member of a registered trade union who is wrongfully expelled from it is entitled to maintain an action for damages for breach of contract against the union in its registered name.

[See *Trade Disputes and Trade Union Acts, 1927* and *1946*.]

Rights and Duties of the Citizen

John Lewis & Co. Ltd. v. *Tims*, [1952] A.C. 676 (H.L.)

When one person arrests another in the exercise of the common law power of arrest, his duty is to take the arrested person before a justice or to a police station as soon as he reasonably can, and not necessarily forthwith.

Christie v. *Leachinsky*, [1947] A.C. 573 (H.L.)

If a policeman arrests without warrant when he entertains a reasonable suspicion of felony, he is under a duty to inform the suspect of the nature of the charge, and if he does not, the detention is a false imprisonment.

Liversidge v. *Anderson*, [1942] A.C. 206 (H.L.)

When the Secretary of State, acting in good faith under Regulation 18b of the *Defence (General) Regulations, 1939*, made an order in which he recited that he had reasonable cause to believe a person to be of hostile associations, and that therefore it was necessary to exercise control over him and directed that that person be detained, a court of law could not inquire whether in fact the Secretary of State had reasonable grounds for his belief. The matter was one for the executive discretion of the Secretary of State. Lord Atkin delivered a strongly dissenting speech which has been much admired.

[See *R.* v. *Halliday, ex parte Zadig*, [1917] A.C. 260 (H.L.) for a similar case arising out of the defence regulations during the First World War, and compare two more recent cases *Nakkuda Ali* v. *Jayaratne*, [1951] A.C. 66 (P.C.) and *Commissioners of Excise* v. *Cure and Deeley*, [1961] 3 W.L.R. 798].

In *Nakkuda Ali* v. *Jayaratne* the Privy Council held that *Liversidge* v. *Anderson* must not be taken to lay down any general rule on the construction of the expression 'has reasonable cause to believe'. The interpretation there should be taken in its war-time context.

Re Mwenya, [1959] 3 A.E.R. 525 (C.A.)

The jurisdiction of the High Court to grant a writ of habeas corpus extends to the issue of a writ to a protectorate (or other such territories) which, having regard to the dominion in fact exercised by the Crown, are under the subjection of the Crown and in which the issue of a writ will be proper and efficient.

Eshugbayi (Eleko) v. *Govt. of Nigeria*, [1928] A.C. 459 (P.C.)

A prisoner or persons on his behalf, may make successive applications for the writ of habeas corpus, whether in a criminal or non-criminal matter to every judge of the High Court in turn.

Re Hastings (2) and (3), [1959] 1 Q.B. 358, [1959] 1 A.E.R. 698 (Divisional Court of Q.B.D.; Divisional Court of Ch.D.)

An applicant for a writ of habeas corpus in a criminal cause or matter has no right to go from division to division or from judge to judge of the High

Court of Justice applying for the writ. When once the proper court according to the rules, a Divisional Court of the Queen's Bench Division, whose order is the order of the one High Court of Justice, has decided the application, the matter is ended. The Divisional Court of the Chancery Division has no jurisdiction to entertain the application.

[See *Administration of Justice Act, 1960.*]

Home Secretary v. *O'Brien*, [1923] A.C. 603 (H.L.)

No appeal lies from an order of a competent court for the issue of a writ of habeas corpus, where the court determines the illegality of the applicant's detention and his right to liberty, although the order does not direct his discharge.

[See *Administration of Justice Act, 1960.*]

R. v. *Taylor*, [1950] 2 K.B. 368 (C.C.A.)

The Court of Criminal Appeal is not bound as rigidly by precedent as the civil courts where the liberty of the individual is concerned. The C.C.A. will depart from a previous decision of the same court where it appears that in the earlier case the law had been either misapplied or misunderstood.

Bowman v. *Secular Society*, [1917] A.C. 406 (H.L.)

A sober and reverent inquiry into the truth of Christian doctrines is no longer against the policy of the law.

Elias v. *Pasmore*, [1934] 2 K.B. 164 (K.B.)

The power the police have at common law to seize documents found in the possession of a person lawfully arrested on a certain charge, which would constitute material evidence of his having committed that offence extends to the seizure of any documents found on the premises where a person is lawfully arrested and which would form material evidence on any criminal charge committed by anyone.

[See the *Incitement to Disaffection Act, 1934*, the *Public Order Act, 1936* and the *Official Secrets Acts, 1911–39.*]

Thomas v. *Sawkins*, [1935] 2 K.B. 249 (Divisional Court)

The police may, without warrant or licence, enter private premises — at least if a public meeting is being held there — in which they have reasonable grounds for believing that an offence (or, at any rate, a breach of the peace) is likely to be committed.

Wise v. *Dunning*, [1902] 1 K.B. 167 (Divisional Court)

The magistrates have power to order a person to find sureties to keep the peace and be of good behaviour if that person's provocative conduct is likely to induce others to commit breaches of the peace, although he himself does not commit any breach of the peace.

Duncan v. *Jones*, [1936] 1 K.B. 218 (Divisional Court)

If a police officer reasonably apprehends that the action of any person may result in a breach of the peace, it is his duty to prevent that action. If the person persists in the action, he may be arrested on a charge of obstructing a police officer in the course of his duty under the *Prevention of Crimes Acts, 1871* and *1885.*

Administrative Law

Kruse v. *Johnson*, [1898] 2 Q.B. 91 (Divisional Court)

In addition to being *intra vires* by-laws must be reasonable — or, at least, not unreasonable. They are not unreasonable merely because particular judges may think that they go further than is necessary or convenient — but a court might hold them unreasonable if they were found to be partial or unequal in their operation between classes, or if they were manifestly unjust, disclosed bad faith, or involved such oppressive or gratuitous interference with the rights of those subject to them as could find no justification in the minds of reasonable men.

Chester v. *Bateson*, [1920] 1 K.B. 829 (K.B.)

A regulation made by the Minister of Munitions debarring any person from applying to the courts, without the consent of the Minister, to recover possession of premises occupied by a munition worker was held not validly made under a power to issue regulations for 'securing the public safety and defence of the realm' (Sec. 1 of the *Defence of the Realm (Consolidation) Act, 1914*.)

Attorney-General v. *Wilts United Dairies*, (1922) 91 L.J.K.B. 897 (C.A.)

Taxation can only be imposed by the authority of Parliament since the *Bill of Rights, 1688*. For levying of money by delegated legislation not to be *ultra vires*, there must be express authorisation in the enabling statute. [The illegal conduct of the Postmaster-General in charging for Wireless licences without complying with the requirements of the *Wireless Telegraphy Act, 1904*, was pointed out in *Davey Paxman & Co. Ltd.* v. *Post Office* (*Times*, November 16, 1954), and the position was regularised retrospectively by the *Wireless Telegraphy (Validation of Charges) Act, 1954*. In that case, the P.O. had to repay the plaintiffs the costs of their licence and of the action.]

Harper v. *Home Secretary*, [1955] Ch. 238 (C.A.)

The courts will not grant an injunction restraining a Minister from laying before Parliament a regulation alleged to be *ultra vires*.

Roberts v. *Hopwood*, [1925] A.C. 578 (H.L.)

The discretion conferred upon local authorities by statute must be exercised reasonably. The fixing by the Poplar Borough Council of an arbitrary sum for wages without regard to existing labour conditions was not an exercise of the discretion given by Sec. 6 of the *Metropolis Management Act*, 1855 ('may . . . allow . . . such . . . wages as the Council may think fit'.) An expenditure upon a lawful object may be so excessive as to enable a court irrespective of its own opinion as to the merits of the expenditure to hold that it could not have been made by a reasonable man. In such a case it is unlawful, and to the extent by which the amount exceeded legality, the auditor is bound to disallow it and to surcharge the excess upon the persons responsible.

Fisher v. *Oldham Corporation*, [1930] 2 K.B. 364 (K.B.)

The police, appointed by the Watch Committee of a borough corporation, if they arrest or detain a person unlawfully, do not act as the servants or agents of the corporation so as to render that body liable to an action for false imprisonment. [Since they are not paid wholly out of the consolidated fund or money provided by Parliament, the Crown cannot be sued in respect of their torts. Hence any action must be brought against the individual policeman.]

Local Government Board v. *Arlidge*, [1915] A.C. 120 (H.L.)

'When the duty of deciding an appeal is imposed on an administrative tribunal those whose duty it is to decide it must act judicially. . . . The decision must be come to in the spirit and with the sense of responsibility of a tribunal whose duty it is to mete out justice.' The rules of natural justice must be followed though the procedure need not follow meticulously that of a court of law.

R. v. *Electricity Commissioners*, [1924] 1 K.B. 171 (C.A.)

'The operation of the writ (i.e. certiorari and prohibition) has extended to control the proceedings of bodies which do not claim to be, and would not be recognised as Courts of Justice. Whenever any body of persons having legal authority to determine questions affecting the rights of citizens, and having the duty to act judicially, act in excess of their authority, they are subject to the controlling jurisdiction of the King's Bench Division exercised in these writs.'

Franklin v. *Minister of Town and Country Planning*, [1948] A.C. 87 (Stevenage Case), (H.L.)

The *New Towns Act, 1946*, empowered the Minister to make an order designating an area as the site of a 'new town' to be developed by a Corporation if he were satisfied, after consultation with local authorities concerned, that it was expedient in the national interest to do so. Usual provisions were made for the making of objections and the holding of a public inquiry. Franklin and other landowners applied to have the order designating Stevenage as the site of a new town quashed on the ground that, before considering objections, the Minister had stated that he would make the order and he was thereby biased in any consideration of the objections. Judgement was given for the Minister on the ground that his function in making an order under the Act was purely administrative; he had no judicial or quasi-judicial duty imposed on him in considering the report of the inquiry, so the question of bias in the execution of such a duty was irrelevant, the sole question being whether or not he had genuinely considered the report and the objections. The local public inquiry was held with respect to the objections only and it was not the duty of the Minister to call evidence in support of the order, since the object of the inquiry was to inform his mind and not to consider any issue between him and the objectors.

[See also *Frost* v. *Minister of Health*, [1935] 1 K.B. 286 (K.B.) and *Offer* v. *Minister of Health*, [1936] 1 K.B. 40 (C.A.), and compare with *Errington* v. *Minister of Health*, [1935] 1 K.B. 249 (C.A.).]

R. v. *Northumberland Compensation Appeal Tribunal*, [1951] 1 K.B. 711 (C.A.)

The Divisional Court has jurisdiction to quash by certiorari the decision of an inferior tribunal where the latter has embodied the reasons for its decisions in its order — has made a 'speaking order' — and those reasons are bad in law. Certiorari is not a remedy which can be granted only when an inferior tribunal has acted without or in excess of its jurisdiction.

[See *Tribunals and Inquiries Act, 1958*, and *R.* v. *Medical Appeal Tribunal*, ex parte *Gilmore*, [1957] 1 Q.B. 574.]

R. v. *Minister of Health*, ex parte *Yaffe*, [1930] 2 K.B. 98 (C.A.); [1931] A.C. 494 (H.L.)

The Court discussed the effect of a clause in an enabling statute which gives to the regulations of the relevant authority such 'effect as if enacted in this Act'. The Court of Appeal held that where the enabling Act provides a particular procedure for the exercise of the power, the exercise of the power is void if that procedure is not followed, notwithstanding the above clause. The jurisdiction of the courts is not ousted, for the question remains: what is a 'regulation' or an 'order' made by the authority? (The House of Lords did not disagree with this view, but held that in the circumstances the order in question was valid.)

Barnard v. *National Dock Labour Board*, [1953] 2 Q.B. 18 (C.A.)

The general principle is that a person or body to whom disciplinary, judicial, or quasi-judicial functions are entrusted may not delegate them to another unless expressly or impliedly authorised to do so. In proper cases where persons would otherwise be without a remedy for an injustice (e.g. where the time limit for certiorari has expired) the Court has a discretionary power to intervene by way of declaration and injunction in the decisions of the statutory tribunals.

[See also *Vine* v. *N.D.L.B.*, [1957] 2 W.L.R. 106 (H.L.).]

Major Statutes affecting the Constitution

The Crown and Royal Prerogative

The Crown Proceedings Act, 1947

Immediately before the Act, the liability of the Crown was regulated by the *Petitions of Right Act, 1860*, which allowed legal proceedings arising out of any matter other than tort, to be brought by petition of right against the Crown, provided that the Home Secretary by fiat gave permission for the proceeding to be brought, and the fiat was very rarely refused. The Crown was immune from liability in tort. Immunity, however, did not extend to the servants of the Crown, who were personally responsible for any injury for which they could not produce legal authority. Thus although the Crown was not liable in tort, the injured party could always sue the particular Crown servant who did the deed, including any superior who ordered him to do it or otherwise caused it directly. In practice, the Crown assumed liability by making a habit of defending actions brought against its servants for torts committed by them in their official capacities, and paying the damages, if any, out of the public funds. For certain purposes this practice was unsatisfactory, and some of the methods were frowned upon by the House of Lords in *Adams* v. *Naylor* [1946] A.C. 543 (H.L.). When *Royster* v. *Cavey*, [1947] 1 K.B. 204 (C.A.) showed that this practice did not always provide a remedy, the need for reform was underlined.

In contractual matters, little change is made by the Act in substantive rules. The petition of right is abolished, and the action can commence as in any ordinary case. In tortious matters the main object was to make the Crown liable in the same way, so far as was practicable, as a private person. It still retains certain privileges in connection with postal services and armed forces, over which the prerogative or statutory powers of the Crown are left unabridged.

Regency Acts, 1937–53

These Acts provide that if the Sovereign is under 18 years of age, the royal functions shall be exercised by a Regent appointed under the provisions of the Acts. (Formerly the appointment of a Regent was *ad hoc*.) The Regent may not give assent to Bills altering the succession to the throne or repealing the Acts securing the Scottish Church.

The Acts provide for Counsellors of State to be appointed during the Monarch's absence from the U.K., or infirmity; and empower certain high officials of the state to declare that 'the Sovereign is by infirmity of mind or body incapable for the time being of performing the royal function'.

(Much of the law regarding Regency is found in these Acts.)

Parliament

Parliament Acts, 1911 and *1949* (see p. 119)

Statute of Westminster, 1931

The equality of the dominions' status was recognised in law as it had previously only been recognised by convention and usage. The statute gave the dominions legislative independence and sovereignty, and extra territorial competence. No British statutes in future would apply to the dominions without their consent.

Provisional Collection of Taxes Act, 1913 (see p. 175)

Army Act, 1955, and *Air Force Act, 1955*

Instead of passing annual Acts to legalize the raising of a standing army and the enforcement of military discipline (as provided by the *Mutiny Act, 1688*), and the maintenance of the Air Force, the new law is that the *Army* and *Air Force Acts* of 1955 expire twelve months after coming into operation unless Orders in Council provide that they shall continue in operation for a further twelve months. Such Orders in Council must be laid in draft before Parliament and are subject to an affirmative resolution by each House. The Acts cannot be continued beyond five years without a further Act of Parliament. (The Acts came into force in 1957.)

Trade Unions

The Trade Disputes Act, 1906

Sec. 1. Procuring a breach of contract (ordinarily a tort) shall not be actionable if done in contemplation of a trade dispute.

Sec. 2. 'Peaceful picketing' is allowed.

Sec. 4 (1). This reversed the decision of the House of Lords in the *Taff Vale* case. It provided that no action against a trade union, or against any of its members or officials on behalf of themselves and all other members of the Trade Union, in respect of any tort, alleged to have been committed by or on behalf of the trade union, shall be entertained by any court.

The Trade Union Act, 1913

This legalised the application of the funds of a trade union to certain political objects set out in Sec. 3, but subject to the condition that any member might claim exemption from contributing to the political fund (cf. the *Osborne* case).

Sec. 3. Contributions of members should not be applied for political purposes unless a ballot has been taken. A member who is exempt from contributing to the political fund should not be excluded from any benefits of the union or placed under any disability.

Trade Disputes and Trade Unions Act, 1927

Coming after the 1926 'General Strike', this Act contained important limitations on trade union rights and immunities. In particular the Act declared to be illegal any strike which '(i) has any object other than or in addition to the furtherance of a trade dispute within the trade or industry in which the strikers are engaged; and (ii) is a strike designed or calculated to coerce the government either directly or indirectly or by inflicting hardship upon the community'. The Act also made contributions to Union political funds a matter of 'contracting in'.

Trade Disputes and Trade Unions Act, 1946

This Act repealed the Act of 1927.

Rights and Duties of the Citizen

The Police Act, 1919

This Act makes it a misdemeanour to cause, or attempt to cause, disaffection amongst the members of any police force, or to induce, or attempt to induce, any member of a police force to withhold his services or to commit breaches of discipline. It also provides the Home Secretary with power to make regulations for the administration, pay, and conditions of service of all police forces in England and Wales.

Incitement to Disaffection Act, 1934

The Act makes it an offence to seduce a member of H.M. forces from his duty or allegiance to Her Majesty; and, with intent to commit, aid, counsel or procure the commission of the principal offence, to have in one's possession any document of such a nature that its distribution amongst the members of the force would constitute the principal offence. The Act enables a Judge of the High Court, if satisfied by sworn information that an offence has been committed, and that evidence thereof is to be found on premises named in the information, to grant a search warrant to the police on their application.

Official Secrets Acts, 1911–1939

These Acts provide for the prosecution of persons who for any purpose prejudicial to the safety or interests of the State: (*a*) approach a place thereby defined to be a prohibited place; (*b*) make sketches, etc. of such prohibited place; or (*c*) communicate to any other person any sketch, documents or information, etc. calculated or intended to be useful to the enemy. It is also an offence to part carelessly with such documents, etc. These Acts prohibit a number of other activities prejudicial to the safety or interest of the State.

Emergency Powers Act, 1920

If at any time it appears to Her Majesty that action has been taken, or is immediately threatened, to interfere on an extensive scale with the supply of food, fuel, light or other necessaries of life, or with the means of locomotion whereby the public or a large section thereof would be seriously affected, Her Majesty may, by proclamation, declare a state of emergency. When a proclamation has been made, and so long as it is in force, Her Majesty in Council may make regulations for securing the essentials of life to the community, and these regulations may delegate to Ministers, etc., such powers and duties as Her Majesty may deem necessary for preserving the peace, securing to the public the necessaries of life, the means of locomotion and the general safety.

Public Order Act, 1936

The Act makes it an offence to use threatening, abusive or insulting words or behaviour in any public place or at any public meeting, with intent to provoke a breach of the peace or whereby a breach of the peace is likely to be caused. The Act makes it illegal for an association to train its members for military purposes. It is an offence to wear in any public place or at any public meeting a uniform signifying association with any political organisation or with the promotion of any political object. It is an offence to carry any offensive or unauthorised weapon to any public meeting or public procession. The Act gives to local authorities on the application of the Chief Officer of Police and with the consent of a Secretary of State, or to the Commissioners of the City of London and of the Metropolitan Police with the consent of the Home Secretary, power to prohibit for a specified period the holding of all processions or of any class of processions within their areas.

Obscene Publications Act, 1959

This increases the right of publication, by providing that a publication for which a charge is made under the Act shall be considered as a whole and allows as a defence that the publication is in 'the interests of science, literature, art or learning, or other objects of general concern to establish or negative which grounds the opinion of experts on the scientific, literary, artistic or other merits of an article may be admitted in any proceedings'.

Administration of Justice Act, 1960

This allows for appeal up to the House of Lords in habeas corpus matters and proceedings in connection with contempt of court (see details of habeas corpus appeals).

Administrative Law

Statutory Instruments Act, 1946

This defines a statutory instrument and provides a standard form of procedure for regulations which are required to be laid before Parliament. It also secures publication of all statutory rules (whether or not to be laid before Parliament) after they are made, by requiring them to be sent to the Queen's printer to be numbered, printed and sold. The Act repeals the *Rules Publication Act, 1893*. In 1944 the House of Commons appointed a Select Committee on Statutory Rules and Orders (*later* on Statutory Instruments) to keep an eye on delegated legislation. (See p. 116.)

Major Statutes affecting the English Legal System

Criminal Appeal Act, 1907

This Act abolished the Court for Crown Cases Reserved, and set up the Court of Criminal Appeal consisting of the Lord Chief Justice and all the judges of the Queen's Bench Division (*Criminal Appeal Amendment Act, 1908*). Three judges constitute a quorum, and in no case is the number hearing an appeal to be even.

A person convicted on indictment may appeal to the Court of Criminal Appeal (*a*) against his conviction on any question of law; (*b*) with the leave of the C.C.A. or on the certificate of the judge who tried him, on a question of fact, or a question of mixed law and fact, or on any other ground which the Court deems sufficient; (*c*) with the leave of the C.C.A., against sentence, unless the sentence is the one fixed by law. (The C.C.A. may increase, quash, or reduce a sentence.)

The C.C.A. must allow an appeal against conviction if they think that the verdict of the jury was unreasonable or cannot be supported by evidence, or that the judgement of the Court below was a wrong decision on any question of law, or that on any other ground there was a miscarriage of justice; but the Court may, although they think that the appellant's point might be decided in his favour, dismiss the appeal if they consider that no substantial miscarriage of justice has actually occurred. If the appeal is successful, the Court may quash the conviction, but cannot order a new trial. The Crown cannot appeal to the Court against an acquittal. The House of Lords is the final Court of Appeal in all cases cognisable by the C.C.A. An appeal may lie from the C.C.A. to the House of Lords if the Attorney-General gives a certificate that the appeal is on a point of law of exceptional public importance, and that it is desirable in the public interest that a further appeal should be allowed. The appeal may be made by either the Crown or the defendant.

Criminal Appeal (Northern Ireland) Act, 1930

An appeal lies to the House of Lords from the C.C.A. in Northern Ireland in criminal cases under similar conditions as from the English C.C.A.

Administration of Justice Act, 1960

In place of the appeal, on the fiat of the Attorney-General, from the C.C.A. to the House of Lords under Sec. 1 (6) of the *Criminal Appeal Act, 1907*, it is provided that the defendant or the prosecutor may appeal to the House of Lords either from that Court or from any decision of a Divisional Court of the Queen's Bench Division in a criminal cause or matter. No such appeal will lie, however, except with the leave of the Court below or of the House of Lords, and leave is not to be granted unless it is certified by the Court below that a point of law of *general public importance* is involved and it appears to that Court or to the House of Lords that the point ought to be considered by that House.

[The Act also applies to Northern Ireland. In Scotland the final appellate Court in criminal cases is the High Court of Justiciary, and no appeals come to the House of Lords.]

Children Act, 1908 and *Children and Young Persons Acts, 1933–35*

These Acts provided that offenders under 16 should be tried in a juvenile court, a court of summary jurisdiction sitting in a different place or at a different time from the ordinary sitting of the Court. They established the principle that young offenders must be treated differently from adults.

Criminal Justice Act, 1948

The trial by the House of Lords at first instance of peers and peeresses for treason or felony was abolished.

Criminal Justice Administration Act, 1956

This set up 'Crown Courts' at Liverpool and Manchester to take the place of criminal assizes, and also to act as Quarter Sessions. They are staffed by Judges of the High Court and the Recorders of Liverpool and Manchester. Sessions are to be held at least eleven times a year.

Tribunals of Inquiry (Evidence) Act, 1921

Upon a resolution of both Houses of Parliament on a matter of urgent public importance a tribunal might be appointed by the Sovereign or a Secretary of State with all the powers of the High Court as regards examination of witnesses and production of documents, for the objective investigation of facts. (It was under powers granted by this Act that the Porter Committee was set up in 1936 to inquire into the Budget 'leakage' through J. H. Thomas and the Bank Rate Tribunal was set up in 1957–8.)

Administration of Justice Act (Miscellaneous Provisions), 1933

This abolished the grand jury for most purposes. It was finally abolished for all purposes by the *Criminal Justice Act, 1948*. In civil cases the Act gives the Court a discretion whether a jury shall be summoned or not; except that a jury must be ordered in case of fraud on the application of the defendant, and in cases of libel, slander, malicious prosecution, false imprisonment, seduction, and breach of promise of marriage on the application of either party, unless the Court considers that the trial will involve a prolonged examination of documents, accounts, or a scientific or local investigation which cannot conveniently be made with a jury.

Juries Act, 1949

This Act abolished 'special jurors' except for the special juries of the City of London in commercial cases. [Prior to this, a distinction was drawn between 'special' and 'common' juries. A special jury was drawn from more well-to-do people than a common jury, the theory being that they would be more intelligent and more able to understand a difficult case than their poorer neighbours. They were also paid for their services, while the 'common' jurors were not. The term 'common' jury is no longer in use.] The Act authorises payment in respect of jury services.

Supreme Court of Judicature (Consolidation) Act, 1925

This re-enacted the *Judicature Acts, 1873–75*, with subsequent amendments which amalgamated the different systems of court into one Supreme Court (High Court and the Court of Appeal), with jurisdiction to administer both law and equity. The Supreme Court has power to make Rules of Court.

Administration of Justice (Appeals) Act, 1934

No appeal lies from the Court of Appeal to the House of Lords save by the leave of the one or the other.

County Courts Acts, 1934 and *1955*

These increased the jurisdiction of the County Courts, which were set up in 1846. Their jurisdiction includes contractual and tortious matters where claim does not exceed £400; equitable jurisdiction where the value of the property, etc., in dispute does not exceed £500; land actions, where rateable value of land is not more than £100; and Probate proceedings where the deceased's estate is less than £1,000.

Restrictive Trade Practices Act, 1956

This established the Restrictive Trade Practices Court to examine restrictive trade agreements registered by the Registrar of Trade Agreements, and to prohibit those found to be contrary to the public interest. The Court consists of five judges of the High Court and not more than ten lay judges.

Tribunals and Inquiries

A large number of statutory tribunals, with jurisdiction to decide legal disputes, have been created since 1900. By 1960 there were over 2,000 tribunals within the supervisory roll of the *Council on Tribunals*. The fifteen member *Council on Tribunals* was set up under the *Tribunals and Inquiries Act, 1958*, following the report of the Franks Committee (*Cmnd 218/1957*). Its role is purely advisory, but it has to report annually to Parliament.

These are some of the more important tribunals:

The National Health Service Tribunals

These hear complaints against medical practitioners and dentists under the National Health Service Acts.

The Lands Tribunal (Lands Tribunal Act, 1947)

This has varied jurisdiction, including questions relating to compulsory acquisition of land by Government Departments and local authorities, such as the value of land and compensation payable under the different compensation acts.

The Transport Tribunal (1947 Act)

This has jurisdiction over railway charges, road transport, harbours and canals and hears appeals from various transport licensing authorities. The tribunal's jurisdiction over railway charges will be removed as far as the British Railways are concerned (but not the London Transport Commission) by a Bill now (May 62) before Parliament.

National Assistance Appeal Tribunals (National Assistance Act, 1948)

These hear appeals from the National Assistance Board on such questions as refusal to give assistance, and the nature and amount of assistance.

National Insurance Tribunals

These decide questions concerning rights to benefit under the *National Insurance Act, 1946*, and the *National Insurance (Industrial Injuries) Act, 1946*. (These questions are determined in the first instance by insurance officers of the Ministry of National Insurance.)

Rent Tribunals

These determine the fair rent for furnished houses under the *Furnished Houses (Rent Control) Act*, 1946.

Pensions Appeal Tribunals (Pensions Appeal Act, 1943)

These hear appeals from the Minister of Pensions concerning war pensions.

Conscientious Objectors' Tribunals (National Service Act, 1948)

These were abolished after the ending of the call up for National Service in 1960.

(The Schedule to the *Tribunals and Inquiries Act, 1948* gives the list of tribunals under the supervision of the Council on Tribunals. Others have been added by subsequent legislation, e.g. by the *Mental Health Act, 1959*, the *Finance Act, 1960* and the *Civil Aviation Licensing Act, 1960*.)

Sources

The leading textbooks on Constitutional Law are by O. Hood Phillips (2nd ed., 1957), E. C. S. Wade and G. Phillips (6th ed., 1961), D. C. M. Yardley, *Introduction to British Constitutional Law* (1960) and F. H. Lawson and D. J. Bentley, *Constitutional and Administrative Law* (1961). For administrative law, the three modern textbooks are: J. A. G. Griffith and H. Street, *Principles of Administrative Law* (2nd ed., 1957); H. W. R. Wade, *Administrative Law* (1961); and S. A. de Smith, *Judical Review of Administrative Action* (1960).

Many of the important cases can be studied in D. L. Keir and F. H. Lawson, *Cases in Constitutional Law* (4th ed., 1954) which also contains valuable introductory comments on different branches of the law, and O. Hood Phillips, *Leading Cases in Constitutional Law* (2nd ed., 1957).

A good account of the legal system is to be found in R. M. Jackson, *The Machinery of Justice in England* (3rd ed., 1960), while for a more historical account, reference may be made to H. L. Potter, *Historical Introduction to the English Law and its Institutions* (4th ed., 1958), or G. R. Y. Radcliffe and G. Cross, *The English Legal System* (3rd ed., 1954).

A. V. Dicey's *Law of the Constitution* (10th ed., 1961) is a classic discussion of some of the important principles of English constitutional law; this may usefully be read in conjunction with Sir I. Jennings, *Law and the Constitution* (5th ed., 1959).

XIV
LOCAL GOVERNMENT

Local Government Structure

The *Municipal Corporations Act, 1835* reconstituted the boroughs on an elective basis. *The Local Government Act, 1888* established the County Boroughs and the County Councils, and in 1894 another *Local Government Act* established Urban, Rural District, and Parish Councils and fitted them into the framework of the administrative county, along with the Non-County Boroughs. The London County Council was set up in 1888, at the same time as the other County Councils. Metropolitan boroughs were established under the *London Government Act, 1899*. In 1900 in England and Wales there were 62 County Councils, 67 County Boroughs, 250 Non-County Boroughs, 28 Metropolitan Boroughs and the City of London, 800 Urban District Councils and 663 Rural District Councils, and approximately 8,000 Parish Councils.[1] In 1960 the equivalent figures were 62 County Councils, 83 County Boroughs, 319 Non-County Boroughs, 28 Metropolitan Boroughs and the City of London, 564 Urban District Councils, 473 Rural District Councils, and approximately 7,500 Parish Councils.

Local Government Finance — England and Wales

RATES AND RATEABLE VALUES

Year (ending 31 Mar)	Total Receipts from Rates £000s	Assessable Value of all Rateable Property £000s	Average Rates collected per £ of Assessable Value
1900	40,734	175,623	4s. 11·8d.
1910	63,261	215,310	6s. 2·8d.
1920	105,590	220,714	9s. 6·8d.
1930	156,312	284,937	11s. 6·8d.
1940	200,567	318,834	12s. 7·5d.
1950	280,195	325,262	17s. 3·0d.
1960	647,000	687,618	18s. 10·0d.

SOURCES.—1900–19, *Annual Reports of the Local Government Board*; 1919–61, *Rates and Rateable Values in England and Wales* (annually from the Ministry of Health, 1919–43, Town and Country Planning, 1943–51, Local Government and Planning, 1951, Housing and Local Government, 1951–60).

[1] From the *Local Government Manual*, 1901.

GOVERNMENT CONTRIBUTIONS TO LOCAL AUTHORITIES

Year (ending 31 Mar)	Government Grants[a] (£000s)
1900	12,249
1910	20,915
1920	48,263
1930	107,828
1940	181,900
1950	294,358
1959	658,804

[a] Consisting partly of grants in aid, and partly of receipts from Local Taxation Account and from the local Taxation Licence Duties, not including capital receipts.

TOTAL EXPENDITURE OF LOCAL AUTHORITIES

Year (ending 31 Mar)	Total Expenditure (£000s)
1900	100,862
1910	166,105
1920	289,353
1930	423,655[a]
1940	578,798[a]
1950	849,099[a]
1959	1,731,287[a]

[a] Expenditure other than out of loans for capital works. Including the repayment of loans by various local authorities to the L.C.C. Consolidated Loans Fund.

SOURCES.—*Annual Local Taxation Returns*; *Annual Reports of the Local Government Board, Ministry of Health,* and *Ministry of Housing and Local Government*; also summarised in the *Annual Abstract of Statistics, 1900–1961.*

Major Legislation Affecting Local Government

Education Act, 1902. This transferred the responsibility for education from school boards and school attendance committees to county councils, county borough councils, and some of the larger county districts.

Local Government Act, 1929. This abolished the guardians of the poor, and transferred their responsibilities for poor law and registration to county councils and county borough councils. It also reorganised the system of grants in aid, creating the general grant, partly as compensation for the complete de-rating of agriculture and the de-rating of industry to 25 per cent.

Local Government Act, 1933. This was a codifying Act covering the structure and constitution of local authorities of all sorts, but making no fundamental change in the law.

Local Government Act, 1948. This Act replaced the block grant by the Exchequer Equalisation grant. It transferred responsibility for valuation from local authorities to Inland Revenue and it provided for revaluation: small houses being valued on pre-war building costs, other houses by reference to pre-war rents.

Local Government Act, 1958. This Act abolished most percentage grants and the Exchequer Equalisation grant, substituting a general grant and a rate deficiency grant. It established Local Government Commissions to recommend alteration of boundaries of local authorities (see below, *Local Government Boundary Commission Act, 1945*). It provided for greater delegation of functions by county councils.

Housing Acts. A series of acts between 1919–59 provided for the building of houses by local authorities with varying rates of subsidy from the Exchequer and from the rates.

Town and Country Planning Act, 1932. This established a general system of planning control which could be adopted by second tier local authorities.

Town and Country Planning Act, 1947. This applied planning control to the whole country, transferred responsibility to county councils and county borough councils, and introduced development charges balanced by a compensation fund of £300 m.

Town and Country Planning Act, 1953. This abolished development charges and the £300 m. fund.

Town and Country Planning Act, 1959. This Act altered the basis of compensation for compulsory acquisition.

New Towns Act, 1946. This provided for the establishment of new towns to be built by development corporations appointed by the Minister.

Local Government (Boundary Commission) Act, 1945. This provided for the establishment of a local government boundary commission.

Local Government Boundary Commission (Dissolution) Act, 1949. This abolished the Local Government Boundary Commission (see *Local Government Act, 1958*).

Children Act, 1948. After the Curtis Committee Report, this Act made counties and county boroughs responsible for all children without proper homes.

National Health Service Act, 1946. This Act transferred local authority hospitals to the Ministry of Health. It made counties and county boroughs responsible for ambulance service, maternity and child welfare, health visiting, home helps, prevention of illness, and after-care, etc.

National Assistance Act, 1948. This repealed the existing poor law. It made counties and county boroughs responsible for accommodation of the aged and those temporarily homeless, also for welfare services for the blind, deaf, dumb, etc. Financial assistance and residual responsibilities were passed to the National Assistance Board.

Party Control in Major Cities

Birmingham

1900 – 45 Conservative; 1945 – 47 Labour; 1947 – 52 Conservative; 1952– Labour.

Bristol

1900–30[1] 1930–37 Citizen; 1938–49 Labour; 1949 Citizen; 1950 No clear majority; 1951 Citizen; 1952–1959 Labour; 1960 Citizen.

Edinburgh

1900–30[1] 1930–38 Moderates; 1938– Progressives.

Glasgow

1900–33[1] 1933–49 Labour; 1949–52 Progressive; 1952– Labour

Leeds

1900–04 Conservative; 1904–07 Liberal; 1907–11 Conservative; 1911–12 Liberal; 1912–28 Conservative; 1928–1930 Labour; 1930–33 Conservative; 1933–35 Labour; 1935–45 Conservative; 1945–51 Labour; 1951–53 Conservative; 1953– Labour.

Liverpool

1900–55 Conservative; 1955– Labour.

Manchester

1900–45 Liberal with Labour support; 1945–49 Labour; 1949–52 Conservative; 1952–53 Liberals held balance; 1953– Labour.

[1] Information on local government party politics before 1930 is in many cases hard to find as records of Councils do not refer to party allegiances, and political parties were not recognised in local government.

Sheffield

1900–13 No clear majority between the Conservatives and Liberals; 1914–1920 Liberal with Labour and Socialist support; 1921–26 Liberal and Conservative unofficial alliance (Labour the largest party); 1926–32 Labour; 1932–33 Liberal and Conservative; 1934– Labour.

SOURCES.—Information given by the Town Clerks of the major towns. *The Municipal Year Book* only began to give details of party control in 1956.

Party Representation on the London County Council, 1898–1961

Year	Councillors (elected)				Total	Aldermen				Total	Majority
	Pr.	MRM	Lab.	Ind.		Pr.	MRM	Lab.	Ind.		
1898	84	34	..	..	118	13	6	..	..	137	Pr.
1901	87	31	..	..	118	14	5	..	..	137	Pr.
1904	83	35	..	..	118	15	4	..	..	137	Pr.
1907	38	79	..	1	118	9	10	..	..	137	MRM
1910	55	60	3	..	118	2	15	..	2	137	MRM
1913	50	67	1	..	118	3	14	..	2	137	MRM
1919	40	68	15	1	124	6	12	2	..	144	MRM
1922	25	82	17	..	124	5	12	3	..	144	MRM
1925	6	83	35	..	124	3	13	4	..	144	MRM
1928	5	77	42	..	124	1	12	6	1	144	MRM
1931	6	83	35	..	124	..	13	6	1	144	MRM
1934	..	55	69	..	124	..	9	11	..	144	Lab.
1937	..	49	75	..	124	..	8	12	..	144	Lab.
	Lib.	Con.	Lab.	Comm.		Lib.	Con.	Lab.	Comm.		
1946	2	30	90	2	124	..	6	14	..	144	Lab.
1949	1	64	64	..	129	..	5	16	..	150 [a]	Lab.
1952	..	37	92	..	129	..	6	15	..	150	Lab.
1955	..	52	74	..	126	..	8	13	..	147	Lab.
1958	..	25	101	..	126	..	7	14	..	147	Lab.
1961	..	42	84	..	126	..	7	14	..	147	Lab.

[a] Plus Chairman, an outsider and Labour nominee.

Pr.—Progressives (Lib).
MRM—Municipal Reform Moderates (Con).
Lab.—Labour.
Ind.—Independent.
Comm.—Communist.
Lib.—Liberal.

SOURCES.—Sir G. Gibbon and R. W. Bell, *History of the London County Council, 1889–1939* (1939). *General Election of County Councillors* (published after each election by the L.C.C.), 1919–61.

Local Government Elections

Since the Second World War the results of Local Government Elections have increasingly been accepted as barometers to the national political mood. They can be misleading. The custom of fighting under national party labels has spread only gradually and sporadically. The fact that, under the triennial system, only a third of the seats on borough and district councils are fought each year causes much confusion (a party may claim a great trend in its favour because it is gaining compared to three years before, even though it is losing compared to the previous year). Moreover the results are very patchily reported and no altogether satisfactory statistics are available. However, the results in the 400 boroughs of England and Wales (excluding London), both county and non-county, do provide some pointer to the national mood (even though the smaller non-county boroughs introduce a very distorting element). Between 3,300 and 3,500 seats are fought each year, to a very large extent on a party basis, and the outcome is fairly accurately reported. The following table is based on information supplied by the Conservative Central Office.

Borough Council Election Results

	Conservative and Conservative-supported Independent	Independent without Conservative Support	Labour	Liberal
1949	1,749	426	1,091	79
1950	1,610	510	1,132	72
1951	1,893	548	883	79
1952	1,138	488	1,718	53
1953	1,571	447	1,448	60
1954	1,498	511	1,438	74
1955	1,604	514	1,470	56
1956	1,358	454	1,614	72
1957	1,292	435	1,642	89
1958	1,307	460	1,705	118
1959	1,545	441	1,399	103
1960	1,750	449	1,137	130

SOURCES.—J. Redlich and F. W. Hirst, (ed. B. Keith-Lucas), *The History of Local Government in England* (1958); *Report of Royal Commission on Local Taxation 1901*, XXIV; *Report of Royal Commission on the Poor Law 1909*, XXXVII; *Report of Royal Commission on Local Government 1924–25*, XIV; *1928–29*, VIII, *1929–30*, XV; *Proposals for Reform in Local Government 1928*, XIX; *Social Insurance and Allied Services 1942–43* (The Beveridge Report); *A National Health Service 1943–44*, VIII; *Report of Interdepartmental Committee on the Care of Children 1945–46*, X (The Curtis Report); *Report of the Local Government Boundary Commission for the year 1947, 1947–48*, XIII; *Local Government: Areas and Status of Local Authorities in England and Wales, 1956*, Cmd. 9831; *Local Government: Functions of County Councils and County District Councils in England and Wales 1957*, Cmnd. 161; *Local Government Finance (England and Wales) 1957*, Cmnd. 209.

XV

TRADE UNIONS

Trades Union Congresses 1900–1960

Date	Place	President	General Secretary	No. of Delegates	No. of Societies Represented	No. of Members Represented ('000s)
3–8 Sep 00	Huddersfield	W. Pickles	S. Woods	386	184	1,250
2–7 Sep 01	Swansea	C. Bowerman	"	407	191	1,200
1–6 Sep 02	London	W. Steadman	"	485	198	1,400
6–11 Sep 03	Leicester	W. Hornidge	"	460	204	1,500
5–10 Sep 04	Leeds	R. Bell	"	453	212	1,423
4–9 Sep 05	Hanley	J. Sexton	W. Steadman	457	205	1,541
3–8 Sep 06	Liverpool	D. Cummings	"	491	226	1,555
2–7 Sep 07	Bath	A. Gill	"	521	236	1,700
7–12 Sep 08	Nottingham	D. Shackleton	"	522	214	1,777
6–11 Sep 09	Ipswich	"	"	498	219	1,705
12–17 Sep 10	Sheffield	J. Haslam	"	505	212	1,648
4–9 Sep 11	Newcastle	W. Mullin	C. Bowerman	523	202	1,662
2–7 Sep 12	Newport	W. Thorne	"	495	201	2,002
1–6 Sep 13	Manchester	W. Davis	"	560	207	2,232
6–11 Sep 15	Bristol	J. Seddon	"	610	215	2,682
4–9 Sep 16	Birmingham	H. Gosling	"	673	227	2,851
3–8 Sep 17	Blackpool	J. Hill	"	697	235	3,082
2–7 Sep 18	Derby	J. Ogden	"	881	262	4,532
8–13 Sep 19	Glasgow	G. Stuart-Bunning	"	851	266	5,284
6–11 Sep 20	Portsmouth	J. Thomas	"	955	215	6,505
5–10 Sep 21	Cardiff	E. Poulton	"	810	213	6,418
4–9 Sep 22	Southport	R. Walker	"	723	206	5,129
3–8 Sep 23	Plymouth	J. Williams	F. Bramley	702	194	4,369
1–6 Sep 24	Hull	A. Purcell	"	724	203	4,328
7–12 Sep 25	Scarborough	A. Swales	"	727	205	4,351
6–11 Sep 26	Bournemouth	A. Pugh	W. Citrine	696	207	4,366
5–10 Sep 27	Edinburgh	G. Hicks	"	646	204	4,164
3–8 Sep 28	Swansea	B. Turner	"	621	196	3,875
2–6 Sep 29	Belfast	B. Tillett	"	592	202	3,673
1–5 Sep 30	Nottingham	J. Beard	"	606	210	3,744
7–11 Sep 31	Bristol	A. Hayday	"	589	210	3,719
5–9 Sep 32	Newcastle	J. Bromley	"	578	209	3,613
4–8 Sep 33	Brighton	A. Walkden	"	566	208	3,368
3–7 Sep 34	Weymouth	A. Conley	"	575	210	3,295
2–6 Sep 35	Margate	W. Kean	Sir W. Citrine	575	211	3,389
7–11 Sep 36	Plymouth	A. Findlay	"	603	214	3,615
6–10 Sep 37	Norwich	E. Bevin	"	623	214	4,009
5–9 Sep 38	Blackpool	H. Elvin	"	650	216	4,461
4–5 Sep 39	Bridlington	J. Hallsworth	"	490 [a]	217	4,669
7–9 Oct 40	Southport	W. Holmes	"	667	223	4,867

[a] Actual attendance owing to the outbreak of war. Credentials were issued to 659 delegates.

Date	Place	President	General Secretary	No. of Delegates	No. of Societies Repre- sented	No. of Members Repre- sented ('000s)
1–4 Sep 41	Edinburgh	G. Gibson	"	683	223	5,079
7–11 Sep 42	Blackpool	F. Wolstencroft	"	717	232	5,433
6–10 Sep 43	Southport	Anne Loughlin	"	760	230	6,024
16–20 Oct 44	Blackpool	E. Edwards	"	730	190	6,642
10–14 Sep 45	Blackpool	"	"	762	191	6,576
21–25 Oct 46	Brighton	C. Dukes	V. Tewson	794	192	6,671
1–5 Sep 47	Southport	G. Thomson	"	837	187	7,540
6–10 Sep 48	Margate	Florence Hancock	"	859	188	7,791
5–9 Sep 49	Bridlington	Sir W. Lawther	"	890	187	7,937
4–8 Sep 50	Brighton	H. Bullock	Sir V. Tewson	913	186	7,883
3–7 Sep 51	Blackpool	A. Roberts	"	927	186	7,828
1–5 Sep 52	Margate	A. Deakin	"	943	183	8,020
7–11 Sep 53	Douglas	T. O'Brien	"	954	183	8,088
6–10 Sep 54	Brighton	J. Tanner	"	974	184	8,094
5–9 Sep 55	Southport	C. Geddes	"	984	183	8,107
3–7 Sep 56	Brighton	W. Beard	"	1,000	186	8,264
2–6 Sep 57	Blackpool	Sir T. Williamson	"	995	185	8,305
1–5 Sep 58	Bournemouth	T. Yates	"	993	185	8,337
7–11 Sep 59	Blackpool	R. Willis	"	1,017	186	8,176
5–9 Sep 60	Douglas	C. Bartlett	G. Woodcock	996	184	8,128

SOURCE.—*Trades Union Congress Report, 1961.*

Formation of the 'Big Six' Unions, 1920–1960

Union	*Formed*	*Major Components*
Amalgamated Engineering Union	1920	Amalgamated Society of Engineers (founded 1851) and others.
National Union of General and Municipal Workers	1924	National Union of General Workers (founded 1889 as the National Union of Gasworkers and General Labourers of G.B. and Ireland), National Amalgamated Union of Labour (founded 1889 as Tyneside and General Labourers' Union), and Municipal Employees' Association (founded 1894).
National Union of Mine-workers	1889 (1945)	Formed as the Miners' Federation of G.B., amalgamated with specialist unions, renamed N.U.M. in 1945.
National Union of Railway-men	1913	Amalgamated Society of Railway Servants, and General Railway Workers' Union, and others.
Transport and General Workers' Union	1922	Dock, Wharf, Riverside and General Workers' Union, National Union of Dock Labourers and other dockers' unions, United Vehicle Workers, National Union of Vehicle Workers and others. 1928 amalgamated with the Workers' Union.
Union of Shop, Distributive and Allied Workers	1921 (1946)	Co-operative Employees, and Warehouse and General Workers amalgamated in 1921 to form the National Union of Distributive and Allied Workers. 1946 fusion with National Amalgamated Union of Shop Assistants, Warehousemen and Clerks.

SOURCE.—*Trade Union Congress Reports, 1920–60.*

Leading Officials of the 'Big Six' Unions, 1920–1960

Amalgamated Engineering Union President

1920	J. Brownlie	1939	J. Tanner
1930	W. Hutchinson	1954	R. Openshaw
1933	J. Little	1956	W. Carron

National Union of General Municipal Workers Secretary

1924	W. Thorne	1946	(Sir) T. Williamson
1934	C. Dukes		

National Union of Mineworkers Secretary

(Miners' Federation of Great Britain, 1920–45)

1920	F. Hodges	1946	A. Horner
1924	A. Cook	1959	W. Paynter
1932	E. Edwards		

National Union of Railwaymen Secretary

1920	J. Thomas and C. Cramp	1943	J. Benstead
1931	C. Cramp	1948	J. Figgins
1933	(*Acting Secretary*)	1953	J. Campbell
1934	J. Marchbank	1958	S. Greene

Transport and General Workers Union Secretary

1921	E. Bevin	1955	A. Tiffin
1940	A. Deakin [1]	1956	F. Cousins

Union of Shop, Distributive and Allied Workers Secretary

(Union of Distributive and Allied Workers, 1921–46)

1921	J. Hallsworth and W. Robinson	1947	(*Acting Secretary*)
1924	(Sir) J. Hallsworth	1949	(Sir) A. Birch

[1] Acting Secretary until March 1946.

SOURCES.—*Trade Union Congress Reports, 1920–60*; *Amalgamated Engineering Union Monthly Journal and Report, 1920–60.*

Membership of the 'Big Six' Unions 1920–1960

(to nearest '000)

Year	AEU	NUGMW	NUM	NUR	T&GWU	USDAW
1920	407	..	900	458	..	..
1921	357	..	800	341	300	100
1922	256	..	750	327	300	90
1923	246	..	750	327	300	90
1924	206	327	800	327	300	93
1925	205	320	800	327	300	95
1926	162	300	800	327	300	94
1927	146	278	725	327	300	100
1928	151	258	600	313	286	109
1929	155	261	600	310	389	115
1930	154	258	600	321	384	119
1931	146	240	600	310	390	121
1932	136	220	500	285	390	127
1933	135	230	500	272	370	131
1934	146	252	500	291	403	134
1935	164	280	500	306	460	145
1936	248	340	518	338	523	158
1937	299	405	538	364	611	172
1938	334	417	584	367	635	183
1939	376	430	589	350	648	194
1940	454	441	589	362	650	223
1941	550	548	580	376	680	234
1942	645	721	599	394	806	254
1943	825	726	603	406	1,089	268
1944	811	661	605	404	1,017	272
1945	704	605	533	410	975	275
1946	723	795	538	414	1,230	374
1947	742	824	572	448	1,264	343
1948	743	816	611	455	1,271	342
1949	714	805	609	421	1,253	340
1950	716	785	602	392	1,242	343
1951	756	809	613	396	1,285	348
1952	796	808	641	397	1,277	346
1953	810	790	669	378	1,259	339
1954	823	787	675	372	1,240	344
1955	854	805	675	368	1,278	347
1956	860	808	674	369	1,264	349
1957	900	804	681	371	1,244	352
1958	888	775	674	355	1,225	353
1959	908	769	639	334	1,241	351
1960	973	796	586	334	1,302	355

SOURCE.—*Trades Union Congress Reports, 1920–61 (Statistical Statements).*

Major Industrial Disputes

(in which more than 500,000 working days were lost)

Dispute Began	Industrial group	Area	Numbers affected ('000s)	Working days lost ('000s)[a]
1900 Apr	Potters	N. Staffs.	20	640
Nov	Quarrymen	Bethesda	3	505
1902 Jul	Miners	Federated districts	103	872
1906 Oct	Shipyard workers	Clyde	15	592
1908 Feb	Shipyard workers	Humber, Barrow, Birkenhead, Clyde, E. Scotland	35	1,719
Feb	Engineers	N.E. Coast	11	1,706
Sep	Cotton operatives	Lancs., Cheshire, Derby	120	4,830
1909 Jul	Miners	S. Wales and Mon.	55	660
1910 Jan	Miners	Durham	85	1,280
Jan	Miners	Northumberland	30	1,080
Apr	Miners	Rhondda	13	2,985
Jun	Cotton operatives	Lancs. and Cheshire	102	600
Sep	Shipyard workers	N.E. Coast and Scotland	35	2,851
1911 Jun	Seamen and dockers	U.K.	120	1,020
Aug	Dockers and carters	London	22	500
Aug	Railwaymen	U.K.	145	500
Dec	Cotton weavers	N.E. Lancs.	160	2,954
1912 Feb	Miners	U.K.	1,000	30,800
Feb	Jute workers	Dundee	28	726
May	Dockers and carters	Port of London and Medway	100	2,700
1913 Jan	Cab drivers	London	11	637
Apr	Tube and metal workers	S. Staffs. and N. Worcs.	50	1,400
Aug	Transport workers	Dublin	20	1,900
1914 Jan	Builders	London	20	2,500
Feb	Miners	Yorks.	150	2,654
1915 Jul	Miners	S. Wales	232	1,400
1916 Mar	Jute workers	Dundee	30	500
1917 May	Engineers	U.K.	160	2,880
1918 May	Miners	S. Wales and Mon.	40	760
Dec	Cotton spinners	Lancs. and Cheshire	100	900
1919 Jan	Miners	Yorks.	150	1,950
Jan	Shipyard workers	N.E. Coast	40	820
Mar	Miners	Various districts	100	600
Jun	Cotton operatives	Lancs. and adjoining counties	450	7,500
Jul	Miners	Yorks.	150	4,050
Sep	Ironfounders	England, Wales, and Ireland	50	6,800
Sep	Railwaymen	U.K.	500	3,850
1920 Sep	Cotton operatives	Oldham and district	400	620
Oct	Miners	U.K.	1,100	16,000
1921 (Dec. 1920)	Shipyard carpenters	U.K.	10	2,200
Apr	Miners	U.K.	1,100	72,000
Jun	Cotton operatives	Lancs. and adjoining counties	375	6,750
1922 Mar	Engineers	U.K.	250	13,650

[a] Where figures for working days lost are not given in the *Gazettes*, they have been estimated.

Dispute Began	Industrial group	Area	Numbers affected ('000s)	Working days lost ('000s)[a]
1922 Mar	Shipyard workers	Various districts	90	3,400
1923 Feb	Jute workers	Dundee	29	950
Apr	Boilermakers	Clyde, E. Scotland, N.E. Coast, Hull, Southampton, Birkenhead, Barrow	30	5,725
1924 Jan	Railwaymen	U.K.	69	500
Feb	Dockers	U.K.	110	510
Jul	Builders	U.K.	100	2,970
1925 Jul	Wool textile workers	W. Riding of Yorks. and part of Lancs.	165	3,105
1926 May	Miners	U.K.	1,050	145,200
May	General Strike	U.K.	1,580[b]	15,000[b]
1928 May	Cotton weavers	Nelson	17	600
1929 Jul	Cotton operatives	Lancs. and adjoining counties	388	6,596
1930 Apr	Wool textile workers	W. Riding of Yorks. and part of Lancs.	120	3,258
1931 Jan	Cotton weavers	Lancs. and adjoining counties	145	3,290
Jan	Miners	S. Wales and Mon.	150	2,030
1932 Aug	Cotton weavers	Lancs. and Yorks.	148	4,524
Oct	Cotton spinners	Lancs. and adjoining counties	130	760
1937 May	Busmen	London	24	565
1944 Mar	Miners	Wales and Mon.	100	550
Mar	Miners	Yorkshire	120	1,000
1945 Sep	Dockers	Birkenhead, Liverpool, Hull, Manchester, London	50	1,100
1953 Dec	Engineers and Shipyard workers	U.K.	1,070	1,070
1954 Sep	Dockers	Port of London and sympathy strikes	45	726
1955 May	Dockers	Various ports of England	21	673
May	Railwaymen	U.K.	70	865
1957 Mar	Engineers	U.K.	615	4,000
Mar	Shipyard workers	U.K.	165	2,150
Jul	Busmen	Provinces	100	770
1958 Apr	Dockers, transport and market workers	London	24	515
May	Busmen	Greater London	49	1,604
1959 Jun	Printing workers	U.K.	120	3,500

[a] Where figures for working days lost are not given in the *Gazettes*, they have been estimated.
[b] Excluding Miners.

SOURCES.—*The Board of Trade Labour Gazette, 1900–17*; *The Ministry of Labour Gazette*. Published monthly, 1918–61.

XVI
CHURCHES

Church Membership Statistics

EXTREME caution should be observed in making use of church membership statistics, as no entirely reliable sources exist giving information about membership or attendance. The last reasonably authoritative figures of religious affiliations in Britain were taken from the 1851 census, though even then there was no compulsion to answer the questions on religion. Since then no census has included questions on religious affiliation. The statistics in the following tables are drawn from the official year-books and handbooks of the various religious denominations in Britain. These are generally collected annually from the local registers in churches. Strictly comparable figures are impossible to obtain for church membership and church attendance between 1900 and 1960. The definition of membership varies greatly from one denomination to another, as does the minimum age for reception into the church. At one extreme, the Roman Catholic Church officially records the Roman Catholic population of all ages, regardless of church attendance. Nonconformist churches with adult baptism, and in the case of the Methodists a probationary period before baptism, are the most exclusive. These statistics give no indication how frequently 'members' of the churches attended services. No precise information is available on the effect of religious broadcasting on attendance at church services. Some studies of church attendance and religious affiliations that have attempted to fill out these necessarily very inadequate figures are: *Religious Broadcasts and the Public*, by the B.B.C. Audience Research Department (1955); "How Many in the Pew?" in *The Economist* of 30 Aug 58; *Puzzled People*, by Mass Observation (1948); *A Survey of Social Conditions in England and Wales*, chapter 18, by A. M. Carr-Saunders, D. C. Jones, and C. M. Moser (1958); and Gallup Poll figures for church membership and attendance.

More general works on religion in Britain in the twentieth century are: E. O. James, *History of Christianity in England* (1949); R. Lloyd, *The Church of England in the Twentieth Century* (2 vols., 1948–50); G. Spinks (ed.), *Religion in Britain since 1900* (1952); R. F. Wearmouth, *The Social and Political Influence of Methodism in the Twentieth Century* (1957); J. Highet, *The Scottish Churches* (1960).

THE CHURCH OF ENGLAND[a]

Parochial Easter Day Communicants

Year	Estimated No. ('000s)[b]	Rate per 1000 of Population aged 15 and over	No. of Parochial Churches
1900	1,902	93	n.a.
1910	2,212	95	15,864[c]
1920	2,194	88	16,156[c]
1930	2,285	80	16,515[c]
1940	2,018	64	n.a.
1950	1,867	58	16,825[c]
1958	2,073	63	18,051[d]

[a] For the area of the 43 dioceses of the Provinces of Canterbury and York. Figures for the 4 dioceses of the province of Wales before 1920 have been excluded for proper comparison.

Under the *Welsh Church Acts* of 1914 and 1919, the Church in Wales and Monmouthshire was disestablished as from 31 Mar 20, and Wales was formed into a separate province.

[b] Includes estimated figures for churches for which no returns were received. No statistics included for extra parochial churches in Armed Forces, universities, prisons, hospitals, etc.

[c] Figures for parochial churches are from *The Statesman's Year-Book* for 1911, 1921, 1934, 1951.

[d] Figure for 1960, from *Facts and Figures about the Church of England.*

SOURCES.—*Facts and Figures about the Church of England*, prepared by the Statistical Unit of the Central Board of Finance. Published by the Church Information Office (1962); *Official Year Books of the Church of England, 1900–1961*; L. Paul, *The Pay and Deployment of the Clergy* (1964).

EPISCOPAL CHURCH IN SCOTLAND

Year	Communicants ('000s)	No. of Church Buildings
1900	46	354
1910	52	404
1920	57	416
1930	60	415
1940	62	404
1950	57	397
1960	57	369

SOURCES.—*The Year Book for the Episcopal Church in Scotland*; *Whitaker's Almanack* (figures for 1910 and 1920); *The Statesman's Year-Book* (figures for 1930 and 1940).

BAPTIST UNION

British Isles[a]

Year	Members ('000s)	No. of Places of Worship[b]
1900	366	2,579
1910	419	2,889
1920	405	2,866
1930	406	2,965
1940	382	3,044
1950	338	3,110
1960	318	3,053

[a] These are statistics actually received from the churches; no estimates are made for churches omitting to return figures.

[b] England and Wales only.

SOURCE.—*The Baptist Handbook, 1900–1960.*

CONGREGATIONAL UNION
United Kingdom [a]

Year	Members ('000s)	No. of Places of Worship
1900	436	4,607 [b]
1910	494	4,721
1920	n.a.	n.a.
1930	490	3,556
1939	459	3,435
1950	387	3,173
1959	212	2,984

[a] 1900 and 1910 figures for British Isles.
[b] Figure for 1901.

SOURCE.—*The Congregational Year Book, 1900–1960.*

METHODIST CHURCH [a]
Great Britain and Ireland

Year	Members and Probationers ('000s)	Churches, etc.
1900	520	9.037
1910	544	n.a.
1920	512	9,013
1930	548	9,070
1940	823	n.a.
1950	776	n.a.
1959 Dec	729	n.a.

[a] Up to 1930 these figures are for the Wesleyan Methodist Church. The Methodist Church was formed in 1932 by a union of the Wesleyan, Primitive, and United Methodist Churches. The United Methodists were themselves formed by a union of three separate bodies in 1905.

SOURCE.—*The Minutes of the Methodist Conference, 1900–1961,* W. S. F. Pickering, *Anglo-Methodist Relations* (1961) gives figures (for England only) for all bodies (1906–1957).

PRESBYTERIAN CHURCH
England

Year	Members ('000s)
1900	76
1911	87
1922	84
1930	84
1940	82
1950	82
1960	71

SOURCES.—1900 and 1911, *The Official Handbook of the Presbyterian Church of England*; 1922–60 *The Statesman's Year-Book.*

THE CHURCH OF SCOTLAND [a]

(Presbyterian)

Year	Total Communicants on Rolls ('000s)	No. of Places of Worship
1901	1164	n.a.
1911	1220	1,703
1921	1278	1,704
1931	1281	2,795
1941	1269	2,507
1951	1273	2,348
1959	1307	2,242

[a] In 1929 the United Free Church of Scotland rejoined the Church of Scotland.

SOURCE.—*The Church of Scotland Year Book, 1961.*

THE ROMAN CATHOLIC CHURCH

Great Britain

Year	Estimated Catholic Population ('000s) [a]	Catholic Baptisms ('000s)	No. of Public Churches and Chapels
1900	5415	n.a.	1,536
1910	5515	n.a.	1,773
1920	5704	n.a.	1,408
1930	6024 [b]	66	1,564
1940	3444 [c]	70	1,802
1950	3884 [c]	87	1,971
1960	4818	112 [d]	3,204

[a] These figures include England and Wales, Scotland, Ireland, 1900–30, and N. Ireland, 1940–60.
[b] This figure is made up of the English estimate for 1930, the Scottish estimate for 1926, and the Irish estimate for 1911.
[c] The figures for 1940 and 1950 include the N. Irish Catholic population taken from the 1937 census.
[d] Figure for 1959.

Roman Catholic Archbishops of Westminster

1892 H. Vaughan (Cardinal, 1893)
1903 F. Bourne (Cardinal, 1911)
1935 A. Hinsley (Cardinal, 1937)
1943 B. Griffin (Cardinal, 1946)
1956 W. Godfrey (Cardinal, 1958)

SOURCE.—*The Catholic Directory, 1900–1960.*

THE JEWISH FAITH [a]

Great Britain

Year	Estimated No. of Jews ('000s)	Approx. No. of Synagogues
1900	160	80 [d]
1910	243	200 [d]
1920	287	200 [d]
1929 [b]	297	300 [e]
1940	385 [c]	200 [e]
1950	450	240 [e]
1960	450	240 [e]

[a] Statistics for 1900 for G.B. and Ireland, 1910 for the British Isles, 1920 for U.K., 1929 for G.B., 1940–60 for G.B. and N. Ireland.
[b] No Jewish statistics available, 1930–34.
[c] Including about 35,000 refugees.
[d] From *Whitaker's Almanack.*
[e] From *The Statesman's Year-Book.*

SOURCE.—*The Jewish Year Book, 1900–1960*

NORTHERN IRELAND
Religious Affiliations
(to nearest '000)

Year	Roman Catholic	Presbyterian	Protestant Episcopalian	Methodist	Others
1911	430	395	327	46	52
1937	428	391	345	55	60
1951	471	410	353	67	69

SOURCE.—Census reports quoted in *The Statesman's Year-Books, 1900–1961.*

Leading Bishops of the Church of England

Archbishops of Canterbury

1896 F. Temple
1903 R. Davidson
1928 C. Lang
1942 W. Temple
1945 G. Fisher

Archbishops of York

1891 W. Maclagan
1909 C. Lang
1929 W. Temple
1942 C. Garbett
1956 A. Ramsey

Bishops of London

1897 M. Creighton
1901 A. Winnington-Ingram
1939 G. Fisher
1945 J. Wand
1956 H. Campbell

Bishops of Durham

1890 B. Westcott
1901 H. Moule
1920 H. Henson
1939 A. Williams
1952 A. Ramsey
1956 M. Harland

Bishops of Winchester

1895 R. Davidson
1903 H. Ryle
1911 E. Talbot
1924 F. Woods
1932 C. Garbett
1942 M. Haigh
1952 A. Williams

The Archbishops of Canterbury and York, and the Bishops of London, Durham, and Winchester have permanent seats in the House of Lords. Twenty-one of the remaining diocesan bishops also sit in the House of Lords, according to their dates of seniority as diocesan bishops. Translation of a bishop from one see to another does not affect his right to sit in the House of Lords. The Bishop of Sodor and Man has no seat in the House of Lords, as he has a permanent seat in the House of Keys, Isle of Man.

SOURCES.—*Crockford's Clerical Directory, 1900–60; Whitaker's Almanack, 1900–61.*

XVII

NATIONAL NEWSPAPERS[1]

National Daily Newspapers

(British Gazette), 5–13 May 1926

Proprietors: His Majesty's Stationery Office. Printed at offices of *Morning Post.*
Policy: Strong opposition to the general strike.
Editor: W. Churchill.

(Daily Chronicle), 1869–1930

Proprietors: E. Lloyd, 1871–1918. Frank Lloyd and family trading as United Newspapers Ltd. Lloyd family parted with their interest in 1918. Incorporated with *Daily News* as the *News Chronicle,* 1930.
Policy: Liberal.
Editors: W. Fisher, 1899. R. Donald, 1902. E. Perris, 1918–30.

Daily Citizen), 1912–Jan 1915

Proprietors: Labour Newspapers Ltd.
Policy: Official Labour.
Editor: F. Dilnot, 1912–15.

Daily Express, 1900

Proprietors: A. Pearson, Daily Express (1900) Ltd. Acquired by Ld Beaverbrook, London Express Newspaper Ltd., 1915. 1954 control relinquished by Ld Beaverbrook to Beaverbrook Newspapers Ltd. Block of shares transferred to the Beaverbrook Foundation.
Policy: Independent conservative.
Editors: A. Pearson, 1900. R. Blumenfeld, 1902. B. Baxter, 1929. A. Christiansen, 1933. E. Pickering, 1957.

(Daily Graphic), 1890–1926. 1946–52

Proprietors: Founded by W. L. Thomas. Owned by H. Baines & Co. Amalgamated with *Daily Sketch* in 1926 (Kemsley Newspapers). Appeared as *Daily Sketch and Daily Graphic* 1926–46, as *Daily Graphic* 1946–52, then as *Daily Sketch.*
Policy: Independent conservative.
Editors: H. Hall, 1891. H. White, 1907. W. Ackland, 1909. A. Hutchinson, 1912. A. Netting, 1917. H. Lawton, 1919. E. Tebbutt, 1923. H. Heywood, 1925–6. A. Thornton, 1946. N. Hamilton, 1947. H. Clapp, 1948–52 (see *Daily Sketch*).

Daily Herald, 1912

Proprietors: Daily Herald Printing and Publishing Society in association with Odhams Press Ltd. Formed Daily Herald (1929) Ltd. (Chairman: Ld Southwood). 49 per cent of shares held by T.U.C.,

[1] The policies of national newspapers between 1900–60 have inevitably fluctuated. 'Policy' should here be taken only as a general indication of the nature of the paper. In very few cases have newspapers been the official organs of a political party.

51 per cent by Odhams Press. 1960 new agreement between Odhams Press and T.U.C.

Policy: General support to Labour Movement, 1912–23, 1960–. Official Labour 1923–60.

Editors: R. Kenny, 1912. C. Lapworth, 1913. G. Lansbury, 1913. W. Ryan, 1922. H. Fyfe, 1923. W. Mellor, 1926. W. Stevenson, 1931. F. Williams, 1937. P. Cudlipp, 1940. S. Elliott, 1953. D. Machray, 1957. J. Beavan, 1960.
(Issued as a weekly paper during 1st World War, launched again as a daily in 1919.)

Daily Mail, 1896

Proprietors: A. Harmsworth (Ld Northcliffe), Associated Newspapers Ltd.

Policy: Independent. Right-wing Conservative.

Editors: T. Marlowe, 1899. W. Fish, 1926. O. Pulvermacher, 1929. W. McWhirter, 1930. W. Warden, 1931. A. Cranfield, 1935. R. Prew, 1939. S. Horniblow, 1944. F. Owen, 1947. G. Schofield, 1950. A. Wareham, 1955. W. Hardcastle, 1959.

Daily Mirror, 1903

Proprietors: A. Harmsworth, Sir H. Harmsworth (Ld Rothermere), 1914. Pictorial Newspaper (1910) Co. Daily Mirror Newspapers Ltd.

Policy: Independent.

Editors: Mary Howarth, 1903. H. Fyfe, 1904. A. Kinealy, 1907. E. Flynn, 1915. A. Campbell, 1919. L. Brownlee, 1931. C. Thomas, 1934. S. Bolam, 1948. J. Nener, 1953. L. Howard, 1960.

(Daily News), 1846–1930

Proprietors: Daily News Ltd., 1901 (Chairman: G. Cadbury, 1901–11). Amalgamated with *Morning Leader*, as *Daily News and Leader*, 1912. Amalgamated with *Westminster Gazette*, 1928. Amalgamated with *Daily Chronicle*, 1930. Continued as *News Chronicle* (see below).

Policy: Liberal.

Editors: E. Cook, 1896. R. Lehmann, 1901. A. Gardiner, 1902. S. Hodgson, 1920–30.

(Daily Paper), 1904 (32 issues only)

Proprietors: W. Stead.

Policy: 'A paper for the abnormally scrupulous'.

Editor: W. Stead.

Daily Sketch, 1908

Proprietors: E. Hulton and Co. Ltd. Daily Mirror Newspapers Ltd., and Sunday Pictorial Newspapers (1920) Ltd. Bought by the Berry brothers, 1926, and merged with the *Daily Graphic*. Name changed to *Daily Graphic*, 1946–52. Subsidiary of Allied Newspapers Ltd. Kemsley Newspapers Ltd. Bought by Associated Newspapers Ltd., 1952. Renamed *Daily Sketch*, 1953.

Policy: Independent conservative.

Editors: J. Heddle, 1909. W. Robinson, 1914. H. Lane, 1919. H. Gates, 1922. H. Lane, 1923. A. Curthoys, 1928. A. Sinclair, 1936. S. Carroll, 1939. L. Berry, 1942. A. Thornton and M. Watts, 1943. A. Thornton, 1944. N. Hamilton, 1947. H. Clapp, 1948. H. Gunn, 1953. C. Valdar, 1959.

Daily Telegraph, 1855

Proprietors: Ld Burnham and family. Sold to Sir W. Berry (Ld Camrose), Sir G. Berry (Ld Kemsley) and Sir E. Iliffe (Ld) in 1928. Absorbed *Morning Post*, as *Daily Telegraph and Morning Post* in 1937. Ld Camrose acquired Ld Kemsley's and Ld Iliffe's interests in 1937.

Policy: Conservative.

Editors: (Sir) J. le Sage, 1885. F. Miller, 1923. A. Watson, 1924. C. Coote, 1950.

Daily Worker, 1930

Proprietors: Daily Worker Cooperative Society Ltd. Descendant of the *Sunday Worker*, 1925–30. Publication suppressed 1941–42.

Policy: Communist.

Editors: W. Rust, 1930. J. Shields, 1932. I. Cox, 1935. R. Palme Dutt, 1936. W. Rust, 1939. J. Campbell, 1949. G. Matthews, 1959.

(Financial News), 1884–1945

Proprietors: Financial News Ltd, 1898 (H. Marks). Incorporated with the *Financial Times* in 1945.

Policy: Finance, independent.

Editors: H. Marks, 1884. Dr Ellis, 1916. H. O'Neill, 1921. W. Dorman and W. Lang, 1921. Sir L. Worthington-Evans, 1924. Sir E. Young, 1925. O. Hobson, 1929. M. Green, 1934. H. Parkinson, 1938–45.

Financial Times, 1888

Proprietors: Financial Times Ltd. Incorporated Financier and Bullionist. Incorporated with the *Financial News* in 1945.

Policy: Finance, independent.

Editors: W. Lawson. A. Murray, 1901. C. Palmer, 1909. D. Hunter, 1924. A. Chisholm, 1938. A. Cole, 1940. H. Parkinson, 1945. L. Newton, 1950.

Guardian (see under *Provincial Newspapers — Manchester Guardian*)

(Majority), 1906 (10–14 Jul only)

Proprietors: Majority Ltd.

Policy: 'The organ of all who work for wage or salary'.

Editor:

Morning Advertiser, 1794

Proprietors: Incorporated Society of Licensed Victuallers.

Policy: Defence of the interests of licensed trade.

Editors: F. Doney, 1894. H. Fyfe, 1902. G. Talbot, 1903. H. Byshe, 1913. A. Jackson, 1924. H. Bennett, 1927. F. Millman, 193?. E. Hopwood, 1947. D. Quick, 1954. L. Forse, 1956.

(Morning Herald), 1892–1900

Proprietors: Morning Newspaper Co. Became *London Morning* in 1898, and *Morning Herald* in 1899. Merged with *Daily Express* in 1900.

Policy: Independent.

Editor: D. Murray, 1892–1900.

(Morning Leader), 1892–1912

Proprietors: Colman family of Norwich. Merged with *Daily News*, as *Daily News and Leader* in 1912 (see *Daily News*).

Policy: Liberal.

Editor: E. Parke, 1892–1912.

(Morning Post), 1772–1937

Proprietors: Sir A. Borthwick (Ld Glenesk), 1876–1908. Lady Bathurst, 1908–24. Absorbed in *Daily Telegraph* in 1937 (Ld Camrose).

Policy: Conservative.

Editors: J. Dunn, 1897. S. Wilkinson, 1905. F. Ware, 1905. H. Gwynne, 1911–37.

(Morning Standard), 1857–1917

Proprietors: Bought from Johnston family by A. Pearson, 1904. Sold to D. Dalziel (Ld) in 1910. Ceased, 1917.

Policy: Opponent of tariff reform.

Editors: W. Mudford, 1874. G. Curtis, 1900. H. Gwynne, 1904. H. White, 1911–17.

New Daily, 25 Apr 1960

Proprietors: The British Newspaper Trust Ltd. Sponsored by the People's League for the Defence of Freedom, the Free Press Society, and the Anti-Socialist Front.

Policy: 'The only daily newspaper in Great Britain independent of combines and trade unions.'

Editor: E. Martell, 1960.

(News Chronicle), 1930–60

Proprietors: Amalgamation of *Daily News and Leader* and *Daily Chronicle* in 1930 (Cadbury family). Bought by Associated Newspapers Ltd. in 1960, and merged with *Daily Mail.*

Policy: Liberal.

Editors: T. Clarke, 1930. A. Vallance, 1933. G. Barry, 1936. R. Cruikshank, 1948. M. Curtis, 1954. N. Cursley, 1957.

(Recorder), 27 Oct 1953–17 May 1954

Proprietors: The Recorder Ltd. (Managing Director: E. Martell). A weekly suburban newspaper 1870–1939, continued as a weekly after 1954.

Policy: Independent. 'Keynote: pride in Britain and the British Empire.'

Editor: W. Brittain, 1953–4.

Times, 1785

Proprietors: Founded as the *Daily Universal Register*, became the *Times* in 1788. Owned by the Walter family, 1785–1908. Bought by Ld Northcliffe in 1908. Owned by J. Astor and J. Walter in 1922. 7 Aug 24, Times Trust formed (including Lord Chief Justice, Warden of All Souls, Oxford, President of the Royal Society, President of the Institute of Chartered Accountants and Governor of the Bank of England).

Policy: Independent conservative.

Editors: G. Buckle, 1884. G. Dawson, 1912. H. Steed, 1919. G. Dawson, 1922. R. Barrington-Ward, 1941. W. Casey, 1948. Sir W. Haley, 1952.

(Tribune), 1906 only

Proprietors: F. Thomasson.

Policy: Liberal.

Editors: W. Hill and S. Pryor, 1906.

(Westminster Gazette), 1921–8 issued as a morning paper.

(See *Evening Papers*).

Major Provincial and Scottish Newspapers

Glasgow Herald, 1783
Proprietors: G. Outram and Co.
Policy: Conservative.
Editors: C. Gilchrist, 1888. W. Wallace, 1907. F. Kitchen, 1909. (Sir) R. Bruce, 1917. (Sir) W. Robieson, 1936. J. Holburn, 1954.

(Manchester) Guardian, 1821
Proprietors: The Manchester Guardian Ltd. (& Evening News). Renamed *Guardian*, 1959.
Policy: Liberal.
Editors: C. Scott, 1872. E. Scott, 1929. W. Crozier, 1932. A. Wadsworth, 1944. A. Hetherington, 1956.

Scotsman, 1817
Proprietors: J. Ritchie and Co. The Scotsman Publications Ltd. (R. Thomson).
Policy: Conservative.
Editors: C. Cooper, 1880. J. Croal, 1905. Sir G. Waters, 1924. J. Watson, 1944. A. Dunnett, 1956.

Yorkshire Post, 1754
Proprietors: The Yorkshire Conservative Newspaper Co. Ltd.
Policy: Conservative.
Editors: H. Palmer, 1890. J. Phillips, 1903. A. Mann, 1920. (Sir) L. Andrews, 1939.

London Evening Newspapers

(Evening Echo and Chronicle), 22 Mar–4 May 1915
Proprietor: E. Lloyd. Merged with *Star*.
Policy: Liberal
Editor:

(Echo), 1868–1905
Proprietors: Consolidated Newspapers. F. Pethick-Lawrence in control, 1901–5.
Policy: Radical, progressive.
Editors: W. Crook, 1898. T. Meech, 1900. (Sir) P. Alden, 1901. F. Pethick-Lawrence, 1901–5.

Evening News, 1881
Proprietors: A. Harmsworth (Evening News Ltd.), 1894. Associated Newspapers Ltd., 1905.
Policy: Conservative.
Editors: W. Evans, 1896. C. Beattie, 1922. F. Fitzhugh, 1924. G. Schofield, 1943. J. Marshall, 1950. R. Willis, 1954.

Evening Standard, 1827
Proprietors: Bought by A. Pearson from Johnston family in 1904. Absorbed *St James's Gazette* in 1905. D. Dalziel (Ld),[1] 1910. Hulton and Co. 1915–23. Incorporated with *Pall Mall Gazette* and *Globe*, 1923. Bought by Ld Beaverbrook in 1924.
Policy: Independent conservative.
Editors: S. Pryor, 1897. W. Woodward, 1906. J. Kilpatrick, 1912. D. Sutherland, 1914. A. Mann, 1916. D. Phillips, 1920.

[1] Ld Dalziel of Wooler, not to be confused with Ld Dalziel of Kirkcaldy who was proprietor *Reynolds' News*, 1914–29.

E. Thompson, 1923. G. Gilliat, 1928. P. Cudlipp, 1933. R. Thompson, 1938. F. Owen, 1939. M. Foot, 1942. S. Elliott, 1943. H. Gunn, 1944. P. Elland, 1950. C. Wintour, 1959.

(Evening Times), 1910–11
Proprietors: London Evening Newspaper Co. (J. Morrison, Sir S. Scott, J. Cowley).
Policy: Conservative.
Editors: C. Watney, E. Wallace.

(Globe), 1803–1921
Proprietors: (Sir) G. Armstrong, 1871–1907. H. Harmsworth, 1907–11. W. Madge, 1912–14. Absorbed by *Pall Mall Gazette* in 1921, incorporated with *Evening Standard* in 1923.
Policy: Conservative.
Editors: Sir G. Armstrong, 1895. P. Ogle, 1907. J. Harrison, 1908. C. Palmer, 1912. W. Peacock, 1915–21.

(Pall Mall Gazette), 1865–1923
Proprietors: W. Astor (Ld), 1892. Sir H. Dalziel, 1917. Sir J. Leigh, 1923. Incorporated with *Evening Standard* in 1923.
Policy: Conservative.
Editors: Sir D. Straight, 1896. F. Higginbottom, 1909. J. Garvin, 1912. D. Sutherland, 1915–23.

(St James's Gazette), 1880–1905
Proprietors: E. Steinkopff, 1888. W. Dallas Ross. A. Pearson, 1903. Amalgamated with *Evening Standard* in 1905.
Policy: Conservative.
Editors: H. Chisholm, 1897. R. McNeill, 1900. G. Fiennes, 1903. S. Pryor, 1904–5.

(Star), 1887–1960
Proprietors: Star Newspaper Co. Owned by Daily News Ltd. Bought by Associated Newspapers Ltd, and incorporated in *Evening News*, 1960.
Policy: Liberal.
Editors: E. Parke, 1891. J. Douglas, 1908. W. Pope, 1920. E. Chattaway, 1930. R. Cruikshank, 1936. A. Cranfield, 1941. R. McCarthy, 1957-60.

(Sun), 1893–1906
Proprietors: T. P. O'Connor. H. Bottomley, 1900. Sir G. Armstrong and W. Madge, 1904-6.
Policy: Literary, non-political.
Editors: T. P. O'Connor. T. Dahle.

(Westminster Gazette), 1893–1928
Proprietors: Sir G. Newnes, 1893. Liberal Syndicate (Chairman: Sir A. Mond), 1908–15. Last issue as evening paper 5 Nov 21. First issue as morning paper 7 Nov 21. Incorporated with *Daily News* in 1928.
Policy: Liberal.
Editors: J. Spender, 1896. J. Hobman, 1921–28.

National Sunday Newspapers
(excluding all those not published in London)

((Illustrated) Sunday Herald), 1915–27

Proprietors: Sir E. Hulton. Renamed *Illustrated Sunday Herald.* Bought by Berry family in 1926 and renamed *Sunday Graphic* in 1927 (see below).

Policy: Independent conservative.

Editors: J. E. Williams. T. Hill, 1926–7.

(National News), 1917–18

Proprietors: Odhams Press Ltd.

Policy: Independent.

Editor: A. de Beck, 1917–18.

News of the World, 1843

Proprietors: News of the World Ltd. (Sir) G. Riddell (Ld), 1903–34.

Policy: Independent conservative.

Editors: Sir E. Carr, 1891. D. Davies, 1941. R. Skelton, 1946. A. Waters, 1947. R. Cudlipp, 1953. S. Somerfield, 1959.

Observer, 1791

Proprietors: F. Beer. Bought by Ld Northcliffe in 1905. Bought by W. Astor (Vt) in 1911. 1945 became the Observer Trust Ltd. Chairmen: Vt Astor, 1945. D. Foot, 1953. Sir I. Evans, 1957.

Policy: Conservative. Independent since 1942.

Editors: F. Beer, 1894. A. Harrison, 1905. J. Garvin, 1908. I. Brown, 1942. D. Astor, 1948.

People, 1881

Proprietors: W. Madge and Sir G. Armstrong. Sir W. Madge, 1914–22. M. L. Publishing Co. Ltd. The People Ltd. Odhams Press.

Policy: Independent.

Editors: J. Hatton. J. Sansome 1913. H. Swaffer 1924. H. Ainsworth 1925. S. Campbell, 1958.

Reynolds' News, 1850

Proprietors: Originally *Reynolds's Weekly Newspaper,* and later *Reynolds's Illustrated News.* Owned by J. Dicks and family since 1879. H. Dalziel (Ld) [1] appointed business manager in 1907. He became the sole proprietor in 1914. Bought by the National Cooperative Press Ltd. Incorporated the *Sunday Citizen.*

Policy: Support for the Labour and Co-operative movements.

Editors: W. Thompson, 1894. H. Dalziel, 1907. J. Crawley, 1920. S. Elliott, 1929. W. Richardson, 1941.

Sunday Dispatch, 1801–1961

Proprietors: Sir G. Newnes. Originally the *Weekly Dispatch* until 1928. Bought by the Harmsworth family. Ld Northcliffe, Ld Rothermere from 1928. Associated Newspapers Ltd. Absorbed by the *Sunday Express* in 1961.

Policy: Independent conservative.

Editors: M. Cotton. H. Swaffer, 1915. B. Falk, 1919. H. Lane, 1933. W. Brittain, 1934. C. Brooks, 1936. C. Eade, 1938. H. Gunn, 1959–61.

Sunday Express, 1918

Proprietors: Sunday Express Ltd. (Ld Beaverbrook).

Policy: Independent conservative.

Editors: J. Douglas, 1920. J. Gordon, 1928. J. Junor, 1954.

[1] Ld Dalziel of Kirkcaldy, not to be confused with Ld Dalziel of Wooler, who was proprietor of the *Evening Standard,* 1910–15.

Sunday Graphic (and Sunday News), 1915–60

Proprietors: Sir E. Hulton. Originally called the *Sunday Herald*, renamed the *Illustrated Sunday Herald.* Bought by the Berry family in 1926, and renamed the *Sunday Graphic* in 1927. Daily Graphic and Sunday Graphic Ltd., a subsidiary of Ld Kemsley's newspapers. Incorporated the *Sunday News* in 1931. Bought by R. Thomson in 1959. Ceased publication in 1960.

Policy: Independent.

Editors: T. Hill, 1927. A. Sinclair, 1931. R. Simpson, 1935. M. Watts, 1947. N. Hamilton, 1947. I. Lang, 1948. A. Josey, 1949. B. Horniblow, 1950. P. Brownrigg, 1952. M. Randell, 1953. G. McKenzie, 1953. A. Hall, 1958. R. Anderson, 1959. A. Ewart, 1960.

(Sunday Illustrated), 1921–23

Proprietor: H. Bottomley.

Policy: Independent.

Editor: H. Bottomley.

(Sunday (Illustrated) News), 1842–1931

Proprietors: Originally *Lloyd's Sunday News.* Sunday News Ltd. United Newspapers Ltd. (W. Harrison). Merged with the *Sunday Graphic* in 1931.

Policy: Independent liberal.

Editors: T. Catling. W. Robinson, 1919. E. Perris, 1924. E. Wallace, 1929–31.

Sunday Pictorial, 1915

Proprietors: The Harmsworth family. Taken over by Ld Rothermere in 1922. Sunday Pictorial Newspapers (1920) Ltd.

Policy: Independent.

Editors: F. Sanderson, 1915. W. McWhirter, 1921. D. Grant, 1924. W. McWhirter, 1928. D. Grant, 1929. H. Cudlipp, 1938. R. Campbell, 1940. H. Cudlipp, 1946. P. Zec, 1949. H. Cudlipp, 1952. C. Valdar, 1953. L. Howard, 1959. R. Payne, 1960.

((Sunday) Referee), 1877–1939

Proprietors: Printed by the Daily News Ltd. Owned by I. Ostrer. Incorporated in the *Sunday Chronicle* in 1939 (which was published in Manchester and ceased independent publication in 1955).

Policy: Conservative.

Editors: R. Butler. R. Donald, 1922. A. Laber, 1924. M. Joulden, 1933.

(Sunday Special), 1897–1904

Proprietor: H. Schmidt.

Sunday Times, 1822

Proprietors: Mrs. F. Beer. Bought by H. Schmidt. Amalgamated with the *Sunday Special* in 1904. Bought by the Berry family in 1915. Bought by R. Thomson in 1959. Thomson Allied Newspapers.

Policy: Independent conservative.

Editors: L. Rees, 1901. W. Hadley, 1932. H. Hodson, 1950. C. Hamilton, 1961.

(Sunday Worker), 1925–30

Proprietors: The Communist Party through nominees. Published daily as the *Daily Worker* from 1930.

Policy: Communist.

Editors: W. Paul, 1925. W. Holmes, 1927.

Circulations of National Newspapers, 1910–1960

National Daily Newspapers

(to nearest '000)

	1910	1930	1939	1951	1960
D. Express	400	1,603	2,486	4,193	4,130
D. Herald	..	750 [b]	2,000	2,071	1,467
D. Mail	900	1,968	1,510	2,245	2,084
D. Mirror	450	1,071	1,367 [d]	4,567	4,545
D. News	200	900	..	..	..
D. Sketch	750 [a]	1,013	850 [d]	777	1,152
D. Telegraph	n.a.	222 [c]	640 [d]	976 [e]	1,155 [e]
D. Worker	..	n.a.	100 [d]	115	73 [f]
M. Leader	250	..	..	..	..
M. Post	n.a.	119	..	..	..
N. Chronicle	800 [a]	967	1,317	1,583	1,206
Times	n.a.	187	213	254	255

Unless otherwise stated the figures are taken from *T. B. Browne's Advertiser's ABC*, 1910–40, and 1950–60 figures are from the Audit Bureau of Circulations, published in the *Newspaper Press Directory*.

[a] Circulation figure for 1915, *T. B. Browne*.
[b] P.E.P.: *Report on the British Press* (1938) gives 1082 for 1930.
[c] From the P.E.P. *Report*.
[d] From the P.E.P. *Report*. Figure for 1938.
[e] *Daily Telegraph* audited circulation figures.
[f] *ABC* circulation in 1956. Latest available figure.

Major Provincial and Scottish Newspapers

(to nearest '000)

	1951	1960
Glasgow Herald	92	79
Manchester Guardian	140	190
Scotsman	54 [a]	63
Yorkshire Post	145	113

[a] Circulation figures for 1951 are not available. The *Scotsman's* circulation was approximately 54,000 in 1955.

London Evening Newspapers

(to nearest '000)

	1905	1910	1930	1939	1951	1960
E. News	300	300	667	822	1,752	1,153
E. Standard	n.a.	n.a.	n.a.	390	862	586
Star	250	327	744	503	1,228	744

All circulation figures for evening newspapers exclude Sporting Editions. 1905–39 figures from *T. B. Browne's Advertiser's ABC*; 1951–60 figures are from the Audit Bureau of Circulations, published in the *Newspaper Press Directory*. Information on the circulations of other evening papers is not available.

National Sunday Newspapers

(to nearest '000)

	1900	1910	1930	1937	1951	1960
Lloyd's Weekly Newspaper	1,250	1,250	1,450 [b]	..	..	..
News of the World	400	1,500	3,250 [b]	3,850	8,407	6,664
Observer	n.a.	n.a.	201	208	450	738
People	n.a.	n.a.	2,535	3,406	5,181	5,468
Reynolds' News	2,000 [a]	2,000 [a]	420	426	712	329
Sunday Dispatch	n.a.	n.a.	1,197	741	2,631	1,520
Sunday Express	..	..	958	1,350	3,178	3,706
Sunday Graphic	..	..	1,100 [b]	651	1,121	890
Sunday Pictorial	..	..	1,883	1,345	5,170	5,461
Sunday Referee	n.a.	n.a.	73	342	..	..
Sunday Times	n.a.	n.a.	153	270	529	1,001

Unless otherwise stated, the figures are taken from *T. B. Browne's Advertiser's ABC*, 1900–30; the figures for 1937 are from the *Report of the Royal Commission on the Press, 1947–49* (Cmd. 7700 and 7690/1949); 1951–60 are the Audit Bureau of Circulations' figures quoted in the *Newspaper Press Directory*.

[a] These figures should be treated with caution. They are from an advertisement in *T. B. Browne's Advertiser's ABC* for 1901 and 1911.
[b] From *Sell's World Press*.

SOURCES.—*The Cambridge Bibliography of English Literature*, Vol. III, pp. 797-8, lists all press directories, pp. 798-846 lists newspapers and magazines. *The History of the Times*, Pt. II, pp. 1130-36 gives a chart of the Metropolitan morning and evening press from 1884–1947. There are several press directories which cover all or part of the period: *T. B. Browne's Advertiser's ABC, 1900–1932*; *Sell's Dictionary of the World's Press, 1900–1921* (including a *Who's Who* of notabilities of the British Press in 1914–21 editions); *Mitchell's Newspaper Press Directory* (became *Benn's* in 1946), 1900–61; *Willing's Press Guide, 1900–1961*. *PEP: Report on the British Press* (1938); *Report of the Royal Commission on the Press* (Cmd. 7700 of 1949, Minutes of Evidence, Cmd. 7317 of 1948); N. Kaldor and R. Silverman, *A Statistical Analysis of Advertising Expenditure and of the Revenue of the Press* (1948); A. P. Wadsworth, "Newspaper Circulations" (in Proceedings of the Manchester Statistical Society, 1954). J. L. Hammond, *C. P. Scott of the Manchester Guardian* (1934); J. W. Robertson Scott, *The Life and Death of a Newspaper (The Pall Mall Gazette)* (1952); A. Gollin, *The Observer and J. L. Garvin* (1960); F. Williams, *Dangerous Estate* (1957).

XVIII
BROADCASTING AUTHORITIES

The British Broadcasting Corporation

The British Broadcasting Company Ltd. was formed by some 300 manufacturers and shareholders on 18 Oct 22, registered on 15 Dec 22, and received its licence on 18 Jan 23. London, Manchester, Birmingham, and Newcastle stations began to operate in November and December, 1922. This was followed by the establishment of the *British Broadcasting Corporation* under royal charter (20 Dec 26), which came into operation on 1 Jan 27. A formal agreement with the Postmaster-General was drawn up on 9 Nov 26. Under the royal charter the B.B.C. was granted a licence for ten years, and was to be directed by a board of governors nominated by the government. The B.B.C.'s second charter was granted on 1 Jan 37, and the third on 1 Jan 47. This was extended on 1 Jan 52 for a further period of six months. The fourth charter was granted on 1 Jul 52.

British Broadcasting Company, 1923–1926

Chairman: Ld Gainford **Managing Director:** (Sir) J. Reith

Board members:

G. Isaacs (Marconi) [1]
B. Binyon (Radio Communication Co.)
A. McKinstry (Metropolitan Vickers)
J. Gray (British Thomson-Houston Co.)
Sir W. Noble (General Electric)
H. Pease (Western Electric)
W. Burnham (Burndept)
Sir W. Bull, M.P.

[1] On the death of G. Isaacs, Marconi's were represented by F. Kellaway.

British Broadcasting Corporation, 1927–1960

Board of Governors

Chairman

1 Jan 27	E of Clarendon
3 Jun 30	J. Whitley
28 Mar 35	Vt Bridgeman
3 Oct 35	R. Norman
18 Apr 39	Sir A. Powell
1 Dec 46	Ld Inman
17 Apr 47	Ld Simon
1 Aug 52	Sir A. Cadogan
1 Dec 57	Sir A. fforde

Vice-Chairman

1 Jan 27	Ld Gainford
1 Jan 33	R. Norman
25 Oct 35	H. Brown
8 Jun 37	C. Millis
11 Dec 46	Marchioness of Reading
1 Aug 52	Ld Tedder
1 Jul 54	Sir P. Morris
1 Jul 60	Sir J. Duff

Governors

1927–31	Sir G. Nairne
1927–32	M. Rendall
1927–32	Mrs. P. Snowden (Vtess)
1932–35	H. Brown
1932–35	Vt Bridgeman
1932–37	Mrs. M. Hamilton
1935–39	Lady Bridgeman
1935–39	H. Fisher

Governors

1937–39	Miss M. Fry	1950–52	Ld Tedder
1937–39	Sir I. Fraser	1950–52	Ld Clydesmuir[2]
1937–39	J. Mallon	1950–52	F. Williams
1939–41[1]		1950–56	Prof. Barbara Wootton
1941–46	Lady V. Bonham-Carter	1952–54	Sir P. Morris
1941–46	Sir I. Fraser	1952–55	I. Stedeford
1941–46	J. Mallon	1952–56	Lady Rhys Williams
1941–46	A. Mann	1954–59	Ld Rochdale
1941–46	H. Nicolson	1955–60	Sir E. Benthall
1946–50	B. Ward	1956–	Mrs. T. Cazalet-Keir
1946–50	G. Lloyd	1956–	Dame F. Hancock
1946–50	Sir R. Peck	1959–60	Sir J. Duff
1946–50	E. Whitfield	1960–	E of Halsbury
1946–46	Marchioness of Reading	1960–	R. Lusty
1946–52	J. Adamson		

Governors appointed to represent national interests

N. Ireland

1952–58	Sir H. Mulholland
1958–	J. McKee

Scotland

1952–55	Ld Clydesmuir
1955–56	T. Johnston
1956–60	E of Balfour
1960–	Sir D. Milne

Wales

1952–60	Ld Macdonald
1960–	Mrs. R. Jones

Directors-General

1 Jan 27	Sir J. Reith
1 Oct 38	F. Ogilvie
1 Jan 42	Sir C. Graves & R. Foot
24 Jun 43	R. Foot
31 Mar 44	(Sir) W. Haley
17 Jul 52	B. Nicholls (*acting*)
1 Dec 52	Sir I. Jacob
31 Dec 59	H. Carleton Greene

SOURCE.—*BBC Handbooks 1928–1961*; *Whitaker's Almanack 1928–1961*.

Television

B.B.C. Television

On 2 Nov 36 the first public service of high definition television was started from Alexandra Palace. The service was suspended from September 1939 until June 1946. The first stations outside London, at Birmingham and Holme Moss (Lancs.) began transmitting in 1951. By 1960, with 23 transmitting stations, B.B.C. Television was within the range of 98·8 per cent of the population of the United Kingdom. The first international link-up was in 1950 with the transmission of programmes from Calais. The Eurovision network was formed in 1954, and by 1960 linked 14 countries.

The Independent Television Authority

I.T.A. was set up by the Postmaster-General under section 1 (3) of the *Television Act, 1954* on 4 Aug 54, for a period of ten years. The whole of the finance of Independent Television depends on advertising revenue, though the act specifically prohibits the 'sponsoring' of programmes by advertisers.

[1] 5 Sep 39, the Board was reduced to 2 members (Chairman and Vice-Chairman) by Order in Council. The Board was reconstituted to its full strength of 7 members in 1941.

[2] 1 Aug 52, appointed Governor to represent Scottish interests.

Independent Television Authority 1954–1960

Chairman

31 Mar 55	Sir K. Clarke
8 Nov 57	Sir I. Kirkpatrick

Deputy Chairman

4 Aug 54	Sir C. Colston
3 Jan 55	Sir R. Matthews
22 Jun 60	Sir J. Carmichael

National Members

N. Ireland

1955–60	A. Chichester
1960–	Sir L. O'Brien

Scotland

1955–58	T. Honeyman
1958–	T. Talbot-Rice

Wales

1955–56	Ld Aberdare
1956–	J. Alban Davies

Other Members

1955–56	Ld Layton
1955–56	Miss M. Popham
1955–57	Miss D. Powell
1955–58	G. Thorneycroft
1955–59	Sir H. Hinchliffe
1956–60	Miss D. Harris
1957–60	T. Summerson
1957–	Dame F. Farrer
1958–	W. Beard
1960–60	Sir J. Carmichael
1960–	Sir S. Caine
1960–	Mrs. I. Graham-Bryce
1960–	A. Cropper

Director-General

1 Oct 54	Sir R. Fraser

SOURCE.—*Independent Television Authority Reports and Accounts 1954–1960.*

The following programme contracting-companies (with their initial controlling interests) have been licensed by I.T.A.:

ABC Television. 1955 (North and Midlands, Saturday and Sunday). Chairman: Sir P. Warter. Wholly controlled by Associated British Pictures.

Anglia Television. 1958 (East Anglia). Chairman: Marquess Townshend of Raynham. Substantial minority interests in the company held by the (*Manchester*) *Guardian*, Romulus and Remus Films, and Wyndham Theatres.

Associated-Rediffusion. 1955 (London, Monday-Friday). Chairman: J. Wills. Fifty per cent controlled by British Electric Traction, and major interest held by Rediffusion.

Associated TeleVision. 1955 (Midlands, Monday-Friday. London, Saturday and Sunday). Chairman: Prince Littler, 1955. Sir R. Renwick, 1960. Originally the Associated Broadcasting Development Co., then renamed Associated Broadcasting Co. Substantial interests held by the *Daily Mirror* and *Sunday Pictorial*, Pye, and Moss Empires.

Border Television. 1960 (Carlisle). Chairman: J. Burgess.

Channel Television. 1959 (Channel Islands). Chairman: Senator G. Troy.

Grampian Television. 1960 (Aberdeen). Chairman: Sir A. King.

Granada Television. 1955 (North, Monday-Friday). Director: S. Bernstein. Wholly controlled by the Granada Group.

Scottish Television. 1956 (Central Scotland). Chairman: R. Thomson (Thomson Allied Newspapers).

Southern Television. 1958 (Southern and South-East England).

Chairman: J. Davis. Formed by the Rank Organisation, the Amalgamated Press,[1] and Associated Newspapers.

T.W.W. 1958 (South Wales and West of England). Chairman: E of Derby. Substantial interests in the company held by E of Derby, J. Hylton, the *News of the World*, *Liverpool Daily Post*, and Imperial Tobacco.

Tyne-Tees Television. 1956 (North-East England). Chairman: Sir R. Pease. A minority interest in the company was held by the *News Chronicle*.

Ulster Television. 1959 (Northern Ireland). Chairman: E of Antrim.

Westward Television. 1960 (South-West England). Chairman: Paul Cadbury.

Independent Television News Ltd. 1955, Editors-in-Chief: A. Crawley, 1955. G. Cox, 1956. This is an independent non-profit making company, to provide a common news service for all the contracting companies. The appointment of the editor-in-chief must have the approval of the I.T.A.

SOURCES.—*I.T.A. Annual Reports and Accounts, 1954–61*; *Investing in Television* in *The Economist*, 9 May 59, p. 553.

Broadcast Receiving Licences 1925–1960

(to nearest '000)

Year	Total	Free for Blind	Sound Only	Sound & Television combined
1925	1,654	..	..	..
1926	2,178	..	..	..
1927	2,270	6	2,264	..
1930	3,092	16	3,076	..
1935	7,012	42	6,970	..
1940	8,951	53	8,898	..
1945	9,710	47	9,663	..
1947 [a]	10,778	50	10,713	15
1950	12,219	56	11,819	344
1955	13,980	63	9,414	4,504
30 Mar 60	15,005	55	4,480	10,470

[a] Licences for television were not required before June 1946.

SOURCES.—*BBC Handbooks 1928* and *1961*.

Sources

Sykes Committee Report on Broadcasting, Cmd. 1951/1923; *Crawford Committee Report on Broadcasting*, Cmd. 2599/1926; *Selsdon Committee Report on Television*, Cmd. 4793/1934–35; *Ullswater Committee Report on Broadcasting*, Cmd. 5091/1935–36; *Hankey Committee Report on Television*, Non-Parliamentary Papers, 1945; *Government Statement on Broadcasting Policy*, Cmd. 6852/1945–46; *Beveridge Committee Report on Broadcasting*, Cmd. 8116 and 8117/1950–51; *Government Memoranda on the Report of the Broadcasting Committee, 1949*, Cmd. 8291/1950–51, and Cmd. 8550/1951–52;

[1] The Amalgamated Press holding in Southern Television passed to the *Daily Mirror–Sunday Pictorial* group when the latter acquired the Amalgamated Press in Nov 1958. Under the terms of the *Television Act, 1954*, I.T.A. was required to ensure that there was 'adequate competition between a number of programme contractors, independent of each other, both as to finance and control'. The *Daily Mirror* group therefore had to sell this interest in Southern Television as it was also the largest shareholder in A.T.V. The holding was sold in Sep 1959 to Associated Newspapers, the Rank Organisation, and D. C. Thomson (the newspaper and periodical publisher).

Government Memorandum on Television Policy, Cmd. 9005/1953–54; G.P.O., *1st and 2nd Reports of the Television Advisory Committee*, 1952 (1953), and 1953 (1954); *Television Act, 1954*; (B.B.C.) *Annual Reports presented by the Postmaster General to Parliament*, 1927–60; *Annual Reports of the Independent Television Authority*, 1954–60 (H.M.S.O.); *BBC Handbook*, 1927–61.

A. Briggs, *The History of Broadcasting in the United Kingdom*, Vol. I.: *The Birth of Broadcasting* (1961); R. H. Coase, *British Broadcasting: a study in monopoly* (1950); B. Paulu, *British Broadcasting* (1956); B. Paulu, *British Broadcasting in Transition* (1961); Simon of Wythenshawe, *The BBC from within* (1953); H. H. Wilson, *Pressure Group: the campaign for commercial television* (1961).

XIX
PRESSURE GROUPS

MANY organised groups have sought to influence legislation and administration in twentieth-century Britain. It is not possible here to offer any full listing or classification of these groups. The names and addresses of many leagues and associations are to be found in each issue of *Whitaker's Almanack* and the *Constitutional Year Book*. The trade associations representing specialised branches of agriculture, industry, and business can be found in *Industrial Trade Associations*, by Political and Economic Planning (1957). Details of the Trades Union Congress and its affiliated unions are to be found in the *Trades Union Congress Annual Reports*. The role of these groups is analysed in *Anonymous Empire*, by S. E. Finer (1958), *British Pressure Groups*, by J. D. Stewart (1958), and *Organised Groups in British Politics*, by A. Potter (1960).

A brief list of the most influential groups would certainly include the following: National Farmers' Union (founded 1908), Association of British Chambers of Commerce (1860), Federation of British Industries (founded in 1916 in succession to the Employers' Parliamentary Council, which was founded in 1898), National Union of Manufacturers (1915); many narrower producers' associations ranging from the National Pig Breeders' Association to the Society of Motor Manufacturers; local authority associations, notably the Association of Municipal Corporations (1873) and the County Councils Association (1889); professional groups such as the British Medical Association (1832) and the National Union of Teachers (founded as the National Union of Elementary Teachers in 1870); groups acting largely within parties such as the Fabian Society (1884) and the Bow Group (1951); and the whole range of 'cause' groups, including the British Legion (1920), the Royal Society for the Prevention of Cruelty to Animals (1824), the Lord's Day Observance Society (1831), the Howard League for Penal Reform (1866), the Women's Social and Political Union (1903), the United Kingdom Alliance (temperance) (1853), the Liberation Society (disestablishment) (1844), the Tariff Reform League (1903), the Free Trade Union (1903), the India Defence League (1933), the Roads Campaign Council (1955), the Campaign for Nuclear Disarmament (1958), the League of Nations Union (1918), and the United Nations Association (1945).

Apart from the general works already quoted, the following are among the most notable studies of individual pressure groups: A. H. H. Matthews, *Fifty Years of Agricultural Politics, 1865–1915* (1915); W. P. Jeffcock, *Agricultural Politics, 1915–35* (1937); P. J. O. Self and H. Storing, *The State and the Farmer* (1962); A. J. Wolff, *Commercial Organisations in the United Kingdom* (1915); H. H. Wilson, "Techniques of Pressure: Anti-Nationalisation Propaganda in Britain" (Public Opinion Quarterly, Summer 1951); A. M. Carr-Saunders and P. A. Wilson, *The Professions* (1933); H. Eckstein, *Pressure Group Politics: The Case of the British Medical Association* (1960); J. Christopher, *Capital Punishment and British Politics* (1962); G. Wootton, *The Official History of the British Legion* (1956).

XX STATISTICAL DATA

1900–1960

	U.K. Population ('000s)	Net National Income (at factor cost)[a] (£m.)	Index Number of Industrial Production (1924 = 100)	Steel Production[b] ('000 tons)	Coal Production[c] (million tons)	Raw Cotton Consumption[d] U.K. (million lbs.)	Agriculture: Cultivated Areas[e] ('000 acres)	Agriculture: Cattle ('000s)	Agriculture: Sheep ('000s)	Wholesale Price Index Number[f]	Retail Price Index Number	Imports and Exports of the U.K: Imports[g] c.i.f. (£m.)	Imports and Exports of the U.K: Exports of U.K. Products[g] f.o.b. (£m.)	Imports and Exports of the U.K: Re-exports[g] f.o.b. (£m.)	Imports and Exports of the U.K. Volume Indices: Imports[h]	Imports and Exports of the U.K. Volume Indices: Exports[h]	
	1	2	3	4	5	6	7	8	9	10	11	12	13	14	15	16	
										(1900 = 100)	(1914 = 100)				(1880 = 100)		
1900	41,155	1,750	73·9		225	1,737	47,795	11,455	31,055	100	91	523	291	63	n.a.	140·0	1900
1901	41,459	1,727	73·6		219	1,569	47,761	11,478	30,830	97	90	522	280	68	176·7	141·4	1901
1902	41,893	1,740	76·4		227	1,633	47,753	11,367	30,057	96	90	528	283	66	182·2	150·0	1902
1903	42,237	1,717	76·4		230	1,617	47,708	11,409	29,659	97	91	543	291	70	183·8	154·1	1903
1904	42,611	1,704	75·7		232	1,486	47,671	11,576	29,105	98	92	551	301	70	185·9	157·4	1904
1905	42,981	1,776	78·3		236	1,813	47,673	11,674	29,077	98	92	565	330	78	187·7	173·0	1905
1906	43,361	1,874	80·2		251	1,855	47,193	11,692	29,210	101	93	608	376	85	193·2	186·0	1906
1907	43,738	1,966	81·6		268	1,985	46,998	11,630	30,011	106	95	646	426	92	195·8	201·1	1907
1908	44,124	1,875	77·1		262	1,917	47,002	11,739	31,332	103	93	593	377	80	188·5	185·1	1908
1909	44,519	1,907	78·9		264	1,824	46,888	11,762	31,840	104	94	625	378	91	193·8	192·8	1909
1910	44,916	1,984	80·6		264	1,632	46,932	11,765	31,165	109	96	678	430	104	197·6	210·3	1910
1911	45,222	2,076	83·0		272	1,892	46,927	11,866	30,480	109	97	680	454	103	203·6	218·0	1911
1912	45,436	2,181	84·2		260	2,142	46,794	11,915	28,967	115	100	745	487	112	219·2	230·0	1912
1913	45,648	2,265	90·5	7,664	287	2,178	46,741	11,937	27,629	117	102	769	525	110	227·1	238·9	1913
1914	46,048	2,209	84·8	7,835	266	2,077	46,643	12,145	27,886	117	100	697	431	95	n.a.	n.a.	1914
1915	44,333	(2,591)	86·4	8,550	253	1,931	46,554	12,132	28,198	144	n.a.	852	385	99	n.a.	n.a.	1915
1916	43,710	(3,064)	81·8	8,992	256	1,972	46,564	12,413	28,777	187	n.a.	949	506	98	n.a.	n.a.	1916
1917	43,280	(3,631)	76·4	9,717	249	1,800	46,212	12,346	27,788	243	n.a.	1,064	527	70	n.a.	n.a.	1917
1918	43,116	(4,372)	73·8	9,539	228	1,499	46,142	12,274	26,981	268	n.a.	1,316	501	31	n.a.	n.a.	1918
											(1938 = 100)				(1938 = 100)		
1919	44,599	(5,461)	81·3	7,894	230	1,526	46,206	12,454	25,048	296	139	1,626	799	165	78	95	1919
1920	46,472	5,664	90·3	9,067	230	1,726	45,953	11,735	23,329	369	159	1,933	1,334	223	78	123	1920

[Sources and Notes to Table.—See p. 223.]

Statistical Data — 1900–1960

	U.K. Population ('000s)	Net National Income (at factor cost)[a] (£m.)	Index Number of Industrial Production (1924 = 100)	Steel Production[b] ('000 tons)	Coal Production[c] (million tons)	Raw Cotton Consumption[d] U.K. (million lbs.)	Agriculture: Cultivated Areas[e] ('000 acres)	Agriculture: Cattle ('000s)	Agriculture: Sheep ('000s)	Wholesale Price Index Number[f]	Retail Price Index Number	Imports and Exports of the U.K.: Imports[g] c.i.f. (£m.)	Imports and Exports of the U.K.: Exports of U.K. Products[g] f.o.b. (£m.)	Imports and Exports of the U.K.: Re-exports f.o.b.[g] (£m.)	Imports and Exports of the U.K. Volume Indices: Imports[h]	Imports and Exports of the U.K. Volume Indices: Exports[h]	
	1	2	3	4	5	6	7	9	9	10	11	12	13	14	15	16	
										(1938 = 100)	(1938 = 100)				(1938 = 100)		
1921	47,123	4,460	73·5	3,703	163	1,066	45,581	11,857	24,198	163	144	1,086	703	107	65	86	1921
1922	44,372	3,856	85·0	5,881	250	1,409	45,458	12,026	23,689	131	117	1,003	720	104	76	119	1922
1923	44,597	3,844	90·0	8,482	276	1,362	33,106	7,764	21,085	131	112	1,096	767	119	82	129	1923
1924	44,916	3,919	100·0	8,201	267	1,369	33,057	7,794	22,239	137	112	1,277	801	140	92	132	1924
1925	45,060	3,980	103·9	7,385	243	1,609	32,920	8,035	23,578	131	112	1,321	773	154	94	130	1925
1926	45,233	3,914	98·4	3,596	126	1,509	32,830	8,177	24,591	122	110	1,241	653	125	97	116	1926
1927	45,389	4,145	113·4	9,097	251	1,557	32,724	8,183	25,208	117	107	1,218	709	123	99	134	1927
1928	45,578	4,154	110·2	8,520	238	1,520	32,617	7,978	24,602	116	106	1,196	724	120	96	137	1928
1929	45,672	4,178	115·8	9,636	258	1,498	32,547	7,890	24,315	113	105	1,221	729	110	101	141	1929
1930	45,866	3,957	110·8	7,326	244	1,272	32,459	7,759	24,669	99	101	1,044	571	87	98	115	1930
1931	46,038	3,666	103·7	5,203	220	985	32,374	7,955	26,374	87	94	861	391	64	100	88	1931
1932	46,335	3,568	103·2	5,261	209	1,257	32,284	8,306	27,204	84	92	702	365	51	87	88	1932
1933	46,520	3,728	110·1	7,024	207	1,177	32,193	8,647	26,651	85	90	675	368	49	88	89	1933
1934	46,666	3,881	121·1	8,850	221	1,322	32,096	8,742	24,944	87	90	731	396	51	91	95	1934
1935	46,869	4,109	130·3	9,859	222	1,261	32,024	8,659	25,062	88	92	756	426	55	93	102	1935
1936	47,081	4,388	142·0	11,785	228	1,366	31,932	8,623	25,040	93	94	848	441	61	99	104	1936
1937	47,289	4,616	150·5	12,984	240	1,431	31,827	8,639	25,541	107	99	1,028	521	75	105	113	1937
1938	47,494	4,671	146·4	10,398	227	1,109	31,755	8,762	26,775	100	100	920	471	62	100	100	1938
1939	47,762	5,037	n.a.	13,221	231	1,317	31,679	8,872	26,887	101	103	886	440	46	95	94	1939
1940	48,226	5,980	n.a.	12,975	224	1,389	31,430	9,093	26,319	135	117	1,152	411	26	(85)	(70)	1940
1941	48,216	6,941	n.a.	12,312	206	965	31,353	8,940	22,257	151	129	1,145	365	13	(70)	(50)	1941
1942	48,400	7,664	n.a.	12,942	205	939	31,204	9,075	21,506	157	137	997	271	5	(65)	(36)	1942
1943	48,789	8,171	n.a.	13,031	199	885	31,058	9,259	20,383	161	142	1,234	234	6	(70)	(29)	1943
1944	49,016	8,366	n.a.	12,142	193	804	31,008	9,501	20,107	164	145	1,309	266	16	(75)	(31)	1944
1945	49,182	8,340	n.a.	11,824	183	717	31,023	9,616	20,150	167	148	1,104	399	51	61	46	1945

1946	49,217	7,974	149·4	12,695	190	813	31,010	9,629	20,358	173	154	1,298	912	50	67	99	1946
1947	49,571	8,587	158·7	12,725	197	815	31,022	9,567	16,713	189	163	1,798	1,142	59	76	109	1947
1948	50,065	9,556	171·7	14,877	209	977	31,062	9,806	18,164	216	175	2,075	1,578	61	78	137	1948
1949	50,363	10,208	182·5	15,553	215	979	31,056	10,244	19,493	227	180	2,279	1,789	58	85	151	1949
1950	50,616	10,762	195·1	16,293	216	1,017	31,126	10,620	20,430	(1954 = 100) 85	185	2,609	2,174	85	85	174	1950
1951	50,225	11,757	201·2	15,639	223	1,024	31,131	10,473	19,984	99	203	3,905	2,582	127	96	174	1951
1952	50,444	12,707	195·9	16,418	227	686	31,163	10,244	21,655	102	221	3,465	2,567	142	88	166	1952
1953	50,611	13,604	207·9	17,609	224	831	31,177	10,444	22,455	100	228	3,328	2,558	103	95	169	1953
1954	50,784	14,535	222·5	18,520	224	892	31,128	10,718	22,873	100	232	3,359	2,650	98	96	177	1954
1955	50,968	15,361	234·5	19,791	222	778	31,103	10,688	22,949	103	242	3,861	2,877	116	107	190	1955
1956	51,208	16,746	234·4	20,659	222	714	31,092	10,907	23,594	107	254	3,862	3,143	144	106	201	1956
1957	51,456	17,675	237·6	21,699	224	744	31,030	10,881	24,796	110	264	4,044	3,295	130	110	205	1957
1958	51,680	18,380		19,566	216	628	31,001	10,956	26,105	111	272	3,748	3,176	141	110	197	1958
1959	51,986	19,124		20,186	206	623	30,873	11,291	27,612	111	273	3,983	3,330	131	118	205	1959
1960	52,383	20,301		24,305	194	599	30,854	11,771	27,871	113	276	4,557	3,536	141	133	216	1960

- - - - - Change in basis of calculation. ( ) Estimated figures.

SOURCES.—

1. Census figures for 1901, 1911, 1921, 1931 and 1951. Figures for other years are mid-year estimates. Figures for 1900–21 inclusive include S. Ireland. Figures for 1915–20 and for 1940–50 relate to civil population only. *Annual Reports of the Registrars General for England and Wales, Scotland, and N. Ireland.*

2. 1900–14, C. H. Feinstein, 'Income and Investment in the U.K. 1856–1914', *Economic Journal*, June 1961. 1914–46, A. R. Prest, 'National Income of the U.K. 1870–1946', *Economic Journal*, March 1948. 1947 onwards *National Income and Expenditure Blue Books.*

3. K. S. Lomax, 'Production and Productivity Movements in the U.K. since 1900', *Journal of the Royal Statistical Society*, Series A, 1959.

4. British Iron and Steel Federation, *Annual Abstract of Statistics.*

5. Ministry of Power, *Annual Abstract of Statistics.*

6. R. Robson, *The Cotton Industry in Britain* (1957), p. 332, Statistics table 1, and information supplied by the Cotton Board.

7, 8 and 9. Figures for June each year. 1900–13 including Isle of Man and Channel Islands. 1914 onwards excluding Isle of Man and Channel Islands. 1900–22 including S. Ireland. *Annual Abstract of Statistics*, Agricultural Departments.

10. Board of Trade and *London and Cambridge Economic Service.* (Supplements in '*Times' Review of Industry.*)

11. 1900–14, A. L. Bowley, *Wages and Income in the U.K. since 1860* (1937), p. 30. 1919 onwards based on the official indices of retail prices as published in *London and Cambridge Economic Service.* (Supplements in '*Times' Review of Industry.*)

12, 13 and 14. *Trade and Navigation Accounts of the U.K.* Board of Trade, annually.

15 and 16. 1900–13, A. H. Imlah, *Economic Elements in the Pax Britannica* (1958). 1919 onwards, *London and Cambridge Economic Service.* (Supplements in '*Times' Review of Industry.*)

[a] Changes in sources at 1914 and 1947.

[b] Great Britain only.

[c] Including S. Ireland, 1900–21 inclusive.

[d] From 1958 a revised bale weight was used in calculations.

[e] Total area under all crops and grass. For Great Britain excluding all holdings under one acre, for N. Ireland excluding all holdings under ¼ acre until 1953, and under one acre from 1954.

[f] 1900–20 on different basis from later figures. 1913–49 covers materials, semi-manufactures and finished products, and is not comparable with later figures (1938 = 100 . . . 1913 = 83, 1950 = 259). 1950–3, new series based on 1948 weights and covers output of manufactured products other than fuel, food and tobacco. 1954 onwards, based on 1954 weights and covers home market sales of all manufactured products.

[g] 1900–22 inclusive, S. Ireland is included. From 1923 direct foreign trade of S. Ireland is excluded, and Imports and Exports include trade of Great Britain and N. Ireland with S. Ireland. There are small changes in coverage from time to time.

[h] 1900–23 inclusive, including S. Ireland. 1900–13 Exports of U.K. products only. 1919 onwards, Total Exports. (1938 = 100 . . . 1913 Imports = 88, 1914 Exports = 173.)

Statistical Data — 1900–1960

	Net Balance of Payments of the U K. on current account[a] (£m.)	Terms of Trade[b] Index No. (1938 = 100)	Price of 2½% Consols (Average for year)	Bank Rate % (Maximum and Minimum for year)	Purchasing Power of £: 1900 = 20/–	Purchasing Power of £: 1960 = 20/–	Foreign Exchange Rates: U.S.A. ($ to £)	Foreign Exchange Rates: France (Francs to £)	Foreign Exchange Rates: Germany (Marks to £)	Total National Revenue[i] (£m.)	Main Sources of Revenue: Income tax[j] (£m.)	Main Sources of Revenue: Surtax (£m.)	Main Sources of Revenue: Customs (£m.)	Main Sources of Revenue: Excise (£m.)	Main Sources of Revenue: Death Duties (£m.)	
	17	18	19	20	21	22	23	24	25	26	27	28	29	30	31	
1900			99·6	6 3	20/–	101/7	4·84	25·1	20·4	140	28	..	26	38	17	1900
1901			94·3	5 3	19/9	100/5	4·85	25·2	20·4	153	35	..	31	37	19	1901
1902			94·4	4 3	19/7	99/4	4·85	25·2	20·5	161	39	..	35	37	18	1902
1903			90·8	4 3	19/4	98/3	4·85	25·1	20·4	151	31	..	34	37	17	1903
1904			88·3	4 3	19/1	97/2	4·85	25·2	20·4	153	31	..	36	36	17	1904
1905			89·8	3 2½	19/4	98/3	4·85	25·2	20·5	154	31	..	35	36	17	1905
1906			88·3	6 3½	19/4	98/3	4·82	25·1	20·5	155	31	..	33	36	19	1906
1907			84·1	7 4	18/8	95/1	4·84	25·1	20·5	157	31	..	32	36	19	1907
1908			86·0	7 2½	18/4	93/1	4·85	25·1	20·4	152	34	..	29	34	18	1908
1909			83·9	5 2½	18/4	93/1	4·86	25·2	20·4	132	13	..	30	31	22	1909
1910			81·1	5 3	18/1	92/1	4·84	25·2	20·4	204	60	3	33	40	25	1910
1911			79·3	4½ 3	17/11	91/2	4·84	25·3	20·4	185	42	3	34	38	25	1911
1912			76·2	5 3	17/3	87/6	4·85	25·2	20·5	189	41	4	33	38	25	1912
1913	194	143	73·6	5 4½	17/3	87/6	4·83	25·2	20·4	198	44	3	35	40	27	1913
1914			74·8	10 3	17/5	88/5	4·87	25·2	20·5	227	59	10	39	42	28	1914
1915			65·5	5	14/2	71/10	4·77	26·3	..	337	112	17	60	61	31	1915
1916			58·0	6 5	11/11	60/7	4·76	28·2	..	573	186	19	71	56	31	1916
1917			54·7	6 5	9/11	50/3	4·76	27·4	..	707	216	23	71	39	32	1917
1918			56·9	5	8/7	43/7	4·76	27·2	..	889	256	36	103	59	30	1918
1919		124	54·1	6 5	8/1	41/1	4·60	29·7	..	1,340	317	42	149	134	41	1919
1920	210	114	47·0	7 6	7/–	35/6	3·97	47·9	145	1,426	339	55	134	200	48	1920
1921		101	48·0	7 5	7/8	39/1	3·73	46·7	268	1,125	337	62	130	194	52	1921
1922	151	109	56·5	5 3	9/6	48/4	4·41	52·8	1,654	914	315	64	123	157	57	1922
1923	140	113	58·0	4 3	10/–	50/10	4·58	75·2	720,000	837	269	61	120	148	58	1923
1924	72	117	57·0	4	9/11	50/6	4·33	81·8	18 billion	799	274	63	99	135	59	1924
1925	46	121	56·3	5 4	9/11	50/3	4·86	106·1	20·4	812	259	69	103	135	61	1925
1926	−15	117	55·0	5	10/1	51/5	4·87	167·5	20·4	806	235	66	108	133	67	1926
1927	82	118	54·8	5 4½	10/5	52/9	4·85	124·0	20·5	843	251	61	112	139	77	1927
1928	123	120	55·9	4½	10/6	53/3	4·87	124·2	20·4	836	238	56	119	134	81	1928
1929	103	120	54·3	6 4½	10/7	53/11	4·84	124·0	20·4	815	238	56	120	128	80	1929
1930	28	110	55·8	5 3	11/–	55/11	4·86	123·7	20·4	858	256	68	121	124	83	1930

1931	−104	99	56·9	6	2½	11/10	59/11	4·86	124·2	20·5	851	287	77	136	120	65	1931
1932	−51	98	66·8	6	2	12/1	61/5	3·58	91·1	15·0	827	252	61	167	121	77	1932
1933	0	96	73·7		2	12/5	63/2	4·30	86·2	14·3	809	229	53	179	107	85	1933
1934	−7	99	80·6		2	12/4	62/8	5·04	76·6	13·3	805	229	51	185	105	81	1934
1935	32	100	86·5		2	12/2	61/10	4·94	74·5	12·2	845	238	51	197	107	88	1935
1936	−18	103	85·1		2	11/10	60/2	5·01	75·7	12·4	897	257	54	211	110	88	1936
1937	−56	109	76·3		2	11/4	57/5	4·94	120	12·3	949	298	57	222	114	89	1937
1938	−70	100	74·1		2	11/2	56/8	4·95	178	12·3	1,006	336	63	226	114	77	1938
1939	−250	101	67·2	4	2	10/10	54/11	4·68	177	11·7	1,132	390	70	262	138	78	1939
1940	−804	n.a.	73·5		2	8/11	45/4	4·03	177	..	1,495	524	76	305	224	81	1940
1941	−816	n.a.	80·0		2	8/–	40/7	4·03	..	..	2,175	770	75	378	326	91	1941
1942	−663	(103)	82·6		2	7/5	37/7	4·03	..	..	2,922	1,007	75	460	425	93	1942
1943	−680	(109)	80·7		2	7/2	36/5	4·03	..	..	3,149	1,184	76	561	482	100	1943
1944	−659	(104)	79·6		2	7/–	35/6	4·03	..	..	3,355	1,317	74	579	497	111	1944
1945	−875	107	85·5		2	6/10	34/6	4·03	203·8	..	3,401	1,361	69	570	541	120	1945
1946	−295	109	96·3		2	6/7	33/6	4·03	480·0	..	3,623	1,156	76	621	564	148	1946
1947	−442	116	90·7		2	6/2	31/4	4·03	480·0	..	4,011	1,189	91	791	629	172	1947
1948	7	118	78·0		2	5/9	29/1	4·03	d	..	4,168	1,368	98	824	734	177	1948
1949	38	117	75·9		2	5/7	28/5	c	e	..	4,098	1,438	115	813	706	190	1949
1950	297	125	70·5		2	5/5	27/9	2·80	980·0	..	4,157	1,404	121	905	724	185	1950
1951	−419	139	66·1	2½	2	5/–	25/3	2·80	979·7	..	4,629	1,669	130	998	753	183	1951
1952	227	129	59·1	4	2½	4/8	23/11	2·79	981·5	West Germany only	4,654	1,736	131	1,024	739	152	1952
1953	179	119	61·3	4	3½	4/8	23/6	2·81	982·8	11·7	4,606	1,731	132	1,042	722	165	1953
1954	204	120	66·6	3½	3	4/7	23/1	2·81	981·6	11·7	4,987	1,893	135	1,100	772	188	1954
1955	−92	122	60·0	4½	3	4/5	22/4	2·79	978·1	11·7	5,160	1,943	139	1,149	865	176	1955
1956	192	119	52·8	5½	4½	4/2	21/4	2·80	982·7	11·7	5,462	2,114	158	1,199	902	169	1956
1957	229	116	50·2	7	5½	4/1	20/9	2·79	f	11·7	5,679	2,208	157	1,207	942	171	1957
1958	345	107	50·2	7	4	4/–	20/3	2·81	g	11·7	5,850	2,322	167	1,262	930	187	1958
1959	90	107	51·8		4	4/–	20/2	2·81	13·77 [h]	11·7	6,016	2,243	181	1,373	909	227	1959
1960	−339	106	46·1	6	4	3/11	20/–	2·81	13·77 [h]	11·7	6,344	2,433	189	1,457	933	236	1960

----- Change in basis of calculation. ( ) Estimated figures.

SOURCES.—

17. *London and Cambridge Economic Service.* (Supplements in '*Times*' *Review of Industry*) and *Balance of Payments White Papers.*
18. *London and Cambridge Economic Service.* (Supplements in '*Times*' *Review of Industry.*)
19. and 20. Bank of England *Annual Abstract of Statistics.*
21 and 22. 1900–14 based on unofficial price index compiled by G. H. Wood, in W. T. Layton and G. Crowther, *An Introduction to the Study of Prices* (1938); 1914–38 based on Ministry of Labour *Cost of Living Index* (*Min. of Labour Gazette*); 1938–60 based on *Consumers' Price Index*, The Treasury (*Annual Abstract of Statistics*).
23, 24 and 25. 1900–39, *The Economist*, figures for the end of June; 1940 onwards *Annual Abstract of Statistics.* Figures are average for the year.
26, 27, 28, 29, 30 and 31. *Finance Accounts of the U.K.*, published annually by the Treasury.

[a] Changes in sources and methods in 1924.
[b] Import price index as a percentage of the export price index. A rise indicates an adverse movement.
[c] 4·03 to 19 Sep, 2·80 thereafter.
[d] 480 to 25 Jan, 864 from 26 Jan to 17 Oct, 1,062 thereafter.
[e] 1,062 to 26 Apr, 1,097 from 27 Apr to 20 Sep, 980 thereafter.
[f] 984·9 to 10 Aug, 1,177·1 thereafter.
[g] 1,177·5 to 24 Dec, 13·74 from 29 Dec (in units of 100 francs).
[h] In units of 100 francs (100 francs = 1 New Franc).
[i] Total national revenue includes Ordinary and Self-Balancing Revenue. Figures relate to year ending 31 Mar of following year.
[j] 1900–10, 'Income tax' covers Property and Income tax. 1910 figure includes arrears for 1909.

Statistical Data — 1900–1960

	Main Heads of Expenditure							Specimen Tariffs			Employment				Permanent Dwellings Built[k]			
												Industrial Disputes[h]						
	De-fence (£m.)	Educa-tion[a] (£m.)	Health, Labour and In-surance[b] (£m.)	Pen-sions[c] (£m.)	Income Tax (Standard Rate in £)	Amount Retained of Bachelor's £10,000 earned income after Income tax and Surtax	National Debt[d] (£m.)	Sugar[e] (per cwt.)	Tea[e] (per lb.)	Excise Duty on Beer[f] (per barrel of 36 gallons)	Total Unem-ployed[g] ('000s)	Working Days Lost[i] ('000s)	No. of Stoppages beginning in year[i]	Workers involved[j] ('000s)	Private Enter-prise[l] ('000s)	Local Authori-ties ('000s)	Total ('000s)	
	32	33	34	35	36	37	38	39 s. d.	40 s. d.	41 s. d.	42	43	44	45	46	47	48	
1900	121	13	..	..	8	9,667	628·9	..	6	6/9		3,088	633	185				1900
1901	124	13	..	..	1/–	9,500	689·5	4/2	6	7/9		4,130	631	179				1901
1902	101	13	..	..	1/2	9,417	745·0	4/2	6	7/9		3,438	432	255				1902
1903	72	15	..	..	1/3	9,375	770·8	4/2	6	7/9		2,320	380	116				1903
1904	66	16	..	..	11	9,542	762·6	4/2	8	7/9		1,464	346	87				1904
1905	62	16	..	..	1/–	9,500	755·1	4/2	6	7/9		2,368	349	92				1905
1906	59	17	..	..	1/–	9,500	743·3	4/2	5	7/9		3,019	479	218				1906
1907	58	17	..	..	1/–	9,500	724·5	4/2	5	7/9		2,148	585	146				1907
1908	59	17	..	..	1/–	9,500	709·0	1/10	5	7/9		10,785	389	293				1908
1909	63	18	..	..	1/–	9,500	702·7	1/10	5	7/9		2,687	422	297				1909
1910	67	19	..	..	1/2	9,242	713·2	1/10	5	7/9		9,867	521	514				1910
1911	70	19	..	..	1/2	9,242	685·2	1/10	5	7/9		10,155	872	952				1911
1912	72	20	..	..	1/2	9,242	668·3	1/10	5	7/9		40,890	834	1,462				1912
1913	77	17	14	1	1/2	9,242	656·5	1/10	5	7/9		9,804	1,459	664				1913
1914	437	18	14	1	1/2	9,242	649·8	1/10	5	7/9		9,878	972	447				1914
1915	1,424	19	14	1	1/8	8,669	1,105·0	1/10	8	23/–		2,953	672	448				1915
1916	2,007	18	14	1	3/–	7,721	2,133·1	14/–	1/–	24/–		2,446	532	276				1916
1917	2,436	22	14	1	5/–	6,721	4,011·4	14/–	1/–	25/–		5,647	730	872				1917
1918	2,238	23	15	1	5/–	6,721	5,871·9	25/8	1/–	50/–		5,875	1,165	1,116				1918

1919	692	39	74	100	6/–	5,813	7,434·9	25/8	1/–	70/–		34,969	1,352	2,591		0·6		1919
1920	292	54	73	110	6/–	5,813	7,828·8	25/8	1/–	100/–		26,568	1,607	1,932	97·5	15·6	252·0	1920
1921	189	59	73	96	6/–	5,672	7,574·4	25/8	1/–	100/–	2,037	85,872	763	1,801		80·8		1921
1922	111	50	61	83	6/–	5,672	7,654·3	25/8	8	100/–	1,563	19,850	576	552		57·5		1922
1923	105	47	59	72	5/–	6,150	7,742·2	25/8	8	100/–	1,298	10,672	628	405	71·8	14·3	86·1	1923
1924	114	48	65	71	4/6	6,389	7,641·0	11/8	4	100/–	1,087	8,424	710	613	116·2	20·7	136·9	1924
1925	119	48	65	70	4/6	6,389	7,597·8	11/8	4	100/–	1,409	7,952	603	441	129·2	44·2	173·4	1925
1926	116	53	75	65	4/–	6,968	7,558·6	11/8	4	100/–	1,751	162,233	323	2,734	143·5	74·1	217·6	1926
1927	117	53	73	62	4/–	6,968	7,554·6	11/8	4	100/–	1,069	1,174	308	108	134·9	104·1	239·0	1927
1928	113	49	76	59	4/–	6,968	7,527·8	11/8	4	100/–	1,273	1,388	302	124	113·8	55·7	169·5	1928
1929	113	50	86	56	4/–	6,968	7,500·3	11/8	..	100/–	1,164	8,287	431	533	140·3	61·8	202·1	1929
1930	110	55	108	55	4/–	6,968	7,469·0	11/8	..	103/–	1,911	4,399	422	307	128·0	55·9	183·9	1930
1931	107	55	121	52	4/6	6,487	7,413·3	11/8	..	103/–	2,707	6,983	420	490	130·7	70·1	200·8	1931
1932	103	52	155	49	5/–	6,103	7,433·9	11/8	4	134/–	2,843	6,488	389	379	144·5	55·9	200·4	1932
1933	107	51	151	49	5/–	6,103	7,643·8	11/8	4	24/–	2,498	1,072	357	136	210·7	56·0	266·7	1933
1934	113	53	151	47	5/–	6,103	7,822·3	11/8	4	24/–	2,124	959	471	134	287·5	40·2	327·7	1934
1935	136	56	162	46	4/6	6,340	6,763·9	11/8	4	24/–	2,033	1,955	553	271	271·9	53·5	325·4	1935
1936	186	59	162	45	4/6	6,341	6,759·3	11/8	6	24/–	1,731	1,829	818	316	275·2	71·8	347·0	1936
1937	197	60	162	44	4/9	6,222	6,764·7	11/8	6	24/–	1,400	3,413	1,129	597	259·7	78·0	337·7	1937
1938	254	62	166	43	5/–	6,103	6,993·7	11/8	8	24/–	1,885	1,334	875	274	230·6	100·9	331·5	1938
1939	626	63	167	42	5/6	5,867	7,130·8	11/8	8	24/–	1,342	1,356	940	337	145·5	50·5	196·0	1939
1940	3,220	63	165	41	7/–	4,965	7,899·2	23/4	8	90/–	709	940	922	299	27·1	15·4	42·5	1940
1941	4,085	66	170	41	8/6	3,921	10,366·4	23/4	8	90/–	252	1,079	1,251	360	6·9	2·9	9·8	1941
1942	4,840	78	186	40	10/–	3,138	13,041·1	23/4	8	118/1½	106	1,527	1,303	456	8·2	1·4	9·6	1942
1943	4,950	80	199	39	10/–	3,138	15,822·6	23/4	8	138/4½	106	1,808	1,785	557	3·3	2·5	5·8	1943
1944	5,125	85	208	40	10/–	3,138	18,562·2	23/4	8	140/7½	106	3,714	2,194	821	3·2	2·4	5·6	1944
1945	4,410	118	219	42	10/–	3,138	21,365·9	23/4	8	140/7½	104	2,835	2,293	531	0·9	0·5	1·4	1945
1946	1,653	150	334	97	10/–	3,138	23,636·5	23/4	8	140/7½	408	2,158	2,205	526	29·9	21·2	51·1	1946
1947	854	182	380	91	9/–	3,637	25,630·6	23/4	8	140/7½	299	2,433	1,721	620	40·9	86·6	127·5	1947
1948	753	213	598	96	9/–	3,501	25,620·8	23/4	8	178/10½	299	1,944	1,759	424	35·6	170·8	206·4	1948
1949	741	242	806	97	9/–	3,587	25,167·6	11/8	2	157/10½	291	1,807	1,426	433	30·0	141·8	171·8	1949
1950	777	253	835	94	9/–	3,587	25,802·3	11/8	2	155/4½	308	1,389	1,339	302	33·0	139·4	172·4	1950

[Sources and Notes to Table.—See p. 228]

Statistical Data — 1900–1960

	Main Heads of Expenditure				Income Tax (Standard Rate in £)	Amount Retained of Bachelor's £10,000 earned income after Income tax and Surtax	National Debt[d] (£m.)	Specimen Tariffs		Excise Duty on Beer[f] (per barrel of 36 gallons)	Employment				Permanent Dwellings Built[k]			
												Industrial Disputes[h]						
	De-fence (£m.)	Educa-tion[a] (£m.)	Health, Labour and In-surance[b] (£m.)	Pen-sions[c] (£m.)				Sugar[e] (per cwt.)	Tea[e] (per lb.)		Total Unem-ployed[g] ('000s)	Working Days Lost[i] ('000s)	No. of Stoppages beginning in year[i]	Workers involved[j] ('000s)	Private Enter-prise[e] ('000s)	Local Authori-ties ('000s)	Total ('000s)	
	32	33	34	35	36	37	38	39 s. d.	40 s. d.	41 s. d.	42	43	44	45	46	47	48	
1951	1,110	274	810	91	9/–	3,598	25,921·6	11/8	2	155/4½	215	1,694	1,719	379	30·3	141·6	171·9	1951
1952	1,404	288	884	100	9/6	3,361	25,890·5	11/8	2	155/4½	490	1,792	1,714	415	43·4	165·6	209·0	1952
1953	1,365	303	903	97	9/6	3,411	26,051·2	11/8	2	155/4½	335	2,184	1,746	1,370	76·3	202·9	279·2	1953
1954	1,436	338	619	419	9/–	3,646	26,583·0	11/8	2	155/4½	269	2,457	1,989	448	109·4	199·6	309·0	1954
1955	1,405	378	652	433	9/–	3,646	26,933·7	11/8	2	155/4½	243	3,781	2,419	659	120·8	162·5	283·3	1955
1956	1,525	434	750	463	8/6	3,873	27,038·9	11/8	2	155/4½	250	2,083	2,648	507	128·7	140·0	268·7	1956
1957	1,430	481	782	490	8/6	3,873	27,007·5	11/8	2	155/4½	297	8,412	2,859	1,356	131·1	137·6	268·7	1957
1958	1,468	523	794	575	8/6	4,341	27,232·0	11/8	2	155/4½	473	3,462	2,629	523	128·4	113·1	241·5	1958
1959	1,475	215	1,209	610	8/6	4,341	27,376·3	11/8	2	111/9½	449	5,270	2,093	645	149·9	99·5	249·4	1959
1960	1,596	204	1,384	634	7/9	4,648	27,732·6	11/8	2	111/9½	335	3,024	2,832	817	166·0	103·2	269·2	1960

- - - - - Change in basis of calculation.

SOURCES.—

32, 33, 34 and 35. *Annual Abstract of Statistics.*

36. *Reports of the Commissioners for Inland Revenue.*

37. *Reports of the Commissioners for Inland Revenue* and information received from the Inland Revenue.

38. *Finance Accounts of the U.K.*

39 and 40. *Customs Tariff of the* U.K. (*Annual Reports of Commissioners for Customs and Excise.*)

41. *Reports of Commissioners for Customs and Excise.*

42. *Annual Abstract of Statistics.* 1921 figure for December, 1922 onwards figures for June.

43, 44 and 45. *Annual Abstract of Statistics, Ministry of Labour Gazette* and *Abstract of Labour Statistics.*

46, 47 and 48., 1919–38 M. E. Bowley, *Housing and the State, 1919–44* (1945); 1939 onwards *Annual Abstract of Statistics.* 1919–44 years ending 31 Mar of following year. 1945 April to December. 1946 onwards Calendar years. For conflicting figures for G.B. see B. Weber, 'A New Index of Residential Construction, 1838–1950', *Scottish Journal of Political Economy,* No. 2, June 1955.

[a] 1900–13, 'Education' includes Science and Art. From 1935 'Education' includes Broadcasting.

[b] 1900–13, the system of classification prevents entries comparable with those for later years. 1949–53, figures cover Housing, Local Government, Health, Labour, National Insurance and National Assistance. From 1954 figures cover

[c] 1900–13, the system of classification prevents entries comparable with those for later years. Before 1954, 'Pensions' equivalent to 'non-effective' charges. 1954 onwards figures cover Pensions, National Insurance and National Assistance.

[d] Debt of U.K. Exchequer, debt created by N. Ireland Exchequer excluded. Bonds tendered for death duties and held by National Debt Commissioners excluded from 1920. External debt arising out of 1914–18 war, excluded from 1935, when it was £1,036·5 m.

[e] Full Customs duty given. In many cases preferential rates apply to Commonwealth trade. Sugar: exceeding 98° of polarisation.

[f] 1900–32 beer of 1,055° specific gravity. 1933–49 beer of 1,027° specific gravity. 1950–60 beer of 1,030° specific gravity.

[g] 1900–20, unemployment figures for certain skilled trade unions available in *Ministry of Labour Gazettes*, figures are given as percentages. No comparable figures of total unemployed before 1921. Figures for insured workers registered as unemployed. Agricultural workers, insurable in 1936, are included from that date. Numerous changes in coverage throughout.

[h] Disputes involving less than 10 work-people and those lasting less than one day are omitted, except where aggregate duration exceeded 100 working days.

[i] S. Ireland included from 1900 to 1907.

[j] Workers involved directly and indirectly. 'Indirectly' involved means those unable to work at establishments where disputes occurred, though not themselves parties to the dispute.

[k] Figures for England and Wales only. Flats are included, and each is counted as one unit.

[l] Including houses built for families of police, prison staff, armed services and

Population

49. BIRTH RATES AND DEATH RATES IN THE U.K.

	Total Births per 1000 Population	Total Deaths per 1000 Population
1900 . .	28·2	18·4
1910 . .	25·0	14·0
1920 . .	25·4	12·9
1930 . .	16·8	11·7
1940 . .	14·6	14·4
1950 . .	16·2	11·8
1960 . .	17·5	11·5

Figures for 1900, 1910 and 1920 include Southern Ireland. Death rate in 1940 based on civil deaths and population only.

SOURCE.—*Annual Reports of the Registrars-General.*

50. AGE DISTRIBUTION OF THE POPULATION OF THE U.K.

(Percentages)

Age Groups	1901	1911	1921 [a]	1931	1939	1951	1960
Under 9	22·2	21·0	18·2	16·1	14·1	16·0	15·1
10-19	20·3	19·1	19·0	16·8	16·3	12·9	14·9
20-29	18·3	17·3	16·2	17·1	15·6	14·2	12·7
30-39	13·9	15·1	14·5	14·5	16·0	14·5	13·7
40-49	10·5	11·4	13·1	12·9	13·1	14·8	13·5
50-59	7·3	7·9	9·6	11·1	11·3	11·9	13·2
60-69	4·7	5·1	6·0	7·3	8·5	8·9	9·4
70-79	2·2	2·5	2·7	3·4	4·1	5·3	5·6
80 and over	0·6	0·6	0·7	0·8	1·0	1·5	1·9
Total	100·0	100·0	100·0	100·0	100·0	100·0	100·0

[a] Percentages for 1921 are for England, Wales and Scotland only.

SOURCES.—Census figures for 1901, 1911, 1921, 1931, 1951. Mid-year estimate 1939 and 1960; Registrars-General of England and Wales, and Scotland, *Censuses of Population*, and the *Annual Abstract of Statistics*.

51. EXPECTATION OF LIFE

England and Wales

(Average future expected lifetime at birth)

Years	Male	Female	Years	Male	Female
1900–02	46	50	1938	61	66
1910–12	52	55	1950–52	66	72
1920–22	56	60	1956–58	68	74
1930–32	59	63	..	..	..

SOURCES.—*Annual Reports of the Registrar-General for England and Wales,* and the *Government Actuary's Department, Annual Abstract of Statistics.*

52. MAIN CAUSES OF DEATH

England and Wales

(to nearest '000)

	1900	1910	1920	1930	1940	1950	1960
Total deaths	588	483	466	455	572	510	526
Due to:							
Tuberculosis	61	51	43	36	27	16	3
Cancer	27	35	44	57	69	83	96
Vascular lesions of the nervous system [a]	41	30	49	41	52	65	76
Heart diseases	n.a.	49	53	90	136	146	153
Pneumonia	44	40	37	28	29	18	24
Bronchitis	54	34	38	19	46	28	26
Violent Causes	20	19	17	22	47 [b]	19	23

[a] All diseases of the nervous system, 1900–30.
[b] Including 22,000 deaths of civilians due to operations of war.

Infant mortality (i.e. deaths under 1 year) per 1000 live births: 1900 — 154; 1910 — 105; 1920 — 80; 1930 — 64; 1940 — 57; 1950 — 30; 1960 — 25.

SOURCE.—*Annual Reports and Statistical Reviews of the Registrar-General for England and Wales.*

53. AVERAGE AGE AT FIRST MARRIAGE

England and Wales

Years	Bachelors	Spinsters
1901–05	26·9	25·4
1911–15	27·5	25·8
1921–25	27·5	25·6
1931–35	27·4	25·5
1941–45	26·8	24·6
1951–55	26·5	24·2

SOURCE.—*Annual Reports of Registrar-General for England and Wales.*

54. DIVORCES

Great Britain

Decrees made absolute

Year	Decrees	Year	Decrees
1910	801	1940	8,396
1920	3,747	1950	32,516
1930	3,944	1959	25,524

SOURCE.—*Annual Reports of Registrars-General for England, Wales and Scotland.*

55. NET EMIGRATION

From Great Britain and Ireland
to selected countries

To	1900	1910	1920	1931	1938	1946	1950	1960
U.S.A.	47,978	75,021	60,067	−10,385	−1,432	45,751	8,541	3,400
Canada	7,803	115,955	94,496	−10,464	−3,974	43,414	6,464	−300
Australasia	6,259	34,657	28,405	−8,760	2,204	8,443	54,581	28,300
S. Africa	7,417	8,314	7,844	−1,263	2,037	2,241	1,912	−3,300

Southern Ireland excluded in 1938, 1946, 1950, and 1960.

SOURCES.—*External Migration, 1815–1950*, N. H. Carrier and J. R. Jeffrey, *Studies on Medical and Population Subjects, No. 6*, General Register Office (H.M.S.O., 1953), and estimates for 1960 in *Whitaker's Almanack*, 1962.

56. NATURALISATION

Total certificates granted by the Home Department or oaths taken in period

1901–10	7,997	1931–40	15,454
1911–20	11,293	1941–50	51,132
1921–30	9,849	1951–60	44,977

SOURCES.—N. H. Carrier and J. R. Jeffrey, *External Migration, 1815–1950, Studies on Medical and Population Subjects, No. 6*, General Register Office, (H.M.S.O., 1953), and *Whitaker's Almanack.*

57. POPULATION OF MAIN CONURBATIONS

(to nearest '000)

	1901	1911	1921	1931	1951	1961
Greater London	6,586	7,256	7,488	8,215	8,348	8,172
S.E. Lancashire	2,117	2,328	2,361	2,427	2,423	2,427
W. Midlands	1,483	1,634	1,773	1,933	2,237	2,344
W. Yorkshire	1,524	1,590	1,614	1,655	1,693	1,702
Merseyside	1,030	1,157	1,263	1,347	1,382	1,386
Tyneside	678	761	816	827	835	852
Central Clydeside	(1,343)	(1,461)	1,638	1,690	1,760	1,802

SOURCES.—*Censuses of Population*, England and Wales and Scotland. Central Clydeside figures for 1901 and 1911 are estimates from B. R. Mitchell and P. Deane, *An Abstract of British Historical Statistics* (1962).

National Income, Output and Trade

58. INDUSTRIAL OUTPUT OF THE U.K.

Value of Production

	£m		£m
1907	1,765 [a]	1952	19,126
1924	3,747	1953	19,944
1930	3,371	1954	20,867
1935	3,543	1955	22,078
1948	12,398 [b]	1956	23,637
1951	18,554	1957	24,884

[a] Including firms in Southern Ireland. Figure covers firms of all sizes; in other years firms employing less than 10 persons excluded.
[b] Great Britain only.

SOURCE.—*Censuses of Production* (gross output). Figures for each year are for industries included in the *Census of Production* for that year. No adjustment for changes in coverage, but these are generally small. The first full census was taken in 1907, and between 1907–51 only at irregular intervals.

Taxation and Revenue

59. SURTAX

Year of Change	Income Level at which Surtax Payable	Maximum Rate in £ Payable
	Exceeding £	£
1909	5,000	6d. on amount in excess of 3,000
1914	3,000	1/9½ ,, ,, 8,000
1915	3,000	3/6 ,, ,, 10,000
1918	2,500	4/6 ,, ,, 10,000
1920	2,000	6/– ,, ,, 30,000
1929	2,000	7/6 ,, ,, 50,000
1930	2,000	8/3 ,, ,, 50,000
1938	2,000	9/6 ,, ,, 30,000
1939	2,000	9/6 ,, ,, 20,000
1946	2,000	10/6 ,, ,, 20,000
1951	2,000	10/– ,, ,, 20,000
1961	5,000	10/– ,, ,, 20,000

SOURCE.—*Annual Reports of Commissioners for Inland Revenue.*

60. ESTATE DUTY

Payable on estate of net capital value £100,000

Death occurred in Period	Rate of Duty %	Duty Payable £
Before 1909	5·5	5,500
1909–1914	8	8,000
1914–1919	9	9,000
1919–1925	14	14,000
1925–1939	19	19,000
1939–1939	20·9	20,900
1939–1940	22·8	22,800
1940–1946	24·7	24,700
1946–1949	30	30,000
After 1949	45	45,000

Where death occurred before 30 Jul 49 additional legacy and succession duties were also payable.

SOURCE.—*Annual Reports of Commissioners or Inland Revenue.*

61. MAXIMUM RATES OF DEATH DUTY

Death occurred in Period	Rate of Duty	Net Capital Value of Estate
	%	£m.
1894–1907	8	1
1907–1909	15	3
1909–1914	15	1
1914–1919	20	1
1919–1925	40	2
1925–1930	40	2
1930–1939	50	2
1939–1939	55	2
1939–1940	60	2
1940–1946	65	2
1946–1949	75	2
1949 onwards	80	1

SOURCE.—*Annual Reports of Commissioners for Inland Revenue.*

Employment

62. SIZE OF LABOUR FORCE

Great Britain
(to nearest '000)

Year	Total	Male	Female
1901	16,312	11,548	4,763
1911	18,354	12,930	5,424
1921	19,357	13,656	5,701
1931	21,055	14,790	6,265
1939	19,750	14,656	5,094
1951	22,600	15,649	9,661
1960	24,436	16,239	8,197

1901, 1911, and 1921 figures cover persons aged 10 years and over.

1931 and 1939 figures cover persons aged 14 years and over.

1951 and 1961 figures cover persons aged 15 years and over.

SOURCES.—*Censuses of Population*, except 1939 and 1960; *Ministry of Labour Gazette.*

63. TRADE UNION MEMBERSHIP

United Kingdom
(to nearest '000)

Year	Members
1900	2,022
1910	2,565
1920	8,347
1930	4,841
1939	6,274
1950	9,248
1960	9,803

Including members of registered and unregistered trade unions. The figures relate to all organisations of employees known to include among their functions that of negotiating with employers to regulate the conditions of employment of their members. (See also pp. 193-7).

SOURCES.—*Abstracts of Labour Statistics* and *Annual Abstract of Statistics.*

64. INDUSTRIAL ANALYSIS OF THE OCCUPIED POPULATION

Great Britain
(to nearest '000)

	1911	1921	1931	1940	1950	1960
Total Working Population	18,351	19,369	21,074	20,676	22,954	24,436
H.M. Forces	n.a.	n.a.	n.a.	2,273	697	518
Total in Civil Employment	n.a.	n.a.	n.a.	17,758	21,993	23,628
Agriculture & Fishing	1,493	1,373	1,259	925	1,161	983
Mining & Quarrying	1,308	1,469	1,385	886	852	761
Manufacturing Industries	6,147	6,723	7,006	7,128	8,510	8,811
Building & Contracting	950	826	1,149	1,064	1,434	1,567
Gas, Electricity & Water	117	180	246	213	353	370
Transport & Communications	1,260	1,359	1,443	1,146	1,781	1,662
Distributive Trades	n.a.	n.a.	n.a.	2,639	2,571	3,284
Insurance, Banking & Finance	n.a.	n.a.	n.a.	370	447	555
Public Administration:						
National	452[a]	706[a]	610[a]	1,793 (National and Local)	619	502
Local	555	773	1,019		743	741
Professional Service	2,678[b]	2,225[b]	2,629[b]	n.a.	1,593	2,138
Miscellaneous	n.a.	n.a.	n.a.	1,594	1,929	2,154
Registered wholly unemployed	n.a.	n.a.	n.a.	645	264	290

The Table shows only the changes in the general pattern of industry over the period. The figures for 1911–31 are based on the Census of Population figures published by the Registrar-General. The figures for 1940–60 are compiled by the Ministry of Labour. The figures are in no cases completely comparable owing to changes in the methods of classification and changes in the age-limits.

[a] Including members of the armed forces stationed in Great Britain.
[b] Personal Service.

SOURCE.—*Annual Abstract of Statistics*, 1935–46, 1938–50, 1958 and 1961.

65. EARNINGS AND HOURS WORKED

Great Britain

Year	Average Weekly Earnings		Average Weekly Hours Worked	
	All Operatives	Men aged 21 and over	All Operatives	Men aged 21 and over
	s. d.	s. d.		
1924	47 9 [a]	56 3 [a]	n.a.	n.a.
1935	48 11	64 6	n.a.	n.a.
1938	53 3	69 0	46·5	47·7
1940	69 2	89 0	n.a.	n.a.
1941	75 10	99 5	n.a.	n.a.
1942	85 2	111 5	n.a.	n.a.
1943	93 7	121 3	50·0	52·9
1944	96 8	124 4	48·6	51·2
1945	96 1	121 4	47·4	49·7
1946	101 0	120 9	46·2	47·6
1947	108 2	128 1	45·0	46·3
1948	117 4	137 11	45·3	46·5
1949	121 9	142 8	45·3	46·6
1950	124 1	145 9	45·6	47·0
1951	136 2	160 2	46·3	47·9
1952	147 3	173 7	45·6	47·3
1953	157 5	185 11	46·2	47·8
1954	166 6	197 8	46·5	48·3
1955	182 3	217 5	64·9	48·9
1956	197 9	235 4	46·7	48·6
1957	204 7	241 6	46·6	48·5
1958	214 2	253 2	46·2	48·0
1959	222 6	262 11	46·3	48·0
1960	n.a.	282 1	n.a.	48·0

Figures cover manufacturing industry and some non-manufacturing industries and services, but exclude coal mining, dock labour, railways, agriculture, shipping, distributive trades, catering, entertainments, and domestic services. 1935, 1938, and 1946 figures are for October, 1940–45 for July, 1947 onwards for April.

[a] Average of four weeks during 1924.

SOURCE.—*Ministry of Labour Gazette.*

Education

66. NUMBERS OF PUPILS IN GRANT-AIDED SCHOOLS

England and Wales

(to nearest '000)

Year	Elementary	Secondary	Total
1900–01	5,772	..	5,772
1910–11	6,062	161	6,223
1920–21	5,902	350	6,252
1930–31	5,572	435	6,007
1937–38	5,098	502	5,600
1950	5,121 [a]	684	5,805
1958	5,967 [a]	1,060	7,027

[a] In 1950 and 1958 Secondary Modern School pupils are included with Primary Schools for comparability with previous years. 1950: 1,095,000 Secondary Modern pupils. 1958: 1,435,000 Secondary Modern pupils.

SOURCES.—1900–50, *Education in 1947*, Report of the Ministry of Education and Statistics of Public Education in England and Wales, (Cmd. 7426/1948), 1950–58, *Annual Abstract of Statistics, Ministry of Education Annual Reports.* After 1958 the basis of calculation changes.

67. NUMBERS IN UNIVERSITIES

Numbers of students taking courses, full- and part-time, in Great Britain

Year	Men	Women
1900–01	20,436	
1910–11	33,111	
1920–21	37,921	14,221
1930–31	46,057	16,255
1940–41	32,083	11,951
1950–51	79,422	22,590
1959–60	92,339	27,602

SOURCES.—*University Grants Committee Reports 1920–60*; 1900–11, *Annual Statistical Reports of the Universities*; and *Annual Abstract of Statistics.*

Housing

68. NUMBER OF HOUSES

England and Wales

Occupied and Unoccupied

(to nearest '000)

Year	Number	Year	Number
1901	6,710	1939	11,263
1911	7,550	1951	12,389
1921	7,979	1961	14,648 [a]
1931	9,400		

[a] Excluding vacant dwellings.

SOURCES.—1901, 1911, 1921, 1931, 1951, 1961 *Population Censuses*; 1939 estimates in M. E. Bowley, *Housing and the State, 1919–1944* (1945).

Transport

Road

69. NUMBER OF LICENSED VEHICLES

Great Britain

	('000s)
1904 Mar	18
1910 ,,	155
1920 ,,	663
1930 Sep	2,287
1940 Aug	2,332
1950 Sep	4,414
1959 ,,	8,606

Covers private cars, motor cycles, buses, coaches, hackney carriages, goods vehicles, trolley buses, tractors licensed to operate on public roads, invalid and exempt vehicles and tramcars.

SOURCE.—*Basic Road Statistics* (British Road Federation).

Shipping

70. TONNAGE REGISTERED

United Kingdom

	'000 gross tons	% of World tonnage
1900	11,514	51·5
1910	16,768	45·0
1920	18,111	33·6
1930	20,322	29·9
1939	17,891	26·1
1950	18,219	21·5
1960	21,131	16·3

Steam and motor ships of 100 gross tons and over.

SOURCE.—*Lloyd's Register of Shipping* (Statistical Tables), published annually.

71. RAILWAYS

Great Britain

	Train Miles (million miles)	Passengers Carried (millions)	Freight[a]	
			Tons (millions)	Ton Miles (millions)
1900	379·3	962·3	416·1	n.a.
1910	386·7	936·0	504·7	n.a.
1920	355·7	1,243·2	332·2	19,173
1930	397·5	844·9	304·3	17,784
1938	420·9	1,237·2	265·7	16,266
1950	384·1	981·7	281·3	22,135
1960	375·4	1,036·7	248·5	18,650

Excluding operations of London Electric Railway, London Passenger Board, and London Transport throughout. Standard-gauge Railways only (except 1900 and 1910).

[a] Including free hauled traffic.

SOURCES.—*Railway Returns*, Ministry of Transport, published annually, and *Annual Abstract of Statistics*.

Miscellaneous

72. LICENSED PREMISES

England and Wales

Number of On-Licences

1900	102,189
1910	92,484
1920	83,432
1930	77,821
1940	73,365
1950	71,814
1960	69,184

SOURCE.—*Licensing Statistics*, Home Office, published annually.

73. BEER CONSUMPTION

United Kingdom

Yr ended 31 March	Million Bulk Barrels
1901	40
1911	35
1921	35
1931	24
1941	27
1951	26
1960	27

Including Southern Ireland, 1900–21.

SOURCE.—*Annual Reports of Commissioners for Customs & Excise.*

74. DRUNKENNESS CONVICTIONS

England and Wales

1905	207,171
1910	161,992
1920	95,763
1930	53,080
1940	44,699
1950	45,533
1960	65,170

Not including other offences under the intoxicating liquor laws.

SOURCE.—*Licensing Statistics*, Home Office, published annually.

75. STATISTICS OF CRIME IN BRITAIN

Great Britain

Years	Indictable Offences known to Police		Total tried in all Courts for Indictable Offences		Non-indictable Offences: Criminal		Non-indictable Offences: Non-criminal	
Average for years	('000s)	Rate per 100,000 of of the Population	('000s)	Rate per 100,000 of of the Population	('000s)	Rate per 100,000 of the Population	('000s)	Rate per 100,000 of the Population
1897–1901	79	249	53	165	103	323	629	1,973
1902–06	90	266	59	176	88	261	642	1,903
1907–11	102	288	65	184	76	216	581	1,640
1914–18	85	246	59	170	57	165	461	1,337
1920–24	107	280	59	154	65	170	491	1,293
1925–29	128	325	61	163	53	136	550	1,339
1930–34	195	484	69	173	46	113	543	1,349
1935–39	267	733	82	224	43	118	682	1,868
1940–44	363	972	111	296	42	112	317	848
1945–49	486	1,278	125	328	46	122	432	1,134
1950–54	481	1,257	128	334	43	118	579	1,510
1959	676	1,690	161	402	58	143	861	2,153

Before 1935–39 the proportions are calculated on the whole population, not on the population over the age of criminal responsibility (8 years). The rise in these proportions in the 1930s is slightly exaggerated due to the use of the corrected figure. The total number of persons tried in the courts refers to the number of appearances before the courts, and not to the number of *different* persons tried in any one year.

SOURCES.—G. Rose, *The Struggle for Penal Reform* (1961), pp. 286-95. *Criminal Statistics* are published annually as Command papers. A summary of statistics can be found in the *Annual Abstract of Statistics, 1900–1961*.

76. POLICE FORCE

(to nearest '000)

Year	England and Wales [a]	Scotland (authorised number) [b]	Ireland (N. Ireland only, 1930–60) [c]
1900	41·9	4·9	12·3
1910	49·6	5·6	11·9
1920	56·5	6·5	11·6
1930	58·0	6·6	2·8
1940 [d]	57·3	6·8	2·9
1950 [d]	62·6	7·2	2·8
1960 [d]	72·3	8·7	2·9

[a] Regular police force at 29 Sep each year.
[b] Authorised police force at 31 Dec each year.
[c] Regular police force at 31 Mar each year.
[d] Figures 1940–60 include policewomen.

SOURCES.—*Annual Abstract of Statistics, 1900–1961*; J. M. Hart, *The Police Force* (1951).

77. PRISONERS

Daily Average Population of Prisons and Borstal Institutions

England and Wales

1900	14,739
1910	20,904
1920	11,000
1930	11,346
1940	9,377
1950	20,175
1960	26,824

SOURCE.—*Reports of Prison Commissioners for England and Wales*, published annually.

78. LIBRARY LOANS

United Kingdom

	('000s)
1896	26,225
1911	54,256
1924	85,668
1935	207,982
1939	247,335
1948	294,000
1959	440,095 [a]

Figures relate to Public (rate supported) Libraries.

[a] Excluding loans from School libraries run by Public Libraries.

SOURCE.—Information supplied by the Library Association.

79. TELEPHONES

United Kingdom [a]

	('000s)
1900	3
1910	122
1920	980
1930	1,996
1940	3,339
1950	5,171
1960	7,864

[a] Including Southern Ireland, 1900–20.

SOURCES.—General Post Office, *Post Office Commercial Accounts*, published annually, and *Annual Abstracts of Statistics*.

XXI
BIBLIOGRAPHICAL NOTE

THIS book does not attempt to provide an extensive bibliography of works on British politics since 1900. That would demand a separate volume and much of its contents would duplicate bibliographies already available. The main sources of factual data used in compiling this book are listed separately in the appropriate sections. There are, however, some works of reference of such major importance and reliability that it seems useful to collect them together as a help or reminder to those involved in research.

Many of the standard and most useful sources for reference are Stationery Office publications. Summaries, guides, and short-cuts to these publications are provided in the Stationery Office: *Catalogue of Government Publications* (annually), the *Sectional Lists of Government Publications*, published by the Stationery Office for individual departments, the *General Index to Parliamentary Papers, 1900–1949* (H.M.S.O.), and the three volumes by P. and G. Ford, *Breviate of Parliamentary Papers* (1900–16, 1917–39, 1940–54).

For reference to day-to-day political events the *Official Index to the 'Times'* is the most complete guide, though before 1906 *Palmer's Index to the 'Times'* is difficult to use successfully and is by no means complete. *Keesing's Contemporary Archives* since 1931 give a concise summary of news reported in the national Press, though they were not published in their present fuller form until 1937. Brief chronologies of the year's major events (including some very minor ones) are printed in the *Annual Register* (since 1954 the *Annual Register of World Events*), which also covers them in greater detail in the main text of the book. Still briefer summaries of the year's events are to be found in *Whitaker's Almanack*.

For biographical details of leading figures in British politics since 1900 the main sources are the *Dictionary of National Biography* (1901–11, 1912–21, 1922–30, 1931–40, 1941–50), the *Concise Dictionary of National Biography, 1901–50*, *Who Was Who* (1897–1916, 1916–28, 1929–40, 1941–50, 1951–60), and *Who's Who*, for those still alive. As supplements to these, for lesser-known figures in the Labour and Co-operative movement see also the *Labour Who's Who*, 1924 and 1927 (The Labour Publishing Company) and the *Herald Book of Labour Members* (1923, with a supplement in 1924). Appointments are recorded in many official sources. The major annual publications are: the *Imperial Calendar and Civil Service List*, *H.M. Ministers and Heads of Public Departments* (published since 1946, from four to six times a year), and the *London Gazette*, where appointments are announced officially, which appears about once a fortnight. Official appointments are also recorded in the annual *Lists* of the *Foreign Office*, the *Colonial Office*, and the *Commonwealth Relations Office*, the *Army*, *Navy* and *Air Force Lists*, the *Law List*, and the *Annual Estimates* of the civil, revenue, and service departments. There are two handbooks on Parliament, giving the names of M.P.s, details of procedure and officials: *Dod's Parliamentary Companion* (annually) and *Vacher's*

Parliamentary Handbook (published from four to six times a year). Extremely valuable sources of reference for the House of Commons are the books *House of Commons* published by the *Pall Mall Gazette* in 1906, 1910 and 1911, and since 1910 by the *Times* after each General Election (1922–4 excepted). Other sources of biographical information are *Debrett's* and *Burke's Peerage*, and *Burke's Dictionary of the Landed Gentry*, the *Directory of Directors*, the *Authors' and Writers' Who's Who*, and other directories devoted to the members of particular professions.

The annual almanacks are also an extremely useful source of information. Amongst these the most notable are: the *Constitutional Year Book* (published until 1939), *Whitaker's Almanack*, *The Statesman's Year-Book*, the *Yearbook of International Organisations*, the *United Nations Yearbook*, and *Britain: An Official Handbook* (published by the Central Office of Information).

The major sources for British statistics are already quoted in notes to the tables on pp. 221-38. The most readily available is the *Annual Abstract of Statistics* (H.M.S.O.). This appears both annually, and in a form covering a ten-year period, since 1945. The *Censuses of Population, Industry* and *Production* though infrequent provide the firmest figures. Much of the information in annual publications is only estimated. The reports of the major revenue departments: the *Commissioners for Customs and Excise*, the *Commissioners for Inland Revenue*, and the *Registrars-General for England and Wales* and for *Scotland* are major sources of statistical information — as are the reports of the other Government Departments, and especially the *Ministry of Labour* with its monthly *Gazette* (until 1917 this was the *Board of Trade Labour Gazette*), and *Annual Abstract of Labour Statistics*. Other major sources of information are *The London and Cambridge Economic Service* published about three times a year in the '*Times' Review of Industry* and the *Abstract of British Historical Statistics* by B. R. Mitchell and P. Deane (1962).

A useful guide to works on British politics is the subject index of the British Museum Library. Bibliographical references can be checked through the *Cumulative Book Index*. For information on many aspects of British politics the *Encyclopaedia Britannica* or *Chambers's Encyclopaedia* may give a lead. Weekly journals, especially the *Economist*, may provide much additional information. Apart from the *Times*, the national dailies are not indexed, which makes reference a slow process. But newspaper libraries generally have their own index system and may be of much help.

No attempt is being made in the book to provide a bibliography for the period 1900–60. An extensive bibliography is already available for much of the period by C. L. Mowat in his book *Britain between the Wars* (1955) and in his article, 'Some Recent Books on the British Labor Movement', *Journal of Modern History*, xvii, No. 4, December 1945. He has also published *British History since 1926*, a select bibliography (The Historical Association, 1960). Other bibliographies include J. Palmer, *Government and Parliament in Britain: a bibliography* (1960, The Hansard Society), E. J. Hobsbawm, 'Twentieth Century British Politics', *Past and Present*, No. 11, April 1957 and H. R. Winkler, 'Some Recent Writings on Twentieth Century Britain', the *Journal of Modern History*, xxxii, No. 1, March 1960.

INDEX

This index lists all major items in the book, but it is not exhaustive; it does not include individual names, except where biographies are supplied, or separate entries in tables and bibliographies. The index of Ministers on pp. 58-88 supplements this index.

THE END

PRINTED BY R. & R. CLARK, LTD., EDINBURGH